IN SEARCH OF
THE PERFECT
M · E · A · L

TO THE KING'S TASTE:
Richard II's Book of Feasts and Recipes

TO THE QUEEN'S TASTE:
Elizabethan Feasts and Recipes

DINNER WITH TOM JONES:
Eighteenth-Century English Cookery

CHRISTMAS FEASTS FROM HISTORY

IN SEARCH OF THE PERFECT
M · E · A · L

A Collection of the Best Food Writing
of Roy Andries de Groot

SELECTED BY
LORNA J. SASS

St. Martin's Press ◆ *New York*

Grateful acknowledgment is made for permission to reprint the articles and excerpts listed below.

"Memories of Youth" originally published as "Holland: A Memorable Feast," *Cuisine*, April 1978; copyright © 1978 by Roy Andries de Groot.

"Service Without a Smile," *Playboy*, May 1973; copyright © 1973 by Roy Andries de Groot.

"Confessions of an Oyster Lover," *The Chicago Tribune*, January 1981; copyright © 1981 by Roy Andries de Groot.

"On Becoming and on Being a Gourmet," excerpted from *Feasts for All Seasons*; copyright © 1966, 1976 by Roy Andries de Groot; originally published by Knopf and reissued by McGraw-Hill.

"The Qualities of Memorable Meals," excerpted from *Esquire's Handbook for Hosts*; copyright © 1973 by Roy Andries de Groot; originally published by Grosset & Dunlap.

"A Formative Dish: Portuguese-style Pork with Fresh Clams," *The Chicago Tribune*, July 9, 1979, copyright © 1979 by Roy Andries de Groot.

"A Quartet of Cooks," excerpted from *Feasts for All Seasons*; copyright © 1966, 1976 by Roy Andries de Groot; originally published by Knopf and reissued by McGraw-Hill.

"A Visit to Roquefort," *Cuisine*, November 1980, copyright © 1980 by Roy Andries de Groot.

"On the Trail of Bird's Nest Soup," *Smithsonian*, September 1983, copyright © 1980 by Roy Andries de Groot.

"Saved by a Recipe: Snowy Soufflé with Green Chartreuse," originally published as "Green Chartreuse Soufflé," *The Chicago Tribune*, September 9, 1979; copyright © 1979 by Roy Andries de Groot.

"Have I Found the Greatest Restaurant in the World?" *Playboy*, April 1972, copyright © 1972 by Roy Andries de Groot.

Continued on page 412.

Design by Giorgetta Bell McRee/Early Birds

Library of Congress Cataloging-in-Publication Data

De Groot, Roy Andries, 1912–1983
  In search of the perfect meal.

  1. Gastronomy.   I. Sass, Lorna J.   II. Title.
TX631.D4 1986   641'.01'3   86-12699
ISBN 0-312-41131-6

First Edition
10 9 8 7 6 5 4 3 2 1

Dedicated to the memory of an epicure
whose pleasure in seeking perfection was equaled
only by his pleasure in writing about it

Contents

PART VI: THE OENOPHILE AT LARGE

Acknowledgments

I would like to give special thanks to my agent, Robert Cornfield, for bringing this project to my attention. Thanks also to Joyce Engelson, formerly of St. Martin's/Marek, for signing me on; to Barbara Anderson of St. Martin's, for adopting the project with such enthusiasm; to Marjorie Tippie for copyediting with such thoroughness; and to Rose Keough for her help in preparing the manuscript.

I am especially grateful to Katherine Hynes de Groot, without whose cheerful cooperation this project would not have been possible.

Foreword

Whenever Roy Andries de Groot dined at Lutèce—which was often during the sixties and seventies—he would always call a few days in advance and say something like, "André, I'm coming on Wednesday. Serve me whatever you're in the mood to cook."

That was de Groot's way of saying that he was coming to Lutèce because he had a hankering for the hearty, no-nonsense regional fare that is typical of my home province, Alsace. He loved *real* food.

"André, did you make me your wonderful homemade noodles?" he would invariably ask soon after arriving at the restaurant. Of course, I always did make him those noodles because he loved them so much. I might serve them with a fillet of sole, a rabbit stew, or coq au vin.

We always looked forward to having de Groot at Lutèce. He was an absolute gentleman with an exquisite palate and despite—or perhaps because of—his blindness, his ability to evaluate the taste of food was remarkable. He always came with his dog and his wife, Katherine, or a companion who carefully described the visual aspects of each dish. As a result, his food writing was always full of vivid detail, as if he'd seen the food with his own eyes.

On his way out, de Groot often stopped by the kitchen for a chat with the chefs, and we always valued his comments. I, for one, never failed to be amazed at his knowledge of food and his prodigious taste memory.

His presence at Lutèce is sorely missed, so I am particularly pleased that readers will now have an opportunity to join him on his delicious journey in search of the perfect meal.

—André Soltner
Chef/Owner, Lutèce
New York City, May 1986

Introduction

On a balmy afternoon in June 1985, I sat in the Greenwich Village loft of the late Roy Andries de Groot and, as the Hudson River swept by beneath the window, listened as Katherine Hynes de Groot sketched the outlines of her husband's life. What emerged from our conversation was the fact that de Groot's gastronomic career was a quest for perfection: the perfect meal, the perfect wine, the perfect pear, the perfect understanding of the unique qualities of Roquefort cheese.

"He had always been a knight on a white horse in search of adventure, and he liked to sweep people off their feet with his vibrant enthusiasm for a subject," recalled Mrs. de Groot. But it was not until the late fifties that de Groot's quest for perfection began to dovetail professionally with his growing passion for the subject of food. Indeed, it was shortly before the time when his limited eyesight deteriorated to total blindness that food emerged as the ideal channel for de Groot's creative energies.

De Groot's extraordinary sense of taste was no doubt intensified by his blindness. (Both retinas were detached during the London blitz, leaving him only partially sighted until 1963.) But he had always had a fondness for good food, and the childhood gastronomic adventures he shared with his Dutch father are vividly recalled in a number of the food pieces included in this volume.

Indeed, during the early years of marriage, he always spent a good deal of time preparing meals for Mrs. de Groot and their two young daughters. "He had a great interest in rare and exotic foods," recalls Mrs. de Groot, "and it was not unusual for him to mail-order an item like crawfish from Green Bay, Wisconsin, and then orchestrate as the whole family prepared a special meal centered around the prized ingredient."

A hearty appetite led eventually to a problem of overweight, and around the time that de Groot decided to leave his public relations career during the mid-fifties, he became interested in the Rockefeller diet. His first book, *How I Reduced with the New Rockefeller Diet*, describes the weight-loss plan that worked very successfully for him and brought national attention to the popular program.

By this time, part of the family's routine activity was to explore the ethnic neighborhoods of New York, and de Groot—in his usual thorough and enthusiastic manner—established an elaborate plan for shopping expeditions and the subsequent preparation of meals from all around the world. The diary he kept virtually every day of his adult life began to reflect his growing interest in recipes and food research, and by 1966 he had developed the enormous and eclectic manuscript that became his first cookbook: *Feasts for All Seasons*.

This impressive work—abounding with carefully tested recipes from around the globe—established de Groot as a food writer of considerable merit. He began doing regular holiday food spots on "The Today Show," where he was affectionately dubbed "Gourmet in Residence." It was also during the late sixties that de Groot began writing a very popular series of features on wine and food for *Esquire*.

His next book, *Auberge of the Flowering Hearth*, is considered a classic of the literature of gastronomy. So evocative are the prose and recipes in this volume that de Groot preserves indelibly the flavors and aromas created by the two memorable female cooks in their charming restaurant in the high Alpine valley of La Grande Chartreuse.

The books that followed—*Esquire's Handbook for Hosts, Revolutionizing French Cooking, Cooking with the Cuisinart Food Processor, Pressure Cookery Perfected,* and *The Wines of California*—were researched with equal zeal; in each case de Groot aimed to write definitive works on the subjects at hand. "He was an indefatigable researcher," recalls Mrs. de Groot, "and he had a meticulous mind for organizing the mounds of material he would gather on any subject of interest."

Indeed, it is the lengthy unpublished treatises on de Groot's final quest—*In Search of the Perfect Meal*—that inspired the publication of this anthology. "This is the story of a perfectionist pilgrimage," he explained at the beginning of a sixty-two–page outline. The book was to have been an enormous undertaking, a grand scheme of typical de Groot proportions. But its author died in 1983 at the age of seventy-three, having written only a small portion of the planned contents.

It is a loss that cooks and readers won't have the pleasure of traveling around the world with a palate of such perfect pitch. Then again, perhaps it is fitting that the book was never completed, for a true perfectionist's pilgrimage—at its very essence—is without end.

—Lorna J. Sass
New York City
January 1986

A Note to the Reader

In editing the following essays, I have made minor adjustments to avoid repetition of content and to eliminate out-of-date price references when they were irrelevant to the text. In a few instances, I have appended de Groot's cookbook recipes to prose that originally did not include them.

Since de Groot experimented with recipe format for most of his professional life, both historical interest and practical considerations dissuaded me from rewriting the recipes in one consistent style.

In an editor's note at the beginning of each article, I have reminded the reader of the original publication date so that he may be better able to place de Groot's observations within the appropriate historical context. Those who know their contemporary culinary history will quickly recognize that de Groot was frequently in the vanguard when it came to recognizing the abilities of a young chef or the development of a new trend.

PART
· I ·

The Making of a
Gastronome

Memories of Youth

When I was young, I led a charmed life. My father, a great six-foot-six Dutchman, was a landscape artist who painted the farm and village scenes of Holland. I was sent to school in England and I spent my summers and holidays with him in a thatched-roofed cottage in the picture-book artists' colony village of Blaricum, about twenty miles southeast of Amsterdam and close to the shore of what was then still (before it was drained) the Zuider Zee.

Those lovely and peaceful Dutch summers are now more than forty years behind me, but, of all the good things I did with my father—the bicycling and camping around the country looking for scenes for him to paint, the sailing on the Zuider Zee in a small ketch with red sails, the late fall speed-skating on the frozen lakes and for mile after mile along the canals—what I remember most vividly is Dutch food. And this, I believe, is because Dutch food, if you taste it with understanding, talks to you, tells you a story about the Dutch character, about Dutch history, and about the dreams and memories of the Dutch people.

If your knowledge of Holland is restricted to a tourist visit of a few days, you may jump to the conclusion that this theory is pure nonsense. When you were there, you found Dutch cuisine bland, heavy, solid—a meat-and-potato-man's diet. Most Dutch gourmets agree that the blame for this international misconception must be placed squarely on the less responsible tourist restaurants of the big cities. When Dutch families eat out, they are not looking for a Dutch menu. No restaurant could possibly

EDITOR'S NOTE: This article originally appeared in the April 1978 issue of *Cuisine*.

improve on what they eat at home. They want to eat French, Indonesian, Indian, or Chinese food. It is left to the innocent tourist to be drawn into a restaurant that claims to be "typically Dutch." Real Dutch family food is light, joyous, and simple, filled with memories for every Hollander of a peaceful, quiet, rural life, rich with the good things of the fresh earth.

Holland, a very small country, has lost the wealth of its colonial empire but has made up for that by becoming one of the most highly industrialized and modernized countries on earth: its chemical and electronics industries lead the world. Although the Dutch compete in mass markets with packaged fast foods and instant mixes, these are not bought in quantity by Dutch housewives. No corner of Holland is further than two hours' drive from the sea; so there is hardly a need for frozen fish. A beef carcass butchered, a strawberry picked, a potato dug anywhere can be delivered to any retail market in the country within three hours; thus, farm freshness of everything is taken for granted.

Dutch families' daily food reminds them that their country was once (and largely still is) one of the richest farm communities in the world. Nowhere, perhaps, is the memory of food perfectionism more vividly expressed than in that unique Dutch institution, *de koffietafel*, the coffee table, which appears on Sunday morning, in varying degrees of luxury, in virtually every home, every hotel, every restaurant.

I shall never forget my first *koffietafel*. When I was about eleven, I left London on a Saturday evening to join my father in Holland. I boarded the "night boat" in the small English port of Folkestone and, bright and early on Sunday morning, I landed at the equally small Dutch harbor of Vlissingen. My father, who was waiting at the bottom of the gangway, drove me at once to the old Brittania Hotel, where we went down to the dining room for *de koffietafel*.

The centerpiece of the buffet was a triptych of whole Gelderland hams, each a different shade of pink, a different degree of smokiness, a different texture. Putting the long knife in my hand, my father gave me my first lesson in how to treat such marvelous hams with the respect that is their due—how to slice them evenly and so thinly that each slice was almost transparent. There was also a platter of sausages: *boterhamworst* (with cubes of white fat like an Italian mortadella), *cervelaatworst* (similar to the German type), *Haagse leverworst* (a beautiful liver sausage with bits of crisp bacon), and *plokworst* (very firm and chewy, a bit like a French *rillett*).

There were eight whole cheeses, including the red cannonball from Edam, the flattish, farm-made rounds from the town of Gouda, the cumin cheese from the ancient city of Leiden, and the *nagelkaas*, nail cheese, so called because it is dotted with cloves that look like nails. There were baskets with almost a dozen different kinds of home-baked breads, rolls, various shades of whole wheat and rye, rusks, raisin and nut breads, plus the blackest pumpernickel, which my father called "Satan's bread." There were mounds of creamery butter, the freshest of newly laid eggs—hard- or soft-boiled, as you pleased—and magnificent jams, with the largest whole strawberries and black cherries I had ever seen. I staggered slightly as I carried my plate back to our table.

After this first ritual feast, we traveled northward from Vlissingen along the eternally straight lines of the Dutch countryside—country roads paved with red brick, often running for miles along the tops of dikes, bordered by rows of trees along the banks of canals. Everywhere we saw, as if drifting across the fields, the multicolored sails of boats and barges and, on every side, the turning windmills.

When we reached my father's house, I was as hungry as the proverbial Dutch hunter, and the housekeeper, Hannah, gave me my first taste of one of the most popular of Dutch family-at-home dishes—all of which are easily remembered by the wild fantasy and lilt of their names. Who can forget *hemel en aarde* (heaven and earth, an apple-and-potato casserole) with pork chops, *snert* (split-pea soup with sliced smoked sausage), *hutspot* (a boiled dinner), *hoppel-poppel* (an egg-and-rum dessert), *oliebollen* (doughnuts), *poffertjes* (fried puffs), *slemp* (a spiced festive drink)? Hannah served me some *hete bliksem* (hot lightning), a simple, unpretentious casserole of fresh potatoes and celery root, lightly fluffed together and then swirled with a sauce of coarsely cut, locally picked apples, all accompanied by grilled, smoked Gelderland pork sausages. With the first bite, I adopted this dish into my life!

My father's house was always filled with his friends, but I confess that I remember the food more vividly than the people. I spent a lot of time in the kitchen with Hannah, and what a wonderful cook she was! Using various combinations of the classic Dutch cheeses, she made at least a dozen different variations of creamy *kaassoep* (cheese soup). She would set a large, whole, still almost alive fish in a baking pan, on a layer or in a nest of sliced newly dug potatoes, and bake it, basting almost continuously with creamery butter, so that the fish absorbed the main part of the butter, while the potatoes absorbed the rest and the juice of the fish. This method of butter poaching is so much admired in France that it is called, on a haute-cuisine menu, *à la Hollandaise*. My favorite ending to any meal was the dish that is really a kind of national dessert of Holland, *pannekoeken*, ovenbaked pancakes served with various traditional regional fillings, but almost always in Blaricum with whole blackcherry preserves and thinly sliced fresh gingerroot.

As I grew older, my father began to show me more of the provinces. We would strap our camping equipment on and then pedal out on our bicycles. The direction we chose was generally aimed at finding the best food in the best place at the best time: northeast to Friesland, the land of black-and-white cattle, for tables groaning with beef, butter, cream, and cheese; east to Utrecht and Gelderland for pigs and poultry. We fished for fat eels in the IJsselmeer. In June, we tried to be in Tiel for the harvest of luscious black cherries, of which we would consume vast quantities in *vlaai* tarts, like enormous pizzas filled with stewed fruits. And always in September we went southwest to the mouth of the Rhine and the innumerable islands of Zeeland to feast on the marvelous Zeeland oysters, salty and tangy, with a faint taste of seaweed; just-caught shrimps; huge blue mussels fresh from their beds; and every other kind of superb seafood.

When the canals and lakes froze, speed-skating became our principal sport. No one can understand the pure joy of it until he has skated flat-out for five miles along a dead-straight canal, each breath making a puff of steam in the icy-sharp air. My skating memories are always involved with *snert*, which is to Holland what fried chicken is to the United States, the universally accepted, beloved standby that appears on every menu. I consider it the world's finest version of split-pea soup, rich and nourishing, with chunks of pork and slices of smoked sausage. Along almost every Dutch canal there are wooden huts that are the winter roadhouses for serving, in exchange for a few cents, a piping hot bowl of *snert* and a mug of steaming cocoa.

Other Dutch dishes bring other memories, some speaking loudly of history. On October 3, a Dutch national holiday, almost everyone eats the traditional dish, a most excellent beef stew called *hutspot met klapstuk*. (*Hutspot* means a dish that is shaken during cooking to prevent it from sticking to the pan, and *klapstuk* refers to the particular cut of meat.) It is traced back to the year 1574, which was a bloody and terrible one for the Dutch. They had been invaded by the armies of Philip II of Spain and, during the entire summer and fall, the ancient Dutch city of Leiden was besieged by the Spanish armies. After five months, when the brave Leiden people had almost been starved into surrender, they were saved by the Dutch hero, William the Silent, who opened the dikes, flooded the surrounding countryside, and sailed a small fleet of flat-bottomed gunboats up to the walls of the city. The Spaniards fled in confusion and the starving Leideners rushed out through the gates to find, simmering on the fire at the abandoned Spanish camp, an enormous black iron pot filled to its brim with a beef-and-vegetable stew. Obviously, this was the *cocido*, the Spanish version of our New England boiled dinner, but if you suggest this to any group of patriotic Hollanders, you will be less than popular. That Spanish stew is today Holland's proudest dish—with memories of a great victory that brought with it national freedom.

Finally, we come to a memory aspect of Dutch food that is pure fantasy. In sharpest contrast to the simple, country-style cooking that we have been discussing, you can find, all over Holland, the fiery spices and red-hot curries of Indonesia. In the major cities, especially in Amsterdam and The Hague, there are Indonesian restaurants prepared to serve you, upon reasonable notice, one of the great banquet feasts of the world, an Indonesian *rijsttafel*, the "rice table," which may include anywhere from fifty to seventy-five different courses. It is a feast that blends various kinds of Indian, Far Eastern, and Chinese spices into the kaleidoscope that the Indonesians call a *slamatan*, the ancient festive dinner of the islands.

And the Dutch still serve a version of the *slamatan* in Holland, because they have decided that food is to be the medium through which they will remember the lost greatness of their days of empire. The great writer Vladimir Nabokov called one of his best books *Speak, Memory*. That should be, also, the perfect description for Dutch food. As you eat it, it speaks to you of memories, of dreams, of adventures and hopes, of losses and victories.

EDITOR'S NOTE: Here are four family-style recipes from de Groot's childhood home of Blaricum.

CHEESE SOUP
(*Kaassoep*)

4 servings (about 1 cup each)

> ¼ cup unsalted sweet butter
> ¼ cup all-purpose flour
> 2 cups half-and-half
> 2 cups milk
> 2 cups grated aged Gouda cheese (see note)
> ½ teaspoon Worcestershire sauce
> 2 to 3 drops red pepper sauce
> Salt
> Paprika

1. Melt butter in medium-size saucepan over low heat. Stir in flour; cook, stirring constantly, until bubbly, about 2 minutes. Stir in half-and-

half and milk. Cook over medium-low heat, stirring constantly, until mixture thickens and bubbles for 1 minute.

2. Place 1 cup of the cheese in blender or food processor; gradually pour in 1 cup of the hot milk mixture; blend until smooth, about 3 seconds. Repeat with remaining cheese and a second cup of the milk mixture. Stir melted cheese mixture into remaining milk mixture in pan. Heat, over medium heat, stirring constantly, until hot but not boiling. Stir in Worcestershire sauce and red pepper sauce; season to taste with salt. Serve in heated soup bowls; sprinkle with paprika.

NOTE: Regular Gouda cheese can be substituted; flavor will be milder.

DUTCH BOILED DINNER
(Hutspot met Klapstuk)

8 to 10 servings

> Dutch Stock (recipe follows)
> 2 pounds top round roast, rolled and tied
> 4 smoked pork chops (about 1½ pounds)
> 1½ pounds boneless stewing lamb, cut into 1-inch cubes
> 2 pounds boiling potatoes, pared, cut into 2-inch pieces
> 8 onions, cut into quarters
> 4 leeks, cleaned, cut into 2-inch pieces
> 6 carrots, pared, cut into quarters
> 2 cups coarsely shredded green cabbage
> 1 small cauliflower, separated into flowerets
> Butter
> Salt
> Freshly ground pepper
> Snipped fresh parsley

1. Make Dutch Stock.

2. Place beef, pork, and lamb in large kettle or stockpot in which all ingredients will fit snugly; surround meats with potatoes, onions, and leeks. Add Dutch Stock to cover all ingredients; simmer uncovered 15 minutes. Add carrots, cabbage, and cauliflower; simmer uncovered 15 minutes. Remove beef (meat will be rare); keep warm. Simmer covered until vegetables are tender, about 15 minutes.

3. Strain broth; reserve 10 cups. Slice beef and pork chops into serving-size pieces; reserve. Mash vegetables with fork until chunky; add but-

ter; season with salt and pepper. Mound vegetables in center of heated platter; surround with meats; keep warm. Cook reserved broth over high heat until reduced to 6 cups. Serve Boiled Dinner with reduced broth and pepper. Garnish with parsley.

Dutch Stock

4 to 5 quarts

> 1 *medium tomato, sliced*
> 1 *tablespoon butter*
> 2 *pounds fresh beef brisket*
> 1 *veal knuckle, split*
> 1 *oxtail (about 2 pounds), cut into sections*
> 4 *ribs celery, cut into 3-inch pieces*
> ½ *cup chopped celery leaves*
> 2 *carrots, pared, cut into 3-inch pieces*
> 2 *onions, with skins*
> 1 *medium white turnip, pared, cut into 1-inch pieces*
> 1 *parsnip, pared, cut into 3-inch pieces*
> 3 *cloves garlic*
> 4 *parsley sprigs*
> 3 *tablespoons salt*
> 3 *bay leaves*
> 2 *teaspoons dried tarragon leaves*
> 2 *teaspoons dried thyme leaves*
> 1 *dried hot chili pepper*
> *Freshly ground pepper*

Sauté tomato slices in butter in skillet until light brown; combine with remaining ingredients in large stockpot. Add water to cover; heat to boiling; skim foam. Reduce heat to low; simmer uncovered 4 hours, skimming foam occasionally. Remove vegetables with slotted spoon, pressing to extract juices. Discard vegetables; reserve meats for other use. Strain broth; cool to lukewarm. Refrigerate covered; skim fat.

DUTCH DOUGHNUTS
(Oliebollen)

About 3 dozen

    1 cake (1 ounce) compressed yeast (see note)
1½ cups milk, scalded, cooled to lukewarm (80° to 90° F)
    2 eggs
    3 cups all-purpose flour
    2 tablespoons granulated sugar
    2 tablespoons dark raisins
    2 tablespoons chopped candied orange peel
1½ teaspoons grated lemon peel
    1 teaspoon salt
      Vegetable oil
      Powdered sugar

1. Dissolve yeast in 3 tablespoons of the milk in small bowl; let stand until bubbly, about 10 minutes.

2. Stir eggs one at a time into flour in large bowl. Gradually add remaining milk, mixing after each addition, until smooth; stir in granulated sugar, the raisins, orange peel and lemon peel. Stir in yeast mixture. Let rise covered until doubled, about 1½ hours.

3. Stir salt into dough. (Dough will be sticky.) Pour oil into large skillet to a depth of 1 inch; heat to 375° F. Fry tablespoons of dough, 6 at a time, turning once, until golden, 5 to 7 minutes. Drain on paper toweling. Sprinkle with powdered sugar.

NOTE: One and one-half packages active dry yeast can be substituted; use very warm milk (105° to 115° F).

HEAVEN AND EARTH
(Hemel en Aarde)

6 to 8 servings

   ¼ cup softened unsalted sweet butter
   2 cups hot mashed potatoes (about 1 pound)
   2 cups unsweetened applesauce
   2 tablespoons sugar
   ½ teaspoon ground nutmeg
   ½ teaspoon salt

Heat oven to 400° F. Beat butter into potatoes; stir in remaining ingredients. Spoon into 1½-quart casserole, lifting peaks with back of spoon. Bake until hot, about 30 minutes. Increase heat to 550° F and/or broil. Broil until surface browns slightly, about 3 minutes.

EDITOR'S NOTE: Here are five recipes that de Groot considered ideal for a brunch menu modeled after the Dutch *koffietafel*. Plan to serve these dishes with assorted cheeses and cold cuts, rolls and/or bread, mustard, and coffee, tea, or beer—if you are in a Dutch frame of mind.

HERRING SALAD

6 to 8 servings

> 2 jars (12 ounces each) herring in wine sauce, drained, and chopped,
>   onions discarded
> 3 cups chopped pared tart apples
> 3 cups chopped cooked pared potatoes
> ¾ cup chopped onion
> ½ cup chopped dill gherkins
> 3 hard-cooked eggs, chopped
> 3 tablespoons vegetable oil
> 2 tablespoons white wine vinegar
> 1½ cups mayonnaise
>   Salt
>   Freshly ground white pepper
> 1 hard-cooked egg, sliced
> 2 dill gherkins, sliced
> 1 pimiento-stuffed green olive

1. Combine herring, apples, potatoes, onion, chopped gherkins, chopped eggs, oil and vinegar in large bowl. Gently stir in 1 cup mayonnaise. Season to taste with salt and pepper. Refrigerate covered with plastic wrap 1 hour.

2. Shape salad on large platter. Spread with ½ cup mayonnaise. Garnish with sliced egg, sliced gherkins, and the olive.

BRAM'S PEA SOUP
(Snert)

10 servings (about 1½ cups each)

> ½ cup dried white beans
> 2 cups dried green split peas
> 4 quarts water
> 1 ham bone
> 2 smoked pigs' feet
> ½ pound salt pork, diced
> 4 leeks, trimmed, sliced (see note)
> 2½ cups chopped onions
> 1 cup chopped celery
> 3 medium potatoes, pared, cut in half
> 2 carrots, pared
> ½ cup snipped fresh parsley
> ½ pound ham, cut into cubes
> 1 teaspoon dried thyme leaves
> ½ teaspoon chili powder
> 1 pound fully cooked smoked Polish sausage, sliced
> Salt
> Pepper
> Pumpernickel

1. Soak beans in water to cover in small bowl overnight. Drain; reserve.

2. Rinse peas in cold water; drain. Heat peas, 4 quarts water, the ham bone, pigs' feet, salt pork, leeks, onion, celery, potatoes, carrots, and parsley in Dutch oven to boiling. Reduce heat; simmer uncovered, stirring occasionally, until thickened, about 4 hours.

3. Remove ham bone and pigs' feet. Remove meat from bones; chop meat; discard bones. Remove potatoes and carrots; puree in blender or food processor. Stir meat and pureed vegetables into soup.

4. Stir reserved beans, the ham, thyme, and chili powder into soup. Simmer uncovered 1 hour. Add sausage; simmer until hot. Season to taste with salt and pepper. Serve with pumpernickel.

NOTE: To clean leeks, cut lengthwise almost to base. Rinse in several changes of cold water and under cold running water. Drain on paper toweling; pat dry.

SHRIMP AND CAULIFLOWER SALAD

6 servings

> 1 *small cauliflower, broken into flowerets*
> 1/2 *cup mayonnaise*
> 1 *tablespoon snipped fresh parsley*
> 1 *tablespoon snipped fresh chives*
> 1 *tablespoon tomato paste*
> 1 *teaspoon Dijon-style mustard*
> 1/2 *pound tiny deveined shelled and cooked shrimps*
> *Leaf lettuce*
> *Radishes*

1. Cook cauliflower in boiling salted water to cover in medium-size saucepan until crisp-tender, about 5 minutes. Drain; rinse with cold water. Refrigerate covered several hours or overnight.

2. Combine mayonnaise, parsley, chives, tomato paste, and mustard in small bowl. Combine cauliflower and shrimps in medium-size bowl; add dressing; toss gently. Refrigerate covered 1 hour.

3. Arrange salad in lettuce-lined salad bowl. Garnish with radishes.

RAGOUT OF VEAL KIDNEYS

6 servings

> 2 *veal kidneys (about 1 1/2 pounds)*
> 1 *quart water*
> 1/4 *cup plus 3 tablespoons unsalted sweet butter*
> 4 *tablespoons dry sherry*
> 1/4 *pound mushrooms, sliced*
> 1/2 *cup chopped onion*
> 1/2 *teaspoon salt*
> 1/4 *teaspoon pepper*
> 1/2 *cup beef bouillon or beef broth*
> 1 *tablespoon flour*
> *Snipped fresh parsley*
> *Toast triangles*

1. Clean kidneys thoroughly. Discard membranes and remove all fat. Cut into 1-inch cubes. Heat water to boiling; boil kidneys 6 seconds. Drain; discard water.

2. Sauté kidneys in 2 tablespoons butter in 9-inch skillet over high heat 2 minutes. Add 2 tablespoons sherry; cook, stirring constantly, 2 minutes. Drain; discard liquid; reserve kidneys. Clean pan.

3. Sauté mushrooms and onion in ¼ cup butter over medium heat, stirring constantly, 5 minutes. Stir in reserved kidneys, the salt, pepper, bouillon, and 2 tablespoons sherry. Heat to boiling; reduce heat to low. Mix 1 tablespoon butter, softened, and the flour on small plate with fork; whisk into kidney mixture. Simmer, stirring constantly, 20 minutes. Sprinkle with parsley; serve with toast triangles.

GOUDA DEVILED TOMATOES

6 servings

6 small tomatoes
Salt
Pepper
1 hard-cooked egg
¼ cup softened unsalted sweet butter
½ cup grated Gouda or Edam cheese
⅓ cup chopped boiled ham
2 egg yolks
Salt
Pepper
2 egg whites
Watercress

1. Heat oven to 375° F.

2. Remove ½-inch slice from tops of tomatoes; scoop out pulp. Discard tops and pulp. Sprinkle insides of tomatoes with salt and pepper. Drain inverted on paper toweling.

3. Remove yolk from hard-cooked egg; mash with butter in medium-size bowl. Chop hard-cooked egg white. Stir chopped egg white, the cheese, ham, and 2 egg yolks into butter mixture; season to taste with salt and pepper. Beat 2 egg whites in small bowl until stiff peaks form. Fold into cheese mixture.

4. Fill tomato cups with cheese mixture. Bake 25 minutes. Garnish with watercress.

Service Without a Smile

On the morning of my sixteenth birthday, in London between the two world wars, my mother, who was a snob, decided that her beer man was no longer giving satisfactory service and fired him. He had begun his week's work every Monday morning by delivering several gallons of light beer that was used exclusively to wash our polished-wood floors, thus bringing up their color and grain. On that particular morning, she had caught him in her drawing room drinking the beer from the pail instead of using it on the floor. When she reprimanded him, he merely smiled. My mother thought that was altogether too forward a gesture. She was convinced that servants should "keep their distance" and provide service without a smile.

Then she presented me with my birthday present: my first formal outfit of white tie and tails. With it came her gratuitous advice: "Whenever you appear in public, always remember that you are being watched, especially by the servants. Learn to demand quietly and to expect the proper service from them. But never expect too much. Always be slightly distant. The servant knows his place and is proud of it. You must know yours and be equally proud."

With this Victorian credo ringing in my ears (a credo that I deeply resented—I was already steeped in the revolutionary writings of Thorstein Veblen and Beatrice and Sidney Webb)—I was launched into the last social whirl of the "old days" in London, Paris, and The Hague. At private and public parties, the ratio was about four servants to each

EDITOR'S NOTE: This article originally appeared in the May 1973 issue of *Playboy*.

guest. I remember one charity ball in London where my date and I walked up a great curving flight of stairs lined on either side with perhaps one hundred footmen in powdered wigs, brocaded coats, white knee breeches, and silver-buckled shoes. I handed my gold-edged invitation to the footman on the bottom step and the card was passed up, hand to hand, exactly parallel with our upward progress in the procession of guests. Finally, at the precise moment when we passed through the great ballroom doors on the upper level, our card was handed to the master of ceremonies and our names were announced in stentorian tones. It was a smart trick of timing.

Service, in those days, was intense and highly personal. On Thursday afternoons, I would often drive out to the country for a weekend house party. Even in an upper-middle-class home, the degree of service offered to guests was, by modern standards, extraordinary. When I swung into the driveway and pulled up at the front door, a footman carried in my suitcase and one of the chauffeurs took over my car, washed it, waxed it, and filled it with gas. Meanwhile, the footman had unpacked my suitcase, laid out my dinner clothes, drawn my bath, and was prepared to shave me. He also stood behind my chair at dinner, woke me each morning with a tray of tea and biscuits, and ministered to every detail of my personal needs throughout each day.

I called him by his last name, Jenkins, and he called me sir. Yet there was not the slightest sense of servility in his manner. He saw himself in terms of a long tradition of high skill and professional standing. He deferred to me as if I were the master, but he looked me very straight in the eye and matched his senior self-assurance with my much younger and less solid confidence. In fact, I often felt that I was on trial before him. He knew all the rules of the social game I was playing and was quite prepared to pull me back if I were about to make a *faux pas.* He even advised me on the various girls at the party.

Jenkins belonged to what in England is still known as the servant class—a term implying no sense of inferiority whatsoever—a class of highly skilled professionals, very proud and independent. Jenkins once said to me, "The other day, the master asked me if I would go out and dig some potatoes in the vegetable garden. Of course, I refused, pointing out to him that I was a house servant. I gave him a bit of a row for it and I think it did him a deal of good. I don't believe I'll have any more trouble with him." This type of man might equally well have been a fine waiter in a great restaurant or a room clerk in an outstanding hotel or a steward on a luxury liner. Perfect service was such a normal way of life for him that a smile would have been redundant.

A few days ago, just about forty-three years after I last saw Jenkins, I experienced the full impact of the change in the concept of service between then and now. I lunched in the automated cafeteria of a suburban New York department store. All along one wall were seven-foot-tall machines, with clear-glass fronts like giant jukeboxes. I put in my quarters, pushed the buttons for beef in Burgundy, and the interior stainless-steel wheels started turning. Small doors opened and closed. A turntable rolled around and my dish came into view, gently slid down a chute, and was in my hand, still ice-cold. The food was on a square plate made of an unburnable, unsoakable, indestructible plastic foam produced by one of the giant gasoline companies. On the wall adjacent to the gastronomic jukeboxes was a row of small infrared ovens. I pushed the timing button marked MEAT STEWS. After about 30 seconds, the door snapped open and my meat was steaming hot, while the plastic-foam remained cool enough to pick up. From other machines, I obtained a bowl of tomato soup, a carton of strawberry ice cream, bread and butter, and a plastic cup of coffee. I was given a disposable cardboard tray, a paper cup of water, plus disposable plastic knife, fork, and spoon. At the end of my meal, I complied with the signs posted all around the room: PLEASE CLEAR YOUR TABLE AND PLACE YOUR GARBAGE IN THE CAN.

In this cafeteria, I was told, three hundred people are served lunch every day under the control of one human manager. During the lunch rush, he gives change, clears the disposable garbage from the few tables where the customers have refused to cooperate with the signs, and, presumably, dutifully kicks any of the machines that might suddenly refuse to operate.

After lunch, I thought about the historic concept of service—of one man earning a dignified and honorable living by serving another. Is the concept dead? If good service still exists, how can one find it? And what can one do to bring it out?

The word comes from the Latin *servitium*, or slavery. There is the key to the problem. In ancient times, one tribe went out and conquered another and held its people in lifelong and unsmiling bondage. Through later centuries, service by slaves (which meant bondage to a particular person) was supplemented with service by serfs (which meant bondage to a piece of land), in many forms and under various names. Service by compulsion was practiced in every part of the world.

In Europe, the ultimate refinement was the feudal system, which began to disintegrate when the cities were built and the young peasants found at least some freedom by leaving the land to work in the new factories. In England, the most significant development in terms of service was the formation of the guilds, which included apprenticeship training as butlers, cooks, footmen, house stewards, gardeners, coachmen, grooms, etc. These British guilds had much to do with the development of a proud, professional service class, which remains the secret ingredient of the great hotels and luxury restaurants of today. Outside Europe, the concept of service was generally imposed by colonial administrators. During their phases of empire building, Englishmen, Dutchmen, Frenchmen, Spaniards, Belgians, and Portuguese carried their ideas about service to native peoples.

The Britisher was always the most obstinate in imposing his traditional way of life. No sooner had the rubber planter settled down in his faraway job than he sent to London for his regular brand of afternoon tea and favorite orange marmalade. He trained the natives to serve him in the English manner. Indian girls became ayahs—English-style nursemaids—for the children. African boys learned to wait at table. Chinese cooks were taught how to prepare English plum pudding.

The Dutch colonial was a good deal more adaptable. He accepted many of the traditions of the Eastern countries where he lived and worked. This is how the *rijsttafel,* or rice table, the marvelous fifty-course Javanese feast, became one of the national dishes of Holland.

On Sunday afternoons, the Dutch planters on Java would gather at the *soos,* the *societeit,* or club, to begin the entertainment with solid slugs of heavily iced Holland gin. The big round tables had a large circular hole in the middle. When you wanted your next drink poured, you would kick gently under the table and up through the hole would rise a *djongo,* a Dutch-trained Javanese boy waiter, in an impeccable white jacket. Having poured more drinks, he would again disappear downward to squat invisibly under the table.

When the gong sounded, everyone walked into the dining room and sat down at long tables for the *rijsttafel.* The snow-white tablecloth was of Dutch linen from De Twente, the Dutch china from Maastricht, the sparkling Dutch glasses from Leerdam. The double doors of the kitchen swung wide open and the procession of *djongos,* led by their *mandor,* or foreman, marched in with military precision. They wore brilliantly colored Oriental sarongs of batik, with *kebajas* (the original Nehru jackets) and bright-colored turbans.

The table service was utterly precise and completely silent. Throughout the meal the boys hovered, watching the guests with total concentration. It was a perfect example of service without a smile.

The American concept of service is different. It has been molded by two overwhelming factors. The first was our traumatic experience with slavery. We have never forgotten Abraham Lincoln's admonition that no man shall say to another man, "You toil and work and earn bread and I will eat it." We still seem to feel that servant and service are vaguely entangled with slave and thus with a sinister implication of inferiority.

One can trace the roots of this feeling in the reports of visitors from Europe in the early 1800s. One of the most perceptive and sensitive of these early travelers was Mrs. Frances Trollope (the mother of the great English writer Anthony Trollope), who traveled around the U.S. for four years and set down her experiences in a book titled *Domestic Manners of the Americans.* Mrs. Trollope said that she found everywhere a horror of any kind of service because of "the reality of slavery." She found "hundreds of half-naked girls" working in the Cincinnati paper mills for less than half the wages they would have received in service. Mrs. Trollope concluded that the natural desire for one person to give service to another was being "paralyzed" by the example of slavery. A little of that paralysis seems to have remained as a permanent part of the American character.

The second factor that has molded the American philosophy of service is the egalitarian vision of the immigrants who landed on our shores in search of freedom. "Every man a king," said Huey Long. The only way you can persuade a young American to do a service job is to tell him that he's on his way to becoming a manager. It is inconceivable that anyone here should consider himself a member of a servant class. This egalitarianism was also sensed by Mrs. Trollope. She felt that Americans were convinced that "any man's son may become the equal of any other man's son" and she found, on the part of people in service, such a deep resentment, such a sense of inferiority, that they were angry and short-tempered, rudely patronizing to their customers, and were continually in a state of "ever wakeful and tormenting pride."

It is the same thread—thinner now and often gilded, but still the same thread—when the manager of a famous American hotel says, as one said to me recently, "People need not be given what they want, provided they can be persuaded to want what they are given." Or when the sommelier in a fancy restaurant sizes up an inexperienced patron, sells him that superexpensive bottle of wine, which he waves around like a baseball bat before oh, so gently placing it in the wicker basket.

Obviously, there is good and bad service everywhere—and usually a lot more of the latter than the former. Yet one is bound to say that the highest expression of luxurious personal service—the service that comes naturally, without a smile—is still most often found in Europe. Not long ago, while flying the Atlantic in the first-class lounge of a BOAC jet, I tried to get to the essence of it in a relaxed after-dinner discussion with the chief steward. With a slightly satiric twinkle in his eye and just a trace of Cockney in his accent, he said: "First off—it takes professional training. I was apprenticed for thirteen years before I became a chief steward. You have to begin by making the customer feel comfortable, relaxed, and confident about your skill. So you act very calmly, speak in a low tone, and are precise with your movements. You must know when to leave him alone, but you must be watching. You have to anticipate. You have to know what he wants a fraction of a second before he knows it himself. You have to be self-assured about your own job and yet you have to make him feel that he's in charge. You might call it an art. We British have been doing it for centuries."

I have found these guiding principles expressed in dozens of ways in such truly great hotels as Claridge's in London, the Ritz in Paris, and the Gritti Palace in Venice. Perhaps Marcel Proust said it best when he expressed his preference for the Paris Ritz: "I prefer to be in a place where there is no jostling." He was right. An absence of fuss, an imperturbability, is the mark of a great hotel as against a merely good one. From the moment one steps into the lobby, one is flattered and made to feel welcome. Every problem is instantly smoothed over.

One evening in his suite at the Gritti Palace, Ernest Hemingway and a group of friends began playing baseball. They used the long-handled, ornamental doorstop as a bat and a rolled-up pair of Hemingway's socks as the ball. With the first swing, the lead weight on the bottom of the doorstop flew off and crashed through the arched window out into the Venetian night. There was an angry shout from the bank of the Grand Canal below.

When he checked out the next day, Hemingway offered to pay for the broken window. "Ah, yes, the window," the manager said. "The flying lead weight barely missed the nose of a gentleman who is, unfortunately, a member of the city council. This gentleman, trembling with rage, came into our lobby with the weight in his hand. However, we calmed him successfully. As for paying for the window, in the three-hundred-year history of the Gritti Palace, no one, to our knowledge, has ever played baseball in any of its rooms. In commemoration of the event, Signor Hemingway, we are reducing your bill by ten percent."

The great hotel provides the unexpected or unusual service without batting an eyelid. When Peter O'Toole registered at the Dolder Grand in Zurich, he called room service to say that he always liked an English kipper for his breakfast. The request was at once reported to the manager, who telephoned his London suppliers and had the kippers flown in on the night plane. Next morning, O'Toole had not the slightest idea that he had caused any trouble.

Service without a smile demands many unusual qualities on the part of the staff. One of the chief among them is tact. Without it, there is always the danger of disaster. Lasserre's, a famous three-star restaurant in

Paris, had a regular customer who often brought his dark-haired wife for lunch but was more often seen dining with a somewhat younger woman, a stunning blonde. One day, after lunch with his wife, when the check was brought by the captain, the customer complained about the price of the wine. René Lasserre, busy at a nearby table, wished he could sink through the floor as he heard the captain say: "It is not as expensive, monsieur, as the Château Margaux you enjoyed so much last night."

Few hotel men are more tactful, more solidly reliable and resourceful than Alberto Scialanga, the manager of the Grand Hotel in Rome. One day, a chambermaid brought him a lady's black-silk nightgown that had been found in the room just vacated by a fairly obscure Belgian count and his wife, who had never stayed at the Grand before. Scialanga had the nightgown carefully wrapped and sent to *madame la comtesse* at her home in Brussels. Three days later, she called him in a furious tone of voice. What about that nightgown? Hadn't the count been alone at the hotel? Scialanga made a lightning decision. He said how happy he was that she had called. He had just been trying to reach her. The nightgown had been sent to the wrong address. Would *madame la comtesse* kindly return it and the hotel would pay the postage. The wife asked what did he mean, the wrong address? He said that the nightgown had been found in room 737. Monsieur had been in room 773. He hoped *madame* would forgive the most unfortunate mistake.

As to supreme service in restaurants, it is ridiculous to discuss only the luxury establishments. Even the smallest bistro can provide the finest service when one is a regular customer, when one's regular waiter knows exactly which is one's favorite table and which dish on the *carte du jour* one will choose before one has chosen it.

At the end of World War Two, quite soon after Paris had been liberated from the German Occupation, I returned after an absence of more than ten years. That day, Paris was poor, cold, gray, and strangely deserted. Full of my own memories, I walked along the Left Bank and, suddenly, I saw one of my favorite cafés, just off the Place St. Michel, which I had known since my days as a student at the Sorbonne. I went in. The electricity was off. The tables were dimly lighted by small, flickering oil lamps. The place was almost empty.

I walked to my favorite table, in the corner near the front window. A man came toward me in a threadbare tuxedo. It was my old waiter. He was so thin that he looked a foot taller than I remembered him. But there was the same expression on his face—the same unsmiling formality. He nodded deferentially: "Your usual *café au lait* and glass of Perrier, monsieur?" Without waiting for my answer, he limped toward the kitchen. He brought my coffee and mineral water, remembering that

I always liked the glass on the left side of the cup. He bowed slightly and walked away. He asked no questions as to where I had been. He offered no comments as to what he had been doing. I closed my eyes. It was as if I had never left Paris.

In the Paris of today, such service is hard to find. Most of the great three-star restaurants have simplified their menus to cut costs. On every horizon, there is the bleak rise of automation—not only the automation of computers but also human automation. More and more service people are being trained and rehearsed with pat, stock phrases, to make each contact with a customer as instantaneous and as impersonal as possible. The stewardess on the transatlantic plane no longer talks to you as she races to serve a hundred dinners. She asks, "How did you enjoy your meal?" but does not listen to your reply. She has already moved on to the seat behind you to ask the same question in exactly the same tone.

To earn good service you must make an effort to bring it out. But sometimes the effort is hardly worth while. Many years ago, I dined in Vienna with the late Ludwig Bemelmans, one of the finest writers on great dining and great drinking. I had no idea at the time that it was to be a special occasion that he would make famous, later, in one of his short stories.

When I met Bemelmans that evening, he was in a state of furious irritation. He had discovered a restaurant with a name so obviously dishonest that even the thought of it had put him in a temper. The restaurant was called Chops from Every Animal in the World. He said: "Let's go there and cut them down!"

Bemelmans called the restaurant and reserved a table for two, using his name and mine. I discovered later that this call instantly threw the restaurant into a panic. The terrified chef called the owner, who was at home but who immediately threw on his dinner jacket and arrived just a minute before we did to meet us in the lobby with a deep bow. He was, obviously, a man with money; equally obviously, he had no artistic taste whatsoever. The latter was apparent from the fact that the name of the restaurant was printed across the front of the building in five-foot-high floodlit red letters.

We were seated at the best table and the owner approached with the menu. Bemelmans imperiously waved it away and, in a very quiet voice, said: "We will each have an elephant chop. . . ."

The owner's body jerked slightly and his face turned ghostly white. But he instantly steeled himself and asked: "And how would monsieur wish the elephant chops to be prepared?"

Without a second's hesitation, Bemelmans replied: "Oh, lightly sautéed, rare, in butter, *à la milanaise*, served with a covering of *risotto*, crossed anchovy fillets and a black olive at the center of the cross."

"That will be very good, monsieur." The owner bowed again and almost ran to the kitchen. For five minutes we calmly sipped our Campari-and-sodas. Bemelmans whispered: "I'll bet any money you like that the name of this restaurant was the idea of the chef and now the owner is out there screaming, 'You fool! What are we going to do?'"

We did not have long to wait. The chef appeared from the kitchen, in sparkling white from the tip of his *haut chapeau* to the hem of his long apron. With calm, deliberate steps, he approached our table, bowed, and leaned over us: "Monsieur has ordered two elephant chops?"

"Yes," Bemelmans hissed.

"Sautéed *à la milanaise*, with rice, anchovies, and an olive?"

"Yes."

"And *les messieurs* have no beautiful ladies with them tonight?"

"No."

"And *les messieurs* expect no other guests tonight?"

"No."

"And *les messieurs* wish only *one* elephant chop each?"

"Yes. Yes." Bemelmans' baby-round face and his bald head were red with rage. "Why all these impudent questions?"

The chef drew himself up to his full height: "Because, I am very sorry, monsieur, but for only two chops, we cannot cut up our elephant."

Confessions of
an Oyster Lover

I am desperately in love with oysters and have spent a large part of my life pursuing them to their beds. I was nine when I tasted my first oyster. I remember it as if it were this morning. My father had a summer home in Holland, where we would spend part of our time in the lovely seacoast district of Zeeland, where the oysters, the Zeelanders, are among the finest in the world. In those days, there were still wild beds in small bays.

On this crisp, sunny day, I remember the wind rustling through the grasses on the sand dunes as my father and I push out our boat to go fishing. The black ducks are flying low. At lunch time, my father maneuvers the boat over one of his pet oyster beds, takes a long rake, and begins bringing up a muddy mess and dumping it into the bottom of the boat. We sort through it, pulling out the good oysters, throwing everything else overboard. I lay out rows of crackers and lemon wedges on the stern seat.

When the Zeelanders are opened, their flesh seems to be the color of priceless pearls. Their aroma reminds me of everything I have ever known and loved about the sea. Their meat is firm, at the same time delightfully tender, with a tiny touch of sweetness. I feel a rush of joy, of pure energy. If oysters are a drug, I am hooked.

Fate seemed determined to associate me with the oyster. After Holland, each summer my mother took me to England, where we would stay in the small town of Whitstable. About sixty miles from London,

EDITOR'S NOTE: This syndicated newspaper article originally appeared in January 1981.

Whitstable was the home of the supreme British oysters, the Royal Natives. I was in my teens and made friends with the captain of a dredging boat. He took me on many of their daily trips to clean, dredge, lay the brood, sort, transplant, and generally housekeep the oyster beds. Vicariously, I became knowledgeable about oysters.

I grew aware of the strange sex-by-remote-control of the oyster, which regularly changes its sex. It may be female for a few months, then male, then back to female, and so on throughout its life. I was jealous of the oyster. It seemed to have the best of both worlds. One day, in an experimental tank of the Whitstable Oyster Co., I observed the sex act of a group of oysters.

There was a slight scratching at the bottom of the tank. One of the males opened his shell about one-fourth inch and puffed out a small cloud of sperm, like tiny whiffs of smoke. All the females around him seemed to catch an infectious excitement. With more scratching, several opened their shells and shot out millions of infinitesimal eggs, which floated through the sperm and were fertilized. This, in turn, excited other males, who sent out more clouds of sperm. As a result of this orgy-at-arm's-length, a new generation of oysters was spawned.

If this had happened on the beds in the open sea, the start in life of the eggs would have been both dramatic and tragic. Millions are gobbled up, almost at once, as a feast for hungry, predatory fish. But there are so many eggs (about 700 million from each female) that millions by the law of averages escape, to be widely scattered by ocean currents for about two weeks, while each egg grows a single, tiny foot, and under it, a supply of natural adhesive.

The miniscule oyster is called a spat. At the end of the two weeks of the only freedom it will ever know, it sinks to the bottom and clamps onto the first solid thing it finds. It cannot maneuver much, so it has to accept the luck of the landing. Sometimes it comes down on a back of a crab and has to move around with its host until the crab sheds its shell.

The spat is now a miniature oyster. If it is lucky, it will have found a near-perfect home in which to grow. The water, from which it draws all its food, must be clean, unpolluted, not too salty. This is why most of the greatest oyster beds of the world are in or near the mouths of rivers, where a continuous flow of fresh water dilutes the salty sea. Also enormously important to the oyster is the seabed around it. Shifting sands can choke and kill it.

In Falmouth, England, there are small deposits of copper under the beds and the oysters develop a coppery color. The Marennes of France absorb chlorophyll from the surrounding seaweed and their flesh becomes delicately green. The environment is so dominant in forming the flavor of oysters that all the oysters of the world are named for the sites where they grow.

The developing young oyster devotes itself to drinking heavily. It can easily pass twenty-six quarts of water through its body in an hour and continue hour after hour. It filters out all the tiny diatoms, peridia, and plankton that it needs for its food. It enlarges its shell. It may be moved by the oysterman from one bed to another to develop certain nuances of flavor and texture. Finally, after a growing period of three to seven years, the oyster is ready to satisfy my craving to eat it live.

My sex education came early from watching oysters in their experimental tanks. I was convinced that eating oysters was the key to male irresistibility. I tried to find proof in learned books on aphrodisiacs. After all, if African tribes eat ground rhinoceros horn, if the Indians of British Columbia swallow the gonads of salmon, if Europeans almost poison themselves with the wings of the Lytta blister beetle (Spanish fly), why could I not find super virility on the half shell? The scientists said I was wrong. But I drew some hope from a British doctor, a London gynecologist, who wrote in a professional magazine:

> Hunger is an appetite common to both sexes, and during their mutual satisfaction of it, a man and a woman can assess each other for a more intimate relationship. In every civilized society, oysters have played an important symbolic role in this preliminary phase of courtship. The oyster signals an extravagant gesture. The diners immediately absorb an abundance of minerals and vitamins, free from any heavy load. So they remain alert.
>
> The simplicity of the oyster leaves the man and the woman free to concentrate on each other. The appetite is stimulated. The physical aura of the oyster is sensual: plump, quivering, round, soft to the touch. To the woman, it symbolizes the womb of the pearl; to the man, the cleft shell with the soft interior reflects the anatomy of the woman. . . . The oyster has always played a major role in the creation of the atmosphere for lovers.

I grew to manhood with the help of oysters. My passion for them became overwhelming. When I did not have the money to buy them, I stole them. I have even poached oysters in the dead of night from closed beds during May, June, July, and August, when after their usual April spawning, they recover their strength by producing a natural starch called glycogen which makes them taste bland and mealy. I cannot bear to be deprived of them.

The world's oyster list is almost as long as the world's wine list and there are quite a few similarities. Both have their great names, varieties, family resemblances, rarities, and prestigious reputations. To be an aficionado, you have to know the top names.

When the hunger hits me in Chicago, I drop in to see Fred Manof, the manager of the Chicago Fish House retail division, where oysters from around the country are distributed to local fish markets and consumers. Fred lets me sit on a barrel in his back room and open a few dozen. I usually skip the Bluepoints because, although they are certainly fine and fresh, this name generally is used in the trade to cover all kinds of medium-sized oysters (average two and a half inches in diameter) from many places, so there is a certain lack of individuality. The same problem applies to oysters called Cape Cods, the general name in the trade for any kind of large oyster. I always insist on picking mine by the place names.

In Fred's back room, I begin with Port Norris mediums from Delaware Bay on the New Jersey coast, followed by the magnificent chewy, fat, rich Cotuits from the bay and village of that name on the south shore of Cape Cod, and then some of the world's finest, the Chincoteagues from the Chincoteague inlet on the Virginia side of Chesapeake Bay.

The oyster heartwater of this country has been Chesapeake Bay for more than 200 years. Besides the lordly Chincoteagues, it gives us the great Kent Islanders, Patuxents, Rappahannocks, and Tangiers. The only challenge to the supremacy of these on the East or Gulf coasts are the Florida Appalachicola Bays.

The first time I visited Puget Sound, the oyster heaven of the Pacific Northwest, I fell in with, what was for me, bad company. My boon companion was the delightful food writer, the late Stan Reed, whose appetite was about as big as mine, who knew everything there was to know about Pacific oysters, and who was more than willing to satisfy my wildest cravings. The first day, we lunched at a famous oyster house in Seattle. Consuming nothing but oysters, we put away $200 worth.

This area is the home ground of one of the supreme food delicacies of North America, found nowhere else in the world, the native miniature Olympia oyster, the shell about the size of a quarter, the flesh the size of a nickel. One normal portion is three dozen, served shucked in their juice in a pedestal glass, set in crushed ice. The supreme taste and texture of these little oysters has to be experienced to be believed. They are among the great specialties of the world. Naturally, their expense is stratospheric. For this kind of gastronomic experience, one does not question cost.

Another North American oyster always worth a detour to its home on Canada's Prince Edward Island, where it is gathered by skin divers, is the marvelous Malpeque. It is so famous that it is distributed by most of the top U.S. fish markets during its short season from October into early January.

The Supremes of the oyster world are relatively few, and they are spread far and wide. I would vote for five or six of North American oysters already named as being truly great. To find and taste the others, you have to travel the world.

On the northeast coast of Brittany, there is the greatest of France: the Belon, the oyster that is almost certainly the world's best-known and most sought after. (When I dined recently at a fancy French restaurant in Hong Kong, they were offering Belons on the half shell, just flown in from France at the equivalent of $5 per oyster.) Belons have been laid down in the cool salt waters off our coast of Maine, so we are getting American Belons from the mouth of the Damariscotta River.

I can count the other great oysters of the earth on my fingers. In England, there are the Whitstable Royal Natives, and the Colchesters, from the small east coast town. In Ireland, there are the fabulous Galway Bays from the west coast. In Belgium, there are the Ostenders, and in the Netherlands, the great Zeelanders. From Australia, the great oysters known all over the Far East are the Sydney Rocks, and from New Zealand, the smaller, more delicate Auckland Bays.

These are the big names. There also are the small joys. I remember a warm, moonlit night in Florida when I was taken to an informal picnic of the superb oysters of the Indian River by my friend, the writer Marjorie Kinnan Rawlings. We drove down the narrowest of sandy lanes, between scrub palmettos, to the water's edge and the shack of Gene, the old oysterman who tended his beds just offshore. When he put on a roast, he promised, "All you can eat for 50 cents." We took our own butter for melting, brown bread, salad, beer, and coffee.

As we turned the last bend on the lane, the orange glow from Gene's fire lit up the oak trees and the long pine tables under them. He had a big sheet of iron, about as big as a king-size double bed, supported on iron posts over a blazing fatwood fire. Gene brought up baskets of oysters from the river beds, dumped them onto the hot iron sheet, raked them into a single layer, and threw over them water-soaked sacking. There was an explosion of hissing and clouds of steam. The oysters sizzled for a few short minutes, and at exactly the right moment, known only to Gene, he pulled off the sacks, raked the oysters to the side with a dramatic flourish, and piled them along the tables. "Don't hold back," he said, "there's more where them came from."

There are thousands of little corners like that all over the world growing incomparable oysters of rare quality, but in such small quantities that their names never will be known except to the connoisseurs who live right there.

Perhaps the sadness of my life is that, however long I live, I will never be able to find all those secret little beds.

THE PERFECT OYSTER KNIFE

To get the full character of a great oyster, you should eat it within five minutes of its being opened. Obviously, you need to arm yourself with an efficient oyster knife and learn the simple trick of opening the shells without hurting either the oyster or yourself. Half the battle is having a well-designed oyster knife, preferably with a hilt to protect your fingers.

HOW TO OPEN AN OYSTER
WITHOUT HURTING ITS FEELINGS

Professionals, when they compete at international festivals, can open fifty oysters in less than four minutes. That is just under five seconds per oyster. My average is about ten seconds, which means that I can open a dozen in two minutes. So can you, with a bit of practice. The point I am making is that opening oysters is no big deal.

Arm yourself with a stiff wire brush and quickly scrub each oyster clean under cold running water. Open them over a bowl in which you have balanced a sieve to catch bits of shell. The flavorful juice runs through into the bowl and is used later. Hold the oyster in the palm of your hand and, with the point of your knife, go in through the hinge. Then slide the knife around until you have cut the muscle that holds the shells tightly together. Throw away the flat top shell. Keep the curved deep shell as the cup in which to serve the oyster. Gently run the knife under the oyster to loosen it from the shell. Spoon over it some of the juice you have reserved in the bowl. Serve the oysters on a bed of crushed ice.

WHAT TO SERVE WITH OYSTERS ON THE HALF SHELL

The delicate, sublime flavor of a great oyster never should be over-powered by anything stronger than a dribble of freshly squeezed lemon juice, and perhaps a few grains of freshly ground Chinese Szechuan pepper, lighter than Indian black pepper. Anyone who insists on dipping a great oyster into a blood-red cocktail sauce of horseradish and catsup should be considered guilty of a criminal offense and executed at dawn. If this kind of sauce is more important to your pleasure than the oyster, do not spend big money on Chincoteagues, Cotuits, or Malpeques. Buy inexpensive, second-grade oysters.

If you insist on having something more fancy than plain lemon juice, there are a few light sauces that are reasonably acceptable:

1. Melted butter with lemon juice.
2. From the Four Seasons Restaurant in New York, chef Seppi Renggli's hitherto-unpublished recipe for a modified mignonette without egg. Combine 3 tablespoons dry red wine (such as Gamay or Beaujolais), 2½ teaspoons to 1 tablespoon white-wine tarragon vinegar, 1 tablespoon minced shallots, and salt and pepper, to taste. Cover; let stand 24 hours. Drizzle about ¼ teaspoon over each oyster on the half shell.
3. A light and lemony mayonnaise.
4. An extremely light remoulade.

WHAT TO DRINK WITH OYSTERS ON THE HALF SHELL

I do not believe in Champagne with oysters. The bubbles overrule their subtle taste. If you want wine, it should be dry and have a lemony tang. If cost is no problem, the top choice is a *grand cru* French Chablis. That is the classic combination. A second choice, at a much lower price, is a French Muscadet from the Sèvres-et-Maine district. For an American wine, choose a dry Pinot Blanc, or a Sauvignon Blanc.

A fine accompaniment I often prefer is a well-chilled tankard of a noble ale or beer. Somehow the prickly bite of the fermented malt is the almost perfect foil to the lusciously soft texture of the oyster.

If you pin me down for specifics, here are the exact beer-oyster combinations I love: Canadian Malpeques with Molson's ale or Ballantine's aged India pale ale; Chesapeake Chincoteagues with English Whitbread pale ale; Northeastern oysters from Cape Cod, or Long Island with Bass ale. Virtually any oyster is uplifted by Guinness stout. Other lagers I have found extremely good are Beamish Irish stout, from Cork, and Worthington ale from Britain.

HOW TO COOK AN OYSTER
WITHOUT CONVERTING IT TO LEATHER

Naturally, on a frozen winter's day, the most attractive food may not be a plate of cold oysters on crushed ice. So serve oysters in a hot state. There are two vital points to be clearly understood. First, an oyster cannot be heated fast, or a moment too long, or it is fit only to resole shoes. Watch the mantle of skin around the edge of the oyster. The moment it starts to crinkle, regardless of cooking method, the oyster is done and must be removed from the heat. Immediately.

Second, cooking a truly great oyster is a waste. Its delicate, sublime flavor will be lost in the heating. These days, great oysters may cost you more than a dollar each. Do not waste that kind of money for an oyster to be cooked. Use fresh oysters, but of the second grade, much less expensive types. The final result in a hot dish will be as good.

Choose your oyster recipes carefully. There are few really good ones. A creamy oyster stew can be fine. Baked oysters sometimes can be fairly good. Fried oysters deep-fried in a mahogany brown, cracker-hard batter crust should be forbidden by law.

One of the best basic ways of cooking any oyster was perfected by the great British author, Dean Jonathan Swift, while he was writing *Gulliver's Travels*. He described it in a famous letter to his lady love, Stella.

"Take oysters, wash them clean; that is, wash their shells clean, then put your oysters in an earthen pot, with their hollow side down, then put this pot, covered, into a great kettle with water, and so let them boil. Your oysters are boiled in their own liquor."

We call this steaming. Put oysters (curved or hollow side down) in a single layer on the top rack of a lidded steamer over boiling water. Cover. Steam exactly 3 minutes, or just until the shells open slightly. Immediately remove from heat.

ONE GREAT OYSTER DISH

The most famous baked dish is oysters Rockefeller, invented about fifty years ago by Antoine Alciatore, the founder of Antoine's restaurant in New Orleans. He did not put it together, as is generally believed, in honor of a visiting Rockefeller. He had run out of snails and thought he could interest his customers in hot oysters as a replacement, provided they were served with a bright green, snail-type sauce. When he had finished his experiments, the green was the color of greenbacks and the whole thing was so rich that he wanted a name that would signify the "richest in the world." The first to come to mind was Rockefeller.

The exact recipe has been kept a secret since then, although hundreds of versions have been published. Recently, I dined at Antoine's with Roy Guste, co-owner and manager. He did not give me the secret recipe, but assured me that the real thing does not contain spinach. So that is one way you can check the authenticity of a printed recipe. My own guess for the real oysters Rockefeller is this.

OYSTERS ROCKEFELLER

4 servings

> 16 *tablespoons unsalted sweet butter*
> 1/3 *cup each minced shallots or green onion, chopped fresh fennel*
> 1/4 *cup chopped celery with some leaves*
> 2 *fairly tightly packed cups coarsely chopped watercress leaves*
> 1/2 *cup chopped parsley leaves*
> 1 *tablespoon chopped fresh tarragon leaves or 1 teaspoon dried*
> 1/2 *cup fine dry breadcrumbs*
> 1/3 *cup dry New Orleans Herbsaint anise liqueur*
> *Salt, pepper, cayenne pepper, to taste*
> 2 *dozen raw cleaned oysters, opened on the hard shell*
> *Rock salt*

1. Melt 3 tablespoons butter in large skillet; stir in shallots, fennel, and celery. Cook and stir 3 minutes. Stir in watercress, parsley, and tarragon; cook and stir 1 to 2 minutes, or until wilted.

2. Put watercress mixture with remaining butter in food processor or blender container. Add breadcrumbs and dry anise liqueur and process until smooth. Add salt, pepper, and cayenne to taste.

3. Put oysters on a baking pan lined with rock salt in a single layer. Put a dollop of herb butter over each oyster. Bake at 475° F until butter is melted and oysters are warm, about 4 minutes.

I know I am supposed to give just one great dish here, but an insatiable oyster lover cannot stop at just one. So here is a second great dish.

SEPPI RENGGLI'S OYSTERS WITH CAVIAR

Take fresh, young spinach leaves of suitable size, each to wrap an oyster, then blanch them for a few seconds in boiling salted water. Rinse them at once under cold water to stop the cooking. Take each oyster, put on it a few grains of Tellicherry black pepper, then ⅛-teaspoon black Belugga caviar. Wrap it completely in a spinach leaf of suitable size, tucking in the sides like an envelope. When you have all your oysters wrapped, put into the top of a steamer and steam until they are just nicely warm, never more than 45 to 60 seconds. Serve instantly on quite hot plates.

On Becoming and on Being a Gourmet

Can this book [*Feasts for All Seasons*], or any book, teach the average person with an average interest in food to be a gourmet? The answer lies in a clear understanding of the meaning of the word "gourmet," which is surely one of the most overworked and ill-understood in our language. Insistent signs in supermarkets invite the shopper into the "gourmet-foods department," where one might almost expect to find magic potions to produce an effortless fine meal. Every day we read and hear the phrases "gourmet cookery," "gourmet recipe," "gourmet kitchen." But the fact is that the word "gourmet" is not just another adjective in the language of salesmanship, like "super," or "fancy," or "special." It is a title that applies only to a person, a title of honor, confirming certain skills that have been learned by study and practice.

Many French historians believe that the word derives from the *gromet* of the court of Louis XIV at Versailles. The noblemen in their châteaux across France were getting restive. The king, fearing that they might conspire against him, ordered them all to Versailles. There, to keep idle hands busy, he created a large number of jobs around the palace. A business manager was appointed to each household department and given the title of *gromet*. (Some *gromets* managed the royal stables and today we still speak of the man who looks after a horse as a "groom.") The duties of the food *gromets* were clearly defined. The royal food supply depended on the French "tithe" system—each producer had to contribute one tenth of his harvest as a tax—but there was serious discontent among the

EDITOR'S NOTE: This piece is excerpted from the introduction to *Feasts for All Seasons* (Knopf, 1966).

farmers, fishermen, butchers, millers, wine growers, etc., and each tried to hold back the best of the produce from the king. The first order of the day, therefore, for the royal food *gromets* was to ride out and bring in the proper amounts of the best foods. They had to be sharp judges of quality and value.

This was half the battle in getting good meals at Versailles. It is *more* than half the battle for the gourmet of today, in a world where the imitation often looks better than the real thing and where price seems to bear less and less relationship to quality. No amount of cooking skill in the kitchen can produce a fine meal on the table, unless it is preceded by selective skill in the market. Far more is involved than simply finding a "good buy." It is a matter of getting the right grade for the right purpose and often the higher-priced grade can be quite wrong. For example, in certain types of slow-cooked beef stews, the best grades of sirloin steak would be much too soft and would disintegrate long before the full flavor had been achieved. Again, the preparation of a concentrated chicken stock, where the accent is more on the broth than on the chicken, should start inexpensively with a tough old hen, which can be simmered for hours.

Since the problem of getting the right grade of the right food at the right time is crucial to the gourmet, a substantial part of this book is devoted to the basic questions of efficient shopping. Which are the best foods in season at various times of the year? How much bone and fat is in the various cuts of meat? How does one find better blends of coffees and teas? Which wines are consistently good from year to year? These are among the multitude of questions which must be answered by the gourmet in the market.

When the best supplies were safely gathered into the storerooms at Versailles, the skilled food *gromets* moved into the kitchens. The huge fires were tended by semi-skilled peasants who could roast or bake according to a traditional "rule." But often the fires grew too hot, or the flour was coarser than usual, or the age of the mutton was misjudged. Then the fixed rule broke down and the *gromets* had to take control to save the royal supper.

The need for flexible judgment in the kitchen is the same today. It is impossible to guarantee a perfect result simply by telling the cook to put X pounds of meat into an oven at Y degrees for Z minutes. In an effort to make this book a guide toward the standards of a gourmet, its recipes take account of the variable factors and go beyond the mere uniting of fixed amounts of ingredients in a rigid series of 1-2-3 steps. Instead there is a clear definition of the result that is being sought and of the signs of progress. How is the taste developing at the halfway point? How soft should the meat feel when pressed after the first thirty minutes? How should the color change?

The final duties of the skilled food *gromets* at Versailles were those of the *officiers de la bouche*—the last tasting before service to the king. As each course was ready to be carried to the dining hall on the enormous platters, usually borne by four men, there was a last checking of seasonings. Finally, at the table, the *gromet*-of-the-day had to taste once more in the royal presence to assure the king that all was perfection—and, incidentally, not poisoned!

This then is our three-way definition of a gourmet: one who can expertly judge food in the market, who has both skill and flexibility in the kitchen, and who shows, at the table, an exquisite sensitivity to the needs and desires of his guests.

The essence of the gourmet's attitude is expressed by two basic qualities of living: respect and integrity. When friends enter the circle of our hospitality, the care we take in preparing the food is a measure of our respect for our guests. To achieve the final perfection at the table, we must begin with respect for the gift of Nature's raw materials. Respect demands that good meat, for example, shall not be spoiled in the oven; that it shall be brought to table at the proper temperature; that it shall be carefully carved to preserve its texture and served in such a way as to enhance its natural flavors. In the market, the gourmet has a right to demand integrity in the growing and distribution of food, whether it be the farmer cultivating his peaches for flavor rather than size, or the butcher cutting his carcasses for maximum quality rather than maximum profit, or the grocer taking care to store his eggs at the right temperature. When fresh fruits and vegetables are allowed to deteriorate through incompetent handling, when the contents of a can fail to fulfill the promise of the label, when a package is deliberately designed to mislead the shopper, these are all reflections of that lack of respect for the customer which is implicit in the phrase "the public won't know the difference."

We believe it to be the responsibility of the gourmet to demonstrate in every possible way that the public *does* know the difference and to demand respect for the good taste and intelligence of the consumer. It should never be too much trouble to write a letter to the president of a manufacturing company demanding the replacement of a poor-quality product. If the first taste of a bottle of wine shows it to be inferior, the bottle should be recorked at once and returned to the wine merchant with a demand for a refund. Above all, the gourmet makes demands upon himself: he must continually raise his own standards and resist the multitude of compromises that are constantly offered to tempt him.

It is perhaps a strange twist that it was an Englishman, not a Frenchman, who expressed the ultimate definition of the attitude of the gourmet. It was Dr. Samuel Johnson who said: "He who does not mind his belly will hardly mind anything else."

The Qualities of
Memorable Meals

Some of the most vivid memories of my life are centered on the dining table. I remember each of my youthful girl friends, not by the ardor of her kisses, but by the best meal with which I impressed her. I can still see, in my mind, the first meal I ever had in Paris at that simple and still wonderful restaurant above Androuet's cheese shop, on the rue Amsterdam. I can still relive (and retaste) my first Provençale lunch, on a terrace overlooking the Mediterranean. And so it goes . . . a lifetime picture book of memorable meals.

The great, the classic dishes—those that are on most of the first menus and that one tastes with renewed pleasure again and again, year after year—are, to me, like the symphonies of Mozart. Each time the waiter presents the beautifully decorated dish at table, each time the conductor raises his baton in the concert hall, it is a new performance of an intimately known work. Each time I pass in review in my mind previous performances by other chefs, other musicians. This magnificent, truffle-stuffed saddle of veal à la Prince Orloff, prepared for me by Chef Claude Colomb at Ernie's in San Francisco? This great performance of the Linz Symphony, under the direction of Maestro Bruno Walter in the hushed Concertgebouw auditorium in Amsterdam? How do they compare with all the other performances of my experience? Could this be the best? Will this evening be supremely memorable? If not, then how should tonight be rated in the long sequence of my plea-

EDITOR'S NOTE: This piece is excerpted from *Esquire's Handbook for Hosts* (Grosset & Dunlap, 1973).

sures? Perhaps the veal had more flavor, perhaps the violins a fuller tone, when I was in Vienna fifteen years ago? Was the sauce more delicate, the flute player more sensitive, in London? The truffles, and the trumpets, more nearly perfect in Salzburg? The interest and pleasure of food, music, and wine continue and increase with every added year of experience. Especially with food, where one can be both performer and critic, the development of one's skill is more than a hobby. It is an art—an art of which one will never tire, because there will always be something new to learn, the art of the gourmet—the art of the memorable host.

THE PERFECT DINNER PARTY

Sometimes on a sub-zero winter's morning, when I wake to the whine of the wind whipping up the Hudson River, I stretch out warmly under my goose-feather eiderdown and half-dream about the perfect dinner party. It's a good time for concentration on thought for food. My mouth is slightly dry and thirsty. My stomach is gently rumbling its request for breakfast. My mind focuses on the various questions one by one. What would be the ideal menu for such a dinner? The ideal wine list? The ideal season of the year? The ideal place and setting? But before any of these questions can be answered I must decide on the ideal list of guests. The perfect dinner can be planned only with particular people in mind.

I have decided that the ideal number for the perfect dinner should be ten, including the host and his (permanent or temporary) hostess. In my half-dream, I assemble my guests from everywhere, past and present. I consider the possibility of bringing back Dr. Samuel Johnson from his witty dinner-table debates in the coffee and chop houses of eighteenth-century London. On second thought—no. When one guest completely dominates the dinner, no one notices the food. When one guest's wit is sharper than the carving knife, it can cut the pleasure of the others. When one of the guests lost his temper during a dinner-table debate Dr. Johnson said, "Pray, what annoys you, sir? Have I said something that you understand?"

I might decide to invite Cleopatra, not only because she was beautiful, but also because her social experience would add charm and luster to the conversation. She would be amusing if not brilliantly witty, sparkling if not supremely intelligent. And it would be fascinating to try, by subtle and tactful verbal dexterity, to find out what she had been really thinking about life and love.

The Perfect Guest List

I believe that there are certain basic rules that must be followed in assembling a compatible group of guests for the perfect dinner party. Couples too much interested in each other simply do not fit into a larger party. Two lovers so feverishly absorbed in their own relationship that they have no eyes or ears for anyone else should dine by themselves. So should couples who are feuding or fiercely competing with each other. A husband and wife whose marriage is on the point of breaking up or two politicians running against each other in a current election would put a damper on the pleasures of the evening.

I think I would invite one solidly united couple (either legally or extralegally) to give a sense of security to the party. I might ask another couple for exactly the reverse reason—that their emotional and sexual relationship, not being precisely known, would challenge the rest of the company to subtle, conversational exploration. I would invite at least one stranger, perhaps an extremely beautiful girl with a slightly mysterious background and with no obviously visible means of support, as a further challenge to the intellectual investigations of the evening. Then, to make sure that my food and wine would be noticed and intelligently discussed, I would like to have two or three gourmets in the party— perhaps representing each of the three great cuisines of the world: a Chinese, a Frenchman, and an Indian. This may be a personal conceit of mine, but it *is* always good to have some of the guests linked by a common interest, to provide at least one safe channel for the conversation. The rules for assembling a well-matched group of guests are basic and not exceptionally complicated.

The Perfect Place and Setting

As to where my perfect dinner should be given, it would be easy to decide instantly that it must be in the top-floor dining room of the great Restaurant de la Tour d'Argent on the Quai Tournelle in Paris—with one whole wall a picture window looking across the Seine to the floodlit Cathedral of Notre Dame de Paris. Or it could be in the terrace dining room of the Palazzo Gritti, overlooking the Grand Canal in Venice. But these choices are too easy and obvious.

Since my perfect dinner party is still half a dream and there are to be no limitations in terms of the logistics of reality, why not serve it in a Swiss chalet on a mountaintop with an immense view of snow-capped peaks turning pink at sunset? But mountaintops, in my experience, are for picnics, with my companion suitably impressed by the superb delicacies I bring out from my insulated shoulder basket. I remember a marvelous dinner on the terrace of the lovely, pink-walled Château Loudenne in the Médoc wine district of Bordeaux, with the evening view sweeping down the vineyard slopes to the wide waters of the Gironde estuary, where the passing green and red lights of the ships reminded us, as we dined, of the great wines of France being carried to the world.

At this point, perhaps, my half-dream begins to fade and a sharper reality takes command of my plans. I am now sure that my perfect dinner party must be around a calm and peaceful table here at home. I can at once think of a superb setting. It could be served in the dining room of Nicholas Roosevelt in his extraordinary house precariously perched at the top of a thousand-foot cliff at Big Sur, on the rocky California coast a few miles south of Carmel. As the entrée was being served, we would watch, through the picture window, the fire-red ball of the sun slowly descending into the Pacific, beyond the Bay of Whales and the Punta del Lobos del Mar, the Point of the Sea Wolves.

Or—and perhaps best, dinner could be served on the magnificent roof terrace of the house of Harry Serlis, on the peak of Russian Hill in San Francisco, with the lights of Fisherman's Wharf and the ships in the harbor almost straight down below us and the view sweeping from the Golden Gate across the Bay to the distant misty Berkeley Hills. I would cover this terrace with a red-and-white-striped tent, open on three sides for the view, but with a roof above us, to give us a sense of privacy from the watching stars.

The time of year should be the late spring, when the San Francisco air is gently warm, and the first fruits and vegetables of the season begin to arrive bright, luscious, sweet, from the central valleys.

The Perfect Menu

For this perfect dinner my menu would be unexpected, unusual, at some points astonishing, a dramatic tour de force. The composition of such a menu would be ruled by the basic principles that I apply to all my menu-planning. You start your guests with something they know—something safe and sound—but done with imaginative personal touches, better than they have ever had it before. If, for example, your guest of honor is a Spaniard, newly arrived in the United States, he will obviously want to try our American food, but will be enormously flattered and pleased if you start him off with a classic Spanish *entreméses variados*, prepared and presented as authentically as if he were still at home.

Next, you begin to take your guests with you on an exploratory trip. The second course may be something they immediately recognize, but prepared in a surprising way, with unexpected decorations, garnishes, and seasonings. As they taste, they think, "Wow!—this recipe is an extraordinary combination, but very good! I must get the recipe and try it myself."

Now you have softened them for the big adventure. You give them a dish that they have never had before. You take them out with you into totally unexplored territory. I firmly believe that the secret of a truly great dinner is to have at least one magnificent, but brand-new-to-almost-everyone dish. It isn't as difficult as it sounds. Once you have discovered such a dish and worked out the techniques of its preparation, you can serve it at dinner after dinner to different groups of friends, until you have exhausted your invitation list. Meanwhile, you can be working up your second "unknown dish."

Finally, after the excitement of the exploration, you come back to a safe and sound dessert. This pattern, of course, can be infinitely varied. The big surprise might be the first or the last course. The flattery of the foreign visitor might be by a soup, a fish, a rare game meat, or the dessert. I shall try to show later that menu-planning, while being infinitely flexible, is not nearly so difficult as some people would have us believe.

Apart from the order and balance of the courses, the "secret ingredient" of a memorable dinner is preparing it with the finest of ingredients. One of the greatest of modern French chefs, Fernand Point, once said, "The secret of great cooking is butter, butter, and more butter." To this I would add the essential elements of cream, of wine, and of fruit brandies. I have never eaten a memorable meal that was produced with skimmed milk and margarine.

Sometimes I consider it good dining-table strategy to challenge directly the obstinate conservatism of a guest. We all know the man who loudly and aggressively boasts, "I don't go for this gormy stuff—I'm a steak and potatoes man!" Okay. So I'll give him what he wants. I'll poach a prime sirloin steak in Madeira, with garlic-flavored mushrooms, then flame it with Armagnac as it is set before him. If his face feels the heat of the fire, so much the better. There will be no potatoes anywhere in sight. Then, just as he thinks he is finished, his potatoes will arrive as a separate course in the form of a *gratin dauphinois*, another version of the baked casserole of the French Alps, in which the sliced potatoes are simmered in milk and heavy cream. I will then ask, nonchalantly, "How did you like your steak and potatoes?"

Before sitting down at table I would serve, for this most perfect of dinners, the one hors d'oeuvre that is universally safe, completely acceptable: large-grained, black Beluga caviar, served on small, canapé squares of black bread, with no more seasoning than a few drops of lemon juice. With this, the driest and lightest of Champagnes, Taittinger, Blanc de Blancs, Comtes de Champagne.

If caviar is not available I might begin with firmly textured, first-quality Atlanta Nova Scotia smoked salmon. The dramatic way of serving it is to have a complete "side of the fish"—a three-foot-long, boneless fillet, with the skin underneath—laid out on a cutting board, with an ultra-sharp sixteen-inch knife, on a side table, so that each guest can cut his own paper-thin slices. I often have this delicacy sent to me by Willy Krauch, a Danish fisherman who owns the last smokehouse actually operating in Nova Scotia. Most alleged Nova Scotia salmon is now smoked in large factories elsewhere.

This help-yourself method of offering it to my guests, although it creates an atmosphere of unlimited luxury, does have its pitfalls. Once, a friend called a few hours before he was due to dine with me and made the usual excuse about a friend, an attorney from a small town somewhere or other, who had unexpectedly arrived in town and could he come too? The friend, apparently, had never seen or heard of smoked salmon. We suddenly, with shocked amazement, noticed him standing in front of the cutting board, not slicing the salmon almost horizontally, but cutting straight down into it and tearing off quarter-pound chunks, which he wolfed down before making the next cut. When I rushed, horrified, to his side, he said, fatuously, "I never, in all my life, ate such delicious fish!"

The Beauty of the Table Frames the Food

Our mouths made clean by the earthy salt of the caviar or the smoked salmon, we carry our glasses with the remaining Champagne to the dining table. It is handsomely decorated, with a carefully planned balance of colors. Tonight, for the formal meal, it is covered with a white cloth, on which the china and silver sparkle with reflected light. My wineglasses are of clear, undecorated glass to dramatize the visual beauty of the wine itself. I never permit flowers as a centerpiece. At worst, their scent can interfere with the bouquet of the food and the wine. At best, unless they are very small, they are a barrier to cross-table conversation. My favorite centerpiece is a bowl of green avocados, their skins waxed so they glow and reflect the lights.

The first course at table would also be my first surprise. I would have had flown in from France, from the great three-star restaurant of the Brothers Troisgros, their *suprême de foie gras en casserole*—the classic, goose-liver pâté, not, in the normal commercial style, boiled, or pasteurized, or canned, or frozen, or disguised with Cognac and Madeira, but just gently, gently baked in a low, low oven until the final result is pink, pure velvet. To cut the extraordinary richness of the foie gras I would serve a lightly sweet wine, say, an Alsatian Riesling, Réserve Exceptionelle of a very sunny year.

Next, just as my guests would be beginning to feel secure about my judgment, I would give them the big shock. I would have had flown in from the Mediterranean coast of France a seaweed-stuffed barrel of the most extraordinary shellfish in the world, *les violets* (don't ask me why they are called "violets"), which are dredged up along the rocky coast between Marseille and the mouth of the Rhône. A wooden cutting board and a hefty knife would be placed in front of each guest.

Les violets are oblong, rectangular shapes, rather like light-caramel slabs of milk chocolate, surrounded by a leathery thick skin. You cut straight through one, lengthwise. Inside, you find it filled with hard, inedible white muscle, but right at the center is the animal itself, a light orange-pink, about the size of a small clam. You dig it out with a teaspoon, season it with a drop or two of lemon juice, and consume a morsel that is more refined, sweeter, more succulent than any clam or oyster you have ever had in your life. The wine is a light, refreshing dry white of the southern Alps, the Crépy from the French shores of Lake Geneva. There is to me a double pleasure in this second course—the delightfully simple balance of the food and the wine plus the informality of a finger-food—an almost picnic-style break in the middle of a formal dinner. It is a trick I use often with all kinds of foods, a trick that always seems to please and relax the diners.

Since the main course is also going to be fishy, there should now first be a touch of meat, which is supplied in the third course by a classic Italian *tortellini al brodo*—a richly strong beef consommé, garnished with tiny pasta dumplings, each filled with an aromatic mixture of ground pork, chicken, sausage, and brains—a superb balance of flavors and textures. This is the moment for the arrival of the long loaves of hot-from-the-oven sourdough bread to be snapped and cracked by the guests with a shower of flying crumbs. The wine is now a raspberry-reddish pink, light, and young Beaujolais, fresh in the bottle from the latest harvest, the Château de la Chaize of the Marquise de Roussy de Sales.

The Cook's Proudest Dish

If there is a single dish in my repertoire that I am most proud of, it is my *timbale du roi Neptune,* which I punningly translate as The Kettledrum of King Neptune. (The Arabic-derived word *timbale* means both a kettledrum and a huge earthenware cooking pot.) It is not, however, the kettledrum, but the immense brown, lidded casserole that now comes to the table as the climax of the dinner. The preparation of its contents has involved many hours of labor. It began with the cooking of several lobsters, their meat chunked and poached by the classic French method *à l'américaine* in butter and white wine, before adding Cognac, crushed fresh tomatoes, shallots, and fresh tarragon. At the same time, in another sauté pan, several dozen crayfish were cooked *à la bordelaise*, with white wine, more shallots, and butter. In a large copper pot a stack of oysters were simmered in Alsatian Riesling until their shells just opened. Also, from a batch of shrimp I had made a shrimp butter by sautéing them, with a blend of aromatic vegetables, adding white wine and a dash of Pernod, then pounding them into a paste and working it into a bowl of softened sweet butter.

Finally all these separate elements had been combined in the huge earthenware *timbale* and linked together by the addition of cream, mushrooms, fresh leaves of tarragon, and a garnish of black truffles. The lid had been clamped on tightly and the *timbale* had been reheated in the oven to encourage the multitude of its internal flavors and savors to unite in a perfect marriage.

The final, dramatic trick is to keep the *timbale* tightly closed until it reaches the table and only then lift the lid. The first cloud of savory steam that bursts out has been known to make the diners dizzy with anticipation.

I originally developed this *timbale* in a series of experiments with Mediterranean shellfish while staying in the tiny fishing village of Carry-le-Rouet on the south coast of France, west of Marseille. I would go down to the miniature harbor at five in the morning to meet the fishing boats coming in with their catch, to buy the all-alive, fishy ingredients for my various gastronomic experiments. There on the dock, at that ungodly hour, I often met the great French movie star Fernandel, who had been born in the village and still had a vacation house there, where he relaxed happily in between his movies and plays. On those early mornings, he was also in search of live fish for a *timbale* recipe that had been used by his family for generations. We exchanged notes and, after I returned to New York and was finally satisfied with my recipe, I sent Fernandel a copy. A few weeks later, I received his answer: "M'sieu, I salute you. This is it! Each mouthful of your *timbale* sings on my tongue like a nightingale. I learned at school that the Greek gods, when they lived on top of Mount Olympus, used to gorge themselves on something called ambrosia! Obviously, it was another name for your *timbale*. I won't even bother again with Grandmère's *recette*."

Graceful Approach to the End

Let us get back to the menu of my perfect dinner. After the supreme climax of the *timbale*, the meal descends, gradually and gracefully, to its close. There would have been, of course, a truly great wine to match the *timbale*, perhaps a Montrachet of the Marquis de Laguiche, from the "Golden Slope" of southern Burgundy, or a great vintage year of the Château Laville Haut Brion, or the Domaine de Chevalier from the Graves district of Bordeaux. As soon as *timbale* and wine were finished (but not before—there must be no clash between wine and vinegar), I would serve a beautifully green, well-dressed salad, to "scrape the throat clean," as a great French gourmet once put it.

Now there would be a new peak of interest at table, as we poured a great (but not too great) red wine to accompany the cheeses—perhaps a Château La Mission Haut Brion or a Château Palmer from Bordeaux, or a Chambertin, a Clos Vougeot, or a Musigny from Burgundy. There would be, perhaps, an international selection of half a dozen cheeses, each in a perfect condition of age and ripeness: probably an English farm-made Cheddar, from the Cheddar Gorge, a not too hard, not too old, crumbly and grainy Italian Parmigiana-Reggiano, a blue-green-veined French Bleu de Bresse, a richly soft and aromatic Norwegian Gammelost, a simple, earthy, peasanty Spanish Queso Manchego, from the region of Don Quixote, and, last but far from least, a well-aged and dry Oregon Tillamook. Each diner would cut his own cheese, on a wide, handsome board, from pieces of not less than a pound each, to give the feeling of luxurious plenty.

The dessert would be my own variation of a classic dish. In Bordeaux there is a much-served dessert called *Saint-Emilion au chocolat*, which came originally from the small, sweet cookies handmade by bakers in the lovely hilltop village of Saint-Emilion. I make my version with the Italian *amaretti di Saronno*, small, almond-vanilla macaroons, still handmade in the Lombardy town of Saronno—cookies of such superb quality that they might well lay claim to be the best in the world. I take a few dozen of these, lightly moisten each one with half a teaspoon of golden Jamaican rum, set them in neatly interlocking layers in a deep serving dish, and cover them completely with a rich, buttery, not too sweet chocolate sauce. As it sets, it seals in both the bouquet of the rum and the chewy crispness of the macaroons. These qualities form an irresistible contrast to the velvety softness of the chocolate—a balance so superb that I have instructed my doctor to offer a portion to me as the final medicine on my deathbed. Then I shall take one taste, and refuse to die.

Last, there would be sharply aromatic little cups of my favorite, "private blend" of Colombian, Brazilian, and Venezuelan coffees, suitably overshadowed by a fine selection of what the French so aptly call *les digestifs:* the Cognacs, Armagnacs, the marvelously dry fruit brandies of Alsace, and, with green Chartreuse leading them, the sweet fruit and herb liqueurs.

The talk now flows with a smooth ease. The table is suffused with relaxation and understanding. Strangers have become friends. The woes of the world have been banished from the room. The thousands-of-years-old traditions of hospitality have been carried forward. The magic of a memorable meal has been achieved.

Naturally, the menu I have just described is a dream. It makes absolutely no compromise in terms of effort, of expense, of the difficulty of getting some of the ingredients, and of the time-consuming work of preparation. It is, however, by no means an impossible dream. My objective in describing it was to define the basic principles—and let me add, with the conviction of long experience, that provided these basic rules are followed, a memorable meal can be produced at reasonable expense and within a reasonable preparation time. Not, of course, that there is, or ever could be, an "instant memorable meal." The art of the true host demands that he make some effort and give something of himself in preparing for his guests.

There are less expensive forms of caviar than black Beluga. There is the excellent pressed caviar and the many forms of salty-tangy fish roe, including the fine tarama, carp roe from Greece. There are sparkling wines less expensive than Champagne, including outstanding American labels, charmingly refreshing sparklers from Seyssel, in the Alpine mountains of the French Savoy, and from Saumur and Vouvray along the Loire.

The essential point is that the opening canapés and wine should be immediately acceptable to all the guests and should express the unspoken thought that the party was carefully planned to offer the best that is possible. I would be very careful, for example, about serving snails as an opening hors d'oeuvre since some people find them intolerable and it would be destructive of the calm atmosphere at the beginning of the meal if one or two of the guests were embarrassed or troubled. The place for the unusual is later in the meal, when the guests are more secure in each other's company.

In place of the expensive pâté de foie gras, there are dozens of outstanding recipes for made-at-home pâtés and terrines, easily and quickly prepared, which I regard as among the most important guest-feeding tools of the memorable host.

It is care and imagination in planning—the skilled use of aromatic herbs in making each dish interesting and unusual, the proper balance between one course and the next—far more than the serving of expensive, imported specialties that can make, even of a simple menu, a memorable dinner. The prize earned by one's efforts is, to me, a rewarding richness of living.

A Formative Dish: Portuguese-style Pork with Fresh Clams

Every important event in the life of a devoted gourmet is punctuated by a memorable meal. This certainly is true for me. I have only to think about some past adventure or crisis, a big change, a turning point, and the picture that appears on the screen of my mind is almost always a scene of beautiful food with the sharp memories of aromas, sounds, and tastes added for good measure.

During World War II, I was in Britain at her so-called "darkest hour." France had fallen to Hitler's armies and the Germans had reached the French Channel coast. It was thought that Hitler might invade Britain at any time.

At night, because of continual air raids, the entire nation was totally blacked out. It was inconceivable to go out for dinner. Food rationing was at its worst point. Fishing had been stopped completely because all fishermen had been transferred to naval war service. Farming was at a low point. There was no gastronomic interest in life.

In the middle of this dreary darkness, I was told that I would be flown to the United States. That was a big and complicated deal. The U.S. was still neutral; American commercial planes did not fly into the war zones. The German air force would shoot down any British plane it caught in the air.

I was told that I would be carried to a neutral place by a secret route, that I should pack my bag and await instructions. Later I was ordered to

EDITOR'S NOTE: This syndicated newspaper article originally appeared in July 1979.

take the train to a small town on the south coast of Britain and to check into a certain small hotel. On arrival I was told to sit in my bedroom and remain dressed.

At around midnight, two members of the British Secret Service came to my room, meticulously searched my bag, my clothes, and myself, then told me that they would blindfold me and take me on my way. I knew from listening that we boarded a bus with other blindfolded passengers.

Soon we were at a dock, then boarding a small boat, then purring over the water, then clambering into a seaplane. Only when we were over the water were our blindfolds removed. We were on our way to Lisbon. We also were told that, if attacked by an enemy plane and strafed with machine gun bullets, we should throw ourselves face down on the floor and hold our hands over the back of our heads. All windows, of course, were completely blacked out.

There was no incident. Within a few hours, we landed safely in Lisbon.

I need hardly describe the amazement, the stunning contrast, the sheer shock of stepping out of that darkened plane into a world at peace—a city of lights and teeming traffic, bursting like a cornucopia with cascades of magnificent food, gushing with wine and well-being. My memories of that dazzling arrival in Lisbon always will be tied up with the main dish I had that evening at my hotel.

It was a classic Portuguese specialty, simple in technique but made extraordinary by its juxtaposition of two apparently incompatible ingredients. It was *ameijoas con carne de porco a alentejana*, garlic-braised young pork with fresh whole clams in their shells.

I was so overwhelmed that, when I heard I would have to wait for a few days before I could get a flight to New York, I decided to investigate the background of the dish.

I went south from Lisbon, across the estuary of the Tagus River, to the fish-catching, wine-growing Setubal Peninsula and to the famous fishing village of Sesimbra. There the clam diggers pile their large, shining clams in great heaps on the beach and sell them to anyone who will pay the going price—housewives, shopkeepers, or wholesale distributors. The moment the heap is gone, that particular team of diggers goes back to work for another couple of hours. The supply of the freshest and best-looking clams is enormous.

Because the pork and clam dish is named a *alentejana,* it is in the style of the farming province of Alentejo, where the best young pigs are raised on a diet of acorns. I went there to investigate and found a gently rolling grassland, its rich green patched with the colors of wildflowers, broken with wheat fields and olive groves, the rambling farmhouses blue and white, with red-tiled roofs.

The lady of the house of one of these farms, hearing that I was a journalist with a particular gastronomic mission, invited me and my friends to lunch in her kitchen and taught me how to prepare her version of the famous pork and clam dish—a specialty that is the most famous of the region.

But you don't have to be Portuguese to reap the magic of this dish. There is virtually nothing to preparing it—no difficulty or serious work and no lengthy preparation time. It is, in fact, a one-dish meal, with elements of picnic informality.

PORTUGUESE-STYLE YOUNG PORK WITH WHOLE CLAMS

4 servings

      2 pounds boneless, lean pork loin, cut into 1-inch cubes
      5 teaspoons medium-sweet Hungarian paprika
      4 cloves garlic, peeled and finely minced
      2 whole bay leaves
        Coarse crystal or kosher salt and finely ground black pepper
   1¼ cups dry white wine
     30 small, very fresh clams in shells, preferably little necks
      4 tablespoons well-flavored bacon fat, or vegetable oil
      2 medium yellow onions, peeled and thinly sliced
    ¼ cup chopped canned pimientos
      1 cup ripe red tomatoes, peeled, seeded, and chopped, or an equal
        amount canned Italian plum tomatoes
        Tabasco sauce
      8 slices firm whole-wheat bread, fried in minimum bacon fat until
        browned and crisp
      4 fresh lemon wedges
    ⅓ cup chopped fresh coriander leaves if available, or parsley or watercress

The Day Before—Marinating the Pork

In a refrigerator bowl large enough to hold all the pork cubes, prepare the marinade by combining the paprika, garlic, bay leaves, salt, pepper, and wine. Stir well, then add the pork, making sure it is thoroughly wet.

Cover and put in the refrigerator overnight. Stir once more before going to bed and again in the morning. This marination can be continued with occasional stirring, for 8 to 20 hours.

Preparing Clams and Stewpot

Scrub the clam shells and soak them in cold water for about an hour. This helps to get rid of most of their sand. Wash the sand from each under cold running water. Throw away any clam that is open (usually a sign of poor health).

Set a large stewpot over medium-high heat and lubricate its bottom with about 1 tablespoon of bacon fat. When it is fairly hot—not too hot—quickly sauté the onion slices until they wilt, usually in 2 to 3 minutes. Then, stop the sizzling by stirring in the chopped pimientos and tomatoes. Turn down the heat so that the bubbling is not too fierce. You are now getting rid of excess water. Season with salt and pepper, to taste. While the bubbling continues, take the pork cubes out of the marinade—carefully saving the marinade—and dry each cube.

As soon as the stewpot mixture begins to thicken, take it out and hold it in a bowl. Wipe the stewpot clean and put it back on medium-high heat. Melt 2 tablespoons of bacon fat and, when hot, quickly brown the pork. Keep the cubes moving around and turning over. Do not crowd them. Do them in batches, if necessary, adding more fat.

Braising, Steaming, Reduction, and Serving

When the pork cubes are ready, work the onion-pimiento-tomato mixture into the stewpot, plus all of the marinade. Heat it to a gentle bubbling. Check and adjust seasoning, as needed, adding a few drops of Tabasco to give you as much peppery flavor as you like. When it is bubbling steadily but gently, close the lid tightly and let the meat simmer for 20 minutes. Then turn off the heat and pour remaining liquid into a sauté pan. Place over high heat and by rapidly boiling (about 5 minutes), reduce liquid to about ½ cup.

Meanwhile, put clams in stewpot. When the liquid has been reduced, pour over the pork and clam mixture, re-cover tightly, and let them steam until the clams open—usually in about 6 to 8 minutes.

During this waiting time, ready deep, hot serving plates, the slices of fried bread, and the wedges of lemon. When the clams are open, serve at once. Whether you present the dish on a central platter, or on individual plates, place the clams, still in their shells, plus the pork cubes in the center; sprinkle with chopped coriander or parsley leaves and surround with triangles of the fried bread.

A Quartet of Cooks

This book is a record of the gastronomic experiences of our family, set down over many years and now arranged for the gastronomic pleasure of other families. One might say that both the experience and the writing began about forty-five years ago, one hot summer's day on a green and grassy bank of the river Danube about twenty miles south of Budapest, where I as a small boy had been taken by my mother for a picnic with Hungarian friends. The meal consisted of the wonderful cold meats of the region, accompanied by a locally grown green pepper with sweet and luscious outside flesh, but with fiery-hot inside ribs around the seed pod. Each picnicker, after cutting a chunk of the pepper, carefully sliced off the inside ribs. The Hungarian host prepared the first pieces for me, but when I asked for more, he gave me as a joke a piece with the rib left on. Greedily I stuffed it into my mouth and at once wept with the pain. For the rest of the day I could hardly swallow. That evening I noted the incident in my diary and resolved, from then on, to take an interest in the preparation of my food.

Accompanying my mother to various European countries, I began to be aware of the variety of national dishes. A few years later, in the kitchen of the family home in London, I began trying to reproduce some of them. In my teens, I founded my first Gourmet Society among fellow students. I was already a fairly accomplished cook when I found and married my Katherine, a blond girl of Scots-Irish descent, who knew the

---

EDITOR'S NOTE: This introduction from *Feasts for All Seasons* (Knopf, 1966) reflects the organization and thoroughness that from the beginning were the hallmarks of de Groot's gastronomic writing.

true meaning of Scottish haggis, tipsy laird, and Irish mutton stew, and admitted me to full partnership in her kitchen. In the requisite time there were two daughters, Christina and Fiona, who should perhaps have been born with boxwood spoons in their mouths.

The family developed into a quartet of busy individualists, each pursuing separate work and study interests. I became a journalist and broadcaster and explored many parts of the world. My wife's work as an actress in the theater took her away from home on national and international tours. In time we cooked in kitchens in London, Vienna, Budapest, Amsterdam, Paris, and across the Atlantic in Chicago, San Francisco, New Orleans, and, finally, in New York.

Through much travel and separation the family has remained bound together by a passion for good eating. Since no member was ever at home all the time to cook for the others, each learned to plan and prepare a first-class meal. The most vivid memories of thirty years of family life are of the feasts around the dining table—a send-off on an important journey, the celebration of a new contract signed, homecomings, theatrical opening nights, publication days. Every celebration was also the fun of planning and working together.

From the beginning, when the girls were just old enough to be fascinated by turning the handle of the nutmeg grater, we tried to make the preparation of food an amusing game. When they came home from school, the meal was already underway, but they took turns on alternate days at being either P. E. (Pony Express) or K. H. (Kitchen Helper), with their weekly schedule up on the wall. P. E. would dash to the stores for last-minute shopping, while K. H. set the table and helped serve the food. At the same time, there were opportunities for self-expression and the development of individual skills. Each, on her seventh birthday, had been given a first solo assignment to mix and bake a simple filbert soufflé cake, and it was a moment of high excitement when the cake was taken from the oven. As the girls grew up, we developed more dishes for special occasions, and each season of our year had its traditional ceremonies.

SEARCH FOR VARIETY

How did we capture the interest and imagination of our young children, in meal planning and preparation? The first rule of our game with food was always to try to achieve variety in the dishes that came to our table. Too many families seem to have too small a repertoire of favorite recipes and repeat them too often. Too many mothers allow themselves to be enslaved by the prejudices of children who, whenever a new dish is suggested, cry "We know what we like!" What they really mean is that they have no intention of liking anything they don't know. Our rule has always been to try anything once. Of course, we also have our favorite recipes to which we return again and again, especially those which celebrate the reappearance of the great seasonal delicacies, but we count any week ill spent if it has not included some gastronomic exploration. Clearly, an entirely new dish, often involving considerable work, is not produced every other day. It is the small daily variations that maintain an attractive suspense. A new sauce or garnish for a favorite vegetable. Different dressings for various salad combinations. Finding new ways to prepare the ubiquitous potato. We refuse to be bound by the standard herb affinities. How dull always to put basil with tomatoes and rosemary with lamb. We vary the blends of our coffees and the combinations of our teas.

For the sake of variety, we refuse to be bound by the concept of an "authentic" or "classic" version of any recipe. Some of our friends are so overawed by the aura of the French high cuisine that they dare not vary a single ingredient, or even the laboriously old-fashioned methods of preparation. Of course we always try to maintain the special character and personality of a regional dish. But many great recipes, like folk songs, travel around the world, adapting to local tastes and traditions, absorbing local ingredients and subtleties of flavor, so that eventually there are many variations, each with its own pleasure. There is a saying in Italy that there are as many ways of preparing the famous fish stew *cacciucco toscana* as there are cooks in Tuscany.

FEAST DAYS OF THE WORLD

The second rule of our family gastronomy has been the exploration of the peoples and cultures of foreign nations through foods. When we travel, we always try to eat in small, unpretentious restaurants where local families dine, so that we "experience" a place through its simple but authentic dishes. At home, while our girls were in school, we thought we might add to their studies on world civilization by celebrating some of the foreign feast days at our own table, with traditional menus, the proper wines, serving customs, often the music of the country, and sometimes even a study of the festive costumes. We began with the *Diplomatic List* of the principal national holidays of the world prepared by the State Department and have gradually enlarged and adapted it. Visitors from far-off countries are always delighted when they find that we know something about their native gastronomy and, in turn, they have taught us some of our most exciting dishes.

In working out these foreign recipes, we regard each unknown ingredient as a challenge. In the "foreign" neighborhoods of large cities we have found virtually every kind of unusual food, generally in small family-owned shops—perhaps among the huge stone crocks filled with olives, the trays of pickled fish, the big burlap sacks of dried produce, the tubs of soft cheeses, or sausages and hams hung on the walls. Combing the foreign quarters of a city has always been one of the particular delights of food preparation for us and we often learn new ways of using the exotic foods in talking to the storekeepers and the other customers.

However, even away from the big cities, the extraordinary development of the international mail-order business has made it easier than ever to shop for foreign ingredients. Friends who live on top of the Black Mesa in Arizona have proved that they can stock a store cupboard full of delicacies simply by building up a card file of mail-order supply houses, as we have done over the years. In today's smaller world, we can all share some part of every feast of every nation.

HIGH VERSUS LOW CUISINE

The third value that has helped to hold our family's interest in good eating is to avoid making a burden of cooking by spending too much time in the kitchen. Except for very special parties a few times a year, we avoid the classic *haute cuisine* dishes which involve complicated and lengthy preparation. Instead, our stress is on what the French call *bourgeois* dishes, prepared with fresh, rather than packaged or processed foods. In our experience, the people who eat with the greatest gusto and satisfaction day after day are the middle-income families of the rich agricultural lands. They raise and kill their own animals, grow their own fruits, vegetables, and aromatic herbs, and seem to make the most economical use of everything they have to hand.

Every region seems to have its native one-dish meal, brought to table in a huge clay pot, and we have learned to reproduce some of them in an American kitchen, using fresh meats and seasonal vegetables. These casseroles, *ollas*, *toupins*, etc., are simple to prepare, improve with keeping and reheating, and are much more time-saving, economical, and delicious than the so-called short-cut foods.

THE GAME OF BUDGET CONTROL

Our fourth rule with food (and the one that is the most unexpected part of the fun) is the "numbers game" that we have made out of cost-saving. Our system involves no formal accounting, yet gives a day-by-day check on expenditures. Let us say, for example, that for one period we set daily costs at $1.50 per person, or $6.00 per day for a family of four. We keep a small diary by the telephone in the kitchen and write in it in red figures the amount that we ought to have spent on any particular day of the month at the $6.00 per day rate. Alongside these red figures, we write in black what we have actually spent to date in the current month. Comparing the red and black figures tells at a glance whether we are above, below, or close to the planned budget. Then, with our recipe cards divided into three separate files, we plan our meals by the following rules:

1. When food expenditures are running close to the average, we choose recipes from the file marked "Regular Family Meals."

2. When we find ourselves spending less than the budget estimate, or when the budget is entirely suspended for a few days in honor of guests, we choose from our file marked "Parties and Feast Days," in which time and cost are subsidiary factors.

3. When the danger signal appears, we turn to the file marked "Budget Pull-Back Meals" and we stay with them until the budget is under control.

Our children have always helped with this budgeting; often they have been more firm than their parents and would forgo a six-pack of Cokes until the budget was back in balance.

THE BEST FOODS OF EVERY SEASON

We discovered very early in our family life that for almost every food there was one time of the year when the highest quality was combined with the lowest price. We began to write down on cards, month by month, the best foods we found in the stores and where they were coming from. We headed these cards "Special Pleasures of the Season," and when we came back to them year after year they told us what to expect: when to start looking for the first good local asparagus, when to expect the first shad, the soft-shell crabs, and the arrivals of all the fruits from the first spring rhubarb to the last of the winter apples.

In each season of the year our meal planning begins not with the haphazard question, "What do we feel like eating tomorrow?" but by looking first at our list of the "Foods in Season," which tells us the foods that are likely to be at peak supply. Planning one's meals by nature's calendar is, after all, the oldest and most fundamental of all rules for good eating.

PART

·II·

Food at Its Source

Caviar from a Gentle Giant

It seems to be the conventional wisdom all over the world that black caviar of the finest quality comes only from the Iranian and Russian coasts of the Caspian Sea. This theory is quite a long way from the hard truth. The finest caviar comes from the finest species of the sturgeon, the giant fish that travels all over the world and has been brought in at forty feet long, weighing more than three thousand pounds. It is perfectly true that international pollution has seriously limited the world-wide distribution of the sturgeon. It is an anadromous fish, which means that, like the salmon, it can switch from salt water to sweet in order to travel up rivers for its spawning. One place where it still comes regularly every year is the huge Gironde estuary of Bordeaux.

If you drive at the proper season northward along the great tongue of land that is the Médoc, you will find more than famous châteaux and great wines. After you have passed the last of the prestigious wine villages, St. Estèphe, the earth becomes more and more sandy and the grape vines fade away. This is grassy, sheep-grazing land, getting stonier and stonier until it comes to a dead end at the Pointe de Grave, the rocky finishing point of the Médoc, quite far out into the Atlantic. It's wild country, with a strong sense of "no place to go." The only way out, without retracing your entire road all the way back to Bordeaux, is to take the ferry from the old broken-down dock at Le Verdon, across the almost five-mile width of the mouth of the Gironde—I have made the

EDITOR'S NOTE: This article is published here for the first time.

trip in stormy weather when the waves washed right over the lurching and plunging boat, swamping the cars on deck—to the Cognac country on the mainland. But let us not leave this corner of the Médoc yet. There are places to see and things to do. Tiny fishing ports face the Atlantic. Shopping villages provide cafés and supermarkets for the local farm families. And at the edge of the water, facing the Gironde, there is an extraordinary little country restaurant of the region.

It is owned and run by a fisherman, his wife, and their two sons. His fishing boat is tied up at a nearby dock, where they also have a smoke-house and a cold room for storage and work. They belong to a family whose various branches have been running restaurants in the Médoc for nearly a hundred years. This little place is called Chez le Pecheur d'Es-turgeon de la Gironde and its main objective is to serve, in season, the black caviar drawn from the fish that has just been caught and is, there-fore, fresher than anything you can get virtually anywhere else. I once arrived here directly from Paris, armed with several hundred dollars' worth of the best black Beluga from Iran and the Soviet Union. We spread them all out in a straight line, including the Gironde black, with none of the tasters knowing which was which. I have never quite re-covered from the shock of that test. I learned the lesson, once and for all, that the prestige of the name and the source of the caviar were of far less importance than its freshness. What mattered was how long had it been in the tin? How long had it been traveling? How long in storage? The Gironde black was a little bit more glutinous than the others, a little bit less perfectly salted, its eggs a shade smaller, but as to its pure flavor, it had a matchlessly fresh deliciousness that put it at the head of the list.

The scene of this test, the little restaurant, Chez le Pecheur, is as simple as the country around it. It looks, from the outside, as if it were a small, typically Médocain farmhouse. Inside, it has something of the at-mosphere of an English country cottage. One soon discovers, in fact, that the house is about three hundred years old. A wood fire blazes in the hearth, perfuming the small rooms with a gentle sweet aroma of smoke. Seated at one of the ten tables, you are served by the two sons, Edouard and Robert, who bring you at once glasses of the cold, dry house apéri-tif—a Sauvignon Blanc of the Médoc. If you get into conversation with the boys, you learn that they are the seventh generation of this family to grow up here in the harsh, stormy beauty of the mouth of the Gironde.

You start, of course, with unlimited quantities of the black caviar. With it, you are served nothing more than thin buttered slices of Madame Lussagnet's house-made brown bread, baked every morning with *crème fraîche*. They don't make the mistake here of serving any of the fussy fol-de-rols, such as lemon juice (which is positively lethal to the sublime taste of caviar), or black pepper, or bits of hard-boiled egg, or chopped onions, or any of the other usual garbage. The total effect of this caviar alone is so utterly delicious that all caution eventually disappears and one consumes one portion after another. You may order Champagne but, somehow, you seldom do. The very dryness and tartness of the Sauvignon Blanc seems to provide a gentle, supporting accompaniment.

The secret of the irresistible freshness of this caviar is that the proprietor of the restaurant, *monsieur le pêcheur* Lussagnet, almost certainly caught this sturgeon in the Gironde yesterday, or the day before. Hurrying back to tie up his boat at his dock, he would have laid out the big fish on the white enamel worktable in the cold room behind the dock, where he and his sons would have started working on it immediately. They would painlessly kill the female by severing her spinal cord and, then, slitting open her belly, would carefully and gently draw out the membrane sacs containing the black eggs—sometimes weighing as much as twenty pounds. Using an ivory comb with bluntly rounded teeth— spaced precisely to match the size of the eggs—and pressing gently, gently with the very tips of their fingers, they separate the eggs from the membrane. Then Papa inspects at close range, touches with fingertips, tastes on the tip of his tongue and makes the vital decisions. How many tiny strips of fat are mixed in with the eggs? How much glutinous oil is covering them? How much salt will they need? The right amount of salt both melts out the fat and oil and improves the flavor of the eggs. Gently, with skilled fingers, he works in the salt.

While Papa was busy with the caviar, the two boys were dealing with the rest of the sturgeon. In short order, they had it beheaded, boned, and skinned. Then they sliced the best parts of the flesh into long fillets, which they took out to the smokehouse at the back. Here the fillets would hang for no more than six hours, instead of the usual several days, in dense smoke from glowing *sarments de vigne*, gnarled and thick vine stocks, regarded in the Médoc as absolutely the best wood for grilling and smoking, since it is supposed to impart a distant winey flavor. The caviar is left to ripen for two or three hours, when the fat and oil gather in liquid form at the bottom of the bowl. It is then drained, carefully dried, and packed into its airtight jars for the restaurant.

After eating our fill of this gorgeous caviar, we order round dozens of cold Belon oysters that arrived by boat from the Breton coast this morning, packed in ocean-soaked barrels of seaweed. The serving of these beauties—in the *bordelais* style, with hot grilled pork *crêpinettes* and a small black truffle—is a dramatic and fast operation. Edouard put his hand down into the barrel behind the *zinc* and moved his oyster knife around the shells so fast that the Belons were before me before I swallowed my last grain of caviar. Edouard said that his average time for opening an oyster onto its half shell was five seconds. These Belons had the briny aroma of an ocean beach on a windy day. They were so fresh they seemed to scintillate and shine—so firm and plump, so vibrantly alive, they seemed to stand up on their half shells aggressively, almost threateningly, as if they were prepared to bite back. Meanwhile, Robert had been quickly frying the *crêpinettes* and he now brought them on a hot platter, each thin round decoratively surmounted by a small slice of black truffle. The *crêpinettes*, miniature pork *rissoles*, were so thin that they had the appearance of lace. I was now free to eat some of the oysters cold from their shells, or combine others with a hot *crêpinette* and a truffle. It is the authentic *médocain* way of serving them, and it is a combination of foods that sparkles and tingles on the tongue.

My next course was a plateful—and that is exactly the right word, since the plate was covered from edge to edge—of smoked sturgeon fillets. I don't know whether it was the absolute freshness of the fish, or the precise timing of the smoking, but here, also, there was a degree of perfection that will not soon be forgotten. It was moist, but there was no sense of oiliness about it and its color was a beautiful creaminess. Its flavor was delicate and subtle and yet, through the smoke, I sensed the aroma of the fresh sturgeon.

Prepared main dishes are not stressed here. You just go on forever with caviar, oysters, and sturgeon. But I couldn't resist trying the two other dishes prepared to order by Madame Lussagnet—her *moules marinière* and her salad of Gironde salmon. Both were uncomplicated in preparation, but made joyously good to eat by the bursting freshness of the mussels from the nearby beds in Arcachon and the salmon hooked virtually a hundred yards from the terrace of the restaurant.

A hundred years ago there were sturgeon in large numbers in all the important lakes and rivers of every temperate zone—including the principal lakes, with the largest Atlantic and Pacific rivers of the United States. The Atlantic Ocean was still teeming with sturgeon. So was the Mediterranean, the North Sea, the Baltic, and the Sea of Azov. But wherever conditions became difficult, the sturgeon left. There used to be sturgeon in British waterways—there is not one today. A few sturgeon still swim up the Po River in Italy but, as the Po region becomes more and more industrialized, the big fish are gradually disappearing. Sturgeon twenty feet long used to swim up the Danube to spawn, as far as Baden, but no more. Around the Black Sea, sturgeon are still being caught by Russian Georgian fishermen, by Romanians, Bulgarians, and Turks, but the catch is now only about 10 percent of what it was at its peak a hundred years ago.

Even as recently as 1967, spillage from the Russian oil drilling in the Northern Caspian and industrial waste flowing down the Ural and Volga Rivers killed more than half a million sturgeon in one year. In fact, in our modern times, the sturgeon might be only an evolutionary oddity were it not for the veritable explosion in the value of the black eggs of the female, which are now among the most expensive foods on earth and may, with some degree of truth, be called the "black gold" of our time.

THE PRICE MAY HAVE BEEN SET BY EIGHT COSSACK IMPERIAL GUARDS OF THE CZAR

The great mystery question about caviar is how and why it became so enormously expensive: Around 1850, there were so many sturgeon in the U.S. that we were able to process as much as 150,000 pounds per year and export considerable quantities to Europe. It was a standard item in American grocery stores. Hotels and restaurants bought their caviar in bulk at an average price of two cents a pound. Although the price eventually doubled to four cents, it then cost the same, weight for weight, as a loaf of bread.

At all the better-class saloons in New York and other big cities, caviar was given away free on the snack counters (after all, its saltiness created thirst) to anyone who had the nickel price of a mug of beer. At the Plaza, or the Waldorf, the caviar also came free with the cocktails at the start of dinner.

On the printed menus of the plush dining cars on the grand old transcontinental trains, a portion of Cape Cod oysters cost exactly twice as much as an hors d'oeuvre of caviar. With your Manhattan, or your Sidecar, you could spend an extra nickel for caviar or the same price for a dish of celery sticks and queen olives. Meanwhile, at about this time, in Russia, the peasants were spreading their black bread with caviar because it was so much cheaper than butter.

I like to think that caviar first broke out of its self-defeating circle of poverty by a dramatic and regal event in 1867. The Czar of Russia, Alexander II, was visiting Paris and so was Kaiser Wilhelm I of Germany. They dined together and the Czar was horrified to discover that the Kaiser had never tasted real Russian caviar. The Czar insisted, at once, that he must send eight of his fastest-riding Cossack horsemen of the Imperial Guard (who, of course, were on duty in Paris) off on the 1,400-mile journey to St. Petersburg to bring back four hundred pounds of caviar for the Kaiser. The Cossacks rode hard, changing horses every day, arriving in St. Petersburg in a snow blizzard. They picked up the four hundred pounds of Beluga, which was valued in the Russian market at the equivalent of twenty cents a pound. In a month they were back in Paris and the Czar personally made the presentation to the Kaiser. The Emperor tasted it, was entranced, and said: "Your Majesty, you have given us superb pleasure and greatly enlarged our gastronomic education. You must allow us to pay for this!" The Czar replied: "Under no circumstances, my dear Kaiser. This is our gift to mark our admiration and respect." But then, as if suddenly struck by a brilliant afterthought, a broad smile appeared on the Czar's face: "However, while charging you not one ruble for the caviar, we *will* allow you to pay the costs of sending my eight Cossacks to St. Petersburg. Our secretary just this morning gave us a precise note of the amount. Here it is." And the Czar handed the Kaiser a small bill for the equivalent of $20,000—or $50 for each pound of that long-distance caviar. On that day, caviar cut through its price shackles—broke through its sound barrier—surpassed its four-minute mile. On that day, caviar became one of the great prestige foods of the world. It has never looked back. Today, with steadily decreasing availability of sturgeon, yet with constantly increasing demand from the wealthiest gourmands, caviar has priced itself into the stratosphere.

THE WORLD CENTER REMAINS THE CASPIAN

In the twentieth century, so far, there seems to be only one large expanse of water where the sturgeon still thrives—although even here there has been a dangerous decline—the Caspian Sea, wrongly thought to be a sea by the early mapmakers, but in reality the world's largest land-locked salt-water lake. It is fed by two enormous rivers, the Ural and the Volga, entering it from the north, and this is ideal for the sturgeon, whose life cycle involves swimming upstream for spawning. The modern problem is that there has been substantial Russian oil drilling development at the northern end of the Caspian, so the sturgeon are congregating more and more at the southern end, which was part of Persia and now belongs to Iran. Americans are hardly welcome in that country, but the British writer Hugo Dunn-Meynell has described a visit to Isfahan, the ancient capital of Persia, "with its broad avenues, graceful bridges and turquoise-domed mosques," which is on the so-called Caviar Coast. He lunched at the legendary Shah Abbas Hotel and his meal began with "a noble mound" of caviar in perfect condition—accompanied by nothing more than well-buttered slices of rye bread.

As the oil wells proliferated at the northern end of the Caspian, the Russians became more and more worried about the future of their caviar industry. So, in 1895, they signed an agreement with the Persians, granting the Russians the exclusive rights to fish and to process caviar along the Persian Caviar Coast. The Russians, of course, labeled their tins in Russian and kept up the fictional impression around the world that the very best caviar was Russian. In fact, they were selling Persian caviar.

The agreement was for thirty-two years and, by the time it expired in 1927, the Shah had learned a good deal about the caviar business. He knew that the price of caviar had exploded beyond the wildest dreams of 1895 and he now wanted a larger piece of the pie. He also wanted the world to begin to learn about Persian caviar and demanded a fair share of the very best caviar for his own personal consumption. The new agreement, after 1927, would allow both nations to fish freely and maintain factories at the fishing port of Bandar Anzaly on the southern Caviar Coast. Very soon the Royal Iranian Caviar Company was founded to compete with the Russian distribution all over the world. In exchange for their rights, the Russians would have to pay immense license fees, enormous rents, plus commissions and taxes of every form and shape. No wonder that caviar continued to get more expensive all the time!

The Shah, also, got pretty well his own way about supplies of the very best caviar for his personal use. There are twenty-six different species of sturgeon and the most magnificent and rarest of them all is the Sterlet, which produces the extraordinary and legendary "golden caviar," so called because the eggs are, in fact, bright golden in color and of an utterly superb flavor. In all the world, only about forty-four pounds of this rarest roe is processed annually. A special clause was written into the treaty between the Persian and Russian governments, ensuring that of all golden caviar processed, 40 percent must go directly to the Shah, 40 percent to the head of the Russian state, and 10 percent each to the respective presidents of the Royal Iranian Caviar Company and the Soviet Caspian Company.

There seems to be little doubt that the Persians were the first to discover the glorious taste of the eggs of the sturgeon. They decided that the black stuff was both good and good for you, so they called it *chav-jar*, "cake of strength." When the Turks picked up the idea, with sturgeon caught in the Black Sea, they adapted the name slightly to *khav-yah*. Although the Russians use our word "caviar" on all their labels for export, they have never adopted the word in their own language. In Russian the black eggs are *ikra*.

The more I learn about the sturgeon, the more it seems to me to have a clearly defined character and personality. With its gentleness, its inability to cope with the pollution and violence of our times, it relies on a trusting nature, unafraid and unsuspicious of humans, slow to sense danger, unable to defend itself. For these reasons, the sturgeon through the centuries has been overfished almost to the point of extinction and treated with incredible cruelty. The most cruel of the early fishermen, at the time of the Czars, were the swashbuckling Cossacks of the Ural Mountains, north of the Caspian. They knew—and so did all the caviar lovers of Moscow, St. Petersburg, and all parts of Europe—that twice a year, as precisely on schedule as the calendar, the sturgeon swam in great shoals up the Ural and Volga rivers. This was the precise moment to catch the females, their bellies loaded with the eggs they intended to lay up river. The first of these migrations, lasting for two weeks, was in the fall, just as the cold weather was starting, with the snow beginning to come down, and it was called *plawnaja*. Since the date of this event was so absolutely predictable, it was preceded, many weeks beforehand, by an extraordinary movement of people all planning to meet, on a certain day, on the banks of the Ural and Volga rivers. From Moscow and St. Petersburg, from the major cities of Eastern Europe, even from as far away as Paris, the caviar buyers started out in their horse-drawn carriages. Each brought with him all his needed equipment: sharp knives to cut open the fish, ivory combs to separate the eggs, a supply of salt and ceramic pots in which to pack perhaps more than two hundred pounds of caviar. Since the weather would be ice-cold and the snow would be falling across Northern Europe, there would be no problem about spoilage during the journey back home.

At about the same time, the Cossack families were packing up in their mountain villages. Everyone came for the fishing—wives, children, grandparents, uncles, aunts, and cousins. They brought tents, household goods, complete cooking equipment—all piled onto their sleds. For the next two weeks, they camped along the banks of the rivers.

When the sturgeon began their run, hundreds of Cossack fishermen stretched hand-held nets across the river and dragged them downstream entangling the fish—until each net was loaded and then pulled ashore. Most of the fish were twelve to fifteen feet long and weighed about three hundred pounds—each female giving about sixty pounds of black eggs. The buyers were waiting and each fish was sold, intact, for immediate cash to the highest bidder. At once, without even first killing the female, the Cossacks cut open her belly and took out the roe. No one was interested in the flesh. The bodies were left to rot at the water's edge. Later, when the fishing was over and the dead fish began to stink, they were pushed back into the river.

The second great run of the sturgeon up the rivers was toward the end of winter, just before spring. Again, it lasted for two weeks and it was called the *bagornaja*. Again, the buyers and their horses struggled through the ice and snow, from all across Europe. Again, the Cossacks came down from the mountains. But now the rivers were frozen, so the technique of fishing was entirely different. A large number of Cossacks were stationed all over a stretch of the ice—each man armed with an ice-ax and a long harpoon. At a signal a cannon was fired, and the noise terrified the sturgeon under the ice. Up to that moment, they had been swimming in straight lines, side by side, headed up river, but now they were thrown into a frightened disarray, thrashing about wildly, hither and thither. Quickly, each Cossack cut a hole in the ice and, if a sturgeon came to the surface at that point, it was harpooned and dragged out. The cannon kept firing, to keep the sturgeon terrified almost to death. When all possible fish had been caught and the rest had fled, the catch was carried to the waiting buyers and there followed the usual bargaining, with the immediate evisceration of the black eggs.

Then the whole circus moved, say, half a mile down river, where the exact operation was repeated—and so on, day after day for two weeks, until they all reached the mouth of the river where it entered the Caspian and the water was too deep for harpoon fishing. During each of these biannual drives, several thousand fish were caught and sold by the Cossacks.

When Alexander Dumas visited the Russian northern Caspian fisheries in the 1850s, he found more advanced methods of fishing by the full-time professional fishermen of that later time, but there was still great cruelty and tremendous waste of a valuable natural resource. Although the males had little or no value, they were killed in equal numbers alongside the females. In the "slaughterhouse," about three thousand fish every day were killed by heavy blows from sledge hammers. Alexander Dumas added: "Although the sturgeon is a powerful creature, capable of knocking over even the strongest man with a blow from its tail, it offers no resistance. It simply utters a loud cry as it is struck, leaps four or five feet into the air and falls dead."

A VISIT TO ASTRAKHAN TO EXPLORE THE CURRENT RUSSIAN METHOD OF CAVIAR PROCESSING

Since Russia signed its caviar treaty with Persia in 1927, there have been some major developments in the world. In 1935, Persia changed its name to Iran. Then came World War II and, for six years, the Russians gave little thought to the making of caviar. Finally, in 1979, the Shah was deposed, the Ayatollah took command and our troubles began. The Ayatollah does not eat caviar and his followers—and that means all the people of Iran—are forbidden to eat it on pain of you-know-what! Yet—through all the crises and difficulties—through the agony of the hostages and all the rest—Iranian caviar continued to be delivered through commercial channels. The Royal Iranian Company simply changed its name to the Shilat Iranian Fisheries Company and sold its caviar to its customers as usual. So much for the power of hard-dollar currency in international commerce.

But the Caviar Coast is, obviously, of less importance to the Ayatollah and, since his advent to power, there has been increased industrialization in this lovely region of flowering lemon trees and orange groves. There is more pollution now in the southern Caspian, the sturgeon population has decreased, and the quality of Iranian caviar has somewhat declined.

The Russian government still, technically, has the treaty with the Iranian government for sturgeon fishing rights in the southern Caspian, but, because of the extreme volatility of current politics in Iran, the Russians decided to move their processing plant away from Iranian soil and back to the Russian port city of Astrakhan, on the northern Caspian coast. This is now the center of Russian caviar processing, where one can explore their system, which differs slightly from the Iranian and is, in some ways, unique. The ancient waterfront city was already an important trading center in the thirteenth century when the "Golden Horde" of the nomadic Tartars led by Batu Khan conquered it, in the course of their mighty, westward drive into Europe. About three hundred years later, the city was taken by the Russians under Czar Ivan the Terrible. Since the Tartars were Muslims, there remain many shimmering, blue-domed mosques and slender minarets, but, also, a Christian cathedral dating from 1700 and a fortress Kremlin built by Czar Ivan. As one strolls about the city, one forms vivid impressions of wide, tree-shaded squares, of soaring entrance portals leading into flower-filled courtyards. But, it is, of course, the docks that are the central focus of the city—for here, for more than a thousand years, the trade with Persia has flowed in, and from here, every morning, the sturgeon fishermen in their twenty-foot-long, flat-bottomed barges move out to check their nets.

Each boat identifies its nets with its own colored marker buoys, usually set in fairly shallow water. The men draw the nets into a tightly closed circle and then carefully inspect the mixed variety of the catch. They are looking, first and foremost, for the major prize—a full-grown female sturgeon with a fat belly. Many of the fish fight and thrash around wildly. Some large eels have poisonous fangs and try to bite. The sturgeon remain perfectly calm with large eyes that seem to be trustingly resigned to the inevitable. All wanted fish, including the male sturgeon, are simply stunned by being hit on the head with a wooden club and thrown into the bottom of the barge for later delivery to the general fish pier. No immediate hurry about that. Suddenly, the cry goes up from one fisherman: "Female sturgeon, *ikra!*" Instantly, all other work stops. This sturgeon must have immediate priority delivery to the special caviar pier. She too is lightly stunned and the old boat puts on full speed ahead (which is, in reality, not much speed) toward Astrakhan.

Within five minutes of landing, the female is lying on a huge stainless-steel operating table in the ice-cold workroom. The staff—almost all of them women—wear white coats and caps but, underneath, are heavily protected by padding and wool, since the temperature of this spotlessly clean "operating room" is kept continuously at two degrees below freezing. The fish weighed in at about five hundred pounds and, since the general rule allows for the weight of the eggs to be about 20 percent of the total, this sturgeon is expected to release about one hundred pounds of best black Beluga.

The first step stresses one of the big differences between the Iranian and Russian systems. The Persians kill the fish before cutting her open to remove the eggs. The Russians are so eager for a perfection of freshness that they are willing to permit the cruelty of cutting open the fish while she is still alive. The Russian "sturgeon surgeon" first uses her scalpel to make an incision under the last caudal fin and then waits for the fish to bleed almost, but not quite, to death, so that she will neither feel the pain nor struggle during the evisceration of the eggs. When the sturgeon is finally comatose, the "surgeon" makes the long cut down the belly and, with gentle fingers, she and her helpers carefully draw out the roe sacs. At once judging and assessing the average size of the eggs, the workers place the sacs on one of a series of stainless-steel grids set into a nearby long worktable. Each grid looks rather like an oversized tennis racquet and each has holes of a different size, so that one can be chosen with holes just large enough for these particular eggs to pass through, while all the membranes and other extraneous matter will be held back.

Now begins the most delicate and difficult fingertip work. Gently and slowly the sacs are deliberately manipulated, lightly pressed, rolled back and forth over the grid, allowing the eggs, singly, to fall through into a large stainless-steel pan. At the same time, the grid holds back the undesirable little strips of fat, debris of ovary, the fibrous skin of the sac and other unwanted bits and pieces. Now the eggs are washed in clear fresh water. Some scum rises to the surface and is skimmed off. Once the eggs are cleaned and drained, it is the moment to call in the head man of the entire operation, the "master salt blender." This is the equivalent of the executive chef of a great kitchen—the judge and decision-maker who can bring to perfection (or bring down in ruins) a great caviar!

I am told that there is, in Paris, a famous caviar connoisseur with taste buds so finely tuned that he can lift a spoonful of Beluga to his tongue and, within two seconds, say: "Aha! That was blended by Poliakov!" For another spoonful, say: "That was by Chernoff." And yet another spoonfull: "Pfui! That was by an apprentice." The story, of course, may be apocryphal, but at least it stresses the truth that the blending of the salt, the judgment as to how much salt, and the choice of the type of salt, make or break the caviar. The black eggs do not become caviar until the salt is added. All connoisseurs know that the Russian word *malassol* is used to define the very best grades of caviar—the word simply means "lightly salted." At any caviar processing plant, the master salt blender is the top dog. I have been told by a Russian expert that, out of every hundred people who study the art and science of caviar processing and become apprentices, only five succeed in becoming top experts. About twenty more become second-rung assistants. The other seventy-five give up and go into some other line of work.

The master blender's first step is a minute inspection of the eggs, often using a powerful magnifying glass. Next, they are lightly touched with the tips of the fingers. Finally, a few may be tasted. Then comes a series of instant decisions. First, is this Beluga good enough in color, quality, and size to be absolutely top-grade Malassol? If so, it will get no more than 4 percent salt. If not, shall it be first, second, or third grade for color? What percentage of salt? What type of salt? It must be chemically pure. Some salts are taken from natural deposits in the Soviet Union, then purified and aged for seven years before being used for caviar. Other high-grade salts are imported from foreign countries.

The batch of caviar waiting to be salted is then weighed in *puds*, the Russian unit of weight for caviar. Originally one *pud* was estimated to be the average "take" of roe from the average two-hundred-pound female sturgeon. Thus a *pud* is equivalent to forty-one pounds. If the caviar is to be processed Malassol, it will be mixed with no more than one to one and a half pounds of salt per *pud*. For lesser grades, there will be substantially more salt.

It is now the responsibility of the master blender to use his own highly experienced and skilled fingers to do the actual mixing—to achieve the most even possible distribution. During this mixing, the last tiny threads of fat among the eggs are dissolved and absorbed by the salt. Then this "pickle" is run off and the caviar is, finally, dry. Immediately, before it loses its pliability, the black Beluga is packed into its tins for shipment. The grade given by the master blender is entered on each label. Then the tin is hermetically sealed and is ready to begin its difficult journey— difficult because the eggs are so delicate and have such narrow tolerance of temperature changes. They must be kept ice-cold, but never allowed actually to freeze. In 1938, when a fault developed in a cold room aboard a transatlantic liner, more than $100,000 worth of caviar was completely destroyed by being frozen into solid ice.

Today, most of the cruelty and all of the waste have been eliminated. Quite apart from the caviar, sturgeon flesh has become a much wanted, fairly expensive food product in international commerce. So the strongest possible steps are being taken to preserve the sturgeon as a species for the future. A proportion of the eggs are being hatched and fertilized in the normal way, so that millions of tiny "fingerlings," as the newly born, two-inch-long babies are called, are being released for their seven-year growth to a reasonable maturity. Very many, of course, do not survive. Nature's rate of attrition is high—about 95 percent of them are normally eaten by fishy predators. Above all, the seasonal catch in each district and region is being more and more tightly controlled—to bring the "take" in balance with the supply. Nevertheless, since 1975 the total Caspian Sea production has continued slowly to decline and, were it not for the revolutionary new developments in the United States, the future of caviar would be bleak.

THE BRIGHT HOPE OF THE FUTURE IS IN THE UNITED STATES

A hundred years ago, there was a caviar industry in the U.S. and its product was considered to be quite cheap and ordinary, relatively unimportant and small scale. Then, the age of uncontrolled industrial pollution wiped it out completely for more than fifty years. Now—as a result of the national effort to purify our waters—and especially in the last ten years—the sturgeon has returned to both our Atlantic and Pacific coasts. In terms of caviar, this brings some good news, many quite difficult problems, and revolutionary new developments of world significance.

The good news is that caviar of outstanding quality is again being taken from sturgeon swimming into the Hudson, the Delaware, the Savannah, in California up the Sacramento, in the Northwest up the Columbia and, wonder of wonders, even at the heart of our land in the Arkansas River. These confirmed reports mean, obviously, that the sturgeon is moving quietly into many other North American waters as well. The key factor is that top-quality, perfection-condition American "dry-grain black" can now command as much as two-thirds the price of equal-grade Russian Caspian. (The nasty little trick of counting fourteen ounces as a pound has been perpetrated by all caviar distributors for about a hundred years. But our Food and Drug Administration has now ruled that the trick is illegal in the U.S. where, it is insisted, a pound is a pound is a pound!)

The good side of the new price structure of our caviar is that all American fishermen are now on a constant lookout for female sturgeon and, when they bring one in, take great pains to keep her alive and fresh until the roe is professionally removed and quickly transported, under proper refrigeration, to the nearest distributor. It means that there is more and more American caviar for all of us, of better and better quality, at prices that, at least, reflect the absence of long-distance importation. There are still a few unreconstructed heathens. I have one game-fishing friend who loves to cut up his sturgeon and fry fillets of it, but who won't touch the roe. I asked him what he does with the black eggs? He replied: "I feed them to my cat."

CHOOSING AND JUDGING THE BEST CAVIAR

Whether you are buying (or ordering in a restaurant) American, Iranian, Romanian, or Russian caviar, the different types are identified and named for the species of sturgeon from which they came. Everywhere, the largest and most expensive are Beluga, from the biggest breed of sturgeon. Each batch or tin of Beluga has a color grading, which must be marked on the label, but this has nothing to do with quality, or taste. Grade 0 is given to the blackest eggs. Grade 00 is for medium-dark eggs. Grade 000 is for lightest pearly-gray. Given any of these color grades, if you want absolutely the top-most quality, look on the label for the word "Malassol," meaning "light salt." As explained earlier, this special treatment is given only to extremely good caviar and it is always substantially more expensive.

The second caviar in price, rarity, and slightly smaller size of eggs may be sold as Osetra, Ocetrina, Ossetrina or Ocetrova, all different names for the same sturgeon. Snobbish Western gastronomes may demand Beluga largely on the score of its prestige, but among Caspian sturgeon fishermen, there is strong preference for the Osetra. These people say that the Beluga is too bland and delicate, while the Osetra has the authentic, lusty, nutty, uplifting flavor of "real caviar" without any trace of fishiness. This is what they choose every time. The color ranges from brownish to light gold. The only definite advantage of the Beluga is the snob visual appeal of the larger eggs.

The third caviar, easiest in availability, third in place and size of eggs, is Sevruga, or Chivrouga, the name of the sturgeon. These little eggs are sometimes almost inexpensive—if one dares to use that word in connection with caviar! Sevruga eggs are not the smallest of all. That honor belongs to the species known as the Sterlet, which provides the tiny eggs of the "golden caviar," which is the most magnificent of all, so great, rare, and succulent that it is never on the market, but is always reserved for heads of state!

Finally, there is "pressed caviar," which the Russians call *pausnaya*, usually at about half the going price of Sevruga—a fairly firm brick, or kind of terrine, which is usually cut into thickish slices with a sharp knife. It is all 100 percent real caviar, but from eggs of the three main types that have been accidentally crushed. They are then pressed together into a loaf shape. Many Russian connoisseurs of high standing consider it absolutely the best way of absorbing the real taste of caviar. They eat black bread with it and drink vodka so cold that it bites the tongue.

The word "caviar" can technically be applied to the roe of any fish. However, the U.S. Food and Drug Administration has recently ruled that only the eggs of the sturgeon may be called caviar. This is to guard against dishonest labeling of the roes of other fish, dyed black with cuttlefish ink, then sold with the implication that they are sturgeon eggs. All the eggs of other fish are now required to be labeled as "roe." One of the best of the "alternatives" is golden whitefish roe, which used to be dyed black, but intelligent distributors—Daphne Engstrom in San Francisco, for example—stress its lovely golden color and sell it as "golden whitefish." She also has a remarkably good, sprightly tasting and textured trout roe, with which I would gladly start almost any meal.

Iceland processes lumpfish roe and takes the trouble to dye it black. But the eggs, to me, have little interest and the blackness merely adds a mournful note to the general disappointment of the experience. There is also a product with the dangerously Russian-sounding name, "maviar," but it turns out to be nothing more sinister than smoked cod's roe.

Without any attempt at coloration, fancy names, or other kinds of show-off, I have been served the roe of such everyday fish as bluefish, bream, carp, dolphin (the fish, of course, not the mammal), flounder, mackerel, mullet, Pacific barracuda, pike, salmon, and, of course, shad. They are all very nice, but, to me, they prove one point beyond question: there is no bargain-rate equivalent to sturgeon caviar.

One of the greatest connoisseurs and eaters of black sturgeon caviar was the supreme bass Russian opera singer, probably the greatest basso profundo voice the world has ever known, the late Feodor Chaliapin. As are many Russians, he was extremely addicted to pressed caviar and thought that its flavor was a concentration of the true essence of the sturgeon roe. I shall always remember the brilliant description of her brief encounter with this great man by the American writer, M. F. K. Fisher, when she was a student in Paris and Chaliapin was a refugee from the Revolution:

> I used to go to a small cellar-restaurant behind the Russian church in Paris, after Sunday services. I always stopped in the bar and drank one or two vodkas and ate pressed caviar . . . That was not long after Paris had filled with refugees from the Revolution . . . And Princes were taxi-drivers . . . I learned the lasting delights of pressed caviar, which I found to be best . . . when the barman hacked it off the mother lump and it had to be chewed and mumbled over in the mouth. Then it went down in a kind of gush of pureness, caviar in essence.
>
> One day I staggered into the bar, dizzy from the most beautiful a cappella singing I had ever heard in my life or in my dreams, and the barman, who by that time recognized me, put down before me on the counter a tough slab of the caviar and a little brimming glass and for an instant I felt very lonely . . . after the strain of standing and kneeling and then standing all morning. But next to me I suddenly saw a big man drinking vodka from a water tumbler and he too was eating pressed caviar, holding it like a slice of bread in his hand, and he was joking with the barman. Something about the vibrations of his voice made me recognize that it was Feodor Chaliapin who spoke and that it had been he, no other in the world, who had sung in church that morning with the choristers. I must have looked the way I felt, awe-struck and flabbergasted and naive, for the barman said something and they both glanced at me and smiled, and then Chaliapin clicked his glass against mine and said "*santé!*" and they went on talking in Russian. It was a strange moment in my life, as strong and good as the taste of

caviar on my tongue and the bite of vodka in my throat. I walked straight out . . . everything was in shadow beside the almost brutal glare of the voice that had so uplifted me in church and then had said *"santé!"* to me. Even now, I blink a little, spiritually, thinking of it.

A Visit to Roquefort

Ever since I was a small boy stealing snacks from my mother's refrigerator, Roquefort has been one of the blue cheeses I have loved best. I never knew what was so special and unique about it, however, until the day I had breakfast in New York with a vivacious Frenchman called Jean-Paul Mittaine. I learned from him, after having eaten this noble cheese for fifty years, the extraordinary story of Roquefort, which has been called "the king of cheeses and the cheese of kings." It can be made—because of a fantastic set of geological factors—in only one place on earth, in certain caves in the mountains of south-central France, near the village of Roquefort-sur-Soulzon. There are hundreds of blue-veined cheeses, but there is only one Roquefort, and its name is legally protected throughout the world.

As I sipped my mundane coffee and orange juice, Monsieur Mittaine, an official of the Fédération Roquefort and president of the French national committee for controlled-appellation cheeses, told me a story that might have been the plot of an historical novel.

For more than two thousand years sheep have grazed on the hills overlooking the Mediterranean coast of southern France. But the shepherds came to realize that in high summer the flaming heat of the southern sun was too great for the sheep, so each spring they would drive their flocks north about seventy-five miles to the mountains, now called the Cévennes, of the region of Aveyron. Here the land had been pushed up

EDITOR'S NOTE: This article originally appeared in the November 1980 issue of *Cuisine*.

by volcanic action into high, arid mesas very much like those of Arizona and New Mexico. In French, these tablelands are called *les causses,* "the barrens" or "the wastelands." On the mesas, where the supply of water was limited, the milk given by the ewes was especially rich and thick, excellent for making into sheep's-milk cheese.

Then one summer—about twenty centuries ago, according to the legend woven into the stories and folk songs of the region—a young shepherd, high on *les causses,* made the accidental discovery that changed the course of local history. A firey sun was beating down and the young man was worried about the lunch in his leather shoulder bag—a large crust of rye bread, a piece of white sheep's-milk cheese, and two apples. Along one side of this mesa was a high mass of rock, known today as Mount Combalou, tunneled with many dark caves. The young shepherd climbed up and set his lunch on a cool ledge in the deep shade of one of the caves, where the sun could not penetrate.

Soon after he descended to his flock, the sheep were attacked by a wolf and in the fray he forgot all about his lunch. Next day, because of the continuing wolf danger, he grazed his sheep on a different mesa. In fact, he didn't get back to the original place for about three months. Then, idly, he climbed back into the cave. He was not surprised to find the bread moldy and inedible, but the white cheese was interestingly shot through with jagged blue-green veins.

The young man was not afraid to taste it; he was used to eating up bits of old cheese. But this piece was quite different. It had remained perfectly soft. It had an interesting aroma and a faintly nutty, definitely tangy flavor. He took some home. All his family liked it too. His father decided that they would put some of their cheeses into the cave to develop the mold. The new cheese was an immediate success. Roquefort was born.

As increasing numbers of sheep farmers jumped in on this good thing, more and more caves about the mesa were used and were penetrated more deeply. It was found through trial and error that only the caves of one particular rock formation—Mount Combalou—had the power to cause the blue-green veins to appear in the cheese. Other caves, some only a mile away, produced no effect. For some 1,800 years thereafter the "magic" caves made the marvelous cheeses enjoyed by Roman Caesars, emperors, kings, and princes, without anyone understanding the magic process in the least. Since the cheese came from a fortress-like rock it was called, simply "Roc Fort," and the same name was given to the hamlet where the cheese workers lived around the base of the huge "strong rock." Only in the nineteenth century did bacteriologists, geologists, and other scientists unravel the secret of why nature allows Roquefort to be made only in one tiny spot on earth.

Millions of years ago, when the earth's crust was cooling and shrinking, the solid limestone that was to become Mount Combalou was subjected to enormous cross-pressures that broke the mass up into huge rocks, tumbled together higgledy-piggledy. The spaces that lay between them varied in shape and ranged in size from the equivalent of an intimate den up to a cathedral with a vaulted roof. These are the many-leveled caves of Roquefort, rather like a cross between an apartment building more than a mile long and a deep coal mine. Geologists burrowing down to the lowest depths have discovered that, as Mittaine says, "broken old Mount Combalou has his feet forever standing in a lake." Under the rock a deep bed of clay holds all the waters that seep down after rainfall in the surrounding region. The lake water is constantly evaporating, and the vapors rise through the interconnecting caves above. The result is that, summer and winter, there is a strong draft of air through every cave, keeping the temperature always at around 45° F and the humidity always at around 90 to 95 percent. When you go into these caves, you find them so icy-cold that you are glad to have a blanket to wear over your shoulders, and so damp that the air on your face feels like a sea-born mist. These are ideal conditions for the "benign and noble" mold microorganisms, existing in the caves for untold ages, which have now been dignified with an official Latin name, *Penicillium roqueforti*. Floating invisibly in the air, growing on every square inch of the walls, in every crevice of the rocks and in every cheese that is placed in the caves for the blue-green veins to develop, this microorganism is found nowhere else in the world. It is the secret of Roquefort.

Roquefort is almost certainly the oldest fine cheese in the world, predating the Christian era. During the Roman Empire, Pliny the Elder wrote of this marvelous ewe's-milk cheese from Gaul which was served at the banquets of the Caesars. From the time of the Emperor Charlemagne (when the name Roquefort first appeared on a document) to the present, Roquefort has received official recognition and legal protection of its identity.

Roquefort is one of the eighteen basic controlled-appellation cheeses of France, and the government will not allow any change in its production that might in any way alter its character. For instance, milk from a different breed of sheep may not be used—it would have a different taste and texture. Only fresh milk may be used; dried milk is forbidden. Not one drop of cow's milk is allowed. No artificial enzymes may be used for transforming the milk into curds; natural rennet from lambs' stomachs only is allowed. No additives of any kind are permitted. Finally, the blue-green veining musts be induced naturally and only in the caves of Roquefort.

As outlined by M. Mittaine, this story sounded almost too perfect to be true, and I felt the strongest desire to visit the caves of Roquefort. At the end of our breakfast together in New York, he invited me to come to the village of Roquefort-sur-Soulzon. Before too long, I went.

PERFECTIONISM IN A WILD AND LONELY PLACE: THE CAVES

We drove to Roquefort over the mountain road from the south and, over the last rise, we saw, in the valley below, the village with its huddle of blue and red tile roofs. Facing us across the valley was the rock "fortress" sharply outlined against the sky—Mount Combalou.

Later, as I walked with our host, Jean Bonnefous, a technical expert involved in Roquefort production research, across the village square toward the entrance to the caves, he told me that, while the magic of the microorganisms remains the same as it has been for twenty centuries, the caves now house a highly modernized production operation, in a subterranean city of eleven stories covering twenty-five acres—a labyrinth within a mountain, with nearly four miles of passageways. The main entrance is, quite unromantically, a huge ramp for the trailer trucks that bring the thousands of plain white cheeses for transformation in the caves and carry away the finished cheeses.

In the visitors' reception room I was handed a thick blanket to hang over my shoulders against the cold and the damp. We went down a long flight of stone steps and through a fairly steeply inclined tunnel to the space called "the first grotto." It was about the size of a church. The concrete floor was level but the walls, rising perhaps thirty feet to an apex, were jagged, raw limestone, broken by hundreds of cracks, crevices, fissures, holes, from which came gentle blasts of cold, damp air. It was air-conditioning on a fantastic scale: at each crack, the air jet was strong enough to blow out the flame of a cigarette lighter.

Then, down another long flight of steps, another steeply sloping tunnel, and I began to feel like the hero of Jules Verne's *Journey to the Center of the Earth*. We entered a huge workshop cave, which somehow reminded me of the chapter house of a monastery. The young dairymaids working here, with white coats over their warm clothes and woolen stockings, are traditionally called *cabanières*, a word of the region meaning "cave women." We watched them salting the cheeses, brushing them and perforating each with the thirty-two holes that allow the mold-laden air to reach the center and begin the development of the veins.

But the main work in the caves of Roquefort is the silent and timeless operation of nature. In one enormous cavern, three hundred feet long and almost one hundred feet high, oak shelves from floor to roof hold thousands of cheeses, resting on their sides and slowly developing. Each cheese is regularly turned by hand. After about three months, each is tested by an expert with a probe, which draws out a sample from the center. On the appearance, smell, and taste of this sample the decision is made as to how near the cheese is to perfection. Some cheeses continue to age for as long as a year.

TESTING 263 TIMES FOR PERFECTION OF QUALITY: THE DAIRIES

The day after the cave visit Jean Bonnefous took me to one of the *fromageries*, the smallish, mostly very modern dairies where the white cheeses are made. The milk from more than seven thousand sheep farms is delivered every morning and evening to these *fromageries*, which are scattered in the various valleys and villages of the mesa region. In the village of Fondamente we went to the dairy, an extremely modern, two-story building, its interior bright with stainless steel, white with tiles, as clean and scrubbed as a hospital operating room—a perfect place for a cheese to be born. This dairy is run by a husband-and-wife team, very suitably named Monsieur and Madame Roc. He is the cheesemaker; she is a biochemist who, in her laboratory upstairs, with her thermometers and acidometers, graduated glasses and microscopes and test tubes, carries out many of the 263 tests made on the fresh milk and on every cheese during the process of production and aging.

The fresh milk brought by the refrigerated tank truck is pumped into open stainless-steel vats about six feet across and four feet deep, holding roughly a thousand liters. Each vat is surrounded by a steam jacket that heats the milk gently to 86° F. A measured amount of natural rennet is added to solidify the milk into curd—the first step in making most cheese. After the curd forms, it is "cut up" by a worker using a tool with strung wires that looks a bit like a small harp. As the curd is cut into cubes about the size of lumps of sugar, the watery whey is released and most of it is drained off. After a few hours the curds are ladled into stainless-steel molds with perforated bottoms. The molds are ranged in long lines on ribbed stainless-steel tables where the draining continues for three days. Then the cheeses are unmolded and salted and placed, well apart, on drying shelves in a room kept at a fairly low temperature. After about six to eight more days they are firm enough to be packed and transported by truck to the caves for "refining," as the process of transformation is called.

AS OLD AS TIME—AS MODERN AS THE HOUR: THE SHEEP FARMS

We spent one lovely, refreshing day with the sheep on top of a high, windswept mesa of *les causses*. Our car snaked uphill over a narrow road bordered with limestone boulders, past flowering plants, bright-green young oaks, and hazel bushes. The road led onto a flat tableland where the wind slapped at our faces. The arid earth was covered with stones and punctuated by clumps of dry grass and blue-flowered thistles. Locusts buzzed through the air. The arc of the blue sky was immense.

Above the sighing of the wind, sheep bells tapped out the song of the mesa. The sheep were at home here. They searched out the delicacies among the dry grasses—the wild sweet clover, the sage and thyme, the verbena. They drank the clear water pumped up for them into round stone ponds. We followed one of the flocks of ewes to a group of stone buildings, low under roofs of curved red tiles.

Inside, the bleating of sheep and the smell of oily wool combined with the purring of electric motors. The ewes were crowding around the latest type of milking carousel. On the revolving platform were twenty-four wedge-shaped pens with, at the head of each, a feeder filled with wheat, which is caviar to sheep. Each ewe fairly jumped into the pen and stuck her head into the feeder, immobilized in total concentration while the strong young shepherd fitted the udder into the milking cup. After the carousel had made one slow revolution, the job was done. The milk was at once cooled and pumped into the storage tank.

I tasted a glass of the fresh milk. It was creamy and thick—the first impression was one of richness on my lips and tongue. Then, it seemed to me to have the brightness, the cleanness, the purity of these wide and windswept spaces. There was also, I thought, a faint sense of those wild herbs cropped so eagerly by the sheep. At that moment I believe I knew why, all my life, I had so much loved the cheese of Roquefort.

Before I left Roquefort I talked with the mayor, Monsieur Benjamin Crouzat, who heads a family-operated production unit (one of thirteen producers) in the caves. He makes about 160,000 cheeses a year, all bearing, in addition to the basic "red sheep" label used on all Roquefort, his own brand name, La Cloche (the Bell). Here is M. Crouzat's advice on buying and storing Roquefort:

• The first thing to remember is that the center of a piece of ripe cheese, at room temperature, should be soft enough to be spreadable, about like a firm pâté. If the cheese is a bit too hard when you buy it, you can ripen and soften it in your own refrigerator (see below).

• When choosing a piece of Roquefort, look at the blue-green veins. There should be plenty of them and they should be fairly evenly distributed. Between the veins, the cheese should be creamy-white, never butter-yellow. Look especially for any browning of the outside—this means that the cheese has been badly stored at too high a temperature.

• It is always better to buy a piece cut from a full-sized wheel (5½ pounds) rather than foil-wrapped miniature wedges, which are too small to ripen satisfactorily.

• To develop, ripen, and soften a fine piece of Roquefort at home, first remove all its foil wrapping to permit air to reach it, then wrap it very loosely in waxed paper. Store it in the vegetable crisper of your refrigerator, where there is an approximation of the cold and dampness in the caves. If the cheese is surrounded by well-washed, still-wet lettuce leaves, so much the better. If the piece of cheese is fairly large, use a thickish, stainless-steel knitting needle to bore a number of holes in it, to allow the damp air to get right to its center and help forward the internal development. Within a few days, you will be surprised to see how quickly it is improving.

• Never eat Roquefort taken directly from the refrigerator. When it is that cold, you miss at least half the pleasure. Cut off the piece you are going to use and let it come to room temperature, allowing at least 2 to 3 hours.

To M. Crouzat's advice I would add that ultimately, of course, you must judge the nearness-to-perfection of your Roquefort by its taste. I think that the extraordinary gastronomic excitement of this cheese comes from the contrast between the almost austere, noncreamy, slightly salty, savory simplicity of the white ewe's-milk cheese, set against the aromatic, complicated, luxurious softness of the blue-green veins. It has a unique quality, simply because there is no other blue cheese made from sheep's milk. A fine piece, properly cared for, would keep in your refrigerator for months, if it were not quite so irresistibly habit-forming.

Wonderful as the cheese of Roquefort is when served on its own with a crisp crust of French bread and a glass of wine, it can also lend distinction to an intriguing range of dishes, as the following recipes demonstrate.

LA FEUILLETE AU ROQUEFORT
(Puff-Pastry Roquefort Tart)

4 to 6 servings

    1 pound puff pastry (see notes)
    4 ounces Roquefort cheese
    ¼ cup unsalted butter
    1½ teaspoons sweet Hungarian paprika
    ¼ teaspoon freshly ground pepper
    1 egg, beaten
    ½ cup heavy cream
    2 teaspoons cornstarch
    1 egg yolk
    1 teaspoon water

1. Divide puff pastry into 2 pieces; roll one piece ⅛ inch thick on lightly floured surface; cut out 11½-inch circle. Fold into quarters; ease and unfold into 9 × 1-inch tart pan with removable bottom. Press pastry gently against bottom and sides of pan. Do not trim edges. Refrigerate 1 hour. Roll second piece of pastry ⅛ inch thick; cut out 9-inch circle; refrigerate 1 hour (see notes).

2. Heat cheese and butter in small saucepan over low heat, stirring constantly, until melted. Stir in paprika and pepper. Remove from heat. Stir in egg until smooth. Mix cream and cornstarch in small cup until smooth; stir into saucepan. Cook, stirring constantly, over medium heat until mixture is very thick, 2 to 3 minutes.

3. Heat oven to 400° F. Pierce bottom of pastry in tart pan in several places with fork. Spread cheese mixture in pastry, leaving ¾-inch space between filling and edge of pastry all around. Cover with 9-inch pastry circle. Trim overhang of bottom pastry to ¼ inch. Mix egg yolk and water; brush edge of 9-inch circle and overhang lightly with egg wash. Fold overhang over top pastry; press and crimp to seal. Brush top of pastry lightly with egg wash. Cut several slits in top. Place tart pan on baking sheet. Bake tart 10 minutes; reduce oven temperature to 350° F. Bake until pastry is puffed and browned, 30 to 40 minutes. Cool on wire rack 10 minutes before serving.

NOTES: Use pastry made from your favorite recipe, or use packaged frozen puff pastry, thawed.

Trimmings can be cut into decorative shapes and refrigerated; apply to top of tart with egg wash before baking.

VELVETY ROQUEFORT VICHYSSOISE

6 servings (about 1⅓ cups each)

  1 cup finely chopped cleaned leeks, white part only
  ½ cup finely chopped onion
  ¼ cup unsalted butter
  1 quarter chicken stock or broth
  2 cups diced pared potatoes
  ¼ teaspoon salt
    Pinch freshly ground white pepper
  2 cups buttermilk
  4 ounces Roquefort cheese, finely crumbled (about ¾ cup)
  2 tablespoons chopped scallion tops (see note)

1. Sauté leeks and onion in butter in Dutch oven over low heat until soft and golden, about 15 minutes. Stir in stock, potatoes, salt and pepper. Heat to boiling; reduce heat. Simmer, uncovered, until potatoes are fork-tender, about 20 minutes. Purée soup, 2 cups at a time, in blender or food processor until smooth. Refrigerate, covered, until very cold, about 4 hours.

2. Stir in buttermilk just before serving. Taste and adjust seasonings. Ladle into soup bowls; sprinkle with cheese and scallions and serve.

NOTE: Minced dill or parsley can be substituted for the scallion tops.

ROQUEFORT AND APPLE OMELET

2 servings

  2 tart apples, pared, cut into ¼-inch slices
  3 tablespoons unsalted butter
  5 eggs, lightly beaten
  2 tablespoons water or milk
    Salt
    Freshly ground white pepper
  ½ cup crumbled Roquefort cheese (about 3 ounces)

1. Sauté apples in 2 tablespoons of the butter in large omelet pan over high heat until just fork-tender, about 1 minute. Transfer to plate.

2. Whisk eggs, water or milk, salt and pepper in medium bowl until blended. Heat remaining tablespoon butter in omelet pan over high heat, tilting pan to coat sides with butter. Add egg mixture; cook, stirring with fork, until eggs begin to set. Sprinkle cheese over one half of the omelet; spoon half the apple slices over cheese. Fold omelet in half; transfer to warm platter. Garnish with remaining apple slices.

BEEF STEAKS ROQUEFORT

4 servings

   ¼ cup crumbled Roquefort cheese (about 1½ ounces)
   2 tablespoons Cognac or brandy
   2 tablespoons unsalted butter, at room temperature
   4 individual beef tenderloin, sirloin, or rib steaks (each 1 inch thick)
   Vegetable oil
   Salt
   Freshly ground pepper

1. Mash cheese and Cognac in small bowl until smooth. Add butter; mix thoroughly to make a smooth paste. Shape into 4 even-sized nuggets; refrigerate, covered, until cold.
2. Preheat broiler. Trim excess fat from steaks; score edges with cuts ¼ inch deep, spaced 1 inch apart, to prevent curling. Brush both sides of steaks lightly with oil.
3. Broil steaks, 5 inches from heat source, until top side is browned, about 5 minutes; sprinkle browned side with salt and pepper. Turn steaks. Broil second side until browned, about 3 minutes; sprinkle with salt and pepper (see note). Transfer to warm plates; top each steak with one Roquefort nugget. Serve immediately.

NOTE: The steaks will be rare to medium rare. If you wish, cook longer. Rare meat will be soft and yielding to the touch; medium, springy and firm; well done, hard and unyielding.

WALNUT AND ROQUEFORT SALAD

4 servings

3 ounces walnut halves
2 to 3 tablespoons white wine vinegar
½ teaspoon freshly ground pepper
¼ teaspoon salt
7 tablespoons olive oil
1 medium head romaine, cleaned, torn into large pieces
½ head chicory, cleaned, torn into large pieces
1 avocado, peeled, pitted, sliced lengthwise, dipped in lemon juice
1 bunch scallions with tops, trimmed, chopped
4 ounces Roquefort cheese, crumbled (about ¾ cup)

1. Toast walnuts in heavy skillet over medium heat, stirring frequently, until golden, 5 to 8 minutes. Remove from skillet; cool and reserve.

2. Mix vinegar, pepper and salt in small bowl. Add oil in thin, steady stream, whisking continuously until dressing is smooth and thoroughly mixed.

3. Combine romaine, chicory, avocado, scallions, cheese, and reserved walnuts in large salad bowl. Pour dressing over salad; toss. Taste and adjust seasonings. Serve immediately.

On the Trail of Bird's Nest Soup: Caves, Climbs, and High Stakes

They are plucked from high on the walls of enormous caves by men who risk instant death while climbing about on bamboo and rattan ladders. They are protected by armed guards and, in some areas, barbed wire is used to defend them against theft. From remote islands in the South China Sea and the Indian Ocean they are distributed, in an atmosphere of secrecy like that of the drug trade, by operatives who sometimes have high connections and invariably make equally high profits.

They are not precious gems or priceless antiquities. They are bird's nests.

Small, snow-white, shaped like a half-teacup, the bird's nest is so revered in Chinese gastronomy—as an aphrodisiac, delicious delicacy, magical booster of health, and purifying sacrament—that in some parts of the world it is virtually worth its weight in gold.

My desire to learn about the nests began in a small Chinese restaurant in Hong Kong while I was eating an extraordinary soup. I was the guest of my friend Fen Dow Chan in a back street of Kowloon, so far from the tourist avenues that the restaurant's name was posted in Chinese ideographs only.

The dining room was extremely comfortable and beautifully decorated. There were figures and fittings of ivory and jade. There was the softness of satins, silks, and tapestries. There was no written menu, but the dish that Fen Dow ordered was immediately translated for me as "nests of sea

EDITOR'S NOTE: This article originally appeared in the September 1983 issue of *Smithsonian*.

swallows with venomous snake and chrysanthemum petals with lemon grass and lotus seeds in soup."

After we had sipped some "Iron Buddha" tea and nibbled on small slivers of preserved goose, the waiter brought in a large tureen and set it on the side table. At this moment, a strange figure entered the room, half-shuffling, half-skating toward us in his black velvet slippers. It was an ancient, bearded Chinese gentleman wearing a long, loose scarlet robe. Hanging by a red-silk cord from his left wrist was a brown-leather bag ornamented with silver-dragon designs, with something, obviously, moving inside. As he reached the tureen, the head of a live snake rose from the bag, its forked tongue darting. With a quick motion, the old man grasped the snake behind the head and, deftly squeezing, appeared to spritz into the soup just a drop or two of the venom.

There could be no question as to the extraordinary excellence of this soup. Its brilliant balance of tastes and textures—its combination of pure simplicity and a rainbow of complicated sensuous flavors—made it the single greatest Chinese dish I have ever tasted. Tiny slivers of snake meat had been shredded into the soup, but the dominant ingredient was the translucent, spaghettilike, gelatinous and glutinous birds' nests. They gave a sense of luxurious richness to the soup. Cutting through the velvety flavor was the citrus tang of chrysanthemum petals and lemon grass.

While we consumed the soup, Fen Dow talked incessantly, unburdening his soul, which, this Sunday morning, was deeply troubled. I had promised to pick him up at his apartment and take him to lunch. But when I got there, I found him still in bed and in terrible shape. On Saturday night he had been "out with the bad boys," and everything had gone desperately wrong. They had drunk too much 110-proof Mao Tai. As the night deepened, so did their troubles. They went to "puff a pipe or two" in one of the clandestine opium houses. This morning his body felt like lead and his spirits were as black as the deepest coal mine. I offered at once to take him to his doctor. "No," Fen Dow said. "More than anything, I must have some bird's nest soup. Help me get dressed and then we'll go to my favorite place."

In the restaurant, after his third large bowl, Fen Dow was visibly recovering. He made clear to me the almost magical esteem in which the Chinese hold the nests of the "sea swallow." It was not just as matter of hunger or nutrition. He was convinced that the soup would restore balance and strength to his body and mind and give him long life, virility and wisdom.

In reality, the white nests are not built by swallows but by one particular small bird belonging to the family of swifts. Because of its comparatively small size the bird is known as a swiftlet, more specifically as the edible-nest or white-nest swiftlet. It builds its nests primarily in sea caves, although some swiftlets nest in inland areas far from the coast. It feeds by swooping through the air, catching flying insects.

When the male is ready to start building the nest, he picks a high, safe place, and out of his mouth comes a secretion from his now swollen salivary glands. This "paste" or nest-cement, as it is called, emerges from his mouth in a continuous thin strand of soft "spaghetti." He weaves it, swinging his small head this way and that, into a nest shaped like a shallow half-cup. As the nest dries, all of the strands stick solidly together and the entire nest is "glued" firmly to the rock wall. In this little haven, the female lays her eggs and rears her young for about two months.

As Fen Dow took each mouthful, he meditated on the tremendous struggles of this tiny bird against the forces of ocean storms and monsoon winds. For centuries the Chinese believed that to create the nest the swiftlet absorbed nothing more than the windblown foam from the sea. Fen Dow believed that he was absorbing with the soup the iodine of seaweed, the phosphorescence that lights up the southern seas at night, mineral salts, and other mysterious natural elements. He consumed them as a concentrated essence of the devotion, endurance, power, strength, and virility of this extraordinary bird. It was at this point that the idea came to me of dropping all my other plans to devote myself to an exploration of the white-nest swiftlet and the worldwide trade in its nests.

I began looking for birds' nests in the restaurants of Hong Kong. On Paterson Street in the Causeway Bay district of Hong Kong Island, I found a restaurant, the Siam Bird's Nest, which served them in about forty different ways. Common bird's-nest recipes include a salty soup as a separate course before the main meal, dumplings, and a sweet dessert soup garnished with fruit. At the restaurant one could also buy beautifully packed boxes of whole birds' nests. The price fluctuates according to the economy, the year's harvest, and the quality of the nests. At that time, the price for top-quality nests in U.S. dollars came to about $4,000 per pound. The most valuable nests are the "white" ones, especially those collected before the female lays her eggs. Another species, the black-nest swiftlet, provides nests that contain their own black feathers and are edible only after thorough cleaning, but these are far less expensive.

I started talking with the owner of the restaurant, Wong Tze-ming, inquiring why he continued to use the name "Siam" for his restaurant when the name of the country had been changed more than forty years ago to Thailand. He replied that his family had had a contract, for more than a hundred years, directly with the kings of Siam (those same kings who were the subjects of *Anna and the King of Siam* and *The King and I*) for the rights to the harvesting of birds' nests in some of the great caves on the Thai coast. Since the contract with the Royal Family was in the name of Siam, he did not feel that he should change it.

It was most probably the Chinese who recognized the edibility of the nests of the white-nest swiftlet. Although a firm date or instance has not been documented, one particular account tells of a Chinese man named Hao Yieng, who had settled in Siam about 1750. He apparently soon discovered that the sea swiftlets built their nests and bred in several caves of the offshore islands and that the nests were of an immaculate white material soluble in hot water. The little bird was thought to be so pure that it derived all its nourishment from the air and from sea spray. Its name, in the local language, was "wind-eating bird." It was said never to have been seen taking any form of solid food.

Perhaps it was to be expected that a performance so ethereal should attract such dauntless gastronomic perfectionists as the Chinese. Hao Yieng must have seen the value of such a commodity, for in 1770 he went to visit the King of Siam with a proposal. He presented all his possessions including his wife, his children, and his slaves, along with fifty cases of tobacco, in return for the rights to collect all the birds' nests in all the caves on two islands. The King agreed. Within a few years, Hao Yieng had a virtual monopoly on the bird's-nest trade and had become immensely rich. Later realizing the great value of these edible nests, the Siamese Crown took over and Hao Yieng released his monopoly. A "corps of hereditary collectors" was created and it was perhaps through this administrative machinery that, eventually, the contract was signed with the Wong family at the Siam Bird's Nest restaurant in Hong Kong.

I then decided to to to Bangkok, where some of the finest nests are found in the huge caves near the Bay of Phangnga. I wanted to know what happened to these excellent nests and learned that a major company now manages the collection and distribution, with most of the nests going on to Hong Kong to be sold. I asked an official if I could acquire a few of the top-quality white nests for my personal use and was given a wooden box, about the size of a standard shoe box, filled with nests in perfect condition. We weighed them on a laboratory scale and they came to a shade better than two pounds. I could have these at the wholesale price—"a little below what we charge Hong Kong"—for $2,000 in U.S. currency, cash. The nests are so light that you get about fifty to each pound. It takes about six nests, plus quite a few other ingredients, to prepare a tureen of soup for four people.

THE SEARCH FOR THE ULTIMATE RECIPE

In search of the ultimate recipe for my newly acquired investment of bird's-nest liquid capital, I consulted a number of the top cooks of Bangkok. Though Thailand produces some of the best bird's nests in the world, it has never accepted the dish as a great specialty and has never incorporated any form of cooked bird's nest into Thai cuisine. However, the King and Queen of Thailand have a superb sense of diplomacy and hospitality. When Queen Elizabeth II paid a state visit, the kitchens of the Royal Palace in Bangkok did not hesitate to prepare roast beef and Yorkshire pudding. Just in case there should be a visit from a high Chinese diplomat, there does exist, in the royal kitchen files, a magnificent recipe for bird's-nest soup prepared with the purest, whitest Thai nests. Two outstanding cooks in Bangkok, both consultants to the kitchens at the Palace, one of whom is Chinese, have given me the opportunity to taste what is alleged to be the unofficial royal recipe.

I have since made this soup in my own kitchen in New York and it has worked extremely well for me—both with the top-grade nests I brought back from Bangkok and with less expensive nests I have bought in Chinese-American food shops. The prices mentioned may have given the impression that birds' nests can be afforded only by the very rich. The top prices are paid only for the very limited quantities of absolutely perfect nests; other grades (including packages of broken bits or "dragon's teeth") are sold at relatively affordable prices.

After my experience in Bangkok I realized that great numbers of nests must flow into the Hong Kong market. They come not only from the coast of Thailand, but also from Malaysia, Indonesia, the Philippines, and Vietnam.

It seemed that most of these shipments were shrouded in secrecy. It was hinted that one man was the "world kingpin" of the international traffic in edible nests. He was said to have contracts with governments, kings and princes, and private owners of islands, and to have a great deal of money to throw around. He was said to control his invisible empire from a minuscule office in Kowloon in Hong Kong. Whether this is just one man or a group of so-called brokers is debatable. Eventually—with the help of friends—I did get to talk briefly to such a man, on condition that I did not publish the address of his office and that I simply call him "Mr. Fred."

His office was in a narrow, nondescript back street, at the front of an entirely inconspicuous small building. The main door was steel-plated and opened only by advance appointment. Both the waiting room and the inner office were filled with a chaotic jumble of samples of items for sale. Instantly recognizable were bolts of silk and carved pieces of ivory and jade. There were also some rolls of barbed wire.

Mr. Fred was a small, round Chinese gentleman of indefinite age, educated in Europe and with a near-perfect command of English. He was impeccably well dressed and positively exploding with energy, opinions, and a torrent of talk. I asked, "Why so much secrecy surrounding the trade in birds' nests?" His smile was almost fatherly, the tone of his voice ever so slightly condescending as he answered: "For the same reason that there is secrecy about shipments of gold bars. Gold is now worth about $400 per ounce. The very best grades of birds' nests are getting close to $300 an ounce. Every time we move a shipment from one warehouse to another, or from a packing room to the airport, we face the danger of hijacking."

I asked about the barbed wire. "If you were the owner of an island," he said, "let us say a remote island with caves where the swiftlets have been nesting, perhaps, for hundreds of years—and you had a contract with me for the delivery of so many thousands of nests per year—you would be extremely worried about the security of your island. It might be invaded at any time by poachers intent on taking the nests regardless of the consequences or the impact on the birds or the caves. Since we have a contract with you, and therefore a financial interest in your island, I am prepared to provide you with various means of defending it."

He explained the high prices: "All over the world, it is a seller's market for birds' nests. Chinese chefs in Chinese restaurants, however small and insignificant, want to be able to have bird's nest soup available, at least to special order, on their menus. And," Mr. Fred added, "the supply never catches up with the demand!" In fact, the demand for birds' nests has pushed prices so high that in 1979 a ship was deliberately sunk off the coast of the Philippines so the owners could collect insurance amounting to $11.5 million on its cargo—nine tons of birds' nests, as well as other valuable commodities. Authorities, when they realized that nine tons represented a staggering harvest of nests, grew suspicious. After the investigation, insurance fraud was proved. All that the ship's hold carried was granite dust worth $8 per ton.

By now I was anxious to visit the birds themselves, so I planned a journey that would take me to Malaysian Borneo, where I would visit the Niah caves in Sarawak and then go on to Sabah to the famous Gomantong caves. But first there was a briefing by the government officials who control the harvesting of birds' nests in the state of Sabah. They presented a thoroughly realistic and scientific point of view.

Since about 1934 there has been an ordinance in Sarawak to protect the birds, permitting the nests to be harvested only every seventy-five days. In the late 1950s when the area was under British Colonial rule, an aristocrat from England trained as a biologist, Lord Medway (now the Earl of Cranbrook), became fascinated by the life cycle of the edible-nest swiftlet. He undertook scientific studies of the taxonomy and biology of the bird, which indicated that the government-regulated period between collections was not long enough. Today at the Gomantong caves in Sabah only two nest harvests per year of the white-nest swiftlet are allowed. The first nest is collected before the eggs are laid. The male then makes a second nest, which is collected only after the fledglings have gone. But despite this policy the harvest recently seemed to decline and the Wildlife Section of the Forest Department has now launched a biological study of the swiftlets.

Lord Medway also found that the bird had a skill even greater than any for which it had been venerated: it can navigate in flight in the pitch-black darkness of the deepest recesses of the caves by echolocation. The bird emits sounds—rather like pebbles rattling in its throat. These sounds echo back from the rock walls and assist the bird in finding its nest.

I was looking forward to finding this immaculate, magical bird at Gomantong and I felt an extraordinary excitement as the small boat set out from Sandakan to cross the bay. After docking and a fourteen-mile drive, we walked the last few miles through rain forest. We entered the main cave and it was huge. The light was dim, coming only from several shafts to the outside. The odor was strong and the ground felt like large soft mounds of loose soil. I realized it was a carpet of guano—a mixture of bird and bat droppings. We sank in up to our ankles as we walked forward, and the surface appeared flecked with dark-gold specks that glittered and seemed to move. A closer examination revealed that these specks were a moving sea of predatory cockroaches burrowing under the surface and patrolling on top for anything that fell. A fledgling bird or injured adult stood no chance of survival on the ground.

The light shaft above us was suddenly filled with swiftlets taking off from their nests as a pair of white-crowned hornbills swooped in on a raid. There were also thousands of bats and we observed large centipedes, crabs, and spiders, as well as snakes and an occasional scorpion. There were several long bamboo and rattan ladders hanging two hundred to three hundred feet from wooden staves wedged tightly into crevices in the limestone of the cave. Several nest collectors were climbing these ladders, carrying flashlights to locate the nests. They used special tools for gently grasping and loosening the nests, which they carefully put in rattan baskets attached to a pulley.

Few collectors have fallen to their deaths, which tells us what tremendous athletic skills they have developed. The ladders are replaced every year, but old ones are left in their rotting condition, possibly to discourage would-be poachers. There are always guards to protect the caves. We watched this incredible spectacle and admired the ability of one collector who took an hour to climb down the longest ladder.

In one year about a million nests may be collected in Sabah alone, worth millions of U.S. dollars on the retail market in Hong Kong. The illegal trade accounts for a substantial percentage of these nests.

I have learned much about the white-nest swiftlet on my journey to the caves and it is comforting to know that current studies will, we hope, guarantee the future of this remarkable bird.

As to the alleged magical nutritive properties of the nest material as food, I have learned that a chemical analysis showed that it is "of very low nutritive value." I shall not send a copy of this report to my friend Fen Dow Chan in Hong Kong.

THE UNOFFICIAL ROYAL RECIPE OF THAILAND FOR BIRD'S NEST SOUP

> 6 whole nests, or 1½ ounces of "dragon's teeth"
> 8¾ cups clear chicken bouillon, or stock
> ½ cup diced raw chicken breast meat
> ½ cup diced lean country-smoked cooked ham
> ½ cup diced lean raw pork
> ¾ cup bean sprouts, washed, topped, and tailed
> 8 quail eggs
> ¾ cup chunks raw chicken breast meat
> 2 egg whites (chicken, that is!), fairly stiffly beaten
> ⅓ cup small slivers raw chicken breast meat
> ⅓ cup small slivers lean country-smoked cooked ham
> 1 cup finely chopped watercress leaves, no stalks
> Coarse crystal sea salt
> Freshly milled Chinese Sichuan pepper

1. Put nests into bowl and pour boiling water over them, just to cover. Leave them to soften for 1 hour. Measure ¾ cup of chicken bouillon and chill, covered, in coldest part of refrigerator. At the end of the hour, using fine-mesh sieve, clean and wash nests by holding them under gently running cold water. Wipe out bowl and put back nests. Cover with cold water and soak for another 2 hours.

2. Meanwhile, begin gently heating remaining 8 cups of chicken bouillon to light simmer and stir in ½ cup each of the diced chicken, ham, and pork. Let them all simmer together very gently, covered, for 2 hours.

3. When the timer rings, strain diced meats from chicken stock and discard them. Now drain nests and add them to stock in saucepan and continue gentle simmering, tightly lidded, for another 2½ hours. During this time the nests will partially melt and give a rich, glutinous body to the soup.

4. Then, quickly blanch the bean sprouts by plunging them, for no more than a few seconds, into boiling water. At once, run them under cold water to prevent softening, drain, dry, and put them aside. Next, soft-boil the 8 quail eggs until yolks are just set by putting them into cold water, heating it to a gentle boil, simmering for 3 to 4 minutes, then at once plunging them into cold water. Shell and hold them for garnishing. Next, put ¾ cup of chicken chunks into the workbowl of a food processor and puree to smooth velvet, with the steel blade. Then add the ¾ cup of cold chicken stock and blend for a few more seconds. Transfer mixture to a bowl, fold in the two stiffly beaten egg whites and hold.

5. About 10 minutes before the end of the 2½ hours of simmering, stir into soup the slivers of chicken and ham, plus the bean sprouts and chopped watercress. Taste for seasoning and add a minimum of sea salt and Sichuan pepper. Be very careful not to dominate or override the supremely delicate and subtle flavor of the birds' nests.

6. In the final moment before serving, take saucepan off heat and gently stir into it chicken-puree mix, which will have two immediate effects: first, chicken will slightly thicken the soup; second, egg whites will add a charming decoration by solidifying into a multitude of tiny suspended white threads. Warm for a few seconds and serve instantly, in small portions. Garnish with quail eggs.

A Beach Picnic in Provence (and a Discourse on Olive Oil and Olives)

The scene is the small wine cellar in the hills facing the sea—the cool air perfumed by the fruity bouquet of olive oil and the pungency of garlic—unquestionably a scene in Provence. We are in the hills above the small Mediterranean resort town of Bandol, famous in the Midi (and beyond) for its charmingly refreshing reds, rosés, and whites. On these slopes are several important vineyards and many small ones, whose labels and names are not widely known, but whose wines are solidly and well made, full of the strength that comes from abundant sunshine. They belong to the Midi in character and style—perfect with the aromatic food of Provence.

No one knows the Côtes de Provence wines, from the finest to the humblest, better than Roger Vergé, the famous chef-owner of the three-star Le Moulin de Mougins, near Cannes, who has been tasting them every day of his life since he came to Provence about thirty years ago. He may have been born in the Auvergne in central France, he may have learned his cooking skills under the supreme chefs of Paris at their great hotels and restaurants. He may have spent the first part of his professional career roaming the world. But, as he says: "I would never have become reconciled to returning to work in France if I had not discovered the joys of drinking, eating, and living in Provence."

Today, on our wine-tasting tour, Roger and I have just reached this small vineyard above Bandol and, since it is approaching lunch time, the

EDITOR'S NOTE: This article is published here for the first time.

owner has offered us the hospitable tradition of a tasting of his wines with a *frotté à l'huile,* a ceremonial "rub of oil." The owner, who does all the work himself, is obviously having a struggle to keep his property in perfect repair. The modest cellar is slightly dilapidated, but scrupulously clean. In the open space at the high double doors in front, before the rows of barrels begin and stretch row upon row, into the dark interior, two empty barrels have been upended as tables. There's a large, flat serving platter covered with nothing more than a thin layer of the best, fruitiest, extra-virgin, cold-pressed, Provençal olive oil. Onto it is evenly sprinkled a substantial quantity of finely minced garlic and coarse salt, *gros sel,* as it's called in French. There's also a huge four-pound round loaf of rough country bread, several hunks of deliberately not-too-strong Provençal cow's or goat's milk cheeses—perhaps a Banon, or a Tomme Arlésienne, or a Côtes-du-Ventous, or a Palette—and a few bunches of freshly picked grapes, the orangey-red Grenache, or the greenish Chenin Blanc. You tear off an irregular chunk from the loaf, rub it around the platter until it is thoroughly impregnated with the olive oil, garlic, and salt, then eat it with cheese and grapes. Your thirst is immediate and strong. Fortunately, at this moment, your host is pouring his cool wine for you. You note the dark color of the red in the glass, its ruby clarity against the light. The perfume is reminiscent of the wild rosemary of a Provençal hillside. So soon after the strong food, the first sip seems almost gentle—but then one seems to sense the taste of more herbs—laurel, savory, thyme—and finally, believe it or not, there follows the lightest touch of peppermint in your throat as the wine goes down. The whole effect is curious, but rather attractive and you're impelled to finish the glass. Now you need some solid food to clear your mouth of the wine. More impregnated bread. More cheese. More grapes. Thirstily back to more wine. More food to balance the stomach. More wine to help digest the food. No one ever stops drinking until all the food is gone.

I cannot get to Provence as often as my tongue would wish, but I can recapture at least the practical part of this ceremony of simple hospitality at any time in my New York home. I cannot provide the general atmosphere of a small Provençal winecellar. I do not even own an empty barrel for upending. But there is no problem anywhere about the making of a *frotté à l'huile.*

Roger Vergé and I were visiting vineyards and tasting wines for a quite unique menu that he was planning for a rather special occasion. I had gone down from Paris to spend a few days with him and his wife Denise at Le Moulin de Mougins to taste his new dishes and to hear reports on his many activities. During our lunch on the first day, he was called to the telephone for an urgent conversation with a high official of the Quai d'Orsay in Paris, the equivalent of the Department of State, or the Foreign Office, of the French government. There were, apparently, two most important "diplomatic personages," representing a major foreign nation, who had been working in Paris for several weeks with the appropriate French officials on a major project. This work had now been completed and they were about to return to their own country. Before they left, the French government wanted to show its appreciation for their hard work by entertaining them for a few days of vacation anywhere in France that they would choose to go. They had asked to see Provence. They had especially mentioned the fact that in Paris they had had a great deal of very fancy and fine food and many of the best wines of the country. In Provence, they wanted to live as if they were Provençal natives, eating the rough, strong, garlicky dishes, drinking the peasanty, powerful wines. They had even heard, vaguely, that *bouillabaisse* was a fish stew that, in its most authentic form, should be served as a beach picnic! If that were true, could it be arranged for them? So the Quai d'Orsay turned to the "first chef of Provence," Roger Vergé. Could these diplomats stay for a few days at Le Moulin de Mougins? Could there be a *bouillabaisse* on a beach for them, for the two secret security men who accompanied them everywhere and for their interpreter? They would arrive within about a week.

These were the preparations in which Roger was now engaged. The organizing and preparation of the *"bouillabaisse* on the beach" were to be in the safe and sound hands of his fisherman friend, Pierrot. Roger liked to tell the story of how he got to know Pierrot and his circle of fishermen down at the old fishing port, the Quai St. Pierre, in Cannes. When Roger first came to Provence, he used to go down to the waterfront every day in the early morning, when the fish boats came in, so that he could learn about the various types of fish that were brought ashore. He asked many questions of the fishermen and Pierrot seemed always the most willing to take the time for detailed and intelligent answers. One morning, there had been a particularly large and magnificent catch of the fish that in French is called St. Pierre, and in English, John Dory. The fishermen decided to have a feast of their own and they invited Roger to be their guest. They produced two enormous earthenware *tians*, the traditional, fairly shallow, glazed open baking dishes of Provence, which they filled with the large, monster-headed, cleaned, and washed St. Pierres. The fish were surrounded by small potatoes, dotted orange-yellow with sprinklings of saffron, lusciously red and round tomatoes, glistening white onions, the bluish-green tints of branches of fresh thyme, the brilliant green of bay-laurel leaves, all contrasting with and magnifying the steely grey of the bodies of the fish. It was a mouth-watering picture, framed by the rich brown of the pot and bathed by the brilliant Provençal sunlight of a May morning. The fishermen carefully carried the two *tians* to their favorite bakeshop at the end of the quai and the baker at once slid them into his bread oven. Then, about an hour and a half later, the *tians* were carried back, each now covered with a crust of pure gold. As they were set down, right there in the open air on the quai, on a neatly stacked pile of boxes, the surrounding air was filled with an extraordinary and magnificent perfume, strong yet subtle, a kind of essence of Provence, always to be remembered. Plates and spoons were provided for the ten participants in this, to say the least, unusual lunch. It was only proper and right that it should be eaten standing up.

As the years passed, Pierrot became a close and firm friend. He taught Roger many of the simple, wonderful *recettes des pêcheurs,* the often unique ways in which the fishermen and their wives prepare the fish at home (generally when they have more than they can sell) in ways to highlight the special qualities of each fish. After reworking some of these recipes in his own kitchen, Roger had included them in his three-star menu at Le Moulin de Mougins and they had become *les grandes spécialités* of the fashionable, rich, often snobbish clientele of international connoisseurs who stayed in the dozen or so luxurious rooms of the auberge (the converted main house of the mill) and dined under the huge umbrellas on the terraces of the gardens filled with the scents of flowers and the songs of birds. It was this expensive and refined atmosphere that the diplomatic guests, their protective agents, and their administrative staff entered when they arrived from Paris.

DIPLOMATIC BEACH PICNIC IN THE GRAND MANNER

Pierrot had chosen a quiet and hidden, small sandy cove on the Golfe Juan, slightly east of Cannes, on the way toward Nice. On this beach, Pierrot had arranged for a huge iron pot to be heated over a wood fire. Pierrot is the advocate of one trick that is always controversial and often rather strongly disapproved of by conservative *bouillabaisse* aficionados. Pierrot believes that, at the very moment when the still-almost-live fish are thrown into the fiercely bubbling bouillon, branches of young green pine should be thrown onto the fire and it should be fanned, so that both the flames and the slightly tarry pine smoke should "lick the top bubbles of the *bouillabaisse,*" giving a delicately smoky flavor to the finished fish stew. I can confirm, from having tasted it several times, that provided the trick is not overdone, the delicate and subtle ambiance of far-off pine smoke is an acceptable and excellent variation of the ancient fish stew.

The principal guests were all in bathing suits and were in and out of the water, swimming furiously to work up a major appetite. It was not exactly a simple picnic, designed for communing with nature, disconnected from the human world. It was just about twenty minutes' drive from here to Le Moulin and Roger had a small fleet of refrigerated mini-trucks going back and forth, bringing all the essentials for complete comfort and near-perfect eating. They had brought, among many things, a small bank of portable refrigerators, now neatly hidden behind a group of rocks. So the white wines, the salads, the cheeses, the desserts, would all be at exactly the right cold temperatures.

Roger was in charge on the beach, with his highly trained team from the restaurant. The wood fire was already burning and snapping on a slight rise at the head of the beach. Near it was the requisite pile of fresh young green pine branches. There was a tall black iron tripod that would be set astride the fire and an immense black iron "witch's cauldron" to be hung by the hook above the flames.

Pierrot, on the other hand, was far less committed to all the niceties, far more devoted to the basic simplicities that were the essentials of a near-perfect Bouillabaisse. He believes, first and foremost, that it is not a dish that belongs to the professional chef and cooks of restaurants and commercial kitchens, but to the amateurs, to fishermen and their wives, to all home cooks who prepare it in their own kitchens. He was horrified, recently, by the announcement from the combined restaurateurs of Marseille, of an "official standardized recipe" for *bouillabaisse*. He thinks it must always be made with the best and freshest fish available and, therefore, the dish must vary every time you prepare it. You cannot "know" *bouillabaisse* after eating one fixed official recipe. You must eat a hundred variations and, then, gradually, you will become aware of the true glory of the *bouillabaisse*!

Pierrot's second great rule is that the fish must be so fresh that they are still "throbbing with life" as they are dropped into the boiling bouillon in the big iron pot. To this end, the fish should not be bought from a market, but should be taken from the sea and landed from the fisherman's boat right at the beach where the *bouillabaisse* is being prepared. So—while Roger and his crew worked on the beach—I decided to go with Pierrot in his boat to catch and collect the right balance of the fish. About a mile out from the bay, in open water at a spot where the bottom was rocky and stony, we found the buoy that marked the spot where Pierrot had set his nets and traps. We dropped anchor and hauled the catch into our boat. At our feet tumbled the *bouillabaisse*.

There was, of course, the *rascasse*, the venomous spider fish that is the one essential element of any great bouillabaisse—also *galinette* (sea hen), red mullet, *girelle* (rainbow wrasse), *serran* (comber), gurnard, *vive* (weaver), *boudroi* (goosefish), *roucaou*, *merlan*, St. Pierre (John Dory), and that supreme delicacy called *loup de mer* (sea bass). There were also crabs, lobsters, and *muraena* eels, so big, fierce, strong, and vicious that their thrashing around could break your arm and a bite from one of them would be poisonous enough to be dangerous. Each of them had to be hit on the head with a heavy wooden club we had brought along for that purpose. But hitting the target on the rapidly writhing head was a difficult game. For more than an hour we wrestled with the fish and then headed our boat back toward the beach.

Meanwhile, because the *bouillabaisse* would have to be prepared and served within a few minutes after our return with the fish, the two opening courses of the picnic menu had already been presented while we were still "out at sea." First there was passed around a huge, wide, handsomely hand-woven Provençal basket of cold salade mesclun aux écrevisses. The word *mesclun* in the local dialect simply means "a mixture"—a tossed blend of all the magnificent greenery that always seems to be available in Provence—uplifted by the chopped leaves of many wild herbs and smoothed by the superb fruitiness of the green virgin olive oil. The top of the salad was beautifully decorated with the curled pink bodies of boiled and shelled crayfish, sliced eggs and wild mushrooms, the tiny black olives of Nice, and blood-red little tomatoes the size of grapes. Then this salad was made unique and memorable by the accompaniment of the two-paste puree, dipping-spreading sauces, both dominant and strong, both in fact representing the pure essence of Provence. The *anchoiado* is a paste (soft enough so that you can dip into it, firm enough so that you can spread it on bread) of salted fillets of anchovies soaking in olive oil, plenty of minced garlic, leaves of wild basil and thyme, some Dijon mustard and a little wine vinegar, with fresh black pepper. At this picnic, it was served with the salad, spread on large thick slices of country bread that had been smokily toasted on the tips of long forks at the fierce fire now flaming under the witch's cauldron. Other pieces of toast were spread with the second great classic "dipping-spreading paste" of Provence, *tapenado*, a puree of the pitted flesh of large black olives, with a relatively smaller balance of salted anchovy fillets in olive oil, plus, of course, as always, minced garlic, vinegar-imbued capers, and a reasonable dose of Armagnac brandy. It has been suggested to me, by American gourmet friends, that the idea of opening a meal with a salad is, nowadays, a cliché. I somehow doubt that this salad at this picnic would be as easily forgotten as a simple cliché!

The second course was an ancient Provençal dish that Roger has more or less reinvented, with complete modernization. He has called it, for many years on his three-star menu, *gibelotte de lapin à la provençale*. (The word *gibelotte*, incidentally, is an old Provençal name for a kind of terrine of fricasseed pieces of meat.) Roger's is a cold aromatic aspic filled with quite large pieces of poached wild rabbit, surrounded within the aspic by leaves of herbs and cut-up bits and slices of multicolored vegetables. The dish is served as an unmolded aspic, decorated with sprigs of greenery, tiny red slices of tomato, orange curls of carrots, black and green olive rings, baby *cornichons*, pickled *griotte* cherries, and sweet-and-sour miniature onions. Whether it is presented in the formality of Le Moulin de Mougins, or at a beach picnic, it has to be eaten in a completely informal style. The chunks of rabbit have not been deboned, so you are pretty well compelled to pick them up with your fingers—even though you will probably be able to find a bone sticking out as a convenient handle—and will have to suck off the aspic and bite off the meat. This has been known to shock some ultra-conservative diners at Le Moulin, but the irresistible delectable tastes and textures of the *gibelotte* seem quickly to melt away all opposition. After you have eaten this extraordinary dish—which seems completely out of character with a supreme three-star chef—you feel somehow deeply satisfied—as if it had all been prepared in her country kitchen by your Provençal grandmother! Again, with this second course at our beach picnic, served with an ice-cold *rosé de Provence*, there was, for the guests, a dramatization of the authentic character of the region.

When the keel of our boat, bringing the fish, grounded to a stop on the sand at the edge of the beach, the witch's cauldron was already more than half-filled with the aromatic bubbling bouillon and the flames were hungrily licking the sides of black iron. The perfumed steam from the big pot was proof enough that it contained salted water and white wine, the best cold-pressed green extra-virgin olive oil, fennel, garlic, onions, potatoes, saffron, tomatoes, and all the spices. As we jumped out of the boat, a battalion of Roger's kitchen team, each armed with sharp knives, leaped aboard and, it seemed, in no time at all, had the fish cleaned, scaled, and, as needed, skinned. The bouillon in the pot was bubbling hard as the fish were dropped in and Pierrot threw his pine branches onto the fire for the requisite smoke. Within fifteen minutes there was the golden liquid pouring through a large copper colander into an enormous bowl containing a small mountain of toasted and garlic-rubbed bread. A second bowl, just about as big, was soon mounded with the fish and shellfish.

A great white sheet had been spread as a tablecloth on the grass under the trees at the back of the beach. Deep soup plates were set out, with silver spoons and tall-stemmed wine glasses, with ice-cold bottles of some of the best white wines of Provence. We sat cross-legged in the shade of the trees, the food and wine in front of us, the view of the Mediterranean before us. Pierrot's magnificent *bouillabaisse* was, indeed, delicately and distantly smoky, with, gently superimposed on all its abundance of flavors and textures, that tiny pouch of the character and personality of the pine trees of Provence. It was certainly among the most memorable of all *bouillabaisses*.

Yet even this supreme occasion proved once again that every *bouillabaisse* has its special and unique attractions, because every one is distinctly different from every other. The great gastronomic writer, Waverley Root, shortly before he died, may have stated the final and ultimate truth about *bouillabaisse*:

> There can be no fixed recipe for bouillabaisse because it is composed of the catch that chance has mingled in the fisherman's net of the day. Freshness is always more important than species. So how can you possibly follow a fixed list? Bouillabaisse is an abstraction. The ideal version would, in theory, have to include all the fish in the Mediterranean. Every time you eat a different bouillabaisse, you open up one more facet of the unrealized whole. By the end of your life, no doubt, the image of the ideal bouillabaisse will have formed in your mind. Perhaps that is why bouillabaisse is such a very great dish. It possesses the tantalizing fascination of the unattainable.

After the glory of our *bouillabaisse*, it seemed entirely impossible that Roger could offer a following course that would appear, in any way, to be gastronomically germane, or sensually significant. But he came up with something extraordinary. It was the result of his working with Edouard Ceneri, the famous cheese *éleveur* (it literally means "bringer-up" of cheese) of Cannes, who, with his wife Suzanne and his daughter and sons, runs the extraordinary cheese shop, La Ferme Savoyarde, on the little narrow market street, the rue Meynadier. Edouard does not believe in simply selling cheese—he considers it his responsibility to make sure that every cheese, before it leaves his hands, is in absolutely perfect condition, precisely ripe and ready to be eaten by the customer. To this end, Edouard maintains across the street from his shop a veritable labyrinth of cold deep underground cellars (they were formerly wine cellars), where each large room is constantly maintained at an exact degree of humidity and temperature, while all the rooms taken together, offer such a wide range of conditions that any cheese, of any type, can be pushed forward, or held back, or have this or that feature developed by merely being held, for a carefully calculated time, in one room or another. Edouard plays with his cheeses as an experimental bacteriologist might juggle with his samples of bacteria growing under controlled conditions in laboratory pans. I have spent many hours with Edouard Ceneri in his shivery cold cellars and have tasted there, I think, more nearly perfect cheeses of every conceivable type than I have ever found gathered together in one place anywhere in Europe or America.

The cheese from these cellars that Roger now presented at our beach picnic was a trick of such a degree of expensive luxury, an example of such blatant "conspicuous consumption" that Thorsten Veblen might have been forgiven for turning in his grave. A whole large round of Brie—what is usually called a "two-kilo," a bit over four pounds—had been brought to perfect ripeness, then cooled down for a few days until it was quite elastic and firm. Then, with the help of a long cheese-cutting wire, it had been neatly cut, horizontally, exactly in half, to convert it into a sandwich. The cut side of each half was then spread with top-quality, sweet Provençale butter and a layer of heavy, thick *crème fraîche*. Meanwhile, just about a pound of the best Périgord black truffles (worth at least about five hundred dollars) had been carefully cut by hand into neat, small, exactly square dice. They were now sprinkled and spread, in a fairly solid layer, all across the center of the inside of the Brie. Finally, a goodly supply of black truffle juice was sprinkled over everything. The top half of the cheese was set back in position and the whole round was replaced in its box, so that it would be prevented from spreading out sideways. Then it was put into the refrigerator and a fairly heavy weight was laid on top, so as to integrate everything inside. The amazing fact is, apparently, that the butter and cream act as conductors of the truffle flavors and somehow carry them to all parts of the cheese, which thoroughly absorbs them. The pressure stays on and the cheese remains untouched for three days.

At last, for our beach picnic, the "doctored" Brie was allowed to warm up to correct eating temperature and was served to us with slices of Roger's homemade walnut bread, which contains the crunchy contrast of uncut walnut halves. As each wedge of now-slightly-runny Brie was cut, the line of black truffles was visible along the center. It was quite true that the delicate, subtle, indefinable, indescribable, faintly earthy, distantly mushroomy, always woodsy scent and flavor of truffles had permeated the entire cheese. Roger was successful in his menu maneuver. For the moment, at least, the *bouillabaisse* had been put right out of my mind!

For the dessert Roger did not try any fireworks. He served us a charmingly light tart of grated fresh coconut with cream and spices from the French Caribbean called *tourment d'amour au rhum de Martinique*. No doubt the "torments of love" were considerably magnified by the substantial amounts—used in the pastry, in the fillings, and sprinkled on top after the baking and just before the serving—of the finest Martinique rum, which in my opinion is almost certainly the finest in the world.

Over the coffee, our talk turned to the magnificence of this meal and how it related to the world fame, in general, of the cuisine of Provence. We all knew the obvious answers. You have only to go with Roger at crack of dawn any day to the Farmers' Market in Cannes to know that the near-perfect weather, the rich earth, the abundant and life-giving sun, produce fruits, salad greens, and vegetables that are incomparable. You have only to pick up branches of tiny tomatoes, still attached to their vines as if they were clusters of grapes, to know why the tomato is one of the kingpins of the Provençal cuisine.

You have only to go to any of the small fishing ports between Nice and Marseilles and watch the sparkling treasure of the fish cascading ashore— in spite of pollution and over-fishing in many parts—or look over the fish laid out for sale on the long trestle tables near the boats by the charming, lovely young fishergirls. In other fishing ports in other parts of the world, the fishwives seem to follow a tradition of loud roughness. They shout, with harsh voices. They slap the fish over to you and dare you to hesitate. Not so in Provence. The girls are gracious and merry-eyed. They are perfectly willing to wait while you make up your mind. They admire you if you are discriminating and take your time. They recognize your innate right to pick your fish carefully. This easy consideration for the requirements of good cooking is also a secret of *la cuisine provençale*.

And what about garlic as a foundation of the cooking—as the essential element of so many dishes to which Provence is devoted—the *aïoli*, the garlic mayonnaise with the fish of the Friday lunch; the *rouille*, the version made with the mashed potatoes and hot peppers; the *brandade de morue*, the pâté of cod, garlic, and olive oil; the *aïgo bollido*, one of the many soups made from garlic-scented water, of which another is the *aïga saou*, the "salted water" of Nice; and, of course, to cut an infinite list short, the *pistou*, the Provençal version of the *pesto* of Genoa. The list— and the jokes about garlic—could fill a book. It was Fred Allen who said that, in Provence, almost everyone should be arrested for fragrancy.

Roger said: "No more jokes about garlic are really necessary. All that needs to be said was told by the British writer, Ford Madox Ford, almost fifty years ago. His heroine, so far as I remember her, was a gorgeously beautiful, divinely tall, shapely as Venus, high-fashion model in London.

In her private life, she was a superb cook, adored Provence, and was hopelessly addicted to garlic. Since she prepared many Provençal recipes, she used quantities of garlic. Now this was London and her work was social. Garlic is all very well in the Roman arena at Nîmes among sixteen thousand civilized Provençaux. But when the lovely model went to her studio, the outcry from her colleagues, from her employers, from the wealthy clients for whom she modeled the clothes, and even the driver of the bus that took her homewards, was an agonized sequence of complaints about the stench on her breath. She was asked to take a leave of absence and not come back until she had cured herself of her heinous addiction. She celebrated her release by cooking for herself a chicken garnished with two pounds of garlic cloves, which she ate with a spoon as if they were *haricots blancs*. For the next week she lived on dish after dish loaded with garlic. Then, on the following Monday, she set out again for her high-fashion studio, convinced that this time she must definitely resign. But at the studio there was no outcry. On the contrary, she was congratulated on the improvement of her skin, her hair, and the beautifully athletic balance of all her movements. She had solved the great garlic problem. She had schooled her organs to assimilate, not to protest against, the sacred garlic bulb. The perfume to which so many unenlightened people object is only on the breath of those who lack the courage to eat all the garlic that their hearts desire." And Roger added: "That's how it is with us in Provence. We don't complain to each other about garlic. We don't consider that there is anything antisocial about it. We consider it as a healthful and joyous herb."

But the deepest and most solid foundation of the cuisine of Provence—the heart and soul of almost every dish—the one factor that makes the cuisine of Provence unique in the world—is the olive that grows on the hills facing the sea and the lovely bright green oil, with the indescribable flavor of fruit, that is still hand-pressed by a few perfectionist artisanal families. It is a dying art. Even fifty years ago, there were hundreds of such hand-tended presses all over Provence. Today, they are numbered in dozens. Ninety-five percent of all the olive oil exported from Provence is mass-produced in mass factories by giant automated machines in the industrial sections of Marseille. The olives are subjected to such high crushing pressures that all the pits and stalks, as well as the flesh, are pulverized and the subtle delicacy of the flavor is lost—overshadowed by a strong sense of acid. Then high heat is applied to the olive mash to expel the last dregs of oil and, with this final maneuver, the lovely green color is also lost. This is the average, relatively inexpensive, olive oil that goes out to shops all over the world.

Olive oil is such an important food, such an essential part of the nutrition of millions of people, that it has recently been the subject of research, of discussion, and of international agreements at the United Nations. Official standards have been set up for the best and purest quality of cold-pressed, extra-virgin olive oil and for all the many grades below this top. National governments have signed agreements to maintain these standards, so that a particular grade of olive oil in one country will be the same as that in another. Olive oil is one of the greatest and oldest of foods in international commerce.

In Provence, since Roger Vergé cooks only with the best hand-pressed oil and since he knows virtually every producer of it, I suggested to him that evening that I would like to explore the artisanal production in Provence. "After all," I said, "if it is going to fade away and disappear, it is something I should experience before the end." Roger agreed to take a few of us on an olive oil tour of Provence.

IN SEARCH OF THE PERFECT OLIVE OIL

The slow decline of olives and olive oil in Provence runs almost exactly parallel to the "great modern change" in the life and work of the Midi— the sunbathed Mediterranean South of France. Before 1800, Provence, despite its dramatic and glamorous history connecting it with the Crusades and the Romans, was a self-contained, simple community of peasant farmers and fishermen, relatively little known to travelers. Then, around 1830, the English aristocracy, longing to find relief from their cold and sunless winters, discovered the climate of Cannes. Soon there were lovely villas all along the coast and thousands of Provençaux, instead of farming, were serving the wealthy visitors. Then came the painters and the writers to make the landscape and the people famous all over the world—Cézanne, Van Gogh, Picasso, Matisse, Daudet, James, Zola—and when the automobile brought mass tourism the isolation of Provence was ended forever. After 1956, the package tour dealt the final blow to the once-simple *douceurs de vie.* Any Provençal could earn a great deal more money with a lot less effort by selling hot dogs at a roadside stand than by hand-pressing olive oil. In the hills behind Cannes, around the town of Grasse, there used to be one hundred fifty-five olive pressing mills. Today, there are four. We set out to find them.

The narrow road climbed toward the hillside that faced the sea— slopes given an almost surrealist ambiance by the distorted, gnarled shapes of the olive trees, some of them said to be about five hundred years old and with trunks more than two feet in diameter. Now, among the universal somber green, there were strange patches of brightly clashing colors: fiery red, lemon yellow, creamy white, brown, purple, silver . . . As we got closer, we found that the clashing colors belonged to huge sheets of plastic laid on the ground around each tree that was being harvested. Then, the whole family, including the children, armed with long poles, began beating the trees to make the ripe olives fall onto the plastic sheets.

Some families don't own a plastic sheet and they, after the beating, get down on their hands and knees in the grass, their faces about six inches from the ground, while they scrabble and search with their hands. As they crawl forward, inch by inch, they give a strong impression that each person has lost a diamond earring, or a dime.

Yet other families—more conservatively purist—do not approve of the damage to the olives and the trees by beating them with sticks. These perfectionist harvesters climb up the trunk to reach some parts of the tree and use stepladders to get to other parts. The final result, by every method, is the same. Baskets of beautifully ripe olives are carried to the nearest pressing mill. These are not the black or green olives we nibble with our apéritifs, drop into our Martinis, or chop into our salads. These Provençal olives are deliberately grown overripe, mushy, and soft, useful for no other purpose than the pressing out of the oil. Nor are they the same from year to year. There are vintages in olives as forcefully and precisely as there are vintages in wine. Absolutely nothing can be done, at the pressing, to overcome the poor weather of a bad year. But when the weather is kind, when the harvesting is carefully completed at the right moment, when the hand pressing is skillfully controlled, then the finest grades of Provençal olive oil are indeed among the best in the world.

Continuing along our road a mile or two, we found the pressing mill to which all these olives would be taken. We came to the miniature hamlet—hardly more than a few houses along the side of the road—of Speracedes and the Moulin Doussan, with its owners Monsieur Aimé Baussy and his wife Charlotte, to say nothing of a small crowd of their charmingly polite and helpful children of every conceivable age. This was the first time I had been actually involved in the making of virgin olive oil and I found the experience so fascinating that I spent the rest of the day "working" at the mill. It has been owned and run by various branches of this family for more than one hundred fifty years. For the major part of that time, the press was actually screwed down by the athletic force of four men straining and struggling at the levers. Today, a more modern press is powered hydraulically, but the operation is still technically considered to be "hand pressing," since there is no automation and the actual degree of pressure is minutely and precisely controlled by the judgment and skill of the operator, turning with his hand a small control wheel.

The olives, as they are delivered in baskets by the pickers from the groves, are put into the press, batch by batch, at the temperature at which they are received. They are not, in any way, heated to encourage their release of extra oil. This is the meaning of the technical definition "cold pressed," which is internationally recognized, on the labels of the finest grades of olive oil. The pressure is then applied to the olives, but only enough to extract the maximum possible oil without cracking the pits. This is the highest quality oil, bright green in color, beautifully fruity in taste, very low in acid, yet still with the delicately bitter after-taste of the olive on the tree. This first, light pressure produces what is technically defined as "extra-virgin" oil, another internationally recognized phrase on all labels in every country and language.

The freshly pressed oil, at this point, is unlikely to be absolutely clean and pure. It will have little bits and pieces of olive flesh, perhaps some herbs and sand from the fields, etc. In the old days, the oil would be left in vats for many days and allowed to settle. Nowadays the job can be done in a few minutes by means of a centrifuge. The oil is then ready, at once, to be bottled or canned.

Monsieur Baussy is now left with the *grignon*, the mash, or olive pulp from the press. Since he is involved in making only the top-grade, extra-virgin oil, he has no further use for the *grignon*. As he described to me what would now happen to his *grignon*, I confess that the story took on, for me, a certain nightmarish quality. All his mash residue would be packed up and sent to one of the mass-production factories in Marseille. There, the first step is to subject the mash to such extremely high pressure that all the pits are broken and ground up into the pulp. Monsieur Baussy said: "If this pulp were then immediately pressed, they might get a certain small percentage of fairly good oil from it. But, instead, they allow the pulp to pile up in warehouses until they have collected a large quantity of different shipments. Only then is the processing continued, but by then the pulp has dried out and deteriorated, so that it does not respond adequately to the pressing, when it finally comes."

The next, very heavy, pressing produces the second-grade oil, which is now bright yellow instead of green and is, relatively, much higher in acid. For the third pressing, a special machine is used in which the pressure chamber is surrounded by a "jacket" filled with continuously circulating boiling water, so that the remaining olive pulp is strongly heated and is thus encouraged (or forced) to give up the third grade of now-rather-thin oil. The last extraction of all is not by pressure, but by a chemical interaction with the addition of the now almost-dry-and-powdery olive residue of measured quantities of carbon sulphide. This chemical extracts the very last 5 to 10 percent of the lowest grade oil. All these different oils are then blended in various ways to produce the "standard olive oils" that are sold at different price levels in shops all over the world. Some of them, in taste and texture, seem to have very little relationship with the fruit and flavor of the olive on the tree.

Monsieur Baussy continued his sad story: "You understand, of course, Monsieur, that these mass-production factories in Marseille are not making Provençal olive oil. They buy *grignon*, mashed residue, not only from me, but also from hundreds of small producers in Spain, Italy, Greece, from many parts of North Africa—and they also receive shipments by boat from more distant places. All these different residues are mixed together and processed at the same time. In my extra-virgin oil here from my Moulin Doussan, you may be able to detect (as I certainly can) a regional character and personality of Provence. But all this is lost when the olives from hundreds of different sources, thousands of miles apart, are mixed and pressed together. One of the principal beauties of olive oil—as a reflection of a local place—is entirely lost."

When at last we said goodbye to Aimé and Charlotte Baussy, they urged us to visit one of their principal competitors, Le Moulin de la Brague in the village of Opio, just outside Grasse. It is claimed to be the oldest olive mill in Provence, with documents showing that it was already in business in 1426. Today, its modern hydraulic hand-controlled press is powered by a huge waterwheel on the outside wall of the mill. Here, also, only the cold-pressed, extra-virgin olive oil is made. The pulp residue is sent by truck to the mass factories in Marseille.

Next day, our journeying was made more difficult by the blowing up of *le mistral*—the still almost-surprising stormy wind that suddenly, at any time, roars down the tunnel of the Rhône valley and seems to spread out across Provence. *Le mistral* (the name means "the master") dominates much of the countryside and farm life. The peasants are cunning and persistent in their efforts to shelter themselves, their gardens, and their houses from the dominant wind. The location of the villages, the placing of each *mas*, or farmhouse, the planting of orchards, among other things, are all regulated by the angle at which *le mistral* strikes that particular place. Remember that it always comes from exactly the same direction. The landscapes of Provence take their visual rhythms from the fear of the implacable "master." The force of that wind never fails to shock me. It doesn't cool the fire of the sun. Instead, it is an angry disturbance, waking you up at night by clattering the shutters and windows, by howling across the rooftops. It keeps up its mindless fury for days. It twangs everyone's nerves until there seems to be anger and the threat of violence in the very air. A woman screamed at the grocery boy in the shop because he did not serve her quickly enough. The waiter in the restaurant lost his temper because I complained that the veal was tough. "It's the *mistral!*" they always say.

In the seacoast area between Cannes and Nice and around Menton, where the steep slopes of the Alpes Maritimes come almost down to the edge of the Mediterranean, there were, in the old days, 128 small, family-owned olive-pressing mills. Today there are only two. I was taken to visit Le Moulin Lottier in Menton, owned and worked by François Lottier and his wife. As I walked into what felt like a cool dark cellar (although it was on ground level), at crack of dawn when the day's work was just beginning, it seemed as if I was stepping back into the ancient, simple Provence, long before the tourist world had discovered it. There were tall arches, huge wooden gears, heavy and solid granite millstones for grinding, with the presses that would accept a single load of almost five hundred pounds of small black Niçois olives, to be slowly converted to dark, thick oil.

After the first, relatively gentle pressing, for the top-quality, extra-virgin oil, the mashed pulp is layered on a series of round mats of nylon, each with a six-inch hole at its center. These loaded mats are then stacked on a vertical spindle, one on top of the other, until the pile is about five feet high. A heavy, strong metal disk is placed on top of the pile to hold it all down and, then, the whole construction is carefully lowered into the hydraulic press.

As the pressure begins, very gently at first, there are only some insignificant, small drippings of the dark, thick oil oozing out at the base of the pile. But as the pressure is slowly increased, the oil begins to rain down and, eventually, the shower becomes a solid downpour. From the press, the oil goes into a centrifuge where the high-speed spinning separates the pure oil from the debris and the dirt. Now there is the bright green color—the taste of liquid ripe olives—the perfume that is at once age-old, fruity, heady, sweet . . . The oil will mellow and ripen in oak barrels for two to three months before it is bottled and delivered to the users.

François Lottier is the third generation of his family to press oil in this mill, which his grandfather built almost one hundred twenty years ago. He thinks that next to Provence, the best olive oils come from certain parts of Italy and Spain. He believes that many oils from other places are not *douce*, because they have a high acid content due to the type of olives grown and the temperature at which they are pressed. Low acidity, *douceur*, is the great quality objective in all the finest olive oils. According to the United Nations standards, if olive oil is to be rated as "extra virgin" it must contain less than 1½ percent of acid. Against this standard, the ordinary plain "virgin" can contain acid up to 3 percent. As with wine, it pays to read an olive oil bottle label, whether it comes from France, or anywhere else.

As the various batches of olive oil age in their oak barrels, they often develop different tastes and textures, because, after all, the original baskets of olives may have come from different slopes with varying exposures to the sun. So there arises the question of blending the oils—of putting together a *cuvée*, as they do with the sparkling wines of Champagne. In Nice, there was a charmingly hospitable tradition that went with this judging and blending. The owner of the mill invited his knowledgeable friends to a tasting. A long trestle table was set up in the mill and down its center was placed a long row of gleaming greenish bottles, each labeled with a secret number for definition, containing the different batches of oil. Then there was served a huge bowl of a salad of white haricot beans, which must be neither cold, nor hot, but tepidly warm. It is called in the Niçois dialect *lu faiou grana en salada.* The ceremony of tasting and judging the oils is called *lou defici.* Each taster put on his plate a portion of the bean salad and then, in turn, sprinkled on different parts of it a few drops of the oil to be tasted. By chewing the beans with the oil, the expert could form a precise opinion of its character, personality, and quality. Gradually, several oils were blended together in precise proportions and retasted. At the end of the long session—and after a vast consumption of white beans and oil—the *cuvées* were decided and made up. (Just in case you would like to try it, the authentic recipe for this Niçois white bean salad is on page 119.)

François Lottier of Menton and Aimé Baussy of Spéracedes do not press enough oil to go beyond their local customers, who have a continuous thirst for every liter that these mills can produce. So there seems to be very little chance that either of them could ever begin exporting to the United States. But there are slightly larger mills that can and do send a small part of their production across the Atlantic. So it is now possible to find, admittedly at a price, the utterly superb, handmade, bright green, cold-pressed, extra-virgin Provençal olive oil. Le Moulin de la Brague, for example, in the tiny hamlet of Opio, between Valbonne and Grasse, is now sending its best oil to New York and that means, I am sure, that it will also be available in other large cities. They are also sending their herbed oil, flavored with bay, fennel, rosemary, and thyme. There is also oil spiced with chili peppers. I confess that I think the plain oil is good for almost everything, including rubbing on my wife's skin. Every morning, first thing, I take a couple of tablespoons of it as a medicine, to clean and lubricate my body. In my kitchen, I use about a pint of it every day—in soups and stews, salad dressings, over tomatoes and certain raw fruits, to poach and sauté vegetables, with fish, game, meats, and poultry, with eggs, fried, in omelettes and scrambled, to think only of the more obvious uses. This oil is of such an absolute supremacy of quality that it uplifts everything it touches—a degree of perfection that is now rare in the world.

EVEN BEFORE THE OIL—CONSIDER THE OLIVE

Perhaps it was the English novelist Lawrence Durrell who first conceived the idea that the olive was in truth "the Lord of the Mediterranean":

> The whole Mediterranean—the sculptures, the palms, the gold beads, the bearded heroes, the wine, the ideas, the ships, the moonlight, the winged gorgons, the bronze men, the philosophers—all of it seems to rise in the sour, pungent taste of these black olives between the teeth. A taste older than meat, older than wine.

I shall always vividly remember my first try to capture Durrell's immense vision of history in the taste of a single fresh olive. I picked a fully ripe black one off the tree in the garden of my friend Madame Ricard at her house among the lonely Alpilles Hills of northern Provence, not far from Avignon. I popped it into my mouth and bit it. I was shocked and almost stunned by the fiercely vicious force of the totally inedible bitterness and sharpness of that little fruit. I spat it out instantly, but my mouth felt as if it had been burned with fire. Madame Ricard came out of her kitchen, laughing, carrying a glass of cold water for me. "Now, perhaps, I had better give you," she said, "my infallible recipe for curing all types of olives and making them at least pungently edible!" She wrote out, then and there, on a small slip of paper, a description of how she soaked the olives for ten days in cold water—changing the water and washing the olives every day. Toward the end of this lengthy period, she prepared an aromatic salt marinade by boiling a quarter-pound of salt to each quart of water, adding plenty of bay leaves, cracked coriander berries, and green fronds of fennel. When this *saumure* was strongly flavored, she let it cool completely. She finally washed the olives once more, put them into jars, and covered them with the aromatic salt solution. Many, many such jars rested peacefully on her shelves—giving her a steady supply of olives until the next harvest. Madame Ricard follows the general practice of curing olives and converting them into an edible food that has been more or less unchanged for at least four thousand years. The little slip of paper she wrote out for me is one of my most prized documents.

I have tried to count the flavors and textures of the olives around the Mediterranean—the various varieties and the different ways they are cured—the contrasts in the aromatic balance and pungency—my total comes to more than a hundred. Some are tiny ovals with pointed ends, some are large and rounded like a walnut—others are the shape of almonds. The rainbow of colors includes bronze, pale green, mahogany, and mauve variations of brown, purple, walnut, and jet black. Some olives come piquant and sharp, soaking in brine. Some are fleshy, luscious and sensuous, resting languidly in their own aromatic oil. Some of them have their pits cracked and are strong with the nutty bitterness of the kernel. Since olives are now shipped all over the world, it is quite as important for the true gastronomic connoisseur to know the gamut of the olives as it is to know one's cheeses and one's wines.

Of those that grow in Provence, my favorites are the tiny, shiny, jet-black Niçois, which Roger Vergé buys from farm wives who cure them in their kitchens and bring them for sale to the back door of Le Moulin. They are oval, pointed at each end, irresistibly spiced with herbs. Then there is the Nyons, round, small, dark reddish-brown, grown around the Provençal city of Nyons. They are chewy, attractively bitter. The third Provençal type is the Picholine, oval, green, with a fresh taste, crisp yet tender, delicate, and mild.

The nearest foreign place that sends its olives to Provence is, of course, Italy. There is the Calabrese, oval, small, bronze-green, generally with the pit cracked, and strongly spiced. The Gaeta is round, small, mahogany in color, always slightly bitter. The Siciliana is oval, small, with the pit usually cracked, attractively bitter and piquant, often strong spiced with fennel, garlic, and hot red peppers.

From the western end of Provence there are imports from Spain, where a different system of curing makes of many of the olives something much nearer to pickles, something crisply refreshing, but almost acid. The one I like best is the largest olive I know, the Sevillana, the size of a big walnut, bright green, with crackly crisp flesh. But Greece seems to produce and export by far the largest number of olives. The Agrinion is almost round, pale bronze-green, meaty, silky, tender, mildly salty. It is named for the town near the Epirus. It is almost like biting into a chewy bit of meat. The Amphissis is named for the town on the lower slopes of the Pindus mountains. It is large, black, salty, yet with the flavor of the purest virgin olive oil. The Chios, from the Aegean island of that name, is small, black, so dry that it is slightly shriveled, like a Moroccan olive.

As you chew it, the juice gradually flows. The Jians is oval, salty, firmly meaty. The supreme Greek olive is the Kalamata, named for the port city in the Peloponnesus, from which it is shipped, almond-shaped, shiny, purplish-black-to-mahogany, elegantly luscious in flavor, yet with a delicately bitter, earthy ambiance, usually split and permeated by its marinade with a quality of old wine. The Nafpaktos, named for the town near the vineyards of Patras, like a small grape, green, usually with cracked pits, meaty, oily, rich, yet with a touch of the sharpness of a sour apple, because it is probably the least ripe of any table olive. The Nafplion, small, oval, green, usually with pit cracked, nutty, fruity, slightly tart. Royal Victoria is very large, black, usually slit, luxurious, and superb in the eating. The Volos, named for the Thessalian port, is grayish-purple; when you bite into it a salty juice runs at once into your mouth, as if it were the fruit of some seaweed on a Mediterranean beach.

Several types of olives are grown in Morocco and eventually cross the Mediterranean to France but, since they are all cured in almost exactly the same way, they all come out very much alike. They are "dry-cured," with a minimum use of oil, by being buried for a controlled length of time in dry salt. Then they are dried in single layers on huge trays in the hot sun until they shrivel and wrinkle as if they were tiny black prunes. Finally, they are hand-rubbed with olive oil. They are very firm when you first bite into them but, as you chew and masticate them, there gradually develops an intense, mellow, delicious flavor with a meaty texture. I place them very high on my list of favorite olives.

Obviously, since virtually all of these olives are nowadays shipped, in barrels or stone crocks, to all parts of the world, you hardly have to go to the Mediterranean for a thoroughly varied and wide tasting. In more and more specialty groceries, you can pick out more and more of the best types from their brine or oil marinades in large ceramic jars, or open wooden barrels. You may also be tempted to try California olives but this is not altogether a happy story. Olive trees do grow rather well in the hot Central Valley of California. But the very large companies that take care of the harvesting, curing, and packing seem to have some ideas that—to a European-experienced aficionado—seem very strange indeed. First, they seem to be convinced that American consumers will not stand for the slightest bitterness of pungency in their olives. So they cure them until they have about as much flavor as if they were balls of water-wetted bread dough. Second, for some reason that entirely escapes me, they do not allow their black olives to ripen on the trees. Instead, they harvest all the olives when they are green and, then, they color the required number of olives black by dyeing them with a chemical additive. No one is suggesting that this is a dangerous chemical. It is ferrous glutanate, much used for adding an iron complement to various commercial foods and, also, in vitamin pills claiming to contain iron supplements. In effect, this iron "rusts" the green olives until they turn black. It does seem to be a bizarre procedure, but it is universal among the large commercial manufacturers of olives in the U.S. The final result is that the black olive is exactly as bland as the green. Every American mass-produced olive tastes exactly the same. There is absolutely no variation whatsoever. It is the ultimate triumph of technical uniformity. But all is not completely lost, even in California. There are a few small family firms that are curing olives and pressing oil in the European tradition.

Just as a few notes of a piece of music will take my mind back to a particular day, a place, an occasion to which the music has become attached—so it is to bite again into a particular kind of olive, to recognize it with sudden pleasure as an old friend and to remember the day, the place, the occasion that its unique taste recalls. Whenever I eat Nyons in Provence, I remember the day of the festival in Arles, when I was sitting at a small sidewalk table in a café, lunching on large slices cut from a crusty *baguette*, sprinkled with green olive oil, then eaten with orange-red tomatoes, an aged mold-flecked hard salami, a large chunk of white Tomme Arlésienne cheese, and a dish of the Nyons olives. There was also, of course, plenty of rough red wine. We were watching the parade. I had always been told about the beautiful women of Arles, but I felt sure it was a romantic dream created by Daudet and Bizet in the light opera *L'Arlésienne*. But, on this day, we were all astonished by the almost universal beauty of the young women, by their long slim noses, by their lithe tall figures, by the athletic grace of their every movement. The parade was serious, but very simple. There were ridiculous bugle bands, followed by drums and fifes, but no one seemed to march in step. The parade was a lazy walk by the young women, the children, the older people, in costumes. They all seemed to have the grace, the sense of occasion, a delightful simplicity and complete absence of show-off. We shouted compliments to some of the beauties—everyone in the café standing up and applauding. There was a special excitement about the ladies who sat on the white horses behind the sunburned horsemen from the Carmargue. Now and then, there seemed to be a subtle Spanish touch when one of the women was wearing a black Cordoba hat. After all, tomorrow there would be a bullfight in the Roman amphitheatre and the *toreros* would be both local young men and imported Spanish professionals.

Whenever I bite into the Picholine olive, I am instantly transported back to night picnics in Provence. As time passes, it is of the mysterious and starry nights that the memories of Provence are mainly woven. It is cool and people take the air. You spread your white tablecloth on the grass near the tow-path of one of the canals. You cut the large slices of crusty bread, sprinkle them lightly with the olive oil from the bottle, and open the jar of home-cooked, boneless fillets of tuna conserved in olive oil. Suddenly, from the dark water of the canal, you hear a bark—and then it begins, the true night sound of Provence, the endless and universal chorus of the barking bullfrogs. It has the quality of an angry and harsh debate. There must be thousands of them. They can be heard for miles. All day, in the woods in Provence, it is the chirruping scissoring of the cicadas. All night, it is the bullfrogs.

SALAD OF WHITE BEANS WITH BLACK PEPPER
4 to 6 servings

An interesting idea is to organize an olive oil tasting around the serving of this white bean salad. Get a small quantity of the best olive oil from Greece, Italy, Provence, and Spain. Line up four matching bottles in the center of the dining table, then have a blind tasting and imagine yourself dining in an olive mill in Nice.

   2 *packages (10 ounces each) frozen lima beans, thawed*
   1 *pound medium yellow onions, thinly sliced*
   1 *medium yellow onion, left whole*
   4 *whole cloves*
   2 *cloves garlic, peeled, minced*
   1 *whole bay leaf*
   1 *tablespoon chopped fresh dill, or 1 teaspoon dried*
   1 *teaspoon crumbled dried oregano leaves*
   1 *tablespoon chopped fresh peppermint, or 1 teaspoon dried*
   1 *tablespoon chopped fresh savory, or 1 teaspoon dried*
  ½ *pound small mushrooms, wiped clean, sliced*
   8 *rashers thick-sliced country-style lean bacon, fried crisp, then crumbled*
  ½ *pound Switzerland Gruyère cheese, cut into medium dice*
   2 *teaspoons whole black peppercorns, coarsely cracked in mortar*
    Coarse crystal sea salt or kosher salt
  ¼ *cup white wine vinegar*
  ⅓ *cup chopped parsley, leaves only*
   1 *cup virgin green olive oil*

NEEDED KITCHEN EQUIPMENT: 2-quart lidded soup kettle, cutting board and sharp knives, wooden spatulas and spoons, large wooden salad bowl.

AVERAGE TIME REQUIRED: About 45 minutes entirely unsupervised soaking and simmering of the beans. Plus an extra 15 minutes for assembling and serving the salad. Twenty minutes of actual preparation.

Thawing the Beans

Put the beans into a lidded soup kettle, at least 2-quart capacity; cover with about 1 inch cold water. Add sliced onions, whole onion studded with cloves, garlic, bay leaf, dill, oregano, peppermint, and savory. No salt and pepper at this point. Cover; allow to thaw and absorb flavors about 30 minutes.

Make sure beans are still covered by 1 inch of water. Heat to gentle simmer and continue until they are perfectly done, usually about 3 minutes. Drain liquid; discard whole onion with cloves.

Preparing the Dressing-Garnish

What is best for the final assembly is a large wooden salad bowl, good looking enough to be brought to the table as the serving dish. Into it put mushrooms, bacon, cheese; toss gently to mix. Sprinkle over 1 teaspoon black pepper, and salt to taste. Begin tossing the beans and dribble in the ¼ cup of vinegar and sprinkle in parsley.

In Nice, this salad is always served lukewarm. Have a small jug of the best available olive oil at the center of the dining table and dribble a teaspoon or two, to taste, over each serving.

Saved by a Recipe: Snowy Soufflé with Green Chartreuse

For about nine hundred years, the Carthusian monks—a fiercely disciplined order of men who do not speak for six days out of every seven—have lived, prayed, and worked in one of the most beautiful and inaccessible of the narrowly enclosed mountain valleys of the French Alps. The place is called La Grande Chartreuse. The word *chartreuse*, which has a Latin root, originally meant "a lonely place." That certainly is an accurate description of the monastery of the Carthusians, near the top of the mountain pass.

Seven men started building the monastery in 1084 and others joined them. The struggle to survive was tremendous. Again and again, avalanches wiped out the buildings and killed dozens of the men. The monks were decimated by bubonic plague and famine. Repeatedly, they were burned out by fire and had to rebuild completely.

For the first six hundred years, they earned their living by mining iron ore in the valley and forging some of the finest steel made anywhere outside Sweden. Most of the battles of the Crusades were won by men wearing armor, carrying shields, and wielding swords forged by the Carthusians. But, by the mid-1600s, cheap, mass-produced steel was becoming available and there no longer was any demand for small-scale forging. The Carthusians seemed to have come to the end of their lonely road.

They were saved by a recipe—an ancient, hand-written, almost-illegible recipe on three sheets of tattered, yellowing paper—which fell

EDITOR'S NOTE: This syndicated newspaper article originally appeared in April 1979.

into their hands accidentally after the death of a rich, old recluse. In the seventeenth century, when medical science was not very advanced, most families had their own recipes for cure-all herbal potions. This was one of those, but it was unusual in the fantastic complication of its ingredients, which included one hundred thirty fresh herbs to be picked on the slopes of the mountains and then dissolved in brandy. One of the Carthusians, who originally had been trained as a chemist, decided to try to work out the recipe and make the potion. He set up a small laboratory, roamed the mountains searching for the herbs, and soon realized that the procedure text of the recipe was not only illegible, but also imprecise. It took him twenty-seven years of experimentation before he had in his hand a bottle of a brilliant-green, sweet, aromatic liqueur. The Carthusians called it, in honor of their valley, Green Chartreuse and it has made the word *chartreuse*—for the valley, for the monks, for the liqueur, and for the bright green color—a household word around the world.

The Carthusians made more of the potion and sold it to the local villagers. They loved it. Some of it was poured into glass flagons, packed into the saddlebags of mules, and taken by the mountain path to the city of Grenoble, where it was sold. Today, three hundred years later, the Carthusians still are making green Chartreuse and the recipe still is their well-guarded secret. Many attempts have been made to break that secret. None has succeeded. Many other green liqueurs have been put on the market, in obvious direct imitation of Chartreuse. Not one, in my opinion, even approaches the original in its rare, aromatic, herbaceous quality. The Carthusians still can live their lonely, silent lives, because their Green Chartreuse now is a worldwide and very profitable business.

Ten years ago, when I climbed into the Valley of La Grande Chartreuse to write an article about the Carthusians and their liqueur, I stayed at a tiny *auberge* in the lower part of the valley and fell in love with the mountain food. I returned several times, stayed many months, and wrote my book, *The Auberge of the Flowering Hearth*. The two Provençal women who ran the Auberge, both marvelous cooks, naturally used quite a lot of green Chartreuse in their dishes. One, which I remember vividly and which I have made many times since in my own kitchen, probably is the best liqueur dessert I have ever tasted. It is partly a soufflé, but not quite—a kind of combination of a soufflé with that famous French dessert, *oeufs à la neige*. The trick is to make it shallower than a soufflé and bake it extremely fast at very high heat to prevent the liqueur from evaporating, so that the final dessert, as it comes to the table, holds and concentrates more of the character and flavor of the liqueur than you would believe possible. In contrast, in all slow soufflés, most of the liqueur has evaporated before the baking is done.

The women of the Auberge called this dessert, la neige à la Grande Chartreuse, an obvious reference to the fluffy-light snow which lies in the valley, sometimes sixteen feet deep, usually from October to February. I like to translate this title as snowy soufflé, but you must not follow the standard soufflé technique. First, do not use a normal soufflé dish, which would be too deep. Use an oval or round baking dish, preferably with straight sides, not more than 2½ inches deep. A French copper tart pan does very well. This magnificent dessert then will come to the table looking like a miniature mountain range of golden-brown peaks, while the inside is like fluffy snow, marbled with pale green liqueur. The taste and texture are extraordinary.

SNOWY SOUFFLÉ WITH GREEN CHARTREUSE

Serves 4

4 *large eggs, yolks and whites separated*
4 *extra whites from large eggs*
½ *fresh lemon*
6 *tablespoons fine confectioners' sugar*
½ *cup Green Chartreuse sweet liqueur*
½ *teaspoon salt*
2 *to 3 tablespoons butter*

KITCHEN EQUIPMENT: Mixing bowl for egg yolks, round-bottomed beating bowl for egg whites, balloon wire whisk (or electric beater), large cookie sheet, French upside-down tart baking pan (best are copper) about 2½ inches deep and 11 inches wide, rubber spatula for folding soufflé mix.

AVERAGE TIME REQUIRED: About 15 minutes of active preparation, plus about 15 minutes of unsupervised baking.

Preparation

Put egg yolks into the mixing bowl and egg whites into the beating bowl, which has been carefully washed, dried, and rubbed all over the inside with the lemon to eliminate the slightest trace of grease, the worst enemy of the proper stiffening of egg whites. Using a small wire whisk, beat the sugar into the yolks until they are lemon-colored and lift up in ribbons. Then beat the Green Chartreuse into the mixture. Sprinkle the salt over the whites and beat them until they glisten and stand up in firm peaks. Be careful not to overbeat them. Preheat oven to 400° F, setting the lower shelf about 2 inches above the bottom of the oven and the upper shelf near the top. Have ready a cookie sheet about as large as the shelves in your oven and cover on one side with shiny aluminum foil.

Liberally butter the open baking dish. Spoon about an eighth of the beaten whites into the yolks and quickly fold together with the rubber spatula. This lightens the yolks and makes them easier to incorporate into the whites. Now quickly pour the entire yolk mixture into the center of the beaten whites. At once use the rubber spatula to fold the two together, never stirring them, but rapidly combining them with lifting strokes to trap in more air, while holding in all the air that is already there. Don't worry about any remaining green and white streaks—too much mixing destroys the miniature air bubbles on which you are relying to make your soufflé rise.

Baking and Serving

The instant the folding job is done, pour the soufflé mix into the buttered baking dish, quickly spreading it out. Set the soufflé on the lower shelf in the oven and, using heatproof gloves, bring the upper shelf down so that it rests about 3 inches above the top surface of the soufflé. Then place the aluminum-covered cookie sheet on the upper shelf, with the shiny side facing downward, to reflect heat down onto the top of the soufflé. Close the oven door gently—never slam it—and do not open it again for 12 minutes. Then check—the soufflé is done when its top is golden brown and is springy to the slight pressure of your fingertips— usually in 12 to 16 minutes, depending on the efficiency of your oven. Serve the snowy soufflé instantly on very hot plates. The diners must be waiting for this dish—it cannot possibly wait for them!

PART
· III ·

The Gastronome
at Large

Have I Found
the Greatest Restaurant
in the World?

Which is the world's greatest restaurant? This impossible question was broached during a Manhattan lunch with a gourmet friend some months ago. We agreed that the food at this particular restaurant was none too good and the service almost too bad. So our conversation turned to great restaurants we had known and I mentioned the almost-perfect cuisine and service of the restaurant of the brothers Troisgros in the small French town of Roanne, about eighty-seven kilometers northwest of Lyons. I had last visited Troisgros back in 1961, when it was rated with only one star in the *Guide Michelin*. Now the brothers had three stars and the gourmets of the world were beating a path to their tables. My friend asked: "Do you think Troisgros might be the greatest?"

Instantly sensing a magnificent opportunity, I said that since I was leaving for France the following week, I would gladly dine at Troisgros and give him a definitive answer, provided he would pay for one of my meals. A few weeks later, after visiting some vineyards along the Rhine, I crossed from Germany into France bound for Roanne, a small, semi-industrial town of about fifty thousand people. Perhaps because it is the center of a large farming, meat-packing, and wine-producing district, it looks a bit like a New England market village. In front of the railroad and bus stations, the single main street opens out into the *place de la gare*, with freight yards, boxcars, and factory chimneys all around. Facing the stations is a row of shops: a camera mart, a supermarket, a hair-

---

EDITOR'S NOTE: This article originally appeared in the April 1972 issue of *Playboy* and reflects the prices of that year. Jean Troigrois died August 8, 1983.

dresser, a display of bicycles and motorcycles on the sidewalk, a gas sta-tion and, on the corner, two shops joined below a vertical neon sign reading TROISGROS.

I remember, when I first saw the sign in 1961, I couldn't believe that the word Troisgros was a family name. How would you like to be called John Threefatmen? I thought the restaurant must be named The Three Fat Men. Not true. Troisgros is the legal name of the owners.

Theirs is the simplest three-star entrance one has ever seen. No can-opy. No doorman. You step straight from the sidewalk into the dining room. A tall and elegantly dressed young woman greets you with: "Good evening, I am Madame Jean Troisgros." She succeeds at once in making you feel that you are being welcomed as a guest in her home. (Her name is Maria and she told me later: "While I am seating the guests, I try to find out what it is essential for us to know in order to serve them as perfectly as possible. Are they *grands gastronomes* who will say, 'Atten-tion! I will give the orders!'? Or are they beginners wanting to learn? At once, I relay the information to my husband or my brother-in-law in the kitchen so that one of them can come out and discuss a suitable meal.")

The modernized country-style dining room is comfortable but not lux-urious. It was almost full and I counted fifty-two people, obviously local businessmen with their wives and children, giving the place the atmo-sphere of a neighborhood bistro. The French chatter was at the level of a roar. At the back, gruff voices at the bar seemed to be debating by shout-ing, and from the open kitchen door came voices raised to an ecstasy of anger. The maître d'hôtel, Gérard, offered the three *prix fixe* menus, at $9, $12, and $16,* tips and taxes, but not wines, included. (The Troisgros brothers say, "Our lower prices are fixed for the service of our local customers. They come once or twice a week and bring us three quarters of our income.")

Two impeccably dressed chefs with *hauts chapeaux* sauntered casually out of the kitchen, grinning broadly, shaking hands, patting shoulders, quipping in high-speed French. Although the two brothers have stayed together and worked together all their lives as if they were twins, Jean and Pierre could hardly be more different in appearance and personality. Jean is six feet tall, with a long face and a manner that marks him as a rebel, a satirist, a man with a faintly mocking outlook on life. Pierre is short and round, with a body so flexible it might belong to a circus clown, but with a determined and serious face. Both are true Burgun-dians in their gaiety, their irreverent laughter, their lightning intelli-gence and wit.

---

*EDITOR'S NOTE: This article reflects 1972 prices.

They "proposed" my dinner in the basic Troisgros way. Printed menus are for conceited tourists who think they know best. Wiser guests leave it to the Troisgros brothers to tell them what is in the cupboard that is not on the menu. It may be a superb pike, caught in the river an hour before—or a brown bear, trapped in the forest by some gypsies, who know that there is always cash available at the Troisgrois' kitchen door. That night, there were live young female lobsters, just arrived by truck from the fishing port of Plougasnou on the Brittany coast. Also, Pierre was just back from a hunting trip in the Loire marshes and offered a wild duck.

The first course on the *prix fixe* menu was the great specialty of the house, *le foie gras frais en terrine*—mixed duck and goose livers baked in a casserole and served cold, in slices that were pure velvet, richer, and softer than I had ever tasted. When Pierre came by, I demanded the secret. He said: "No secret. We bake the livers very slowly. The terrine is just heated in the oven, then taken out, wrapped in seven thicknesses of woolen blankets, and left on the kitchen table to cook itself overnight."

Then came the lobster, prepared *à la cancalaise*, Cancale being a small seaport in Brittany. "The secret is in the way you flame the lobster," Pierre pointed out. "You pour the Calvados into the pan, never over the lobster, and let only the flames lick the flesh, so as not to overpower the marvelous natural taste." With the shellfish, I had an excellent 1966 Chassagne-Montrachet—a noble white burgundy.

Pierre's roasted wild duck arrived garnished with peaches glazed in Vermont maple syrup, an unbelievable combination that turned out to be unbelievably magnificent. The sweetness had been cut by a touch of vinegar and what was left was the perfect foil for the gaminess of the undercooked flesh. It was all a very fragile balance that a red wine would upset, so Pierre chose a rich and soft 1966 Meursault—a private bottling especially to go with this dish.

Then came a well-laden cheese cart and, finally, Pierre's specially prepared dessert: a *mille-feuille*, so light that one half expected it to float away, filled with whipped cream and covered by a layer of glazed fresh raspberries.

With the coffee, there appeared at my table the grand old man of the Troisgros family, *papa* Jean-Baptiste—the most imaginative, most intelligent, most irrepressible, most ribald, most suspicious, and yet most charming Burgundian I know. He was carrying an ancient, dusty, unlabeled bottle, which he opened at the table and poured into brandy snifters. He said he had found it in a corner of the cellar and wasn't quite sure what it was but guessed that it might be a *marc de Pommard*, privately distilled and bottled by one of their Pommard suppliers and sent to Troisgros as a Christmas present about forty years ago. It was smooth nectar—approximately as powerful as liquid dynamite—but with a body, bouquet, and flavor that were near great.

I shall hotly deny that it was this brandy that brought me to the point of decision. As I sipped, I thought of the overall qualities of the dinner. It had been astonishingly light—with never a trace of that blown-up feeling that inevitably seems to accompany a "great meal." One could sum it up by saying that there had not been the slightest pomposity about the food, the service nor the welcome. This perfectly uncomplicated food is the final and absolute overthrow of all the show-off *haute cuisine* that arose out of the extravagant excesses of luxury under Louis XIV at Versailles.

I turned to Jean-Baptiste: "How did you achieve this quality? How was it done?"

He said, "Our results may appear simple, but our methods are complicated. Stay with us a few days; my boys and I will show you."

As the dining room began to empty and the pressures of the evening decreased, Jean-Baptiste took me to a table in the bar, opened a bottle of Champagne and told me the story of how this extraordinary restaurant was created out of the vision of a single family, over three generations and seventy-five years. In the 1890s, Jean-Baptiste's father ran a popular café in the Burgundian wine capital of Beaune. There, just before the turn of the century, Jean-Baptiste was born. "You see, *monsieur*, I was in the restaurant business the first day of my life. By the time I was seven, I could recognize all the different brandies blindfolded. I learned to taste food and wine with the customers. Those earthy Burgundians taught me that with food, the most important thing is quality and simplicity, while with wine, it is quality and complication."

By the time he was twelve, Jean-Baptiste was already dreaming of being the proprietor of a great restaurant. At twenty, he broke away from the Beaune bistro, went to the small wine town of Chalon-sur-Saône, and soon opened his own Café des Négociants (Café of the Wine Shippers). He married his Burgundian Marie and they had two sons, Jean and Pierre. Jean-Baptiste said, "When I took each, in turn, to be baptized, I first checked the holy water in the font and surreptitiously dropped in a pinch of salt and a few drops of fine olive oil. Then I asked *monsieur le curé* to please also baptize the baby as a good chef. I don't believe he did much, but I did think I detected a few stirring motions in the gestures of his right hand over the baby."

Jean-Baptiste saved his money in a sock in the mattress and decided to move on to a larger place in a busier town. He found the present property, on the corner of the station square in the "big city" of Roanne, where he could convert the entire ground floor into a bistro. They moved in 1930. From the first day, Jean-Baptiste was determined to make his bistro the most popular in town. He had exactly the personality for the job, the manner and voice of a sly clown, the skill of a master storyteller, with the ability to retail the town gossip in terms so malicious and ribald that the stories were only a hairbreadth from slander. Soon the bistro was jammed from morning to evening with people playing the local card game, tarots, rolling dice, and listening to Jean-Baptiste, over endless cups of coffee and glasses of *pastis.*

Under *papa* Jean-Baptiste's firm and persuasive guidance, it never occurred to Jean and Pierre not to become chefs. *Papa* warned that if they wanted to be masters of the art, they would have to spend at least ten years learning the classic techniques in the major restaurants of Paris. In 1944, as soon as Paris was liberated, Jean, at eighteen, headed for the big city. Pierre soon followed and *papa's* parting advice was, "Stay with your brother and work together." They were together at the Pavillon d'Armenonville in the Bois de Boulogne. Together at the Hôtel Crillon. Together at Drouant. Together at the Restaurant de la Pyramide in Vienne.

Finally, Jean became the fish chef and Pierre the sauce chef at the foremost *haute cuisine* restaurant of Paris, Chez Lucas-Carton, where the kitchen was ruled with a rod of iron by a magnificent disciplinarian known to every chef in the city as Le Père Richard. Today, both brothers feel that the classical training they got from him was the major force in their gastronomic education.

In 1954, when the ten years of apprenticeship were up, Jean-Baptiste sent a message to his boys: *"Maman* is tired of cooking. I give you my bistro. Come home and run it. Love, *Papa."*

It arrived at the crucial moment. Jean said, "We were bored to death with the endless repetitions of the classic *haute cuisine*—a waste of money and time."

Pierre added, "Not only is *haute cuisine* finished—its excesses disgust me. Okay. So if you have to spend three days to make a spun-sugar windmill to decorate a dish, make it, but then don't try to break it up and eat it. Send it to a museum and display it in a glass case."

In 1955, they were back home, together. Not long after, Jean met his wife Maria at the Roanne press ball. Pierre brought his girlfriend, Olympe, from Paris. "She was a waitress at one of the restaurants where we worked," Pierre whispered slyly. "I made love to her in the cold room between the carcasses of beef. One day, the chef opened the door and said, 'Oh, excuse me,' and slammed the door at once. He was a good chef." The day after each girl was married, she moved into the Troisgros house and became a waitress in the restaurant under the all-seeing eye of *papa* Jean-Baptiste.

"He was very hard," said Maria, "but now we all realize that he was right. He taught us the discipline of the search for perfection. Now, I believe, that is the mainspring of my life. It involves us all. Even our fourteen-year-old daughter, Catherine, will rush to me and say, 'Quick, look, *Maman.* That gentleman sitting alone in the corner. He seems to want something.'"

Although the two brothers were now classically trained chefs, they never had the slightest intention of converting *papa's* bistro into a temple of *haute cuisine.* Jean said, "We began changing the bistro into a restaurant, but very gradually. Our philosophy was *la cuisine simple,* but prepared as if we were trying to be a great restaurant."

After two years, in 1957, *Michelin* gave them one star. Then, in 1966, they moved up to two stars. Finally, on March 15, 1968, at crack of dawn, the copies of the new *Michelin* reached the bookstall of the railroad station. Jean strolled across the street and bought a copy. There they were. Three stars.

"Does it make a tremendous difference?" I asked.

Jean said, "Yes. In the tension of the atmosphere. When we had two stars, people came, relaxed and said to us, 'Oh, *la la!* You are simply marvelous! You deserve three stars!' Now they come in glowering and say with their eyes, 'Are you really *that* good? Prove to us that you are worth the long journey we have made!'"

For the next few days, I was involved in a fascinating experience. The Troisgros family invited me behind the scenes of their world of daily struggle toward excellence. The first morning, I was down at six-thirty with Olympe and Pierre, for *l'ouverture,* the opening up of the place before the staff arrives. At seven, the *chef de cuisine,* Michel (who is second-in-command to Jean and Pierre), and two assistant cooks were in the kitchen beginning the *mise en place,* the putting in place of every ingredient and tool that would be needed for the day's cooking. By seven-fifteen, two waiters were ready to serve the thirty-odd town customers who come in on their way to work for a *café au lait* and a croissant.

Meanwhile, Pierre concentrated on the food supplies. This was not a market day, so he took me to his small office for a bout of long-distance telephoning. There was a call from the village of Modane on the Swiss border. The wholesale agent there reported that the fishing boats from Yvoire had been out the night before on the Lake of Geneva and had brought in a good catch of the only kind of blue trout the Troisgros will accept: about two pounds and slightly red inside the gills. They would be shipped live by refrigerated truck and reach Roanne in about six hours.

The next call was from Dublin. There had been a good haul the night before in Galway Bay of the Irish mussels that the brothers think are the best in the world. They would be shipped live, in tanks, by boat to the Breton port of Roscoff, and then by refrigerated truck to Roanne. Another fishing company called from Nantes, at the mouth of the Loire, to report what had been caught that morning in the way of crabs, *langoustes*, lobsters, scallops, shrimps, etc. An amateur fisherman in Vichy called to say that he had hooked five large salmon in the Allier River the day before and to ask how many he should bring over.

By ten o'clock, the kitchen staff was in full operation and Jean had come downstairs to take charge. It had been raining early that morning and three schoolboys appeared at the back door of the kitchen carrying bags of live snails they had gathered in the woods. Jean inspected them, weighed them and paid off the boys from the iron cashbox. Two girls arrived to report a noisy mob of frogs on the pond behind the flour mill. Jean showed them the traditional way of catching frogs without damaging them. He brought out a square of bright-red *bouclé* silk, crumpled and rolled it into a rough ball, attached it to a line about six feet long with a short, whippy rod. He said, "You drop the red ball onto the surface of the pond. The red infuriates the frog, who attacks it and gets its teeth stuck in it. At that precise moment, you jerk up the ball with your right hand and, with your left, catch the frog as it falls."

Precisely at eleven, lunch was served to the staff. At eleven-thirty, the five Troisgros children came home from school and joined the family lunch. At noon, a great bell clanged and every man rushed to his post, ready for the first storm of the day. About sixty businessmen came in with their clients and friends. Almost unanimously, they ate two courses and spent about $3.50 per person. No menus were necessary. Maria knows the budget and taste of every one of them. I lunched in the back dining room with the businessmen and ate what most of them were having—an extremely popular Troisgros specialty, creamed marinated chicken in red wine vinegar.

By about two o'clock, the first storm was over. Jean and Pierre took me on a quick tour of the outskirts of Roanne to visit some of the amateur gardeners who grow fruits and vegetables to the Troisgros' specifications. Then we dropped in on their favorite *boulanger*, Claudius Dufour. Claudius bakes for Troisgros twenty-six kinds and shapes of breads and rolls and delivers them warm from his ovens five times a day. Next, we drove out to a green valley where we found, almost hidden among the trees, the two-hundred-year-old Moulin de Sainte-Marie. The water in the tiny river was running fast, turning the mill wheel at a clanking clip.

The owner, sixty-year-old Pierre Debus, a classic French country type who might have stepped straight out of one of Daudet's *Lettres de Mon Moulin,* showed us the first-quality grade of Canadian durum wheat that he mills for Troisgros into a coarse, unbleached flour.

At dinner that night, I ordered from the least expensive, $9 menu. I began with a terrine of wild rabbit (served in small individual crocks) that Pierre had shot in the forest. There followed one of the supreme Troisgros specialties, mussel soup—a rich fish broth, with cream and saffron, aromatic and glutinous, garnished with wine-poached mussels. For the main course, veal kidneys in a mustard sauce. With the mussels, I drank a fine white Burgundy, a 1966 Pouilly-Fuissé Château Fuissé, and with the kidneys, a 1966 red Volnay-Santenots, which the Troisgros serves Burgundian style in a polished pewter jug. After the almost unlimited choices from the cheese and dessert carts, Jean offered, with the coffee, a *marc de framboises,* a brandy distilled from raspberries. "At five-thirty in the morning, *monsieur,"* he told me, "I'm driving you the thirty kilometers to St.-Christophe, to help me buy some live Charolais beef."

As the sun rose, we were driving along the beautiful gorge of the Loire, where the river is narrow and white water races among the rocky pools. Already the amateur fishermen were out, some with rods and lines, others with the large, round conical nets. "They're all friends of ours," said Jean. "We'll get the best of what they catch." The valley opened out into the rolling vineyards of the Côtes Roannais, one of the minor classified wine areas, where we called at the vineyard of another Troisgros friend, Paul-Pierre Lutz, so that Jean could order a couple of barrels of Rosé d'Ambierle, the light carafe wine served at the restaurant. Then, over the hills to the village of Iguerande, to order three drums of walnut oil from the hundred-year-old pressing plant of Jean Leblanc. Next, to the lovely Romanesque village of Marcigny and the goat farm of Madame Jeannine Shalton, who showed us her herd of snow-white females, all kept in a continuous state of milk production by the industrious activities of a single, lordly, jet-black *boue,* who seemed well satisfied with his life's work. We loaded the back of the station wagon with four boxes of the small Marcigny cheeses, each about half the size of a Camembert, then headed toward St.-Christophe.

As we approached the village, the air was filled with the distant lowing of thousands of cattle. The Charolais beef sale is the most famous in France. We rounded a bend in the narrow road and suddenly faced a sea of cattle—almost four thousand on sale that day. The owner stands by the head of the animal and firmly proclaims its magnificent qualities— even if it's the scruffiest beast you ever saw. The buyer walks around the animal, prodding it with a stick and loudly pointing out its faults. The seller asks double what he expects to get. The buyer offers half of what he expects to pay. Then the violent trading begins.

A beef animal bought by the Troisgros brothers will usually weigh about a thousand pounds. They take only the *contre-filets*, the two long backstrips of lean meat, which include all the best steak and roasting cuts—about 10 percent of the carcass. The rest is at once resold to retail butchers. Before leaving St.-Christophe, soon after nine A.M., we had a "meat-handlers' breakfast" at the Restaurant Chenaux, next door to the slaughterhouse. The place was jammed with about three hundred of the brawniest men one has ever seen, most of them in blue-denim shirts that hung down to their knees. We started with a half-liter pot of a powerful, rough red Rhône wine. Then came a mountainous dish of beef stew. The meat seemed very fresh. Next, a well-aged Marcigny goat cheese, which had a certain gastronomic relationship with the beef. The smell reminded me of an unventilated cattle barn on a hot day. This monster meal cost a dollar.

Back in Roanne in time for lunch (but hardly hungry), I asked if I might kibitz with the kitchen crew. The six cooks are commanded by Jean, Pierre, the *chef de cuisine*, Michel, and the *chef pâtissier*, André. Jean is mainly at the stoves. Pierre cuts all the meat. Michel takes care of the fish and the sauces. At the same time, each of the bosses is inspecting, picking at, and tasting everything. A bowl of salad is ready to go into the dining room. Pierre looks at it, pulls out a leaf and tastes the dressing, then roundly bawls out the boy who made it, throws the salad into the garbage, and orders a rush replacement.

One has no feeling of anything being measured or cost-accounted. Mounds of butter, jugs of thick cream, and bottles of wine are everywhere and seem to be added to everything in unlimited quantities. Everyone communicates continuously by shouting—ill-tempered and tough shouting when the going is rough and mistakes are made, jocular and satiric shouting when things go well. The practical joke is never far below the surface. André walks across the kitchen carrying a tower of empty aluminum cake pans. Pierre, at the butcher's block, flashes out his foot and trips him. The deafening crash of the pans sets the whole kitchen to a roar of laughter. André, not amused, yells at the boys, "Pick 'em up!" and stalks off to his corner.

As each order is yelled in and confirmed by Jean's answering shout, he takes down the proper pan for that order and sets it, empty, as a reminder, on the stove. He claims his system is foolproof, but by the time there are ten empty pans, he has been known to mutter, "What the bloody hell is supposed to go into this one?" At moments one senses, perhaps, the secret of the lifelong relationship between the two brothers.

Pierre has the force and the fury: he does the bawling out. The boys watch him with a certain fear. Jean has the charm. He flashes his smile. He jumps in with soothing words. The boys watch him with adoration.

The pressures mount to a peak. The orders are like a barrage of machine-gun fire. One has the vague feeling of a crew of white-coated seamen trying to keep their ship afloat in a hurricane. The blare of noise, the figures rushing hither and thither, the irresistible chaos of enticing smells, the heat and spitting of the frying, the clang of pots, the bloomp-bloomp of chopping knives, all beat down with enveloping force until one feels dizzy.

Yet, in reality, everything is proceeding normally, everyone is efficiently absorbed. A boy is quickly shelling a bowl of beautiful, pink crayfish. Michel is adding a shower of bright-green sorrel to a brilliantly yellow sauce. André is making patterns with peach halves on a tart shell. Pierre watches everything and misses nothing. He could take over any job, from anyone, at any moment, and do it better. Everyone knows this and the effect is both disciplinary and exhilarating. One feels sure that if Jean suddenly felt himself fainting from the heat of his fires, he would, before letting himself fall to the floor, take the piece of beef out of the oven to avoid its being overcooked.

Lunch was over, the afternoon was restful, and, by dinnertime, I was again ready to face the joyous riches of the Troisgros' cuisine. On the third evening, I ordered from the $12 menu. Since this is the dinner chosen by about 90 percent of the tourists, it includes most of the Troisgros' specialties listed in the *Guide Michelin.* My meal began with a dish of pink, cold poached crayfish on a bed of chopped green leaves, lightly set off with a tomato-tinged yellow mayonnaise. Next, the dish that has been most often acclaimed by French gourmets as Troisgros' most brilliant creation: a thin *escalope* of fresh salmon, covered by a faintly acid sauce made with sorrel, vermouth, white wine, lemon juice, and copious quantities of butter and cream. "The trick is to add the finely chopped sorrel not more than ten seconds before you pour the sauce over the salmon," Jean pointed out. "The sorrel melts, but its flavor is captured." The main course was an *entrecôte* of Charolais beef, with a complicated red Beaujolais sauce, thickened with beef marrow. The wine with the fish was a 1964 white Burgundy, Puligny-Montrachet, while the beef deserved and got a magnum of 1961 Chambertin-Clos de Bèze—a great wine.

After cheeses and desserts, Jean offered, with the coffee, a privately distilled, unlabeled marc made from wild plums, which, in finesse and richness, made many a Cognac seem weak and uninteresting. The meal was a gastronomic triumph.

. . .

The following day, after breakfast, I reluctantly packed my bags. It was time for me to leave. Jean and Pierre came up to my room and said that they would all be greatly honored if I would have my farewell lunch with the family and staff in the private dining room. I felt equally honored by the invitation. It was a meal of perfect simplicity—a fitting end to a memorable visit. There was a salad of the last local green beans and tomatoes of the season. There was a whole pike, caught that morning in the gorge of the Loire, served with *la sauce à la manière de Grand-maman*—creamy, lemony, with the faint taste of shallots and speckled with the green of fresh tarragon. Then a beautifully balanced *aiguillette de boeuf*, a stew with sweet baby carrots aand small boiled potatoes. For the wine, they reminded me of my visit to Monsieur Lutz by serving his charming Rosé d'Ambierle. Then came the Marcigny cheese to remind me of Madame Shalton's goats. Then the last raspberries and strawberries of the season—and Champagne for the final toasts.

I raised my glass and gently goaded them: "Here's to your future. You are world-famous, you have more business than you can possibly handle. Here's to your rebuilding this place as a three-hundred-seat restaurant. You have had large financial offers from Paris. Here's to your opening a great restaurant there."

Jean laughed: "If I wanted to be a businessman, I wouldn't be a chef."

Pierre said: "I want to stay in the kitchen. I enjoy cooking with my brother."

The big bell clanged for twelve o'clock. Everyone hurried off to his battle station. I was left alone in the private dining room with *papa* Jean-Baptiste. For a few moments, we sipped our Champagne in silence. Then I asked: "What do you think is the essence of the Troisgros philosophy?"

"When my boys were young," he said, "we used to go into the country together and, when we saw the Charolais cattle in the fields, I said, 'Look, how they are at peace. They are at one with the earth—in perfect harmony.' We try to achieve that harmony in this house. I believe our clients sense that harmony in the foods they eat here and the wines they drink here. Our essence, *monsieur*, is that our cuisine reflects the marvel of the earth."

Is this the greatest restaurant in the world? My mother once told me that she took me to my first restaurant when I was two years old. Since that day, I calculate that I have eaten in 12,474 restaurants around the world. As far as I can remember, not one of them was ever as good as Troisgros.

The Brothers Troisgros and the New Low-High Cuisine

I was having breakfast with chef Jean Troisgros on my last day at his great three-star restaurant in Roanne. We were eating *les petits oeufs de poules naines à la coque*, boiled baby pullets' eggs straight from the nest. We dug out the inside of each egg—hardly more than a single mouthful—with *mouillettes*, narrow fingers of toast very lightly spread with hazelnut-flavored farm butter. In the middle of the table was a big bowl of Montmorency cherries just picked from the tree, a basket of croissants hot from the oven, and a jar of Jean's own whole-strawberry jam.

I had just completed eight working days with Jean and Pierre, tasting and testing in their dining rooms and kitchen many of their marvelous culinary inventions. They had presented me with copies of some of their recipes and had recorded on my tapes their detailed advice. Now, Jean was discussing their basic gastronomic philosophy.

I said that I considered him and Pierre to be the leading exponents of the so-called "new-new cuisine" of France—the new approach to great French eating that is widely known as the "new Low-High cuisine." I knew what it was in terms of eating at the table, but I wanted Jean to give me a definitive statement of its basic principles.

We were joined at this point by one of the top gastronomic writers of France, Christian Millau, who was on a restaurant tour and had stayed

---

EDITOR'S NOTE: This piece is excerpted from *Revolutionizing French Cuisine* (McGraw-Hill, 1975). The "new Low-High cuisine" was de Groot's term; he was among the first American journalists to distinguish the food phenomenon commonly referred to as *nouvelle cuisine*.

overnight at the Hotel Troisgros. Christian and his partner, Henri Gault, publish the most prestigious of French food and wine magazines, *Le Nouveau Guide de Gault-Millau.* Breaking open his first egg, Christian was more than ready to join the discussion of the new developments in the gastronomy of France.

"In ancient China," Christian began, "when a Chinese host invited a friend to a feast, he said: 'Come. We will eat fat.' And in the great, historical family portraits in the Louvre or the Rijksmuseum, the men and women of nobility and wealth are always shown as being much fatter than the ordinary working people. Even in more modern times, the idea of the jolly and successful fat man was part of the unchanging tradition of society. Think of Mr. Pickwick in Charles Dickens. But that whole concept has been buried by our current generation. It would have been a twentieth-century tragedy if our great chefs had failed to recognize the new trend. Let us be thankful they have decided to be involved."

"I think we all understand," Jean added, "that the new international interest in health and weight control is not just a passing fad, but a permanent new direction in gastronomy. So we *cuisiniers* are adding our grain of salt to the new movement. We are helping to make a pleasure out of a necessity."

"It is much more than that," Christian said. "Such great cooks as Jean and Pierre, Michel Guérard, Jacques Manière, Roger Vergé, and many others are, in fact, inventing a superb new cuisine, almost without butter, cream, other fats, starches, or sugar. It is *la nouvelle révolution française.*"

What emerged from the discussion was that this new-new Low-High cuisine is not a slimming diet. It has nothing to do with the mineral oil and sugar substitute recipes of what the French call *la cuisine diététique.* This new-new cuisine still gives first priority to the high pleasure of great eating—but it is great eating that is at the same time digestible, healthy, light, natural, and simplified by the exclusion of most of the carbohydrates and sugars, of flour-thickened sauces and starchy stuffings. The idea is that you should continue to eat in the style of high cuisine but with low likelihood of gaining weight and low prospects of damage to health. The eternal roller-coaster ride—the ups and downs of undisciplined stuffing followed by agonizing self-denial—is eliminated once and for all. It is indeed the new French revolution.

"Well, a gastronomic revolution is hardly something new in French history," said Jean. "In the last three hundred years, there have been more cuisine revolutions than political. The progression of French eating—in every way as temperamental and volatile as our French character—has never gone forward in a logical straight line. It has twisted and turned. It has been through violent upheavals. It has had amazing up-surges and disastrous collapses."

Before the early 1500s, there was no such thing as a French cuisine. Eating was still at what you might call the near-caveman stage. The women who slaved over the hot fires never sat at table with the men. The long trestles of rough boards had neither place settings nor knives, forks, or spoons. The men sat in their hunting clothes on long benches. When the huge joint of still partly raw, spit-roasted meat was placed in the center of the table, they drew their daggers from their belts and slashed off huge chunks, holding them in their hands. Having no nap-kins, they simply waved their bloody, greasy, sticky fingers in the air to dry them. At table, France was in no way ahead of England, Germany, or Spain and was far behind the civilized nobility of Florence, Rome, or Venice.

The first gastronomic revolution was brought to France by Catherine de' Medici, daughter of Lorenzo of Florence, when she became engaged to the Duke of Orléans (later, King Henry II). * On a visit to her fiancé, she was horrified by the food and the manners at table. So, in 1533, when she left Florence to become Queen of France, she brought with her sixteen crack Florentine cooks and a whole wagon train of herbs, spices, and vegetables, including a green leaf that grew wild on the Florentine hills but had never before been tasted in France—*spinaci.* (This is why, on a French menu, any dish with spinach is still called *à la florentine.*) Male-chauvinistic Frenchmen dislike admitting that the basic foundation of *la grande cuisine* (as well as the prototypes of handmade, silver cutlery) were imported into France by an Italian woman.

The next revolution in French cuisine began in 1682, when Louis XIV completed the palace of Versailles and, as part of its immense show-off, launched the wildest era of conspicuous consumption of food. When the king dined, an almost endless parade of huge and highly decorated dishes passed before him, each borne on the shoulders of four men. He would take one bite from each, then wave it back to the kitchen for later reheating and serving to members of the court and their guests. The royal waste of food was one of the seeds of the French Revolution—it has passed into tradition with the famous argument at the gates of Ver-sailles over the relative merits of bread and cake. Meanwhile, all the noblemen in their own châteaux in every part of France were imitating

---

* EDITOR'S NOTE: As Catherine was merely fourteen when she arrived in France, and as there had been a constant exchange of culinary expertise between France and Italy over the preceding cen-turies, we believe Catherine's influence to be overstated here.

the king and hiring the most brilliant cooks they could find. Cooking became (and still is) one of the most honored of French professions.

The era of super luxury came to a crashing end in 1789 when the Bastille was stormed and noble heads were soon being neatly sliced off by the guillotine. The thousands of chefs all over France—fearing that they would be classified as boot-lickers of the rich and also sent to the guillotine—went underground. For almost fifteen years, *la grande cuisine* disappeared. Great eating was automatically associated with the oppressors of the people and was not even mentioned in whispers.

By about 1800, the chefs, having exhausted their savings, had to do something. The famous Parisian *cuisiner* Beauvilliers is generally credited with the brilliant idea that changed the life of France. He decided to demonstrate his devotion to Democracy by opening a restaurant at which he would offer for the delectation of the *bourgeoisie* the greatest dishes he had created for his former noble employers. Beauvilliers slyly called it his "Restaurant of the Republic—Palace of Equality," and it was instantaneously such a raging success that other chefs in hiding opened their own luxurious restaurants in virtually every city of France.

The greatest name to emerge from this tremendous resurgence of French gastronomy was Antonin Carême, who raised *la grande cuisine française* to its highest peak of all. He cooked for the kings of France and England, as well as for the Czar of Russia.

Under the world-wide influence of Carême, which lasted one hundred years, until the appearance of Escoffier, grand dining became more and more an ostentatious and snobbish status symbol, more and more committed to excessive waste. Ice was not yet being used as a preservative and Carême had only four simple ways of preventing mountains of food from going bad: salting, smoking, sun-drying, or marinating in vinegar. To hide the off-taste . . most fish and meat, sauce was piled on top of sauce, filling was stuffed inside filling. A banquet might last for eight hours and offer a hundred separate dishes.

The next revolutionary change came just before 1900 when Escoffier almost single-handedly brought *la grande cuisine* into the twentieth century. He had primitive ice boxes that enabled him to change many of the techniques and codify the basic rules of French grand cooking. But he was still planning his menus for bored czars, emperors, and kings to whom sumptuous waste was a way of life. He was still gilding the lily. It was still very much *la grande cuisine*. Then, after Escoffier died, a thousand chefs continued to try to imitate him, while the world and its sybaritic mood gradually changed as food abundance gradually became food shortage. It was again time for a change—another turning point in French gastronomic history.

THE COURSE OF HISTORY IN A SINGLE DISH

The roots of the new-new Low-High cuisine are clearly seen in the evolution of one of the most famous dishes of *la grande cuisine*. Its name is known to every serious gastronome: *selle de veau à la Prince Orloff*. In the middle 1800s, the Russian Prince Orloff was Minister in Paris for Czar Nicholas I and was a regular customer at the then-famous Parisian Restaurant Tortoni, where the *chef de cuisine* was the great Urbain Dubois. When Orloff returned to St. Petersburg, he persuaded Dubois to go back with him as his personal chef, and Dubois stayed in St. Petersburg for twenty years. There was plenty of good veal in Russia, but Orloff disliked the taste of it. So he kept urging Dubois to mask the flavor of the meat with all kinds of aromatic stuffings and sauces. Finally, perhaps in desperation, Dubois created the famous dish in which an entire saddle of veal is slit across the bones in dozens of places—each slit is filled with a complicated mixture of a *duxelles* or minced mixture of chopped wild mushrooms and shallots, a *soubise* or garnish of onions and aromatic rice and layers of sliced foie gras and black truffles; everything, finally, is covered by a Mornay sauce loaded with grated Gruyère cheese. When all this was reheated and browned, the flavor of the veal disappeared. Prince Orloff felt that a great new dish had been created and gave his name to it as a crown jewel of *la grande cuisine française*.

Just about a hundred years later, Julia Child included a simplified version of the recipe (leaving out the super-expensive foie gras and truffles) in the first volume of her *Mastering the Art of French Cooking*. A friend of mine, a young man who is a highly skilled amateur cook, tried Julia's recipe for a party. Afterwards, he wrote me about it. He admires Julia and follows every fine shading of her instructions. After he had browned and braised the solid piece of veal, he thought it smelled and tasted marvelous. He almost wondered why the rest of the recipe was necessary. He minced the mushrooms and sautéed them with shallots for the *duxelles*. He sliced the onions and sautéed them for the *soubise*. He kept thinking hungrily of that beautifully browned veal waiting in the pot. Julia's instructions worked perfectly. The mushroom *duxelles*, by itself, tasted fine. The onion-rice *soubise*, by itself, was elegant. He whipped up the white Mornay sauce with butter, flour, milk, heavy cream, and grated Gruyère. The veal was sliced open and stuffed in layers. Then it was covered with the sauce, more grated Gruyère, and oodles of melted butter and browned and bubbled in a hot oven. Not a single square inch of the original veal was visible.

After dinner, with the help of some good Cognac to open them up, the cook persuaded his guests to talk frankly about the veal main course.

They thought that the solid veal at the center was lovely, but its character was too much masked by the stuffings and sauce—unnecessarily gussied up. The dish seemed too complicated—overluxurious—absurdly pretentious.

Was this a purely American reaction? Would a French gourmet have agreed? Recently, James de Coquet, the much-admired food and wine columnist of the Paris newspaper, *Le Figaro*, wrote: "In this dish, the attractive veal is put into the minority by the sauce, the *duxelles* of mushrooms, the *soubise* of onions, the slices of black truffles and all the other unnecessary impedimenta. It finishes up as a dish that is ruined!" De Coquet went on to report that when Chef Urbain Dubois ended his service in Russia and returned to Paris in 1870, he wrote a cook book for the average French housewife in which he said: "The ambition of every good cook must be to make something very good with the fewest possible ingredients." Thus, in the view of James de Coquet, Dubois himself wrote the epitaph for his own veal Orloff! Perhaps—a hundred years too soon—he was sounding the first clarion call for the new-new Low-High cuisine?

At breakfast in Roanne, I turned to Jean Troisgros, who, as all young cooks must, had begun his training with the classical techniques. "Would you," I asked, "be willing today to prepare a saddle of veal Prince Orloff?"

Jean fairly snorted: "No! Never! That's an antique, a museum-piece, good for a professional cooking competition. It was one of the dishes I prepared when I won my 'Best Chef of France' award, quite a few years ago. It was an interesting exercise for a young chef. But not for his customers. First, you have to cook the veal. Then you have to spoil it by letting it cool down. Then you have to cut it open in a dozen places to make sure it dries out. Then you have to dominate it with foie gras and truffles *and* an onion *soubise and* mushrooms *and* a cheese Mornay *and* what else? Then you must reassemble it. Then you must reheat it. Then you must be crazy!

"It would be far better to serve the veal as a plain roast," Jean continued, "perfectly hot and savory from the oven. If you want a *soubise* of simmered onions with it, serve them, freshly prepared, in a separate dish. The mushrooms, also freshly sautéed, in another separate dish. And if you absolutely insist on foie gras with it, then have it as the first course of the meal. I would agree with that menu. With all the ingredients of a veal Orloff served separately and in the proper order, you can make a very digestible and pleasant menu, but if you bang them all together inside the meat, I predict you'll be sick!"

Jean's attitude toward veal Orloff is the best possible illustration of the most basic principle of the new-new Low-High cuisine—the continual drive, with every recipe, toward simplification. Jean dislikes veal Orloff because it is an endless repetition, because it offers no opportunity to the cook to be inventive, because it is overcomplicated, overrich, and indigestible.

WHO INVENTED THE LOW-HIGH CUISINE?

Very few great new ideas are the flash of a single mind. Most evolve from the constructive interplay of the thoughts of many specialists. The new-new cuisine is no exception. Almost thirty years ago, after the end of World War II, I talked to the two greatest chefs since Escoffier about the future of French gastronomy. The magnificent Alexandre Dumaine was still at his Restaurant de la Côte d'Or in the village of Saulieu. The giant, Fernand Point, was at his Restaurant de la Pyramide in the town of Vienne just south of Lyon. Although both were brilliant masters of *la grande cuisine*, both were convinced that it must be modernized and simplified. They wanted to cut down on the enormous catalog of classic sauces. They wanted, gradually, to eliminate the overaromatic and overrich garnishes and stuffings. They believed that good ingredients should be tasted for themselves.

Chef Paul Bocuse was trained by *papa* Point and absorbed these ideas. Soon after 1965, when Paul won three stars for his superb restaurant at Collonges-au-Mont-d'Or, I visited him and recorded our discussion. He told me about his *nouvelle cuisine*. Dozens of classic dishes had been adapted by Paul and his disciples (called by their *ancien régime* critics of that time "the gastronomic Mafia"), but as I tasted these dishes, I sensed an ambivalent attitude in their preparation. These young chefs seemed to me to be unsure whether their clients would be willing to switch from the completely rich to the completely light. So they compromised with half-light, half-rich dishes. While loudly proclaiming that they were going forward, they were still looking backward. My disillusionment was fairly complete when Bocuse and his colleagues formed a trade association and named it La Grande Cuisine Française! Ten years later, Paul's recipes had moved much closer to a convinced lightness and simplicity.

The second major attempt to modernize *la grande cuisine* came from the brilliant, young chef Michel Guérard when he was still running his Paris bistro, Le Pot au Feu. He decided to go the whole way and convert some classic dishes into dietetic slimming recipes, complete with mineral oil, sugar substitutes, and low-fat yogurt. I bow to no one in my admiration of Michel's imagination and skill, but, frankly, I find no pleasure in mineral oil. Other Young Turk chefs of Paris have picked up some of Michel's ideas and are now promoting *la cuisine diététique*. Michel calls his version *la cuisine minceur*.

Then, on a visit to chefs Jean and Pierre Troisgros, I was served their duck with fresh figs (page 148), and their sirloin steak with lemon and capers (page 150), and I knew that the perfect balance between *la nouvelle cuisine* and *la cuisine diététique* had been precisely achieved. It was the new-new cuisine—the Low-High cuisine—the new revolutionary gastronomy of naturalism and simplicity. How had it been done? I asked Jean Troisgros, "Did you invent it?"

"No. Not at all," Jean replied. "As you know, I followed Paul Bocuse as the assistant chef to the great Fernand Point. He first laid down the principles of a truly light, simple cuisine. We often discussed the fact that we did better work (and were happier) when we cooked as we pleased, rather than when we were blindly and slavishly following the inexorable and inflexible rules of *la grande cuisine*. We wanted to cook specially for each of our clients—as if they were guests in our own house. We began preparing each dish slightly differently each time. In one evening, I might try twenty variations of sea bass. That was the start of the great urge to experiment."

"Was that when you began cutting out the butter and cream?" I asked.

"Not altogether. We still use butter and cream, but in new ways that eliminate the old indigestibility and super richness," Jean said. "What was wrong, in the old days, was the endless cooking and reducing of the butter and cream. They used to put in gallons of cream and pounds of butter and flour, then boil it down—concentrating and reconcentrating the fats and the starches. That was why the old cuisine was so unhealthy. Today, we use butter and cream without endless boiling, with complete protection of the essential lightness. Come, let me show you."

We had talked so long over breakfast that it was almost lunch time and Jean took me to the kitchen where Pierre and his brigade were preparing for the midday rush. "Look," said Jean, "there is not a single sauce simmering in advance on the stove. The butter is still in the refrigerator. So is the cream. When the first customers arrive, we start from scratch. That is a basic principle of the new-new cuisine. No stale flavors—no washed-out feeling—of anything that has been boiling on the stove for hours and hours."

"How do you give body to your new-style sauces?" I asked.

"The word *roux* has been eliminated from our dictionary," Jean continued. "That eternal and inevitable butter-flour mixture used for thickening everything in sight, which never provided any flavor of its own, has been thrown out of the kitchen window. Now, we thicken our sauces by reduction—a simple process which not only provides a better body to the sauce, but also concentrates and sharpens the flavor—an essence, a magnification of the basic character of the dish. Finally, at the very last moment before serving, we melt in a small quantity of butter or cream, with no cooking at all, to complete the sauce with a sense of light and simple softness."

"How do you lighten and simplify your desserts?" I asked.

"Instead of throwing in masses of processed sugar," Jean said, "we now draw out the natural sweetness of very ripe fruits—we reduce and concentrate the natural grape sugars in sweet wines. This brings a natural quality to our desserts—a much better, healthier, and more satisfying way to end a meal."

"Not all of those ideas," I countered, "are absolutely new."

"Certainly not," Jean said, "some of what we do comes straight from Grandmother. Her cooking somehow went out of fashion. The snobbish gourmets of Paris looked down their noses at it, because they thought it was too simple. So they turned back to the super-fancy-pants, show-off cuisine of the kings of France at the Palace of Versailles, as interpreted by Escoffier. For nearly a hundred years, Escoffier has eclipsed Grandmother. Now, our new-new cuisine is a return to Grandmother, but with this difference—it is now being modernized and perfected by professional chefs, using to the maximum their imaginations and skills. Our new-new cuisine is, speaking in culinary terms, the concentration to an essence of French bourgeois country cooking, which, after all, has always been ultimately the best. The difference, now, is that we cook things less and that we avoid excess. What I hate most is the cuisine where there is too much of everything—too many embellishments in the dish—too many garnishes on the plate—and totally too much of everything everywhere for the diner to eat without after-dinner discomfort. Excess serves no purpose. In our new-new recipes there is no excess of anything."

REVOLUTIONARY, YET PRACTICAL ADVICE FROM PARIS

From Roanne, I returned to Paris and recorded a series of talks with one of the most brilliant *cuisiniers* of the city, chef Jacques Manière, at his famous and great bistro, Le Pactole, on the Boulevard St.-Germain. He, too, has accepted the Low-High concepts, but interprets the new movement in his own special way. I asked whether he thought that the new-new cuisine was as good as the old.

"It is perfectly possible to have a *grande cuisine* with marvelous flavors and savors," Jacques replied, "yet dramatically low in butter, cream, and all other fats. I have been experimenting more and more in my own kitchen with low-fat and low-sugar dishes—yet trying to avoid any compromise in the pleasures and satisfactions of great eating. I must say that I am enchanted with my own food!"

I asked him what kinds of foods he used for his Low-High dishes.

"Clearly," Jacques continued, "one must turn toward those creatures of which the flesh is less fatty, less rich. These include capon and chicken; nonoily fish such as sea bass, sole, and turbot; fatless cuts of lamb and veal; steamed liver; lobster and crayfish; mushrooms; mussels; shrimp; veal brains and sweetbreads . . . all these are thoroughly low in fat and not exactly sad to eat!"

I ask how he planned his menus around these dishes.

"Once you have chosen the main dish, you plan the first course and the dessert for the most perfect possible balance. You can add many different kinds of vegetables, undercooked, of course, without butter, and, to end the meal, nothing more than ripe fresh fruits. You can add body to your sauces with low-fat white or pot cheese. If I occasionally use a small amount of oil, it is to add flavor and therefore I use very small quantities of such strong oils as first-pressing green olive, or cold-pressed walnut. If, occasionally, I dare to enrich a dish with a minimum addition of, say, basil butter, I allow myself this luxury because I have saved so much in other directions."

Which cooking methods did he prefer?

"Many of my dishes are steamed, or cooked wrapped in aluminum foil or parchment paper—a method which requires no pre-buttering of the cooking vessel and which holds in maximum flavor. To balance the absence of fatty richness, I make everything strongly aromatic with such characterful herbs and spices as basil, whole green peppercorns, shallots, tarragon, and thyme, among others. I use no added sugar whatsoever in my desserts. I rely entirely on the natural sweetness of the fruits. If you take very fresh fruits and simply mash them lightly with a fork, then freeze them, you can produce superbly refreshing sherbets. I drink one glass of wine with every meal—to help sustain the pleasures of the table. Instead of coffee with cream and sugar, I drink smoky lapsang souchong—China tea so full of character that nothing need be added. Great menus can be planned by the intelligent balance of the simplest of preparations."

ROAST DUCK WITH FRESH FIGS

4 servings

At their restaurant, chefs Jean and Pierre Troisgros serve several varieties of domestic and wild duck prepared in many different ways. This recipe, to me, is one of the greatest of their repertory—partly, perhaps, because it involves none of the standard, unimaginative, sticky-sweet dressing up of the duck. Here there are no sugar-glazed oranges, no syrup-soaked peaches; the only sweetness is the natural juice of the fresh figs—the natural savor of the duck predominates.

> 2 Long Island ducks (one about 2½ to 3 lbs and one about 4½ to 5 lbs)
> 1 lemon, cut in half
> 1 medium yellow onion, peeled and chopped
> 2 medium carrots, scraped and chopped
> 2 green Pascal outer celery stalks, destringed and chopped, with leaves
> 3 sprigs fresh parsley
>   Coarse crystal salt to taste
>   Freshly ground white pepper to taste
> 12 whole figs, fresh in season or canned Kadota
> 2 ounces French Orgeat, almond syrup
>   About 2 cups chicken bouillon
> 1 cup white wine, preferably Sancerre
> 2 tablespoons minced shallots
> 2 tablespoons sweet butter

About 2½ Hours Before Serving—Active Work About 1½ Hours, Plus About 1 Hour of Unsupervised Maturing and Resting

Preheat your oven to 350° F. Rub the ducks, inside and out, with the cut sides of the lemon halves. Then thoroughly prick the underside skin to allow the excess fat to run out. Place them on a raised rack in an open roasting pan and roast them until the breasts are nicely pink (but not by any means bleeding rare)—usually in no more than 45 to 50 minutes.

Meanwhile, prepare a 2-quart saucepan in which you will cook the duck bouillon. Put into it the chopped onion, the chopped carrots, the chopped celery stalks and leaves, and the 3 sprigs of parsley, with salt and pepper to taste. Pour in a pint of cold water and bring it rapidly to a boil, then stir, reduce heat to gentle simmering, and let it continue, covered, until the duck carcass is ready to go in.

Next, turn your attention to the figs. (If they are canned, first drain all syrup.) Put them in a 1-quart saucepan. Dribble over them the 2 ounces of Orgeat, then pour over enough of the chicken bouillon to cover the figs. Heat this up to gentle simmering and let it continue, covered, to warm and puff up the figs—usually in 5 minutes. By this time the bouillon should be vaguely sweet with fig juice. Lift out the figs and keep them warm in a covered container. Now boil the fig bouillon hard to reduce it, so that its sweetness concentrates and sharpens. When it has reduced by about half, and it is nicely sweet, then turn off the heat and hold, covered, until it is needed later.

About 1½ Hours Before Serving—Resting the Duck While Making the Sauce

As soon as the ducks are pink, put the larger one into a covered casserole or *cocotte* and let stand tightly lidded over extremely low heat on top of the stove. It should stay there, very gently ripening in its own juice for an hour. (This is the secret Troisgros trick with duck—to complete the cooking very slowly in an enclosed, steamy space. Pierre said: "When the flesh rests for an hour, its muscles decontract and the meat slowly softens and increases in flavor.")

Now deal with the smaller duck. Carve off its breast, legs, thighs, and wings and put them in the covered casserole with the larger duck. Using large poultry shears and a Chinese cleaver, cut the remaining carcass of the small duck into, say, 8 pieces and put them in the 2-quart saucepan of bouillon. Press the duck carcass pieces down in the saucepan fairly tightly and then, if necessary, add more water just to cover. Continue the simmering, covered, until the bouillon is needed later.

Skim off all the fat from the oven pan in which the ducks were roasted. When only the juices remain, set the pan over a top burner and deglaze it with the cup of white wine, thoroughly scraping the bottom of the pan with the edge of a wooden spoon. Pour this deglazed mixture into the simmering duck bouillon.

About ½ Hour Before Serving—Completion and Assembly

Preheat your grill. Strain out the solids from the duck bouillon, returning the bouillon to the saucepan and now boiling it hard to reduce it and concentrate its ducky flavor. Reheat the fig bouillon just to bubbling. (Pierre said: "You are now at the crucial moment for the perfection of this dish. You must taste continually both the duck bouillon and the fig stock, so that you can judge the precise moment when they should be combined. The balance you are seeking is very delicate. If you allow the sauce to become too sweet, it will dominate the duck. If you get it dead right—a very delicate and gentle sweetness—it will glorify and magnify the duck. Use your judgment. Keep it light. Avoid the slightest heaviness or thickness in the sauce. Above all remove every scrap of fat.") At the right moment, pour the fig stock into the duck bouillon and add the 2 tablespoons of minced shallots. Continue boiling hard to keep on reducing the combined sauce. Start warming your 4 serving plates. Place the figs on an open grill platter and quickly glaze them under the grill for hardly more than a minute or two.

Now carve the duck (both the whole large bird and the parts from the smaller one), set out the portions on the plates and garnish them with the glazed figs. Keep warm until the sauce is ready. As soon as the sauce has exactly the taste and texture you want, turn down the heat to below simmering and grind in a fair amount of white pepper. (Pierre said: "You must be able to taste it, but there must not be so much that it pricks your throat. There must be enough pepper to cut across the sweetness of the sauce. Also, never allow it to boil once the pepper is in, or you will get a bitter taste.")

Finally, when the sauce is dead right, keeping it just below simmering, perform the professional operation of *monter au beurre*, mounting with butter. Melt onto its surface, sliver by sliver, the 2 tablespoons of butter, to give the sauce, as Pierre put it, "A touch of luxurious velvet." Pour the sauce around, not over, the duck and figs on the plates. Then rush them, very hot, to table. Because of the slight sweetness of the sauce, red wine is not quite right with this duck, so the Troisgros brothers served me a noble, luxuriously rich, soft yet strong white Meursault from the Côte d'Or of Burgundy. At my New York table, I might serve a rich California Pinot Chardonnay from the Alexander Valley in Sonoma.

SLICED SIRLOIN STEAK WITH LEMON AND CAPERS

4 servings

The first time you taste juicy, rare, and tender sections of beefsteak, served in a soup plate with a natural sauce *au jus*, but distinctly flavored with lemon juice and the acid of capers, it comes almost as a shock—it is so completely different from any previous gastronomic experience. By the second or third bite, you begin to realize that it is an extraordinarily successful combination of flavors—the sauce bringing out and magnifying the juicy meatiness of the sirloin. And this is achieved without *béarnaise*, hollandaise, butter, cream, or flour. With the well-known soothing effect of lemon juice on the digestion, you could eat a couple of pounds of steak in this way and never feel the slightest sense of overfullness. You should prepare, to go with this, a nice mixture of light, seasonal, fresh vegetables, preferably poached or steamed, to be served around the meat as a colorful *garniture jardinière*.

> Beef sirloin steak, about 1½ inches thick (about 2 to 2½ lbs)
> 1 tablespoon butter
> 1 tablespoon pure green virgin olive oil
> 2 tablespoons peeled and chopped shallots
> 2 tablespoons lemon juice, freshly squeezed
> 2 tablespoons red wine vinegar
> 1⅓ cups beef bouillon
> 5 tablespoons demi-glace brown sauce *
> 3 tablespoons capers, drained
> Coarse crystal salt to taste
> Freshly ground white pepper to taste
> Small handful of chopped parsley
> ¼ cup chopped tarragon, fresh leaf in season

Preparation in About 25 Minutes

Preheat your oven to a keep-warm 175° F. Cut every scrap of fat away from the sirloin steak and slice the remaining lean into strips, each about ⅜ to ½ inch thick and about 2 to 3 inches long. Set a heavy frypan over high frying heat and, when it is good and hot, quickly lubricate its bottom with the 1 tablespoon each of butter and olive oil. Within a few seconds, as soon as they start smoking, drop in the sirloin strips, batch by batch, moving them around and turning them over almost continuously, so that they brown and crust slightly on the outside but remain juicy, rare, and tender inside. It is all done in seconds rather than minutes. As fast as the strips are removed from the frypan, they should be kept warm on a platter, covered, in the oven. Lower the heat under the frypan to medium frying and put in the 2 tablespoons of chopped shallots, stirring them around until they are just colored, usually in not more than 20 seconds. At once hiss into the frypan the 2 tablespoons each of lemon juice and vinegar with the 1⅓ cups of beef bouillon. Stir thoroughly.

EDITOR'S NOTE: Cooks doing this recipe are advised to consult a basic French cookbook on the preparation of *demi-glace*.

Continue turning down the heat, but keep the liquid bubbling hard to reduce it, concentrating its flavors and thickening it—usually for 2 or 3 minutes. Work in, tablespoon by tablespoon, the 5 tablespoons of *demi-glace*. Keep boiling hard to continue reducing for about another 5 minutes. Add the 3 tablespoons of drained capers. Add salt and pepper, to taste. Add the small handful of chopped parsley and the ¼ cup tarragon. Now put your strips of sirloin back into the sauce and reheat them in it for not a flash more than 10 seconds, or you will commit the crime of overcooking the meat. Serve instantly in very hot soup plates with about ¼ inch of sauce in the bottom. Provide your guests with a soup spoon for the sauce. Accompany the dish with a red Burgundy—or a noble California Cabernet Sauvignon from Sonoma—and drink a toast to the Burgundian skill of the brothers Troisgros!

The Make-or-Break Politics of the Guide Michelin

The *Guide Michelin*, claiming to be as irreproachable as Caesar's wife, has become a sacred cow. It is the largest-selling and most influential gastronomic guide in the world. There is no book on any subject published in France that sells more copies. It can make or break any restaurant; the award of one star increases business by an average of 50 percent. The people who put together the *Guide Michelin* obviously consider themselves the world's supreme judges of gastronomic taste. They never give a reason for any of their decisions. They never make statements to the press. They almost never grant interviews. The *Guide's inspecteurs* operate with the secrecy of the C.I.A. They do not need to plan assassinations; the suicides follow automatically. In 1966, when the two-star Relais de Porquerolles in Paris was dropped from the *Guide*, its chef and owner, Alain Zick, shot himself.

The main business of the Michelin company, as almost everyone surely knows, is the making and selling of automobile tires, and the *Guide Michelin* may very well be the world's most successful promotional idea. This is the fundamental fact about the *Guide*. Its raison d'être is to encourage the motorist to tour on wheels—wheels preferably cushioned by Michelin tires. In the early days of the company, Michelin tire salesmen were ordered to check out, at company expense, the bistros and restaurants on the roads around the country. Their reports produced the

---

EDITOR'S NOTE: This article originally appeared in the July 1976 issue of *Esquire*.

first little *Guide Michelin* in 1900, which was given free by gas and repair stations to the then three thousand-odd motorists of France.

Each year the *Guide* was expanded. Its success was extraordinary. The Michelin Tire Company flourished. So did the roadside restaurants of France. Then André Michelin, one of the founders, began differentiating among restaurants, awarding a star to the better ones. Finally, in 1931, he developed the two promotional slogans that are perhaps the most successful in the history of product salesmanship. Some restaurants were given two stars and said to be "worth a detour"—worth a little extra use of your Michelin tires. A very few restaurants were given three stars, "worth a special trip"—worth quite a lot of wearing friction between the rubber and the road.

Today, of course, the checking of restaurants is done by a special corps of full-time, trained *inspecteurs*, who roll around France in their cars, transmitting their daily confidential reports back to headquarters like a kind of gastronomic secret service.

It's all done with supreme efficiency, and therein lies the reason the *Guide* today misses some of the better bets. An *inspecteur* calls for a reservation a few hours ahead of his visit, but he never orders any specialty that might require lengthy preparation. He operates on the assumption that he will want to continue his journey and cannot dally too long over his meal. When he arrives, he chooses only from the printed menu and expects to be served efficiently and fast. Each *inspecteur* has a daily quota of about twelve hotels and restaurants to inspect, and he covers roughly a hundred miles each day. After each restaurant visit, the *inspecteur* fills out a checklist, rating on a scale from zero to five such factors as the size of the portions, the speed of the service, the cleanliness of the table-cloth, the comfort of the chair, as well as the quality of the ingredients, the doneness of the meat, etc. The *inspecteur* makes no personal decisions as to the rating of the restaurant. The decisions are made by the editors in Paris on the basis of the documentation. The testimony of the point system is not to be challenged.

Michelin is conservative. The decor of the restaurants it lists must be restrained. The welcome must be traditionally correct. Michelin does not look with much favor on the new, lighter, so-called Low-High cuisine now being practiced by many of the Young Turk chefs. On the average, they are rated substantially lower than the traditional chefs. My strong impression is that the old men of Michelin are holding back, waiting to see whether this new cuisine will achieve popular approval beyond the acclaim it has already drawn from connoisseurs and professionals.

For its part, Michelin sets the rules for the restaurants. Each restaurant must obey or be ignored. The *inspecteurs* have internalized these rules to an absurd degree. After a superb dinner in the once-starred restaurant of a small hotel in central France, the owner joined me for coffee and related the "little incident" that had cost this restaurant its star:

"A few years ago, my father, a rather short-tempered man, was having an argument with his staff about money. He unfortunately lost his patience with them and suddenly one morning closed the restaurant, saying that he would not reopen it until they became more reasonable. On that precise day, as luck would have it, an important-sounding gentleman called up for a reservation for one for dinner. My father said he regretted that the restaurant would be closed for several days. There was a veritable explosion at the other end of the telephone. The voice said that he was an *inspecteur de Michelin* and that it was an inflexible Michelin rule that a restaurant which was stated to be open on Wednesday must be open on Wednesday. My father explained his staff problem. The imperious voice said that that had nothing to do with Michelin and that he would be required to report that the restuarant was not meeting its Michelin obligations. The following spring, our restaurant was dropped from the *Guide* and, over several years, was not reinstated. The problem, it seems, had nothing to do with our food."

Sometimes, admittedly, it goes the other way. At a country *auberge* in western France, the lovely young wife of the chef/owner told me that, a few months before my visit, an old gentleman with a very self-assured manner had made a telephone reservation for dinner and a room for one. At table, just as she was serving the terrine of crayfish, he became ill and could not eat. She helped him up to his room, brought up a tisane of mint tea and dosed him with aspirin. The next morning, recovered, he approached the front desk to pay his bill and noticed instantly that the dinner had not been charged. He insisted that he must pay for it. *"Non, non, m'sieur,"* said the lovely *patronne,* "you did not eat it." He produced his card: "I am an *inspecteur de Michelin* and our rules force me to pay for everything I order." The following spring, the *auberge* was elevated to two stars in the *Guide Michelin.*

For fifty years Michelin wrote its rules for restaurants and pretty well made them stick. Then came the first serious challenge. The second of the great French tire companies is La Société Pneumatique, Kléber-Colombes. Its president, coming out of a famous provincial restaurant after lunch while on a business trip across France, noticed a car drive up on Kléber-Colombes tires. But when the driver got out and walked into the restaurant, he was carrying the red *Guide Michelin* under his arm. Not good for the prestige of Kléber-Colombes! At that moment, the decision was made to bring forth a *Guide Kléber gastronomique.*

The man chosen to direct and edit the new *Guide Kléber* was Jean

Didier, an expert gastronome who was determined that his *Guide* would not be a carbon copy of the *Michelin* but would adopt new approaches to restaurant reviewing. Didier believes fiercely in personal judgments on gastronomic matters. He brought out his first edition in 1952 and has been slowly catching up with Michelin ever since. Not having the large Michelin budget, he does without a corps of traveling secret agents. Instead, he relies for most of his information on a constant stream of reports from "resident correspondents" in virtually every city and town of France, and they are encouraged to express their personal opinions. In his Paris office, he told me: "I have banished completely the word *inspecteur*. To me it smacks of police supervision. Our policy is to treat restaurateurs with respect for their independence and individuality. I would not dream of ignoring a good restaurant, or of dropping it from our pages, just because I had been personally irritated by some quirk of the proprietor."

Because it gathers its information on a local basis, the *Guide Kléber* has been steadily "discovering" more and more of the back-street bistros that are patronized by local businessmen and their families, where the top specialties of the chef and his best menus are generally ordered a day or two in advance. Didier also believes in leading his readers to small, off-the-beaten-track country restaurants that prepare the specialties of their regions. Traditional high cuisine is not his main concern. He strongly advises his readers to try the *nouvelle cuisine,* the new Low-High cuisine of the revolutionary young chefs. Because he is less conservative than Michelin, Didier moves faster almost all the time. In 1966, he gave his highest accolade to the restaurant of the brothers Jean and Pierre Troisgros, now almost universally accepted as the greatest restaurant of France. Meanwhile, Michelin struggled with itself for another two years, until 1968, before it could overcome its resistance to the simplicity of the Troisgros setting and award three stars. For its courage, as well as its clarity and speed of decision, I would not travel in France without the *Kléber* alongside the *Michelin* on the front seat of my car.

Then, just as the inevitable "battle of the guides" was becoming a fascinating sideshow to French gastronomic touring, there burst onto the scene a third major candidate for restaurant-rating honors. The brilliant and revolutionary French food critics Henri Gault and Christian Millau brought out their own restaurant guide, not quite as comprehensive as the others—claiming to cover only two thousand restaurants where the *Michelin* rates more than three thousand—but so sparkling with brilliant, brash, opinionated, satiric, and witty commentary that it seems almost to be thumbing its nose at its two predecessors. There was nothing for it, for me, on my recent tours of France, but to take along the three guides and continuously compare them. The results are very interesting indeed.

In Paris, if you ask any resident gastronome to name the single cuisinier who is consistently most dramatic, most exciting, most inventive, the chances are nine to one that the name would be Jacques Manière, the chef/owner of the small, bistro-style Le Pactole on the Boulevard Saint-Germain. Jean Didier found him in 1969 and awarded his restaurant the annual Challenge Prize of the *Guide Kléber* as the "discovery of the year." Naturally, we all raced to Le Pactole and were enchanted. Critic Naomi Barry wrote in 1969 that Manière's cooking was so extraordinary that "all the professional gastronomes of Paris are part of the Pactole clique." In 1974, Manière was discovered by Craig Claiborne, who called Le Pactole "perhaps the most frequently discussed and generally praised restaurant" in Paris and reported that the food "bordered on the sublime." Exactly one week later, Gael Greene jumped onto the bandwagon with the cry that Manière's food was "miraculous . . . haunting . . . spectacular," the work of a "gastronomic superstar." Last year [i.e., 1975], critic Joseph Wechsberg wrote that "serious eaters in Paris" regard Manière as "one of the most brilliant artists on the city's culinary stage," with one dish after another that is "a gastronomic masterpiece."

The *Kléber* gives Le Pactole the equivalent of two stars with the comment: "His cooking is a perpetual exaltation." The *Guide Gault-Millau* awards Manière its highest rating, equivalent to three stars, putting him in the same gastronomic league as all the top restaurants of Paris. Their comment is a hymn of praise: "A fabulous cuisine, audacious, fantastic, with incomparable excitement . . . inventive to the point of genius . . . Manière at his best is the greatest cuisinier in the world; even at his worst he is still very, very good." Yet for the *Michelin*, Jacques Manière does not exist. No stars. Not even a mention of his name in the smallest print.

Neither Manière nor Michelin will comment on this unbelievable blackout. But there are rumors around Paris about "the night of the duck." It is whispered that, one evening, an imperious gentleman came to Le Pactole to dine alone. He insisted that he must have Manière's famous duck with green peppercorns. Manière, with a full house, agreed to prepare it if the diner did not mind waiting for thirty minutes. The diner promised to wait, but after only fifteen minutes walked into the kitchen and started nagging Manière. The imperious gentleman got the hot duck and its green-pepper sauce in his face. In between gasps, he screamed: "I am an *inspecteur de Michelin!*" To which Manière replied: "I very much regret that fine duck."

On my latest visit to Paris, I checked up on the current status of Jacques' cuisine. After tasting and retasting his chicken steamed with crayfish and lobster, velvet calves' liver steamed with black truffles, scallops steamed under seaweed laid on a bed of black caviar butter, raw salmon with chives, I could not possibly have awarded him less than three stars. To be sure, Le Pactole is a very small restaurant, not particularly luxurious, not air-conditioned, with slightly rickety chairs and tables—factors that always loom large in the Michelin mind. But even in Michelin's terms, Jacques Manière deserves two stars.

At Le Restaurant Clovis, in the Hôtel Windsor, around the corner from the Arc de Triomphe, the chef de cuisine is Daniel Météry, thirty-year-old Young Turk of the *nouvelle cuisine*. Trained by the Troisgros brothers, by Paul Bocuse, and by Michel Guérard, at nineteen he won the national award as the Best Apprentice Cook of France. He also was chef saucier at Maxim's.

Jean Didier's *Klèber* awards Météry the rough equivalent of one star and praises his inventions of fish poached in cider vinegar and fricassee of chicken with lime juice. The *Gault-Millau* also gives him the equivalent of one star and praises his "cuisine full of inventiveness . . . which should soon conquer all of Paris." But for the *Michelin*, Météry does not exist. No stars. No mention of his name.

From my own visits, I remember with lip-smacking pleasure Météry's marvelously light and simple Low-High preparations of lobster swimming in a bouillon, scallops with saffron in their natural juices, and his quite marvelous *mirliton de Normandie*, an irresistible dessert layered with fruit, honey, and nuts. For these and the impressive luxury and modernity of his restaurant, another two stars forgotten by the *Michelin*.

If you drive across central France on the old main highway from Lyon to Tours, you pass through the minuscule village of St.-Gérand-le-Puy, where there is a tiny restaurant, housed in a former stable, owned and run by the greatest unknown chef of France, Lucien Sarrassat. When I dined with him not long ago, I ordered his famous crayfish in Champagne, and in my presence in the kitchen, he poured in a whole bottle of Champagne Dom Pérignon, worth about twenty-five dollars. This is one reason why he is known among the gastronomes of the nearby spa city of Vichy as "the madman perfectionist." He prints no menu. His clients telephone a couple of hours ahead and he tells them what has been brought in by his fishing and hunting friends, what cuts of magnificent

Charolais beef are hanging in his larder. At his eight tables it is custom cooking for connoisseurs.

The son of a local pastry chef who once worked under Escoffier at the Ritz, Lucien was apprenticed at the age of twelve to the great chef Rabette in the kitchen of the Majestic in Vichy. Lucien stayed seventeen years and rose to become *chef de cuisine.* Then he bought the tiny stable and converted it to Chez Sarrassat, which has remained unchanged for thirty-five years.

The *Guide Kléber* awards Sarrassat the equivalent of one star; the *Gault-Millau* awards him the equivalent of two. The *Michelin*, apparently, has never heard of him.

Every dish Lucien has ever served me over the past ten years remains vividly in my memory: his various Lyonnais sausages, for which he chops and works the meats entirely by hand, his partridge in Champagne, his memorable thyme-flavored red-wine sauce on steaks of wild boar, and his extraordinary dessert, the best *mille-feuilles* I have ever tasted in my life, which he beats like a jazz drummer with fans of six forks in each hand. In spite of the smallness and rustic simplicity of his eight-table dining room, I could not give him less than three stars for such cooking—three more to be added to the forgotten score of *Michelin.*

Right among the sand dunes of St.-Girons-Plage, on the southern Atlantic coast, you find what looks like a typical Cape Cod shore-dinner shed, called Au Rescapé, serving the superb cuisine of its cook and owner, Mimi Lensalade. She is one of France's best-kept gastronomic secrets. Her cooking is supreme in the region. Her fish are caught on the beach at her front door and can come to table fifteen minutes out of the sea. With her ducks and geese from local farmers she makes foie gras from the livers, the famous *lou magret* from the sliced breasts, pickled *confit* from the legs and wings, and extraordinary pâtés and rillettes, aromatic with the local herbs, from the rest of the body. Her meals are unforgettable in their earthy, natural sincerity.

The *Guide Kléber* awards her the equivalent of one star and *Gault-Millau* says, "Everybody along the Landais coast knows Mimi." The *Michelin* lists her in its smallest print but offers nary a star. After lunching on Mimi's spit-roasted duck hearts, I would wildly give her two stars. Oh, yes, I forgot Mimi's tart of plums with Armagnac *à la landaise.* It could easily put her up to two and a half stars.

There is the mysterious case of one of the great chefs of France, Georges Garin, who for more than thirty years owned and ran one of the finest restaurants of Paris, Chez Garin, with a steady two stars. The supreme skill of those hands produced dish after dish of wondrous clarity and precision: chiffonade of Breton lobster, roast woodcock with fresh truffles, gratin of crayfish. Two years ago, Georges, approaching retirement and hungry for warm southern sunshine, left Paris and opened his semi-retirement bistro, Le Lingousto, in the village of Solliès-Toucas in Provence. There those same hands are producing and serving his classic dishes, plus his new interpretations of some Provençal specialties.

Because Garin has moved, Michelin has stripped him of both his stars and lists him as if he were just an ordinary, unknown roadside grill. This is tantamount to saying that he is now too old to maintain his supreme skill. Obviously, from all the reports, this is pure nonsense. I somehow suspect that on my next visit with Georges I will find two more forgotten stars.

Another tantalizing mystery: Ten years ago, the Restaurant de la Côte d'Or, in the northern Burgundian village of Saulieu, was possibly the supreme three-star restaurant of France. It was owned and run by the chef universally acknowledged to be the greatest *maître de cuisine* since Escoffier, Alexandre Dumaine. About five years ago, when Dumaine retired and sold the restaurant to his young disciple Chef François Minot, Michelin at once conservatively reduced the stars to two. Minot was never able to win back that third star, and last year he sold La Côte d'Or. The new chef is a twenty-year-old Young Turk of the new Low-High cuisine, Bernard Loiseau, trained by the Troisgros brothers.

Both the *Kléber* and the *Gault-Millau* maintain La Côte d'Or's two stars. The *Michelin* has not only removed both the stars but has dropped the famous restaurant from the book. Can it be that they refuse to accept a young revolutionary of the *nouvelle cuisine?* When I have sampled Bernard Loiseau's new menu I may just find two more forgotten stars.

In the southwestern village of Urt is a country restaurant with the seductive name Ferme Napoléon (Napoleon's Farm). The twentieth-century Napoleon here is Chef Jean Néry, who, according to the reports, never fills in those annual questionnaires from guidebooks.

In spite of unanswered letters, Jean Didier of Kléber paid Néry a visit and awarded him the equivalent of one star with the comment: "Although Monsieur Néry apparently does not care about being in any guidebook, we crown him nevertheless for his superb *saumon en papillote* cooked over a smoky wood fire." Gault and Millau praised Néry in a magazine article as a "discovery of the year." But the unanswered questionnaire was an insuperable problem to Michelin. Chefs who do not answer Michelin's mail do not get into the book. I propose to seek an audience of the emperor to discover whether his crown should sparkle with one more forgotten star.

Chez Ruffet is a country bistro in the village of Jurançon, where the chef has the intriguing name Milou Larrouy. *Gault-Millau* awards him the equivalent of one star and says: "A charming old country house, delightfully simple, where one is served, at a price that is more than honest, regional specialties that are quite marvelous, on a menu that is astonishing in its abundance . . . with fresh foie gras flavored with apples, fish from the local river, breast of duck, wild mushrooms, local cheeses. . . ." Both *Kléber* and *Michelin* have missed Chez Ruffet. One more forgotten star?

Finally, I shall go back to a delightful and tiny bistro I discovered last year in the small town of Segonzac, in the Cognac country north of Bordeaux. It is a true back-street bistro, called La Cagouillarde, which can best be translated as The Snailery, because its *grande spécialité* is the *petit gris*, the local small snail of the Charentais region known as *la cagouille*. The chef is twenty-year-old Jean-Marie Colombier, who prepared for us a memorable one-star lunch. I'll admit my delight with La Cagouillarde was distinctly enhanced by the knowledge that it was my own discovery. I may just give La Cagouillarde three stars—one from each of my forgetful guidebooks.

I do greatly admire the *Guide Michelin*. For more than seventy-five years it has helped us all to eat and live better—an admirable record of service. And I have never found a really bad place falsely praised by Michelin. But it seems to be afraid of sending us to a small restaurant where the food is superb, the ambience very simple, rustic, and not luxuriously comfortable. This is a form of Victorian snobbery that may have been the fashion when André Michelin started his guide at the turn of the century but is no longer valid in these modern times, when an earthy naturalism is the order of the day. Remember that the *Michelin* is now a venerable seventy-six years old—an age when one prefers security to discovery, when one moves slowly, when one ponders before acting. This is the reason, I am quite sure, why all the restaurants above have been left in the shadow of oblivion by the forgotten stars of Michelin.

One final question, which I am often asked: Will there be, anytime soon, a *Guide Michelin* for the United States? That brings us right back to where we started—to the fundamental mission of the *Guide Michelin*. In 1968, the Michelin Tire Company of Lake Success, New York, made a formal announcement: "The Michelin steel-belted radial tire has been gaining in popularity since its introduction into the United States. . . . It is, therefore, inevitable that consideration would be given to a pub- lication for the United States." Good. But let them send some younger *inspecteurs,* and let them be a little more adventurous on this side of the Atlantic.

How to Get a Great Meal at a Great Restaurant

A famous British recipe for rabbit pie begins: "First catch your rabbit. . . ." The problem is the same in getting a great meal. First find your great restaurant. The search is not easy. For every truly great restaurant dedicated to the perfect service of superb food, there are a hundred where the chief concern is the dramatic manipulation of luxurious show. What is the use of a Honduras-mahogany pepper mill the size of a young cannon if the filet mignon being peppered is cold? How justifiable is it to flame the *faisan au foie gras à la Souvaroff* with specially doctored brandy to produce a fireball of H-bomb dimensions if the meat of the bird then tastes as if it had been soaked in nitroglycerin? What good is a side-table performance with a giant coffee machine as complex as the atom smasher at the Argonne Laboratories if the resultant potion is the kind used by the Borgias to get rid of their enemies?

For many years I have used a simple yardstick, a kind of instant measure of the sincerity or fraudulence of a restaurant. I call it my "fire-and-ice test."

I dined not too long ago in a Chicago restaurant much publicized for its luxury. So deep was the crimson carpet that it would have been a help to have had snowshoes to reach one's table. Sweet music came from an orchestra dressed, it seemed, in the uniform of the Czarist Cossack Guard. The menu came on yellowing sheets of parchment, handwritten in gold ink, about the size of one of Mao Tse-tung's wall posters. The

EDITOR'S NOTE: This article originally appeared in the July 1969 issue of *Esquire*.

prices were liable to be mistaken for the annual report of General Motors.

The names on the page seemed to be flickering in a golden light and I was shocked to find myself surrounded by massive flames. At the table to the left, a dish of crabs Casanova was blazing mightily. To the right, a roast guinea hen was afire from stem to stern. In front, a burnt offering of crêpes Suzette. Behind, bacon-wrapped oysters glowing on a sword. And in all directions, flaming cups of *café diable*.

The captain now approached, bowing as if he were trying to kiss my feet. In his tailcoat of midnight blue, I mistook him, at first glance, for the Earl of Snowdon. He was flanked, in military formation, by six waiters. Almost kneeling, they begged me to begin with the *grande spécialité de la maison:* a salad of hearts of palm, Chinese water chestnuts, capers, and bananas, with an Oriental spice dressing.

My order taken, the captain and his escort backed off, bowing at each retreating step. As they neared a table engulfed in sheets of flame, I feared that they would all be incinerated.

A long time passed. Then the silver-plated kitchen doors opened, and a line of gleaming wagons moved slowly to my table. Busboys stood at attention. The first wagon carried such a load of ice it looked like a model of the North Pole. Resting on it was a boat-shaped silver dish, carved and fluted as if it had come from the workshop of Benvenuto Cellini. And there was my salad, arranged as a tropical garden. As the captain placed it before me, the orchestra was stilled. Surely, as I lifted the first taste to my mouth, they would break into the Triumphal March from *Aïda.* It felt like an epic moment in the annals of gastronomy.

There was only one flaw. The salad was, if not exactly hot enough to burn my tongue, considerably above the overheated temperature of the room. The principal ingredients had, obviously, just been taken out of cans stored on shelves in the hottest part of the kitchen. Clearly, they had not had any serious contact with the ice. At this warm temperature, the four ingredients exactly canceled each other out, while the peppery red dressing gave the whole thing the ambience of a Texas barbecue.

For one of the later courses, I had ordered a bottle of Champagne. It, too, was rolled in on a gleaming wagon, the bottle resting horizontally on top of—not immersed in—a crushed iceberg. Half a dozen waiters then went through a performance worthy of the Bolshoi Ballet. The glasses were sluiced with ice and twirled with napkins. The bottle was picked up by one waiter, ceremoniously wiped by a second, the seal removed by a third, the cork drawn by a fourth. . . . When the Champagne was poured, it was just below boiling.

Finally the proprietor joined me over the Borgia-type coffee. I asked him whether he didn't agree that a great restaurant could hardly merit that adjective if it placed all the emphasis on show at the expense of the food? Surely elegance symbolized by fire and ice was fake elegance?

The proprietor was in a candid mood. He admitted the melancholy truth, but neatly flicked the blame onto the shoulders of his customers. He described the new generation of expense-account patrons:

"They spend lavishly on food and drink as a status symbol. They know almost nothing about gastronomy, but they are uniformly delighted and impressed by ostentatious service. They don't understand a word of the menu, so they ignore it. They look around the dining room and if they see a table in flames, or an attention-getting bottle the size of the Eiffel Tower, they say: 'Give me what that guy's having.' They think *boeuf à la mode* is something with ice cream on top. They wouldn't lower themselves to order the *plat du jour*, even if it were the best thing in the house. We have to serve our customers what they demand. A restaurant, after all, is a profit-making business. If they want to buy a show for a customer or a girl friend, we'll send them that. It isn't an idea that the restaurants have dreamed up. It's a crazy by-product of our crazy times."

All this is buncombe. There have always been (and always will be) restaurants fraudulently catering to fools.

The truly great restaurant—where the total concentration is on perfect quality and impeccable service—is one of the unifying factors of the world. One can dine in one of these establishments anywhere on earth, with the assurance that the food and the service will be entirely consistent. Once you have learned to find your way through the menu and to get your way with the staff while ordering, say, *le loup de mer des golfes flambé au fenouil et au Ricard* at La Mirabelle in New York, or *le veau à l'ananas au Kari, sauce hollandaise* at Le Gavroche in London, or a *filet de turbot dugléré* at Prunier's in Paris, or the *faison brabançonne* at La Couronne in Brussels, or the *coeur de filet Empereur* in the Borgia Room of the Hostaria dell' Orso in Rome, you will feel at home in any great restaurant from Madrid to Madras, from Beirut to Bangkok. The menu (apart from a few local specialties) will be in French and punctuated with *les plats classiques*. The wine list will be as invariable as the rising of the sun. The chefs, busboys, waiters, captains, maîtres d'hôtel (even if they are charming and attentive Orientals) will most likely have been trained in Paris or Geneva and will most certainly speak fluent French and English. The rules of the great eating game are the same everywhere. And this is the essence of the matter. There are rules. They must be learned.

To begin, there are some hard facts to be faced. A great and successful restaurant is a very profitable business venture, a high-pressure supermarket of cooked foods where every member of the service staff is a skilled salesman. The attack on the customer's sales resistance begins with the maître d'hôtel at the door of the dining room. This gentleman is no longer (as the romantic writers are so fond of describing him) a dodderingly dignified figure with the face of a scholarly marquis who expresses his degree of respect for the regular customers by the depth of his bow. The twentieth-century maître d'hôtel is a calculating technician, a cross between Sherlock Holmes and a professional mind reader. He has developed a special skill, which the Germans call *Fingerspitzgefühl*, a virtually untranslatable word that means, in effect, that he has radar beams radiating from his fingertips. During the five seconds or so that you are walking toward him, he is assessing you in microscopic detail, from the assurance of your step to the authority of your voice. Immediately he places you in one of four categories of customers. You become either a Skunk, a Monkey, a Lion, or a Tiger.

This rating system of the clientele is a fact of life in all the great and fashionable restaurants of the major cities (above all, in New York and Paris). The restaurant is benefited by certain types of guests and injured by others. Beautiful women and handsome men, superbly well dressed, lift the gaiety and pleasure of the entire dining room. Others are neutral and nondescript and will profitably pad out the far corners. Yet others will depress the room and must be rigorously excluded. These are the Skunks.

However, if you appear well enough dressed, well enough behaved and with a wallet pocket that bulges suitably, or if the maître d'hôtel simply decides that you are an unknown quantity worth the risk, you become a Monkey.

The name originated in the thirties at El Morocco, where the less desirable guests were seated in the crimson-curtained back room, which was known to the staff as the Monkey House. There was a similar room at "21," known among the waiters as the Dog House, with a separately printed menu offering only a few of the less exotic dishes and each of these at exactly double the price charged in the main dining room.

In judging Monkeys, restaurateurs are not infallible. Henri Soulé, the late proprietor of the once-famous Le Pavillon, admitted a bad mistake. Two ladies came in for lunch. They did not impress him particularly. He led them to a faraway table deep in Siberia where they sat down without protest. He was faintly surprised when they did not consult him about the menu but immediately ordered *quenelles de brochet à la Nantua*. When they left, the taller of the two said to Soulé: "You have a nice restaurant. It's a pity that you don't know your New York." A few minutes after they had gone, he learned that it was the former Mrs. Nelson Rockefeller.

This matter of seating is of supreme importance in getting a great meal. Roger Chauveron, the owner of Le Café Chauveron, likes to say that every table in his restaurant is desirable, but some are a good deal more desirable than others. The seating arrangements at any great restaurant are as arbitrary as the pew list for a Royal Coronation at Westminster Abbey.

The curious fact is that all social lions want to see and be seen as they dine. They do not want to eat in comfortable privacy in an inner room. The most sought-after tables are those virtually in the entrance lobby where there is continuous traffic. The small corner table nearest the front door of The Colony was always reserved for the Vanderbilts whenever they wanted it. Marlene Dietrich preferred to sit at a tiny and uncomfortable table in the center of the floor of the entrance room, where she could greet and be greeted as people passed in and out. The favorite table of the Duke and Duchess of Windsor at Le Pavillon was so close to the front door that their Royal Highnesses received a blast of cold air every time it revolved.

You will never achieve one of these desirable tables if you are classified as a Monkey. The maître d'hôtel will lead you to a back-of-the-room table "in Siberia." There, he will convey his opinion of you to the captain by a lifted eyebrow signal and as a result, you will receive less than the best service, and though you may get a good meal, it will not be a great one and you will pay more than the people sitting at the best tables.

Some Monkeys panic when they see the menu prices and try to extricate themselves with some such remark as: "I'm not very hungry. I'll take an omelet, but make it a little on the raw side." Or: "Could I get a hamburger? But I prefer it *bien cuit.*"

The best tables are filled by the Lions and Lionesses. These star guests are on the most-wanted list of any great restaurant anywhere. They bring with them prestige and publicity by their newsworthy names, by the influence of their business, political or social positions, or simply by the revolting size of their bank accounts. I am told that one visit by Jackie Kennedy to any top New York restaurant, duly reported the next day in the gossip columns, is worth $10,000 in new business. If she comes back two or three times, the place is permanently jammed. So it's hardly surprising that Lions get the best tables, the most efficient waiters, and the best food at what amounts to discount prices.

So much for Lions, Monkeys and Skunks. The fourth—and most important—category of restaurant diner is the Tiger. The best definition of who and what he is was given me one night when dining in New Orleans on a *coeur de filet de boeuf marchand de vins* with Roy Alciatore, the owner of Antoine's, the greatest regional restaurant in the U.S.

He was talking about the Louisiana Lions (a temperamental and demanding cross-section of the old Southern families at the turn of the century) who had made the restaurant famous under his grandfather, Antoine, and his father, Jules. "Today," he said, "our clientele has changed. Our name is so well known nationally that we are largely filled by gastronomically innocent tourists."

Although some two hundred superb dishes are listed on the still-magnificent menu, nine out of ten guests order the oysters à la Rockefeller, the pompano *en papillotte*, or one of the other overpublicized and somewhat overrated specialties. "But," continued Alciatore, "the people we most enjoy serving are the knowledgeable gourmets with finely developed tastes and a sharp judgment of our cuisine. They make demands on us. They pick up the captains and waiters on the slightest laxity of service. They send dishes back to the kitchen with critical messages to the chef. They keep a restaurant great. We only wish there were more of them."

This is the perfect definition of a restaurant Tiger: a patron without public name or influential position, but with the knowledge and assurance to dominate any restaurant and to bring out the best that is in it. And the beauty of it is that the art of Tigermanship can be learned by almost anyone. It takes reasonable intelligence, an average degree of social grace, some well-cut clothes, a few spare dollars, a period of steady practice, and the right information. What follows here is a short basic course.

FIRST FIND YOUR GREAT RESTAURANT

The surest way to find a great restaurant is through the personal advice of a first-class gourmet who dined there the night before. This time element is crucial. Beware of the man who sends you to a "marvelous little place" he knew two years ago. A truly great restaurant is always delicately balanced on a peak of perfection. It can lose its chef (or be sold to a crass new owner) and a few months will find it in the wide valley of mediocrity. If you can ask a local member of one of the great international wine and food societies, you are on safe ground. The French-oriented Confrérie des Chevaliers du Tastevin has chapters in many major cities. In London, there is the Wine and Food Society; in Paris, Le Club des Cent. Members of such organizations, if they can be reached, can give impeccable advice.

Failing this, one turns to the more trustworthy gastronomic guides to the major eating areas of the world. The best, not surprisingly, are written in French, by Frenchmen, for French tourists. They can be specially ordered from any bookshop that deals in foreign editions. Once you have found an interesting and readable gastronomic guide, take it to bed with you and study it as if your life depended on it.

If all advance planning is impossible—if you suddenly land in a strange city, without friends and without guides—say a prayer and ask around. I once landed in Amsterdam at nine in the evening, at the peak of the tourist season, hungry and without a hotel reservation. In the airport terminal building, I walked to the car-rental desk. An intelligent and charming young man began writing out my contract for an Opel Kapitan. On a sudden hunch I said to him: "If, in the next few minutes, you met the most beautiful and desirable girl in the world and she said yes, yes, yes to everything you asked, where would you take her to dinner this evening and where would you stay the night?" He laughed, thought for a couple of minutes, then wrote on a slip of paper the names of three restaurants and two hotels. I went to the nearest telephone booth. The first of the hotels gave me a room overlooking the Prinsengracht Canal on the top floor of a converted sixteenth-century house. I have been back there a dozen times and would never dream of staying anywhere else in Amsterdam. A telephone call to the second restaurant on the list, an Indonesian bistro, established that it would be open until two A.M. and that a table would gladly be reserved. The bistro turned out to be a small place on a short and narrow back street near the docks, frequented by Indonesian seamen. It served me an unquestionably great forty-dish *rijst-tafel*. Three days later, I had another *rijsttafel* at the most expensive and glamorous Indonesian restuarant of midtown Amsterdam. The bistro's was better!

ZEROING IN ON THE TARGET

It is suicidal to make the first visit to a great restaurant without a reservation. It is almost equally fatal simply to call and make a reservation for "Mr. John Smith." The result will be a table in the darkest far corner, probably behind massed potted palms next to the kitchen service door and attended by an apprentice-waiter who may spill hot consommé down your neck.

A young couple I know was driving through Connecticut one evening and suddenly decided to dine at the Stonehenge Inn. The owner of that gastronomic paradise, Albert Stockli, although he hates to admit it, has an uncontrollable antipathy to loud checked shirts. My friend was wearing one. Trying not to look at the shirt, Stockli regretted that no table was available. This was a true statement.

The couple drove down the road to the nearest phone booth. The young husband dialed the Stonehenge, changed his voice slightly and asked for a reservation. Within the five minutes intervening, two parties had left, so he got his reservation immediately. Back at the inn, the young man said to Stockli: "I talked to you on the phone. Remember? Now we have a reservation." Stockli, who admires a good politician when he sees one, gave the young couple a highly desirable table and sent them a bottle of '62 Mercier Réserve de l'Empereur with his compliments.

Before you lift the phone to make a reservation, work out your personal ploy. Never call as yourself. Either change your voice slightly, or have someone call for you, saying that he or she is the executive assistant of Mr. John Smith, who is . . . You must work out not more than five words to establish the importance of your business and/or social position. You could, for example, be the president of the International Resting House Corporation. (There is always a lot of noise at the restaurant end of the telephone and misunderstandings are conveniently frequent.) Or it might be said that you are the brother of the Ambassador of the Republic of Roaringtania. Pick your own titles.

The most outrageous ploy in restaurant history was used by A. J. Liebling during the time of U.S. Prohibition when he was doing a gastronomic tour of Burgundy. Through a friend he started the rumor that he, Liebling, was an American millionaire bootlegger, who had come to Burgundy to buy wines in order to stock a transatlantic liner as a fabulous "bateau cave" that would eventually be sailed to New York, then hoisted like a lifeboat out of the water and moved at dead of night into a specially built skyscraper with a false hinged front. On that basis, Liebling got to eat more great meals and drink more great wines in a month than most people are able to command in their entire lifetime.

When speaking to the maître d'hôtel, be sure to gabble all the names and titles at high speed and in a lofty tone of such assurance as to imply that it is simply inconceivable that the maître d'hôtel does not already know all about Mr. Smith. If he asks for any of the names to be repeated, ignore him and proceed at once to the second part of the message: "Mr. Smith is considering dining with you, but before he decides he would like to see your menu. We will send a messenger within the next thirty minutes. Please give him copies of both your luncheon and dinner menus. Then perhaps we'll call you back and make a reservation." Sometimes the maître d'hôtel is so impressed that he offers to send his own messenger. Do not accept, unless you are living in the most luxurious apartment building in the city, or are staying at the most expensive hotel. Send your messenger. Sharpen your red pencil.

Although, of course, it is not absolutely essential to do it every time, sending for the menu in advance does achieve two important objectives. You have established John Smith's name at the restaurant. You will be able to analyze the menu in your own time.

THE LANGUAGE OF A GREAT MENU

The menu tells you a great deal about the restaurant and its owner. First, its physical appearance. It should be a simple card, or single folder, quite light to hold and it should not be enclosed in any sort of fancy cover. If it is oversized or overheavy—if it looks like a leather-bound book, embossed or encrusted with gold, or if it has any tricky gimmicks about it— begin sniffing the air for a tourist trap. Next, the general appearance of the text. Is it clearly printed in an orderly arrangement? Are the *spécialités de la maison* made to stand out, either in different-colored ink, or written in by hand, or in a box, or under a special heading? Above all (and this is crucial), there must be no explanatory paragraphs describing the dishes in salesman's terms. If such nonsense appears on your menu, cancel your plans at once. A great restaurant must assume that its customers know the elements of high cuisine. (It is normal, of course, at any restaurant to ask the captain to describe a dish with which you are unfamiliar.)

Faced by a new menu, in leisurely relaxation, I take my red pencil and begin to mark it. First, I cross out all the dishes which I never eat in a restaurant. When I place myself under the gastronomic care of a great kitchen, I want to taste dishes that are the product of the brilliant skill of its staff. I do not want things that come out of a can or that I could prepare for myself in two minutes at home. Among the hors d'oeuvres, I am not interested in *le demi pamplemousse,* half a grapefruit. Or *les sardines à h'uile,* a couple of sardines. For the same reason, I never order caviar or pâté de foie gras in a restaurant. Nor am I much interested in a plain "bifteck," such as "le Sirloin," or "le T-Bone," since these are my more-or-less regular fare at home. I apply the same considerations to every dish on the menu, down to the last dessert.

I have now usually eliminated about one-third of the menu and the dishes that remain are of two types: the *spécialités de la maison* and the universal preparations of *la haute cuisine.* On my first visit to a great restaurant, I try to balance my dinner between the two. The chef and his staff are on trial. I am willing to let them give me some new experiences, but the measure of their skill lies in their approach to perfection in the classic dishes. One of the best tests is a *petite marmite Henri IV,* the marvelous clear bouillon with a taste precisely balanced between beef, oxtail, chicken, and aromatic vegetables, all entwined with the delicacy of fresh herbs. Other classic tests are a simple *poulet rôtie à l'anglaise*, a *sauce béarnaise*, or a *boeuf au Chambertin*, with exactly the right quality of vintage wine.

Now you are ready to lift the telephone and again call the maître d'hôtel. Once more the "executive assistant" speaks for John Smith, saying that the big man is pleased by the menu and wishes to reserve. . . .

THE ARRIVAL OF THE TIGER

Punctuality in arriving at a great restaurant is more important than at a private dinner party. The hostess is sure of her guests, even when they are a few minutes late. Restaurants get dozens of reservations every week from punks who neither show up, nor have the decency to call and cancel. No restaurant can be expected to hold a table (especially for a new and unknown customer) longer than thirty minutes. I avoid arriving five minutes early. That gives the maître d'hôtel the excuse to ask me to wait at the bar. Many inferior restaurants use this trick to increase bar profits. I absolutely refuse to play their game. If the maître d'hôtel insists that my table is not ready, I demand that my party be seated on chairs in the lobby away from the bar, and I stick out my long legs to make sure that as many people as possible trip over them. This almost always ensures a table within a couple of minutes.

As soon as you are seated, you can begin to judge how you are being rated by what happens next. If the maître d'hôtel bows and departs, leaving matters in the hands of the captain, you are being rated at about C. If the maître d'hôtel stays and offers to discuss the menu, you are around B. If, however, the proprietor appears suddenly from nowhere, is introduced by the maître d'hôtel and offers to help, you have achieved A.

Next, you face a thorny and controversial question. If you order high-proof cocktails, your rating is immediately and substantially diminished. I once saw Piero Fassio, the proprietor of the Blue Fox in San Francisco, when he heard an order for double Martinis all around, turn his head and stride away. On the other hand, if you order low-alcohol apéritifs (my invariable favorites: dry Spanish sherry, vermouth Cassis, or Kir), you have taken the first step toward being accepted as a gastronomic brother.

THE HUNGRY TIGER COMPOSES THE GREAT MEAL

As soon as the menus are in hand, I always say: "Give us a few minutes to consider." Although I have analyzed the menu earlier in the day, I now check it carefully for any last-minute changes. Perhaps a new *plat du jour,* or a *plat bourgeois,* has been written in by hand. I make firm proposals to my guests. I have nothing but disrespect for the host who sits back and says to each gueest: "What would you like?" He is evading his responsibility as a gourmet and will never compose a great meal. How can he possibly plan the wines if one person is eating chicken and another, venison? Yet an important part of the special ambience of a great restaurant is the luxurious multiplicity of superlative choices and I try to keep them all dangling as I nod to the captain to indicate that I am ready to order. I never do so at once. First, I start a discussion with him and invite his suggestions. If this is our first meeting, the conversation is crucial and potentially high-pressure. To gain the true cooperation and respect of this man, one must understand the conflicting psychological forces that drive him.

His job compels him, first, to be a salesman. Early this morning, the owner (or manager) of the restaurant started his working day by going to the kitchen to inspect the cold-storage larders and confer with the chef. They reviewed what foods were left over, how they would be served up and presented to the customers, and how urgently they had to be sold. Obviously, the stewed *boeuf à la mode française* will hold (and even improve) for several days; the *salade de crabe à la mayonnaise* will not. Together, owner and chef plan the "hard-sell dishes" of the day. The owner moves to the dining room, where the service staff is assembled, captains in front, and gives instructions on which dishes to push.

To counter this form of pressure the Tiger must not allow himself to be confused. Instead, he must appeal to the other, more idealistic side of the captain's nature. Certainly, if he thinks that the customer is a sucker, he will never give him an even break! But the moment the captain realizes that he is facing a Tiger gourmet, determined to compose a truly great meal, he rises at once to his own pride in his skill and devotion to the traditions of fine service. He feels a sense of participation in a rare adventure. He begins ministering to a pleasure he understands. He is won over.

There have been dozens of occasions when an enthusiastic captain has advised me, even against the interests of his employer, as to the state of the kitchen and the larder. He has been in and out of the kitchen all day. He has overheard the chef swearing at the rump of veal. He is aware of the traps behind some of the fancy names on the menu.

I remember once asking about the *côte de veau grand'mère à la mode périgourdine*. *"Oh non, m'sieur,"* whispered the captain, "the veal was tough this morning." I asked about the *canard bigarade au Grand Marnier*. *"Non, m'sieur,"* he said, "there were no fresh ducks this morning, so we are using frozen."

A truly great meal is almost impossible without this happy cooperation. How to achieve it? The first essential is to establish your authority. There are some ploys that may help.

You suggest that the meal might very well be started with some *ikra.* If the captain admits that he does not know what that is, you draw yourself up and, in your most austere and superior voice, point out that the word "caviar" does not exist in the Russian language. While he is momentarily off-balance, you plunge in with a question about what kind of caviar they have in stock. You let him know that you understand precisely the differences between Beluga, the name for the very large eggs from a sturgeon often more than twelve feet long, Ocietrova, the medium-sized eggs from a fish about six feet long, and Sevruga, the small eggs from a fish about four feet long. Finally, you slam down your advantage by asking point-blank how many ounces of caviar the restaurant serves per portion (it should be about two ounces). At this point, not intending to order caviar anyway, I say that the caviar is obviously unsatisfactory and proceed to order something else.

Yet, although ploys may be useful tools, there is no "instant method," no quick, slick, or trick way to gain the cooperation and respect of the staff of a great restaurant. You must simply have done your homework. You must be able to prove that you know as much (or more) about food and wine as does the captain. Like a jigsaw puzzle, piece by piece (usually starting with the main entrée and balancing the earlier and later courses against it), the parts of the great meal are fitted together. The pressure relaxes. But if the greatness is to be consummated, continuous vigilance is essential at each succeeding step.

HOW TO AVOID DROWNING IN THE WINE

Although this may sound to be heresy, I do not believe that a great meal demands the accompaniment of very great wines. Some great restaurants with outstanding cellars list wines of such rare and extraordinary vintages, of such complexity and subtlety of flavor—sometimes of such dominance and power—that they can completely overshadow the food. A superbly great wine does not accompany the food—the food has to be chosen to accompany the wine. For example, nothing brings out the qualities of a rare vintage red Bordeaux or Burgundy more than a piece of Swiss Bagne cheese. Nothing does more for a great white Graves, or a Montrachet, or a Corton-Charlemagne than the simplest of poached white fish, with the gentlest of Sauce Mousseline. An exceptional red Rhône is best brought out with goat cheese. Great vintage Port is never better than with freshly shelled walnuts. And as to the rich Moselle and Rhine wines of the greatest years, they are best sipped slowly by themselves, after a carefully planned light and small dinner. Hardly the ingredients of a great restaurant meal! Another point is that the true appreciation of such very rare wines requires a quiet and contemplative atmosphere, not the gay and noisy hubbub of public dining.

Finally, since a restaurant has to add to the price of a bottle a share of the storage and service costs, great wines can be extremely expensive on restaurant wine lists. In New York, the price is often five times the retail tag of the same bottle in a wine store. A noble wine at $20 in the store may be $100 in the restaurant. In Paris, the markup is about four times. In London and other major European cities, about three times.

But whatever the wines chosen, one must maintain absolute discipline over the sommelier, or wine steward, as to the classic rules for the service at table. They are founded on the practical experience of a thousand years, yet it is surprising how often they are broken by even the best of restaurants.

When it is time to serve the first wine, the sommelier brings the unopened bottle, so that the label (and especially the vintage year) can be verified and the seal checked for leakage. The bottle is opened in your presence and you are immediately handed the cork for inspection as to security and for smelling as to moldiness or mustiness. If you have any doubts, voice them at once. The sommelier then pours a small quantity (usually about an ounce and a half) into the host's glass and stands, bottle in hand, awaiting approval. Note whether the glass is the right shape and size for this wine. Swirl it around in the glass, inhale the bouquet; taste, judge, and check the temperature. Take your time. In normal circumstances, I spend about five seconds on the tasting, before either nodding my approval or refusing the wine. If it is acceptable, but too warm, I send it back to the cooler. If it is too cold, I suggest to my guests that they warm their glasses with the palms of their hands.

When the second wine is to be served, the waiter must remove the first glass, but if there is still wine left in it, he must ask: "Do you wish to finish your wine?" The empty bottle is left at the table, in case there is any later query. I never hesitate to ask for the label to be soaked off for my files.

At the end of the dinner, when the coffee has been served, the assumption, in a great restaurant, is that the conversation among the diners is now mellow and philosophical and that it should not be interrupted. So the waiters do not normally clear the last of the wine glasses or the empty brandy snifters, but stand aloof, unless called, until the host signals the end by asking for the check.

The final and absolute rule is that you should drink exactly what you like and should not allow yourself to be influenced by any considerations of prestige or status, even in the greatest of restaurants. When John F. Kennedy was a Senator and sometimes dined at a great Manhattan restaurant, he occasionally ordered a glass of milk. A pint bottle was brought to the table neatly hidden in a small silver bucket of ice.

HOW TO FIGHT WITHOUT ACTUALLY DRAWING BLOOD

Now the food begins to come to the table and the blade of one's judgment is removed from its sheath. Again, the rules for serving are classic and there is every sound and practical reason for seeing to it that they are maintained. The food is brought to a side table for "finishing" and serving, not for the purpose of putting on a huge and flaming dramatic show, but to allow the diner to control the final arrangements. The captain presents the dish and waits for the host to nod his approval and give his instructions. There may be a choice of rare or medium, light or dark, etc. The vegetables, garnishes, and sauces are served individually, after the plate has been placed before the diner, so that he can control the exact amounts. When everyone is properly served, the maître d'hôtel should appear, look over the entire table, and bow to the host, signifying that the service is up to the standard of the restaurant. Then, the moment of truth. Is it up to my standard?

Nothing will more quickly build your prestige with this restaurant—nothing will more solidly ensure that you get better and better service each time you come—than the proof that you can recognize within the first two mouthfuls any mistake or fault of slapdash preparation. If you have ordered the *terrine de canard sauvage et de faisan truffé*, and if it comes padded out with veal and ham and mushrooms, you call over the captain and send the offending dish back to the kitchen. When you order *tournedos à la Rossini*, and find that the slices of paté de foie gras and black truffle on top of the filet mignon have been replaced by a tired piece of liver sausage and a mushroom, you refuse it.

If there is one thing that American restaurants lack, it is customers with courage enough to send back mediocre food. Yet one must be secure in one's judgment. The brash young man who, to show off to his girl friend, sends everything back, will be (and should be) put on the Skunk list of that particular restaurant the following day. Equally unacceptable is the man who eats half the dish—and then sends it back. He makes himself ridiculous.

Sending a dish back, of course, also disorganizes the tight kitchen timing of the meal. If you return a soup or an omelet, you must expect to wait about fifteen minutes for a replacement. To replace fried or grilled meats, or grilled fish, or roasted chicken, or a cheese soufflé, you will have to wait about thirty minutes. For a complicated *plat composé*, often as much as fifty minutes.

I remember giving a farewell dinner for a friend who was leaving for several years of work in Europe. The hors d'oeuvres, the soup, and the fish were perfect. The entrée was to be *le carré d'agneau aux primeurs*, with the lamb lean and pink. When it was served, it was running in fat, grossly overcooked and instead of being prepared *aux primeurs* (with fresh garden vegetables), it was *à la languedocienne* (slathered in garlic butter). I sent it back. It could not be replaced in less than forty-five minutes so we changed to a cold *caneton rôti en tranches en gelée de son jus*.

The desert was to be a *soufflé flambé aux marrons*, accompanied by a Champagne Dom Pérignon. As soon as the soufflé was presented, we saw that it was severely overcooked. We mentioned this to the captain, who agreed at once, but asked us to taste it. The crust was thick and hard. The inside was almost as firm as a cake. I sent it back. We were so disgusted that we refused to wait for any replacement, but ordered fruit and cheese. The wine steward came to open the Champagne. I told him that we no longer wanted it, but would change to a Port with the cheese.

Quickly he took off the seal from the Champagne bottle and said: "You see, *m'sieur*, it is already opened."

I simulated a voice of cold fury: "You may open it if you wish, Victor, but I have not the slightest intention of paying for it."

He half-threw the bottle back into the ice bucket in such a way that my friend's wife was slightly splashed. I turned the restaurant inside out and had the proprietor at my table in one minute flat. He offered abject apologies and canceled all charges for the dinner.

I did not "never go there again." It was obviously an unlucky night. My good relations with the owner and the chef (who came out to apologize the next time I was in for lunch) were cemented by this adversity. It is still a great restaurant.

HOW TO CHECK THE CHECK WITHOUT GIVING THE APPEARANCE OF BEING UNABLE TO AFFORD THE PRICE

There is much less opportunity for a restaurant to overcharge for a great meal than there is for a plumber to overcharge for the repair of a toilet. The precise price of every dish chosen (plus any cover or service charge) is clearly printed on the menu. The main problem, when the check comes, is psychological. By the time the second Cognac has been finished and the diners have all relaxed into a rosy state of euphoria, there is an atmosphere of such pampered luxury that any cold question of accounting is an insulting sour note. The late Fernand Point, owner of the famous Restaurant de la Pyramide, once told me at the end of a supreme meal: "For such a dinner one does not ask the price." This is restaurant propaganda. One *does* ask the price. And one makes sure that no improper charges have been included and that the addition is sincere. Yet despite my care, I admit that I have been fooled.

This happened in Venice, where I went to lunch at a small *taverna* on the Bacino di San Marco with my dog, Ñusta. (Venice is nice to dogs; they are allowed in everywhere.) I took a table on the covered terrace overlooking the canal. The maître d'hôtel took my order, then said: "And your dog, *signor*, what would she like?" I avoid feeding Ñusta in public places. I don't want her to get into the habit of looking for food. So I tried to fob him off by saying, "Oh, she doesn't care about eating." A few minutes later, I was surprised to see all the fuss made over the dog. First, a napkin was placed on the floor in front of her. Then she was served, in a silver bowl, consommé containing slivers of prosciutto. Then, spaghetti with bits of fish on a silver platter. Finally, cubes of steak covered with melted butter. Ñusta loved it all. When she had finished, the waiter wiped her mouth with the napkin.

I drank up my coffee and asked for the check. The total was staggering. I called over the maître d'hôtel and said: "Is this mine?"

"Yes, *signor*, that is your correct bill."

I pointed out that I had had the *zuppa di verdura* at 200 lire and the *fegato alla veneziana* at 650.

He agreed.

Then what was this *prosciutto in brodo* at 450? And this *spaghetti alle vongole* at 450? And this *filletti San Pietro al burro* at 900? And why are there two cover charges?

"For the dog, *signor*."

"For the dog?"

"*Sì, signor.*"

My lunch cost 1,000 lire. Nusta's almost 2,000. The waiter insisted that I had ordered it. I had to pay.

HOW TO TIP LIKE A TIGER AND LEAVE LIKE A LION

When the great dinner comes to its rosy end and one is troubled by the high cost of the tips, there is a consoling thought in remembering how many people were involved in the magnificent occasion. You were ushered in by the doorman, your coats taken by the hatcheck girl, led to the table by the maître d'hôtel, order taken by the captain, apéritifs poured by the barman, serviced by two waiters and probably three bus-boys, the wine bottles found by the cellar steward and served by the sommelier, your food ordered from the market by the kitchen steward, its storage controlled by the *garde-manger*, its preparation supervised by the *chef de cuisine* and various parts cooked by five *sous-chefs* and perhaps three apprentice assistants, your dishes washed and pans cleaned out by five *plongeurs*, your check prepared by a cashier, the whole place run by a manager and/or a proprietor. Thus, your dinner required the services of thirty people. The average in a great restaurant is about one employee for every three diners.

The first principle of tipping, I am convinced, should be that the tip reflects the degree of the diner's satisfaction with the service. I do not agree that the tip should be a fixed 15 percent added to the bill without a moment's thought. If the service has been less than perfect, the tip might be 12½ percent or even 10 percent. Restaurant proprietors, when they speak frankly, agree that a variable tip makes for better all-around service. If you add the tip to your bill, remember that the waiter gets it all, even though the captain did a large part of the work.

If you want the captain to receive a part of your general tip, you write the amount on the check and indicate "P.P." (*pour partager*, to be divided) against it. On this basis, if the service was good, add a tip of 20 percent. On the other hand, if the captain has performed special services, I may leave off the "P.P.," so that the waiter gets the whole of the write-in tip. Then I tip the captain separately, usually one dollar for each person served. The sommelier gets one dollar for each bottle. I think it unnecessary to tip the maître d'hôtel at each visit since he shares the captain's tip, but if I am a regular customer, I give him something special at holidays and at the start of his vacation.

I am strongly opposed to overtipping. All of us have seen an overrich and overfoolish man leaving a great restaurant in a green snowstorm of dollar bills. Waiters are glad, of course, to make an extra-fast buck, but they hardly respect the overtipper. The next time he comes in, he gets exactly what he deserves: extra-deep bows and a lot of showy servility, but less, rather than more, gastronomic service.

The chair is drawn back. I stand up from the table. Swaying slightly, I correct my balance and concentrate on laying the groundwork for the next great meal. Deep down in the heart of each captain and waiter there remains the touch of an artist. He longs to know what I really feel about the evening's performance. This is the moment when every well-deserved thank you is not only due, but is worth its weight in gold for the future. A squeeze of the arm to the busboy. A press of the shoulder to the waiter. A touch of the hand to the captain. Congratulations on the meal to the maître d'hôtel. If the proprietor appears in the lobby, it is not enough to say that everything was fine. Mention some extra-special detail for praise, so that he realizes how observant you are. The most fundamental of all principles is that in a great restaurant, a great meal comes only to the diner who can build and maintain a great reputation.

Bistaella

Which is the most spectacular dish of the most magnificent restaurant in the world? The question haunts me. Even my shortest list—one of, say, a supreme half-dozen names—is not exclusively French. It has to include an extraordinary, tiny restaurant hidden away in the *medina,* the old native quarter of the beautiful city of Marrakech, on the edge of the Sahara. The owner-chef is a Frenchwoman from Paris who has mastered the superb preparations of the great classical dishes of Morocco. Two of the top French food critics have called her restaurant the most brilliant, most luxurious, most sumptuous in the world. The sequence of accidents that made all this happen is as fantastic as her food and her setting.

It is only a short walk from the casino and grand hotels of *l'hivernage,* the garden district, to the *medina*'s narrow, cobbled, twisting alleys. Passing through an ornate archway, you walk between high, whitewashed, cracked walls. A huge oak door patterned with bright metal studs bears a small, highly polished, brass plate announcing La Maison Arabe. The door is locked, and your ring brings an Arab boy, resplendent in uniform, who bows low, precedes you up the stairs, and shows you into a magnificent dining room that seats only twenty-five guests. The pure white arches and walls are brilliantly decorated with multicolored mosaic tiles and hung with rich tapestries. You sit cross-legged among mounds of embroidered silk cushions at low, embossed brass tables. As the service of the meal begins, your hands are bathed in perfumed water. There is no

EDITOR'S NOTE: This syndicated newspaper article originally appeared in March 1978.

printed menu: you discuss your meal with the owner. You begin to ask questions. . . .

In the years before World War II, the autocratic ruler of Marrakech was the Pasha El Glaoui, who maintained a harem of three hundred. Despite this excess of available entertainment, the Pasha preferred the companionship of beautiful Frenchwomen. On a visit to Paris with two of his sons, El Glaoui met lovely Madame Helen and promptly invited her to Marrakeech. Madame, with her daughter, Suzy, accepted and fell so much in love with the place she decided to stay.

The Pasha gallantly offered to help set them up in Marrakech in any way they desired. Madame said she would like to open a restaurant serving the superb Moroccan food that had so enormously impressed her at the dinner parties at the palace. El Glaoui thought for a moment and then came up with the big idea. Among the three hundred women of his harem was the quite aged Rhadija, who was a supremely good cook, but so bad tempered that she continually caused trouble among the other women. The Pasha would solve his problem and Madame's by transferring Rhadija out of the palace and into the kitchen of the new restaurant. A house was quickly found in the *medina* and sumptuously redecorated, and soon La Maison Arabe opened to supreme praise.

Suzy learned Arabic in the hope of being able to talk to Rhadija, but that old harridan became more difficult and obstinate with every passing month. She took orders from no one. She refused to allow the French owners to step inside her kitchen. Since Rhadija was approaching seventy, the Frenchwomen began to fear for the future of the dazzling recipes. Rhadija would give not a word. Then, as she began to feel her life fading, she longed to make the pilgrimage to Mecca. For that, she would need money.

So began a fantastic sequence of what we might call Arab recipe trading. For every batch of money, Rhadija had to agree to allow Suzy to work beside her in the kitchen on a particular recipe, making notes on the ingredients, the spices, and the techniques. In this way, almost fifty superb, traditional Moroccan recipes—recipes passed for generations from mother to daughter—were transferred from Rhadija to Suzy and, for the first time, fixed on paper.

When Rhadija finally died, Suzy took over in the kitchen. One evening before he too died, Pasha El Glaoui came to dine at La Maison Arabe. He declared that Suzy's French touch, added to the classic techniques of Rhadija, made the dishes better than they had ever been before.

Suzy has never published any of the recipes. They are special versions of classic Moroccan dishes, their sources wrapped in mystery. But I have been able to reconstruct (and adapt for American ingredients) Suzy's most incredible and spectacular dish at La Maison Arabe. The *bistaella* is the classic Moroccan pigeon pie with eggs, almonds, lemon juice, and a marvelous array of spices, all enclosed in a crackly crisp crust of paper-thin layers of pastry. It may very well be the world's greatest dish.

As with all supreme dishes, it is the product of many cultural influences. Yet its source remains a mystery. It probably came to Morocco from Andalusia in Spain during the Moorish occupation. The Andalusian word *pasteles*, meaning a food surrounded by a pastry crust, relates, possibly, to the Moroccan Berber word *bestila*, a dish of poultry cooked in butter and saffron. But the idea of enclosing the poultry in a buttery-flaky crust almost certainly was picked up by the Moors in Damascus, where the trick may have been learned from reports brought back from China by Marco Polo. Chinese spring rolls are still made from pastry skins.

Historically *bistaella* remains a mysterious dish. But there is no mystery abut making it. Here in the United States it can be made with pigeon squabs, chickens, or a pheasant and with an excellent imitation of the authentic crust from the modern versions of Greek filo or Hungarian strudel pastry sheets. We find this one of the most rewarding of all our recipes.

BISTAELLA

6 servings

> ½ teaspoon saffron filaments, or, as second choice, ground or powdered saffron
> ¼ cup dry white wine
> 4 to 5 pounds pigeon-squabs (usually 4 whole birds), or the same weight in 2 chickens, or one 2½ to 3 pound plump pheasant
> 2 whole fresh lemons
> Coarse crystal salt and freshly ground black pepper
> 5 tablespoons butter
> About 1 quart top-quality first-pressing olive oil
> 2 cups finely chopped onions
> 2 tablespoons chopped fresh coriander leaves
> 1 clove garlic, peeled and finely minced
> 2 teaspoons finely minced fresh ginger root, or, if unavailable, ½ teaspoon dried powdered ginger
> 6 tablespoons chopped parsley, leaf only, no stalks

- ¼ teaspoon red cayenne pepper
- 1 small, dried red chili pepper, washed but whole
- 2 cinnamon sticks (2 inches each)
- ½ teaspoon ground cumin seed
- 1½ teaspoons ground turmeric
- 2 cups clear chicken bouillon
- 1½ cups blanched slivered almonds
- 5 tablespoons confectioners' sugar
- 1 tablespoon ground cinnamon
- 8 large eggs
- 18 to 26 sheets of filo pastry, according to thickness (available at Greek bakeries or groceries, or from fancy food stores)

TIME INVOLVED: Active preparation about 2¼ hours, plus 30 minutes unsupervised poaching of the birds, plus about 45 minutes final oven baking. But the job can be divided between two days, as indicated below.

The Birds

Set the saffron to soak in the wine. Stir them together in a tiny saucepan, then heat gently, stirring steadily, just to the blood heat of your finger. Turn off heat, cover, and let stand until needed. The alcohol in the wine draws out and dissolves the saffron oils, creating the best possible effects of color and taste in the dish.

Clean and refresh the birds by rubbing them, inside and out, with the cut sides of half lemons. If using squabs, leave birds whole, if chickens or pheasant, cut into largish pieces. Rub flesh on all sides with salt and pepper, then hold aside. Choose an enameled-iron pot or heavy Dutch oven with tightly fitting lid and a good frying surface, put it over medium-high frying heat, and put in 3 tablespoons each of butter and oil. When they are good and hot—but not yet browning or smoking—put in the birds and lightly brown them on all sides. As they are done, take them out and place them on a platter that will catch their exuding juices. The moment the pot is empty, put in the chopped onions and sauté them quickly until they are just soft, usually about 5 minutes. Working quickly to avoid evaporation of the flavor oils, mix in "Suzy's secret sequence" of the aromatic herbs and spices: the chopped coriander leaves, the minced garlic, the minced ginger root, 2 tablespoons of the chopped parsley, the cayenne, the chili, the cinnamon sticks, the ground cumin, the ground turmeric.

Now pour and stir in the chicken bouillon and, at the same time, add the saffron and its wine, taking care to dip the little saucepan into the liquid in the pot to capture all the saffron oil. Increase heat to bring the liquid quickly to boil, then at once put back the birds and any of their juices into the pot. Pack them in neatly but not too tightly, and adjust the heat for a steady, not-too-hard bubbling, but enough to provide steam inside the pot. Clamp on the lid. After 30 minutes check the bird flesh (which should be nicely soft, but not falling off the bones) and, if necessary, continue the poaching a few minutes longer.

The Almond Filling

While the birds are poaching, set a heavy pan over medium frying heat and put in 1 tablespoon each of butter and oil. When hot, add the slivered almonds and keep moving them around until they are lightly browned. Remove them with a slotted spoon; drain on and dry with absorbent paper. Then toss them in a large mixing bowl with 2 table-spoons of the confectioners' sugar and 1 teaspoon of the ground cin-namon. This is both the almond filling for the bistaella and the decoration for its top. Hold these almonds aside, covered.

The Flesh Filling

The moment the birds are done, lift them out of the pot and replace them on their platter to cool. Now turn the heat full up under the pot to boil the liquid very hard, to reduce it to about ¾ cup, thus blending and smoothing out its flavors. Fish out the cinnamon sticks and chili but do not strain the sauce. This is another of the secret tricks. Stir quite often during the reduction, which, on our stove, usually lasts 15 to 20 min-utes. Then turn off the heat and let the sauce cool.

Working on a cutting board with a small sharp knife, remove every bit of skin from the cooled birds and, according to your taste, either discard it or dice it fairly finely and put it into the storage bowl for the meat filling. Remove every bit of flesh from every bone and cut into bite-size cubes. Leave small irregular bits as they are. Put everything into the meat storage bowl and cover it.

(At this point, you can stop the entire operation and restart at a later time. Simply refrigerate in separate covered jars the almond mixture, the flesh of the birds, and the reduced contents of the cooking pot. When you restart, bring everything to room temperature—about 2 hours—be-fore continuing with the next operation.)

The Egg Filling

Squeeze ¼ cup of lemon juice and hold it ready. Also have ready the remaining tablespoons of chopped parsley. Break the eggs into a large mixing bowl and beat them, with the lemon juice and parsley, until they are just frothy. Turn on the heat under the cooking pot of sauce and, as soon as the liquid begins to feel hot to the tip of your finger, pour in the eggs. While continuing to heat it, stir the mixture continuously with a rubber spatula, carefully scraping the bottom, where the eggs will first congeal. It is the basic process of scrambling eggs, but in an excess of liquid. Do not expect all the liquid to be absorbed. You are aiming for soft curds, just stiff, but certainly not dry or hard. The instant the eggs are done, remove them from the hot pot or they will overcook. Spoon the eggs into a storage bowl with some of the extra sauce to keep them moist while waiting for the assembly of the pie. Cover. You now have the three components for the filling of the *bistaella*: the almonds, the eggs, and the meat.

The Assembly Line

We have observed *bistaella* being made by Moroccan cooks in a Moroccan kitchen. The ideal arrangement is a team of three people. One holds a soft pastry brush, stands before a pile of sheets of filo pastry (always kept covered with a damp towel), dips the brush into a small bowl of oil, and quickly and completely paints each sheet before it is lifted. The second lifts the painted sheet by its top edge and, sliding the back of the hand underneath it to support it, hands it to the third cook, who precisely places it in position on the oiled baking pan or sheet.

Just before this production line starts moving, preheat your oven to 425° F. Also, choose the baking container on which you will construct and cook your *bistaella*. For our 10-inch pie, we use a 14-inch Spanish steel paella pan about 2 to 3 inches deep. (A pizza pan of about the same size would do.) For turning over the pie, we invert over it a 15-inch cookie sheet. The pie could also be constructed and baked on such a sheet, but there is a slight danger of excess oil dripping off and starting a small fire in the oven. You should set a grill pan underneath to catch the drips.

Now the teamwork begins. It must all go as quickly as possible to avoid the most serious danger: the tendency of the filo sheets to dry out and become brittle if left unattended for even a few seconds. They must, all the time, be kept damp with moistened towels and all exposed parts must be kept oiled.

Oil the baking pan. One by one, lay filo sheets in it—each off center—so that about 2 inches of it are hanging over the edge of the pan, ready, eventually, to be folded back over the filling. Each new oiled sheet is laid down at an angle to the one immediately below it, so that by the time you have laid down about 8, 9, or 10 sheets you have covered the entire circumference of the pan. You must decide how many sheets according to their thickness. Your primary requirement is a solid, reasonably unbreakable base on which to spread the filling.

Reserve ¼ cup of the cinnamon-sugared almonds, divide the remainder in half, and spread one half in a neat, single, 9-inch-circular layer at the exact center of the filo-covered pan. On the almonds, neatly spread half the scrambled egg mixture, using a slotted spoon and leaving behind as much as possible of the liquid. On top, make a neat layer of all the diced and squared flesh of the birds, packing the pieces close together in a solid circle. Cement the pieces into place with the rest of the eggs and finish with the rest of the almonds. Finally, dribble on any flavorful juices from the bowl that held the bird flesh.

Now return to the teamwork for sealing the pie. Brush a little more oil over all the exposed pastry dangling over the edge all around the pan and then fold the sheets back over the filling. At the same time, use your fingers to gently press the pie into a neatly rounded shape. Next, one by one, lay four sheets exactly centered on top of the pie.

Now invert a cookie sheet (or second pan) over the pie and quickly turn it over. It is wise to hold a basin underneath while turning, in case some excess oil runs out. Oil the exposed ends of the pastry sheets and bring them up and over the edge of the pie. Turn it back onto its original pan and lay as many more sheets on top as you think are needed to form a secure covering for the pie. You may go up to 10.

Decide which is the better looking side of the pie and place that downward in the baking pan. Paint the top side with oil, slide the pan into the center of the oven, and forget it for 10 minutes. Then, if the top surface is lightly browned (if not, wait another 5 minutes), turn it over using the reversed cookie sheet, get rid of any excess butter on the baking pan and slide the pie back into the pan with the official top now uppermost. Give a quick painting with oil, and wait for it to brown (usually about 15 to 20 minutes). If the top is getting too brown, while the sides remain too pale, you can hold back the top by covering it with a "hat" of aluminum foil. There will be no harm to the filling if the *bistaella* stays in the oven up to 45 minutes.

While the pie is still piping hot, decorate its top by sprinkling—in any design—with 3 tablespoons of confectioner's sugar and 2 more teaspoons of ground cinnamon. Finally, sprinkle over the top the reserved sugared almonds. Bring the *bistaella* to table on a hot platter and with a very sharp, serrated knife cut it into wedges. Moroccans eat this food for the gods with their fingers.

Moroccan menu notes: A Moroccan host would consider this dish so supremely important that he would never dream of offering anything ahead of it. Guests must come to it with their hunger in full bloom and their taste buds untouched by any canapé or other solid morsel. It would be proper, though, to wash your taste buds and your hands. The guests first recline on very low couches covered with tapestry rugs and are handed tall, narrow glasses of lightly sugared mint tea. Then two boys circulate, one carrying a silver basin and pitcher of perfumed water that he pours over your hands, the other bearing soft towels with which he dries your hands. This completed for everyone, the host rises and begs the guests to partake of his entirely inadequate meal.

Devout Mohammedans do not drink alcohol, but we think that the richness of the *bistaella* calls loudly for the light, fruity refreshment and relatively uncomplicated personality of a fine Beaujolais or a Gamay-Beaujolais from Napa, Sonoma, or Monterey in California.

At La Maison Arabe, Suzy would accompany or immediately follow her *bistaella* with a choice of exquisite salads served in small mounds on a huge copper platter. Each refreshing mixture would have the subtlest touch of sweetness to link it to the *bistaella*. One salad might be tiny cubes of orange flesh perfumed with orange flower water and just touched with grated cinnamon. Another might be miniature hearts of baby Bibb lettuce, a little salt, a lot of freshly ground Tellicherry black pepper, a few drops of the best olive oil and Spanish sherry vinegar, a few grains of cinnamon, and a sprinkling of fine sugar.

After such rich pleasures, perhaps a simple, white goat cheese, some Arabic *lavash* bread, a mouth-watering fruit sherbet, a bowl of fresh fruits, and Turkish coffee.

In Marrakech, there would be bright flowers on the table and around the room. Remember, in Marrakech, it is always summer. At dinner women wear light and lovely caftans; the men wear multicolored silk shirts. Everything is informal. Laughter and love are a part of every scene. As for the background music at dinner, instead of the thumping and wailing of native Arab music, we would turn to the region where the Moorish culture perhaps reached its highest peak: the province of Andalusia in Spain. Our music of the evening would be a guitar strumming the Spanish rhythms that remain as deeply influenced by the Moorish culture as is the magnificent food on the table.

Almost Nine Hundred Years Later — The Same Path to the Same Grandeur

We took the last sips of our coffee at the Auberge des Deux Mondes. Monsieur Michel drove the car across the old bridge over the River Guiers. We turned sharp left and climbed steadily in first gear toward the cleft in the granite wall towering above us. We were heading toward the same valley of peace as were Hugues and Bruno with their six companions almost nine hundred years before.

The cleft has been widened by blasting out a rock ledge for the road above the white-foamed river. The sign at the entrance pointed upward: Route de la Forêt Domaniale—St.-Pierre-de-Chartreuse. The road turned and twisted blindly. It rose sharply. Our engine whined in low gear. The cliffs seemed to be leaning over us. On our right, there was a sheer drop into the gorge of the tumbling river. On our left the cliff stepped forward and blocked our way. The road tunneled through it. A right-angle bend. Another small tunnel. Fifty yards of sunlight. A third tunnel. A hairpin bend. One more tunnel.

As soon as we were through the narrow Porte de la Fourvoirie, the rock walls opened out and we were in a forest of old beeches (many must have been almost a hundred and fifty feet high), brown, green, red, and yellow. My ears were suddenly alert to every sound. My nose was aware of the essences of the earth. The scene was dominated by the orchestra of life and movement among the trees. From the gorge below there came

EDITOR'S NOTE: This piece is excerpted from *The Auberge of the Flowering Hearth* (Bobbs-Merrill, 1973). This title is still in print with Echo Press (1983) in hardcover and Ballantine (1984) in paperback.

the bass roll of rushing water. Above, the treble voices of the birds. They seemed unconcerned with our intrusion.

Monsieur Michel is intimate with these forests. He named the birds and their cries. From high on the cliff came the harsh klaxon hoot of the *coq de bruyère*, the Alpine grouse. Its mate was joyously gabbling as she fattened herself on ripe blueberries and raspberries. Nearer, there were the excited cackles and screams of the wild pheasant; also the high whistles of the mountain thrush, when she stopped gobbling juniper berries. There was the angry chattering of the rock partridge; lonely calls from the quail; and the raucous complaints of woodcocks. Farther away and higher up, there came piercing cries of wild moorhens and hazel grouse. Skunks and squirrels darted across the road as we traveled slowly.

Monsieur Michel said that sometimes at night his headlights had caught leaping foxes and hares. In the fall, on the highest slopes, he had hunted the "prince of the valley," the long-horned chamois; on the gentler slopes, he had found mountain deer. In the deeper forests he had tracked the *marcassin*, the young wild boar. When he fished in the clear river pools, Monsieur Michel caught rainbow and speckled trout. And at night he stalked and netted angry croaking frogs.

The trees closed in above us—an airy vault of gold and green lace. Then, quite suddenly, they opened out. Our road leveled. We were inside the security of the Valley. The gorge widened between the mountains. The Valley appeared as a vast oval amphitheater. Around the highest circle, soaring against the sky, there were the sharply chiseled, dazzlingly white peaks. Just below, wreathing around each peak like a dark green collar, then merging into the second circle around the amphitheater, were the forests of evergreen pines. Below, marching down the slopes to the floor of the Valley as if they were the spectators in the amphitheater, were the brightly colored, curving sweeps of the beeches. On the floor of the Valley, in the ring of the arena, rich green pastures surrounded the now-quiet river, with miniature herds of cattle and sheep. And, in the very center of the ring, with wisps of bluish wood smoke rising from its cottage chimneys, was the tiny village of St.-Pierre-de-Chartreuse. It was an immense and self-assured scene.

Our paved road skirted the northern slope of the Valley. It remained high, with the downward sweep to our right. Below, a narrow winding gravel road followed the river and crossed it over an ancient stone bridge. Huge rocks seemed to block the course of the river, which disappeared beneath them, under a boiling, frothing whirlpool, with a thunderous roar. Early travelers along this road reported it as a terrifying experience. But our new road remained high above the white foam, continuing toward the center of the Valley, where it would turn and descend the steep hill to St.-Pierre-de-Chartreuse. We did not go as far as the hill. We stopped on a high spur above the village. We had come to a group of grey stone buildings. One was low, solid and square, its stone washed in light beige and partly covered by rambler roses. There was a small hand-lettered sign above the door: AUBERGE DE L'ATRE FLEURI.

From the wooden gate, the flagstone path led through the roadside front garden, with lilac and rose bushes, geraniums, and hydrangea. We were met at the front door by the two ladies who own and run the Auberge. Its business manager and maître d'hôtel was a slightly plump, vivaciously voluble lady from Provence, Mademoiselle Vivette Artaud. Her partner, the lady-chef, was a slim, ascetic-looking, and quietly shy lady from Marseille, Mademoiselle Ray Girard.

We stepped at once into Le Hall, the central lobby and meeting place of the house. There was a warm, indoor smell of bread and fruit. The first piece of furniture, near the door, was an old *levain*, a low, heavily lidded oak chest in which yeasted bread dough was left to rise. Next to it, against the wall, was a *pétrin*, a timber box with a sloping bottom in which the risen bread dough was kneaded before being transferred to a *maie*, in which it was pressed into the shapes of loaves. I wondered whether these old chests were still being used in this house.

Le Hall was a large room and its first, most striking feature was its mirror-shiny, perfectly smooth paved floor of natural *ardoise*, slate flag-stones in a dark and rich green. The floor established the informality of the room.

Then one's attention was drawn to the fire in the open hearth, which dominated the room with a feeling of comfort, gastronomic satisfaction, hospitality, warmth, and welcome. The pile of huge beech and pine logs crackled and roared on a firebrick platform raised above the floor. More logs were stacked below the hearth. The opening must have been almost six feet high and five feet wide, framed by golden brown tiles and covered, above, by a canopy of polished copper with a valance of heavy leather to hold in the smoke. This open hearth pierced the central wall of the house. One looked through it, past the flames, into Le Salon. The hearth served both rooms with its flickering glow and shining warmth. But much more than that. This hearth also played its classic medieval role in the preparation of food. From its roof there hung a black wrought iron chain with a hook for a heavy cauldron. There were grill bars and black iron basting cups at various heights. In front there was a turning spit. There were covered holes in its floor, where iron pots could be set for slow heating under the glowing embers. There were warming shelves and iron tripods. There were chimney hooks for smoking hams. In spring and summer, when there is no fire in the great hearth, it is hung with antique copper cauldrons and pots filled with flowering and green plants. This is why the house is called The Inn of the Flowering Hearth (L'Auberge de l'Atre Fleuri).

We climbed the curving stairs to a room with casement windows over-looking the peaks and the Valley. We settled in and rested. Then Mademoiselle Vivette announced that she thought the midday sun was warm enough for us to lunch in the sheltered garden. On the wall at the left, as we stepped out through the French windows at the back, there were two freshwater tanks filled with live crayfish and rainbow trout. The air was soft and sweet, the view overwhelming. In the noontime hush, noises floated up from the village below: children shouting, crashes from the barns, water splashing into buckets. The sun had broken up the clouds and everything glistened. In our garden we were enclosed by the sounds of bubbling and rushing water from a stream at one side racing down over the rocks. Some of the water was piped off to a fountain, sparkling and splashing. We sat down to the first of the extraordinary meals of the Auberge. . . .

MENU OF
The Arrival Lunch

APÉRITIF: KIR DE PROVENCE

Soufflé aux Fromages des Alpes
(*Soufflé of Alpine Cheeses*)

WHITE, CRÉPY DE SAVOIE, FICHARD

Civet de Lièvre à la Chartreuse
(*Ragoût of Wild Hare in Red Wine*)

Homemade Buttered Noodles

RED, BEAUJOLAIS VILLAGES DE BROUILLY, EN CARAFE

Salade de Cornette au Lard
(*Salad of Belgian Endive with Crisped Bacon Dressing*)

Fromages:

Picodon de la Drôme　　　　　　　　Père Ernest du Dauphiné
Pétafine des Hautes-Alpes

Glace à la Noix de Grenoble
(*Homemade Walnut Ice Cream*)

Café

ENZIAN BRANDY OF MOUNTAIN GENTIAN

This magnificent lunch was based almost entirely on the local specialties of the Alpine region. It immediately established the extraordinary skills of Mademoiselle Ray in preparing the foods and of Mademoiselle Vivette in perfectly serving and precisely balancing them with the right wines. From this first occasion onward, the cuisine of the Auberge was made memorable by their approach to the food as a picture set off by the frame of the wine. For each dish, the frame was never so bold as to dominate the picture, nor so shy as to be overwhelmed.

This was especially true with the cheeses. Instead of offering us a huge cheeseboard with fifteen or twenty choices, Mademoiselle Vivette limited us to three types of exactly the right strength to complement and conclude the remaining red wine.

Even her opening Kir was quite different from the usual. She proved how much variety can be achieved in even the simplest of apéritifs by varying the white wine from the traditional Chablis. Instead, she used a dry, fruity, nonvintage white Rognac from a small vineyard near the Provençal village of Marignane about twenty miles from Marseille. One can get dozens of other effects with other white wines, mixed with the usual tablespoon per glass (more or less, to taste) of a first quality Crème de Cassis distilled from the black currants of Dijon.

The soufflé was unusually aromatic and richly textured from being made with two Alpine cheeses of powerful character: the French Gruyère des Alpes and the creamy yellow Tome de Savoie. These local cheeses have a strong affinity for the charmingly light Savoy white wines. Today, Mademoiselle Vivette chose a young vintage Crépy from the French slopes above the Lake of Geneva. Its aroma filled our noses as it was poured from its slim tall bottle. It was aromatic, full-bodied, slightly crackling on the tongue. For later lunches Mademoiselle Ray prepared several more soufflés, each distinctly different, each showing the variety that is possible from the same soufflé recipe (see page 196), with different combinations of cheeses and wines.

Mademoiselle Ray's friend Georges Cloitre had brought her a wild hare that he had shot on the mountain slopes of Les Entremonts above his village of Saint-Philibert. She had hung it in the cool outside larder for a few days. Then she had cut it up and marinated the pieces with herbs and a strong red wine of the Côtes du Rhône. Finally, it had been gently, gently simmered in more red wine, and to give a slight touch of aromatic sweetness to the gamy meat, she had flamed it with a glass of the local Green Chartreuse (see recipe page 197).

The accompanying *Beaujolais de l'année* (meaning, "of the last harvest") was the one that Mademoiselle Vivette had brought back in her car from her last tasting and buying trip. The Beaujolais country, after all, is only about seventy-five miles from the Auberge.

What the French call *la cornette,* or *la chicorée,* is chicory to the British and Belgian endive to us. The stalks were chunked and tossed with green scallion tops, crisped, crumbled bacon, and garlic-rubbed croûtons, then dressed with hot bacon fat and tarragon wine vinegar (recipe, page 199).

To finish the wine, Mademoiselle Vivette presented three very local, little-known-outside-the-region, simple cheeses. The crumbly, salty Picodon is made by shepherds from goats' milk and ripened in sandstone pots. During this process the cheeses are pricked, or *pico*-ed. Hence the name.

The Père Ernest is a fresh milk, young and creamy rich cheese that comes wrapped in straw, with a quite wonderful aromatic character.

The Pétafine is made from mixed cows' and goats' milk, slightly enriched with olive oil, then faintly flavored with Champagne.

Since walnuts are one of the principal crops on the agricultural plains around Grenoble and the Alps, it was to be expected that Mademoiselle Ray would make the richest and best walnut ice cream I have ever tasted. The freshly shelled nutmeats were skinned and pounded by hand into a pulp before being mixed with the cream base (recipe page 199).

With the coffee, there were tiny glasses of the famous Enzian, a clear dry brandy distilled from the yard-long roots of the yellow mountain gentian flower, which grows on the high Alpine slopes. A remarkable half-flowery, half-nutty flavor.

SOUFFLÉ OF ALPINE CHEESES
(Soufflé aux Fromages des Alpes)

4 servings

With this basic soufflé, dozens of variations of flavors and textures are possible, simply by changing the combinations of the cheeses. French cooks generally serve this as a first course, filled with various fresh cheeses as they are at their seasonal peaks of quality. In France there is much awareness of the seasonal cycles of the hundreds of different cheeses.

    ¼ *pound Gruyère cheese, French or Swiss*
    ¼ *pound Alpine Tome of Savoy, or a sharp-flavored alternative*
    5 *eggs*
    ½ *lemon*
    4 *tablespoons sweet butter*
    ½ *cup all-purpose flour*
    1 *cup milk*
    ¼ *teaspoon ground mace*
    1 *teaspoon coarse crystal salt*
    Freshly ground black pepper

About 1 Hour Before Serving—Active Preparation About 30 Minutes—Unsupervised Cooking About 30 Minutes

Grate both the cheeses and measure precisely ⅓ cup of each, then mix them and hold. Separate the 5 eggs, placing each yolk in a separate cup. The whites should preferably be assembled for later hand-beating in a round copper bowl that has been lightly rubbed with the ½ lemon to eliminate any slight film of fat. In a 1½-quart saucepan, melt the 4 table-spoons of butter and smoothly work in the ½ cup of flour. Heat gently, stirring continuously. At the same time, in another saucepan, heat the 1 cup of milk until it is just too hot to touch, then gradually blend in the butter-flour *roux*. Continue heating gently, still stirring, until it thickens. Then turn off heat and let cool, until it can again be touched. Blend in egg yolks, one at a time. Again, gently reheat, still stirring and carefully scraping bottom and sides, until mixture thickens to consistency of custard and drips lazily from spoon. Blend in combined cheeses, continuing to heat and stir until they are melted. Add ¼ teaspoon mace, 1 teaspoon salt, and pepper to taste. Turn off heat and let cool while you beat egg whites.

    Turn on oven to 325° F., setting lower shelf about 2 inches from bottom of oven and upper shelf near the top. Beat whites until they first glisten, then stand up in stiff peaks on balloon whisk. Using a rubber spatula, lightly and quickly fold one-third of whites into cheese mixture, then pour all of it back into the remaining whites in the beating bowl. Lightly and quickly continue folding—do not overdo it—do not worry about a few remaining white streaks. Pour instantly into a 1-quart unbuttered soufflé dish and put on lowest shelf of oven. Adjust upper shelf so that it is about 3 inches above top of still-unrisen soufflé, then invert a shiny cookie sheet on this upper shelf to reflect heat downwards onto the top surface. Gently close oven door—never slam—and do not open for the first 25 minutes. Then check every 5 minutes. Soufflé is ready when top is golden brown, probably with large crack, and is springy to the touch—usually in about 30 minutes. Rush it to table and serve instantly on very hot plates.

RAGOÛT OF HARE WITH GREEN CHARTREUSE
(*Civet de Lièvre à la Chartreuse*)

Serves 4 or more people, according to size of hare

In France this is a dish of the fall hunting season, but in the United States, in fancy game shops, hares are also available throughout the cold winter months. Our store-bought hares are usually called "Belgian" or "Canadian," which does not mean that they come from those countries (any more than a Bermuda onion comes from the island)—it's the type of hare (or onion) that came originally from you-know-where! Best of all, of course, is when a hunter friend brings back his own hare.

> *Whole hare with its liver, usually about 5 pounds*
> 3 *bay leaves, crumbled*
> 2 *or 3 cloves garlic (to taste), finely minced*
> 1 *tablespoon crushed juniper berries*
> 1 *teaspoon dried thyme*
> 3 *medium yellow onions, chopped*
> 6 *shallots, finely chopped*
> 1 *bottle strong red wine, perhaps medium-priced regional Château-Neuf-du-Pape*
> ¾ *pound dark-smoked bacon, thickly sliced*
> ¼ *cup green Chartreuse liqueur*
> ⅓ *cup all-purpose flour*
> ½ *cup heavy cream*
> *Coarse crystal salt and freshly ground black pepper, to taste*

Three Days Before—Marinating the Hare—Active Preparation in About 15 Minutes

Assuming that the hare has already been cleaned and skinned, cut it up into pieces as for fricassee. Hold the liver separately. Assemble aromatics for marinade in a bowl large enough to easily hold hare pieces: 3 crumbled bay leaves, the finely minced garlic, 1 tablespoon crushed juniper berries, 1 teaspoon rosemary, 1 teaspoon thyme, the 3 chopped onions and the 6 finely minced shallots. Mix these dry ingredients, then pat them around pieces of hare as you pack them into bowl. Gently pour over the bottle of red wine. Cover and refrigerate for 3 days, moving pieces of hare around and turning them over two or three times each day.

On the Day—About 2½ Hours Before Serving

Remove hare pieces from marinade, carefully scrape off adhering herbs and wipe flesh completely dry. Cut up entire ¾ pound of bacon slices into inch-square pieces and fry until crisp. With slotted spoon, remove crisp bits and hold. In remaining hot bacon fat, sauté hare pieces until lightly browned on all sides. Then, piling them up in frying pan, flame them with the ¼ cup of Green Chartreuse. Pack them loosely into a tightly lidded oven casserole and sprinkle them with ⅓ cup flour. Turn on oven to 325° F and set shelf so that casserole will be exactly in the center. Put the ½ cup of cream and the liver into the jug of an electric blender and turn on to medium-high speed for only a few seconds, until both are combined into a thickish puree. Blend this into the marinade, adding salt and pepper to taste, then gently pour, including all herbs, over hare pieces in casserole. Bring up quickly to boiling over high heat on top of stove, then cover tightly and place in oven to simmer until hare is done—usually about 2 hours.

Serving at Table

Crumble the crisp bacon and sprinkle over hare on serving platter. Surround with crisp triangles of fried bread and homemade noodles. The wine to drink can be a domaine-bottled vintage Châteauneuf-du-Pape.

SALAD OF BELGIAN ENDIVE WITH CRISPED-BACON DRESSING
(*Salade de Cornette au Lard*)

4 servings

Excellent whenever the endive is in season—usually from October through April. The Salade de Cornette of the Alps is not exactly the same variety as the Belgian endive imported into the United States, but the general ambiance of this salad as we can make it here is almost exactly the same, as they are very close—both members of the *chicorée*, chicory, family.

6 *average-size Belgian endive*
4 *green scallions*
8 *rashers dark-smoked, thickly sliced bacon*
8 *teaspoons tarragon wine vinegar*
1 *cup garlic croûtons, fried in advance*
   Coarse crystal salt to taste
   Freshly ground black pepper to taste

About 10 Minutes Before Serving

Wipe the 6 endives clean with a damp cloth, cut them into ½-inch chunks and separate the leaves directly into the salad bowl. Finely chop the green tops and white bulbs of the 4 scallions and toss them in the bowl with the endives. Cut the 8 rashers of bacon into small pieces and fry until crisp. Let cool slightly, then add the 8 teaspoons of vinegar and pour everything—fat, vinegar, and crisp bits—over the endive. Toss lightly with the 1 cup of croûtons, plus salt and pepper to taste, then serve at once.

HOMEMADE WALNUT ICE CREAM
(*Glace à la Noix de Grenoble*)

4 servings

When I first went to the Alpine region of the Dauphiné—which is the "walnut capital" of France—I had difficulty with the word *noix*. It means, in general, a "nut"—any nut, of any kind—but in the Dauphiné it also means, quite specifically, the walnut for which that region is famous. A warning: This ice cream can only be made with fresh walnuts, still in their shells, within a few months of the harvest. The secret trick is that the halves of nutmeat must be fresh enough and oily enough so that they can be skinned. This slightly tricky operation is simply not possible with old nuts or pre-shelled nutmeats. So—in France, this is a seasonal fall dish.

> 1 *pound fresh walnuts in shells, to provide* ½ *pound of nutmeats*
> 2⅔ *cups heavy cream*
> 1⅓ *cups milk*
> 9 *egg yolks*
> 3 *cups (about* ¾ *pound) confectioners' sugar*
> 1 *teaspoon cornstarch*

Active Preparation Is About ¾ Hour—Freezing in 1 Hour—Several Hours of Ripening

Rope in as much help as possible for the shelling of the walnuts and the skinning of the halves. Pound them to a puree with a pestle and mortar. (Some cooks do this job in an electric blender, but this involves some loss of the vital oil.) Mix the 2⅔ cups heavy cream and the 1⅓ cups milk, bring up almost but not quite to boiling, then add the walnut mash. Turn off the heat and leave the walnut oil to permeate the liquid.

Beat the 9 egg yolks with the 3 cups of sugar until mixture is smooth, and so thick that it forms ribbons on the beater. Then, working gradually and stirring all the time, incorporate into the eggs the warm nut-milk and the 1 teaspoon cornstarch. Now heat the mixture very gradually over a low flame, stirring continuously and carefully scraping the bottom and sides of the pan, until you have a thick pouring-custard that runs lazily from the spoon. Remove from heat and continue stirring for a few minutes to cool. Then pour into icebox bowl and cool in refrigerator.

Freeze by any of the standard methods—in rotary machine, in icebox freezer, or in an electric or hand-turned tub freezer—with ice and salt. Then let the ice cream ripen in the freezer for several hours before serving.

FIRST VARIATION: One extra cup heavy cream, whipped, may be folded into the cooled mixture just before freezing.
SECOND VARIATION: One or 2 cups of extra walnut meats, coarsely chopped, may be worked into the ice cream as it thickens in the freezer.

HOMEMADE FILBERT ICE CREAM
(Glace aux Noisettes)

4 servings

This is basically the same as for the walnut ice cream, with only the difference in the nuts and in the manner of handling them.

Replace the walnuts in the above recipe with 1 pound of filberts in their shells, which will produce about ½ pound of nutmeats. These also must be skinned before pounding, and this is done most easily by first lightly sautéing the nutmeats in butter over a medium-high frying heat until the skins become crisp and flaky—usually in about 5 minutes. Then remove every last little bit of skin before pounding the nutmeats to a puree, continuing as described in the recipe above for the walnut ice cream.

An Indian Village Feast on the Road to Darjeeling (and a Discourse on Tea)

When my Indian friends in Calcutta offered to drive me the three-hundred-odd miles north to Darjeeling, I realized that we would be crossing the great agricultural plain of West Bengal and I asked whether it might not be possible for me, on the way, to get some impression of the life of the country villages and, perhaps, even to taste the authentic, simple, village food of this northeastern part of India. My friends were at once most helpful and sympathetic. They thought they might be able to arrange for us to be invited, as guests of honor, to a village feast, a ceremonial banquet that is a regular ritual in this part of India. So letters were written many days in advance and telephone calls were made to certain district head men and, sure enough, the final happy result was that we were invited to a feast in one of the villages more or less on our way. We would have to let them know one week in advance of the precise day of our coming, since the preparation of between forty and fifty dishes was a complicated and slow process. On the day finally set for the feast, my friends warned me to wear easy old clothes, as I would be eating with my fingers and a good deal of food, both liquid and solid, would be splattered all over me.

When we reached our village, the entire male population—it must have been about a hundred men—all dressed in their most colorful clothes, greeted us with applause, shouts of welcome, and warmly hospitable embraces. The head man of the village, surrounded by the lesser

EDITOR'S NOTE: This piece is published here for the first time.

officials, placed wreaths of flowers around our necks. In the center of the village, there was a small open plaza and here a kind of tent had been set up, made from woven mats suspended from poles and ropes, forming a good solid roof against the sun, but with all four sides open, so that the feast could be watched from the surrounding houses. Apparently, it is the tradition that, while the women prepare the dishes for the feast, they do not join in the eating of it, but watch it from their windows.

Inside the tent, all was ready. Somehow, from somewhere, the villagers had found a Western-style dining table and a service for six of china, glasses, and cutlery. These were the only receptacles and tools available for the entire feast. At the other end of the tent, there was a low wooden dais, covered with a kind of light sackcloth, on which, obviously, the diners would sit cross-legged. Between these two ends of the tent—between the dining table and the dais—all the rest of the company would sit cross-legged on the ground. I asked my hosts who would sit on the dais. The head man replied: "Only minor officials—not important enough to sit at the table with our honored guests." I felt I should make a gesture. I announced that I had decided to sit cross-legged on the dais and eat in the true Indian style. My words—immediately translated into Bengali—were greeted by the entire company with wild applause and cheers. We took our places and the feast—which would last five hours—was launched.

The foods—served by young men—were brought in, generally on huge wooden platters and we were each provided with a wooden plate. It all continued through the middle of the day and on during the afternoon, with the bringing in and formal presentation of twenty-one separate meat and vegetable dishes, virtually each one accompanied by great mounds of snowy white rice.

For all this, there was not a single tool offered to me of any form or shape, at any time. There was never even one of the tortilla-like *chapatis* that Indians often use to scoop up their foods. There was nothing for it but to dig in with the fingers of my right hand and, when I had squeezed together a ball of rice and the ingredients of the dish, I would lift it quickly to my mouth. This was dirty business. With almost every dish there was a very runny, generally fiery-peppery-hot sauce, which ran down my wrist, my arm, dripped off my elbow, and formed pools in my lap. It didn't take many courses to put me in a pretty mess.

We began with a fish and lentil curry, then continued with a vegetable I had never tasted before, plus reassuringly familiar fried slices of eggplant and nicely browned slices of potato. Then came a second fish curry, but completely different from the first. After that, four kinds of flat, dry rissoles, each made from a different dried bean, cooked with herbs, mashed with spices, and fried. There followed lentil soup, fried flowerets of cauliflower, then another vegetable entirely unknown to me, a curry of cubes of pumpkin flesh, a dish of mixed poached green vegetables and, as a kind of sweet/sour break in the meal, delightfully refreshing slivers of sun-dried mango. Its pungent tartness cleared my palate and made me ready to go on.

But, as dish followed dish, my appetite and my capacity were rapidly diminishing. When the last dish came, I tasted only a pea-portion of it and pushed it away from me. I surveyed the mess I was in—I seemed to be covered with hot sauce from the hair of my head to the laces of my shoes. I was ashamed of myself. Then, my Indian friends pointed out that I was probably cleaner than anyone else at the feast. The "expert" diners had not only splashed themselves all over, but also the floor of the dais around them, the screens and even the roof of the tent—such was the eagerness, energy, and enthusiasm of the feasting.

I turned to my friend: "A magnificent feast! Thank you for bringing me."

"Glad you've enjoyed it, so far," my friend replied. "The second half should be even better."

At that very moment, the young men filed in with a procession of platters, bowls, jugs, pitchers, as the head man announced that the feast would now continue with twenty-two different desserts!

I groaned in anguish: "I simply can't eat another bite."

My friend spoke very quietly and seriously: "You can't see the women at the windows of the houses all around us, but all their eyes are on you. The blinds may seem to be drawn, but they are looking through every chink and crack. They started cooking for you five days ago. They worked all through last night. If you reject a single dish, the woman who cooked it is socially destroyed. If you show pleasure, you have made the cook a social queen. This feast will be their principal subject of conversation for the next ten years. So—go ahead and eat."

I feasted on sweet rice, a dozen combinations of milk and sugar, baked, boiled, fried . . . I rolled my eyes with pleasure again and again, I patted my belly. I pursed my lips and kissed my fingers. I tried my best to give each of those hidden women a brief moment of glory.

In spite of the sad condition of my stomach, I even found some of those desserts quite fascinating. There was a creamy rich mash of co-conut wrapped in a crackly-crisp pastry crust—a dramatically successful juxtaposition. There was a kind of praline boiled down from the sweet sap of a native tree—more exciting than maple sugar. The last dessert of all was a liquid blend of milk, rice, sugar, and thinly pureed bananas. How to drink it, without a cup or a spoon? The traditional method of the village was simplicity itself. You held out your two hands cupped together and the waiter poured in a portion of the sweet soup. Then you lapped up the creamy dessert as if you were a kitten at the milk bowl.

A lovely young girl appeared at one end of the tent to sing a short recital of folk songs. Her voice accompanied by the gentle drone of the *tamboura* and the rhythmic thump of the *tabla* was hauntingly beautiful. As her voice faded and the music ended, the sun was setting and it was time for us to continue our journey. But our hosts refused to let us go without a snack to fortify us on the road. Their idea of the perfect stirrup cup after a forty-three-dish meal was a huge pitcher of spiced, sweetened Darjeeling tea and a platter of boiled milk curd balls soaked in rosewater and swimming in a bath of sugar syrup.

As we drove on, I thanked my friends for having given me the chance to taste this authentic cuisine of West Bengal. I added a fear that was in my mind. I wondered whether I had deprived these villages of a store of food they probably needed for themselves. My friends assured me that, if I returned to the village ten years from now, I would find those good people still talking with undimmed pleasure about the great feast when the American journalist did them the honor of choosing their village for a ceremonial visit. I still feel their warmth coming back to me from all that distance and I do hope to return there one day and greet them and thank them for having feasted me and welcomed me in a style worthy of true Indian hospitality.

We spent the night in a small hotel in a nearby town and, of course, slept as if we were the Babes in the Wood. Next morning, in the crisp sharpness of the cool dawn, we continued our journey to Darjeeling. We were still on the great plain of West Bengal, but we would soon have to begin climbing sharply, since the town of Darjeeling, in the foothills of the Himalayas, is at the peak of an eight-thousand-foot mountain. Long before the name of Darjeeling became world-famous for its tea, the town was called, by the British colonials who ruled India, "the queen of the hill stations." This meant in the Anglo-Indian lingo of the Victorian era, a resort with cool pure mountain air, with a fairly peaceful small-town life and gorgeous views of the supreme Himalayan peaks—a place where British officials, worn down by the torrid heat and steaming humidity of Calcutta, could renew their health and strength with British-style country resort living. So they developed their private estates and built their baroque luxury hotels and, for a hundred years, they took the road that we were now traveling.

In the earliest days, the transportation was by coach and horses, with the journey taking seven days. Then they built the railroad—including the sensational British-designed, narrow-gauge up the mountain—and the travel time was cut to twenty hours—a speed that first made possible the idea of "a Darjeeling long weekend." Today the jets and the helicopter have brought the time down to three hours. On the ground, cars are faster and roads are better, but there are now political problems. Since the partitioning of India, parts of the independent nation of Bangladesh stretch out between Calcutta and Darjeeling and, on some routes, you have to spend time arguing with border guards and customs officials.

When we reached the small West Bengali town of Siliguri, our road crossed the Mahanadi River and entered the gorge that leads you up and up out of the alternating dusty winds and damp mists of the plain and at last into the high hills. Here the road, for fifty miles, runs alongside the extraordinary "toy railroad"—with its almost ridiculously small locomotive and four matching passenger cars that has been running back and forth every day for more than a hundred years between Siliguri and the Tibetan monastery at Ghoom, just outside Darjeeling. Rail and road run alongside each other and, in the fifty miles of a "roller-coaster ride," they rise almost eight thousand feet. At one point, the twist in the canyon is so sharp that the little train has to reverse itself and back into a siding, before it can go forward again around the corner. The British historian, Stephanie Stokes, told me that the idea for this trick was suggested to the chief construction engineer by his wife, who thought that, if dancers could reverse when they got themselves into a tight corner, why couldn't a train do the same?

After about two and a half hours of driving along one of the most difficult of roads among some of the most beautiful of jungle scenery— with sweeping carpets of orchids in densely perfumed flower among the great clumps of bamboo—the jungle falls away and the tea plantations, or "tea gardens," as they are universally called, interspersed with the white houses of the planters, take over the landscape. The tea bushes, in their serried ranks are dark green—the earth between them is bright red. The bushes are planted about four feet apart and they are pruned to grow about waist-high, for easy harvesting. If it were not pruned, a tea bush might become a tree as much as fifty feet tall. The river runs at the bottom of the valley. There is only a narrow ribbon of water now, with silver sand on either side, but the rocks are worn smooth by the force of the torrent during the monsoon, when a hundred inches may fall within three months. This is why Darjeeling tea is planted on such steep slopes. The leaves need the water to develop their perfume oils—but the roots must have constant drainage.

The town of Darjeeling is built, in concentric and descending circles, around the peak of an eight-thousand-foot mountain that was once called, in the Hindi language, Dar-jo-ling, the throne of the mystical thunderbolt. Virtually every house is at a different level and the gradients between them are so steep that, often, the chimney of the house below is level with the front door of the house above. Many of the connecting streets are simply long flights of steps. Other streets are so steep that all wheeled traffic (whether powered by motor, horse, or man) is barred by local law. Today, Darjeeling and its seventy thousand people (an amazing amalgam of races, religions, languages, and interests) is run by Indians, but the place is Victorian-British to the core. It was they who discovered it, nothing more than a group of abandoned mud huts and a burnt-out Buddhist temple. It was they who took it over, planned it, designed it, and built it—within the frame of their memory of polite country living "back home" in England. The British have gone from India, but their presence remains tangible in Darjeeling.

The wealthiest neighborhood, of course, is the highest in town, Birch Hill, with big stone English-style houses surrounded by large gardens. The streets are quiet and tree-shaded. The mailboxes at the street corners are painted firehouse red (as in England) and you drive on the left side of the road. When I walk around the courtyards of St. Joseph's College, I half feel myself back at Oxford. The two young girls ambling along over there across the street, wearing serge jumpers and bright red ribbons in their hair, are probably the daughters of wealthy British businessmen in Calcutta—students sent away from the fetid heat of the big city to the boarding school attached to the Loreto Convent, here in the healthy air of the mountains. The same story, almost certainly, with those two boys over there, dressed in formal grey flannel trousers and blue blazers.

The story goes that, in 1835, the head man of the British East India Company was paying a purely social visit to the Maharajah of Sikkim, one of those miniature Himalayan mountain states. The Britisher, in the course of after-dinner conversation, said that, although Dar-jo-ling had no usable buildings of any kind, he was very impressed by the beauty of the setting, by the marvelous view of the great mountain, Kanchenjunga, and by the perfection of the weather (which remained at a temperature of around 50° F, summer and winter), so that he would like to build a country estate there, to be able to get away from Calcutta as often as possible. The Maharajah, in a very friendly mood, replied that he would be delighted to discuss some properly legal transfer arrangement. The British government had to become involved and, at once, the whole thing became intensely political. The hill that is crowned by Darjeeling is very close to the point where three of the miniature Himalayan mountain states meet—one being Sikkim, the other two Bhutan and Nepal. The favorite sport of these three Maharajahs was to raid each other—toy soldier-type skirmishes and battles—but, still, a good many people were killed, a lot of property destroyed, and, most annoying of all to the British, the smooth and orderly flow of profitable British trade was disrupted. Now—if the British could gain control of the triangle of land around Darjeeling, they would have an effective buffer between the three troublesome mini-states. They signed treaties with the Maharajah of Sikkim for British control of more than a thousand square miles of Himalayan foothills around Darjeeling—an area that became an important division of the State of West Bengal.

As soon as they took over, the British began building up Darjeeling in concentric circles araound the crown of the hill and with all possible English amenities. At the top, as I have said, are the rich, private houses. In the next circle, below, the various clubs and a group of mammoth, baroque, Victorian-style hotels, most of them, now under Indian management, still operating—the largest, the Oberoi–Mount Everest, the second, the Windermere. Both still offer food with a fairly strong English accent. When the church clock strikes four, you can order Darjeeling tea with biscuits in the garden at the Windermere, or Darjeeling tea with bread and butter and imported honey at the Oberoi.

Below the hotels, the next circular tier around the hill is the Chaurasta, the Mall, a kind of park-walkway that encircles the hill with benches and trees, where you begin to be aware of the extraordinary mixture of peoples and races, of languages and religions, that mix to make up the population of Darjeeling. The dignified slim man, sitting on the bench, impeccably dressed in a dark business suit, reading an airmail copy of the *London Times,* is a Parsi, whose ancestors came from Persia and whose religion is Zoroastrian, involving the worship of fire. The lean tall man, walking fast, wearing a bright amber turban, is a Hindu Manwari. If you were to take off his turban, you would find his head absolutely clean shaven except for one plaited loop of hair at the very top. This is the "handle" by which the gods will haul him up to heaven when he dies. The Bengali man, dressed in the *dhoti* is carrying his little baby on his shoulder while his wife holds her *sari* shyly across her face. The holy man passing by in the crimson toga, twirling a prayer wheel and murmuring *mantra* prayers is a Tibetan lama. The short little man with the broad muscular shoulders, carrying a long curved knife in his belt, is a Gurkha warrior from Nepal. The Indian soldiers, in uniform, are here because we are so close to the Chinese border. The gorgeously dressed "royal personage" with the jeweled turban over there is obviously a visiting prince fron Rajasthan. There are sheiks from the Punjab and dark Dravidians. Perhaps the most striking of all are the few that are left of the original inhabitants of Dar-jo-ling from the time long before the British came—the Buddhist Lepchas from Sikkim. The men never cut their hair and braid it in two long pigtails often down to the backs of their knees. At the same time, they carry dangerously large, fierce swords. Mixed with all the colors of this dazzling scene are tourists from every part of the world.

Below this "parade ground," Darjeeling continues to cascade down the hill, tier by tier, for at leat another five hundred feet to the market, the bazaar, the *lal* at the bottom rung. Here, among the arguing, bargaining, jostling crowds, the total mixing of languages, races, and religions amounts almost to total chaos. Hindi may be the *lingua franca,* but many still speak English and, for the rest, the negotiations are pursued in Bengali, Bhutani, Nepali, Sikkimese, Tibetan, and variations. The food shops, especially, have to take into account all the complications, taboos, and traditions of Buddhism, Hinduism, Islam as well as Christianity. The creeds of the various customers are easily recognizable. The Hindu Man-wari young women wear brilliantly colored *saris* and gold rings on their toes. The Nepali women wear large nose rings and the ladies from Tibet always seem to wear black kimono-style robes. All is diversity. Darjeeling gives the impression of being a microcosm of the world.

Yet there was one person who came to Darjeeling who turned out to be the most important visitor in the town's history. He profoundly influenced its life and the life of the entire region. In 1849, there appeared on the scene Dr. Archibald Campbell, a botanist and plant pathologist who was interested, among many things, in orchids and wild mushrooms—but, as he pushed his way through the jungle forests up and down the hills, testing the soils and noting the run-off patterns of the rains, he conceived the brilliant idea that the slopes around Darjeeling might be ideal for growing tea. Obviously, it could not be the ordinary tea bush of the damp plains of Assam—it would have to be a plant a good deal hardier than that. So he began experimenting in cross-grafting the mountain tea bushes of China with the perfumed plant of Assam. Dr. Campbell was successful and produced the Darjeeling tea variety that has been only slightly modified in the last hundred years. The British government was so pleased with him that they made him Governor of Darjeeling and he ran the place for twenty-two years. In the early 1850s, the first tea gardens were planted and, by 1860, Darjeeling tea was an important and growing economic factor in the region. Workers came from all the neighboring states and greatly swelled the population of Darjeeling town. At the same time, as the label of "Darjeeling tea" began to be more widely known, the town became less and less isolated. Before long the dawn jet from Calcutta's Dum Dum airfield and the helicopter from Baghdogra made the trip a matter of two or three hours. Darjeeling became more and more crowded. In 1959, when China invaded Tibet, hundreds of refugees flowed in. Population is now over seventy thousand and under severe pressure.

I am often asked a most difficult question. With so much population pressure—with such a constantly increasing demand for the limited living space—with races and religions that have been actually warring with each other for thousands of years—why has there been no explosive friction in Darjeeling? One cannot give a hard, pragmatic "Western-style" answer. One must explain with the mystical philosophy "of the East." Darjeeling is just thirty-five miles from the "Great Holy Mountain"—the third highest peak in the world—Kanchenjunga. As with all huge mountains, the twin peaks, glistening pure white with eternal ice and the ten surrounding lower "attendant courtier peaks," are completely hidden much of the time by swirling clouds. But when they do appear—and they are then visible from every corner and level of Darjeeling—they are a sight of almost indescribable beauty, magnificence, and overwhelming power. Sometimes, in the early morning, the entire valley below is filled with black and grey clouds and white mist, so that all of Kanchenjunga's immense base disappears completely and the white peaks appear disconnected from the earth, suspended in space. At other times, there is a ring of clouds halfway up the mountain, so that the twin peaks appear as lonely sentinels in the sky. Occasionally the mountain is seen through a purple haze, as if a scrim curtain had been mysteriously drawn down. Almost every view, every day, adds to an infinity of variations.

One of the wonders of the world is to experience, on a cool, clear morning, the dawn coming up over Kanchenjunga. Very early, while it is still quite dark in Darjeeling, you climb to the top of Tiger Hill, which is higher than the town. Then, you look steadily toward the North. Long before the rays of the rising sun reach you and the town and the valley below you, they bathe the white peaks of the mountain, which then stand out in the all-surrounding darkness as bright, pure gold. Within a few minutes, Kanchenjunga, so to speak, "passes on its gold" to its lower, surrounding peaks, while the main mountain turns to an azure blue. This, in turn, descends to the lower peaks, while Kanchenjunga turns to roseate pink. This, too, is "passed on down"—a visual equivalent of a repeated theme in an orchestral symphonic poem. At this moment, the blood-red ball of the sun appears rising in the East and the light of day comes first to Darjeeling town and, then, more slowly, to the deep surrounding valleys. Experiencing the sunrise over Kanchenjunga is one of the supreme mystical events of a lifetime. But to see the full moon rise over the mountain, on a clear night, is pure surrealism.

To return, then, to our question about the peaceful qualities of life in

Darjeeling, the greatest force of Kanchenjunga is not its visual beauty, but its emotional and psychological presence. In Darjeeling, Kanchenjunga seems to bring everthing, all of life, down to a reasonable, and even small, perspective and scale. How could you haggle unfairly about the price of a bag of beans in the presence of Kanchenjunga? This was once a Buddhist settlement and there is an ancient local Buddhist proverb: "Just as the dew is dried by the morning sun, so will your cares disappear in the presence of The Lord Kanchenjunga."

BEYOND DARJEELING—THE TEA GARDENS

The moment you leave Darjeeling, there is virtually no place to go but down—down into one valley or another. Almost every slope has been cleared of the original jungle growth and is now dark green with close rows of waist-high tea bushes in perfect geometric squares—the bushes four feet apart, the rows four feet high, each bush four feet high. The soil has the essential high content of acid and low balance of chalk or lime, which encourages the development of the perfumed oils in the leaves.

The narrow and badly surfaced roads that lead down into many of these valleys are so steep that they zigzag continuously on narrow, turning and twisting, treacherous shelves cut out of the sides of the mountains, with often no barrier against a sheer drop of a thousand feet. At one moment, you drive through the semi-darkness and dripping dampness of a still uncleared section of jungle—at the next moment you are under the fierce heat of the sun, across an open clearing. Then your way is barred by the furiously rushing torrent of a river, or by a two-hundred-foot waterfall thundering down into a canyon; you cross on a wooden bridge that is no more than two solid tree trunks cut down and stretched across, with loose, uneven planking laid between them, just the width of your wheels with a few inches to spare, but no rails or sides.

Between the sections of tea plantations are the thatch and wattle huts of the Nepali coolies who work in the tea gardens. Near their primitive homes are the tall, urn-shaped tombs of their ancestors, shaded by ancient holy trees. The bushes, through the year, give several harvests—each called a "flush." The "first flush," always the most delicate and smallest, usually comes at the beginning of April when the spring sap rises and produces, at the ends of the branches, the fine growth of pale tips. After these have been picked, the bushes remain dormant until the start of the monsoon in June or July, when the heavy rain causes the throwing out of a mass of new shoots that, even with steady picking from sunrise to sundown six days a week, is fully renewed every five or six days. This massive series of flushes lasts through the summer rains, often into September or October. Every day, during this period of maximum pressure, the "factory" of a fair-sized estate will produce, finish, and pack several thousand pounds of Darjeeling tea, ready for shipment to all parts of the world.

The work day begins at about six in the morning, as soon as the sun comes up over the far ridge and throws enough daylight into the depth of the valley. Then the "plucking" (as the harvesting is called) is started by the various groups. The "best teams," the most efficient and fastest pluckers, always assigned to the most difficult sites and the best bushes, are the young women—the unmarried girls and the young wives, athletic, competitive, intelligent, lithe, strong, and tireless, they stay and work together in one part of the garden. The "second team," a bit less efficient, slightly slower, is made up of the older women, the pregnant wives, and those carrying young babies with them. By long-standing tradition the "third team" is made up of the men, who work together, but always at a distance from the women. The official reason (and a perfectly true one) is that the women chatter all the time—the rhythm of their voices seeming to match the movements of their skillful fingers—while the men prefer to work almost completely in sileence. A second reason for the tradition, obviously, is that it avoids any troublesome love or sex entanglements, or marital problems between families.

The tea bushes are interspersed by tall shade trees, usually the Indian *sal*, with fanlike branches that protect the tea leaves from the fiercest heat of the midday sun. The overseers (mainly senior Nepali Gurkhas), each holding up an umbrella against the sun, stand along the line of the plucking women, who are sweating profusely as they work. Each woman takes two rows of bushes, which are exactly four feet apart—but the branches spread out and interlock, so she must push her way through as she works her way forward, plucking to left and right. She is, in fact, highly skilled in terms of her nimble fingers, perfectly coordinated with her sharp eyes and instantaneous judgment. She is looking for the bud at the tip of the young shoot and the first leaf or two below it, depending on the required quality and tenderness. If she plucks too much stalk, there will be hard bits in the finished tea. If she plucks a shoot that is underdeveloped, the future growth of the bush will be retarded and a good part of the later leaf will be lost. The truly expert plucker takes only the ripe tips, but gets all of them. At the same time, she decides so quickly and works so fast that her basket is full and she can go up to the weighing station and collect her first fee.

Naturally, it is to the advantage of the owners of the tea garden to make the plucker's work as easy and efficient as possible. In this damp and tropical climate, the growth of weeds is tremendously fast. Every few days, on the earth underneath each tea bush and around its main stem, there springs up a dense "ground jungle of weeds," including small climbing vines that begin at once to entwine themselves around the branches of the bush. This problem is solved in advance of the pluckers by a small army of athletic young men armed with knives, small scythes, and sickles, who move along the rows, throwing themselves on the ground at each bush and wildly flailing their arms. From a distance they appear to be demons, cavorting, dancing, leaping, pouncing on their prey—cutting and slashing the wall of weeds around each tea bush that would impede the pluckers. Behind the group of "angry young men," the overseers walk sedately with their umbrellas, urging the slashers to greater effort. This battle will be constant every day through the three or four months of the monsoon growing season.

WEIGHING-IN AT THE END OF THE DAY

At the top of the hill above the main plantation of the garden is the "weighing hut" and, since this always involves a calculation of money, with the danger of a disagreement, one of the assistant managers of the garden is always present at weighing time. When he arrives for the daily ceremonial, he puts a bullhorn to his lips and his distorted voice echoes and resounds across the valley: "Come. Come. Come now. Come and weigh in your leaf." The young women—each carrying her full basket on her head—always come up the path much faster than anyone else. They seem to scamper rather than walk. The brilliant colors of their blouses and head-shawls make a dramatic contrast as they move along the somber green of the tea bushes.

At the hut, they swing the baskets from their heads without spilling a single leaf and then, chattering and laughing, press around the weighing machine. The overseer weighs each basket on a big spring balance, while the assistant manager writes down in triplicate the name of the plucker and the weight. He hands a copy on a small slip to the plucker. Each woman at once spikes it on the pin that holds her blouse and shawl. Later, perhaps nearer the end of the week, these little slips will be exchanged for money at the treasurer's office.

Each plucker is paid a regular weekly wage and for this is required to weigh in a minimum of twenty pounds of leaf every day. For each pound over the minimum there is a bonus—extra *rupees* to be spent in the bazaar on bright trinkets, or toys, or a length of brilliantly colored cloth.

The best pickers can easily exceed the minimum—often bringing in forty pounds of leaf on a good day.

At the weighing hut, the leaf is transferred from the baskets to big sacks and loaded onto the backs of small, strong ponies—each capable of carrying huge sagging bundles up to three hundred pounds. The men shout to their ponies and they struggle forward up the steep path for the two miles to the "factory" at the top of the ridge. The last pony is loaded with its grotesque burden. The file moves up, the hooves cracking and sparking on the hard rocky path.

The overseers settle down crosslegged in the shade, untie their bundles of food and bottles of slightly cold tea. The pluckers go home to their families. The assistant manager heads for his bungalow on the grass plateau down by the river and dinner with his wife and children. The work of another day is done.

TEA IS MANUFACTURED IN A FACTORY

On arrival at the factory, the sacks of fresh leaf are first taken up by conveyors to the top floor of the building, called "the loft," where the leaves will be slowly dried over gentle heat and begin to wither. When they are first brought in they smell delicately of ginger root but, as they wither, the perfume gradually becomes more fruity and the scent of apples seems to predominate.

The shriveled leaves are then rolled between huge rollers of perfectly polished brass—the pressure precisely adjusted so that the leaves are slightly bruised and crushed. This breaks down the cell walls, so that the enzymes, tannins, pectins, caffeine, and aromatic oils are brought to the surface and exposed to the air, to start the fermentation.

From here the tea goes down chutes to the fermenting rooms where, on immense cement tables with shiny, smooth surfaces—and everthing as sanitary and scrubbed as a hospital operating room—the tea is thinly spread out and left slowly to ferment. The long room becomes filled with a mellow, rich perfume of tea. The color of the bits of leaf spread out on the vast tables turns slowly to a coppery red. This is the tricky time. Now, almost minute by minute, the experts are watching it, picking up small handfuls here and there, sniffing it very close to the nostrils, noting that the fruity perfume is now being transformed into the nuttinesss of almonds, with the combination of spices that is unique to Darjeeling.

The fermentation must be stopped at the precise moment when the perfection of quality has been developed. Then, at that moment, the tea must be "fixed and sealed" by being completely dried in the hot, fired drums on the floor below.

Down there, the woodburning furnaces are already at the correct temperature. Each furnace has its "stoker," who keeps one eye on his fire in the belly of the machine and the other eye on the great hot drum, above it, where the tea will come down from the upper floor on the flexible copper conveyer belt. Each stoker seems almost to be a guard, standing at attention, waiting for the call to instant action. The conveyor belt is still polished and shiny but, after carrying a few thousands of pounds of fermented tea, the belt will be stained a dull ochre from the continuous contact with the tannin. Among the multiplicity of aromas in the firing room, I remember a sense of dry toast and burnt sugar.

After being completely dried, the tea is sifted for grade sizes through the varying meshes of the different shakers and sorters. In the packing room, the empty tea chests are ready-lined with seamless tinfoil or aluminum and snow-white, soft tissue paper. Finally, the boxes are tightly closed and moved out to the loading platform for the trucks.

The monsoon and the plucking were about over on my last day in the tea gardens of Darjeeling. I shall always remember the final scene at the factory. The huge packing room—a handsome, light space, with a highly polished oak floor and tall windows looking out over the gardens—was now almost completely empty, except for one minor operation. There was a small amount of leftover finished tea, but not enough of it to make it worthwhile to run one of the big machines. So a white sheet had been spread in the center of the packing room floor and this tea had been dumped on it, making a heap about, say, three feet high and five feet across. Now, around this heap, in a perfect circle, there squatted a group of colorfully clothed Indian women, grading and sorting by hand this last tea of the season. They discarded the bits of stalk by tossing them neatly onto one bamboo tray. They separated leaves of different sizes onto other trays. Their fingers moved with lightning speed. Their bodies swayed in rhythm with the swings of their bare arms. And—in rhythm, it seemed, with all these movements, they were singing a gentle, low, simple song. It was a leisurely and lovely little picture of life and work in Darjeeling that I will not forget.

A FEW PRACTICAL NOTES ON BUYING AND BREWING
THE BEST-VALUE DARJEELING AND OTHER TEAS

Although, in general, in all the world of teas, Darjeeling is my favorite, I don't drink it exclusively. Even the most exciting taste begins to pall with endless repetition and I always find stimulation in change, experimentation and variety. There are several hundred types of Darjeeling teas—grown in different valleys and at various heights from about a thousand feet up to almost seven thousand feet—but of all teas, grown in all countries, there are more than three thousand varieties. What a challenge for a lifetime of comparative tasting! Many of these teas, naturally, are so different that they simply cannot be compared. Who would dare to set a cup of delicate, almost flowery, subtle Darjeeling against the brash smokiness of a Chinese Lapsang Souchong, or the biting, puckering, tannic power of an "Iron Buddha," or the sheer aromatic force of a Formosa "Black Dragon" Oolong? Yet, without point by point comparison, I can still measure my sensuous pleasure in each one for its particular purpose at its particular time of the day.

Let us agree, at once, that we do not allow ourselves to be led by fancy labels and proprietary names put out by the large, international, tea-blending companies. Because some famous British firm sells "Queen X's Breakfast Blend," there is no social requirement that I have it on my breakfast table. I prefer to buy my teas by their varietal names rather than by the commercial names of the shippers. I am not one of those who believes that the "Orange Pekoe" on a label is the name of some rare and exquisite tea—instead of the standard trade definition of the shape and size of the leaf inside the package. Any tea, from the very best to the very worst, can be an Orange Pekoe. The story of how this phrase became so completely misunderstood, as the result of somewhat irresponsible advertising by Sir Thomas Lipton at the turn of the century, is charmingly and tactfully told by James-Norwood Pratt in his book *The Tea Lover's Treasury*.

In 1890, Thomas Lipton was already a millionaire grocery store owner, with a chain of hundreds of shops all over Britain. He became interested in getting into the tea business in a big way. He went to Ceylon and found so many bankrupt landowners that he was able to buy tea plantations, left and right, at virtually knock-down prices. Returning to Britain, he decided to mass-market his tea at a per-pound price that was less than half what was being charged by his principal competitors. The Lipton advertising slogan was "Direct from My Tea Garden to Your Teapot!" His sales were soon so enormous that his own estates were able to supply only a tiny fraction of his huge volume. Yet his advertising continued to give the distinct impression that he grew every ounce of the tea he sold.

During his travels, Lipton picked up a good deal of the technical jargon of the professional tea tasters and blenders, including, as a definition of leaf size, the phrase "Orange Pekoe." Lipton thought it had such a nice, poetic, romantic sound to it that he decided to print it on every one of his packages and include it in all his advertisements, stressing the pure fiction that "Orange Pekoe" was a rare and superior type of tea. Lipton wsa the showman of the tea business. The millionaire grocer became the multimillionaire tea merchant.

Other professional definitions of leaf sizes have been equally misused. For example, such phrases as "Young Hyson," or souchong, or "fannings," have no reference to quality of type of tea. In fact, "fannings" is the almost powdery leaf that passes through the last and smallest meshed sieve—just one grade above "dust." None of them should be despised. The fannings of a great tea is many times superior to even the largest leaf of a very poor quality. The point is that these words have nothing to do with quality—neither in Darjeeling, nor anywhere else.

Nor do I ever buy a tea just because it is labeled "Earl Grey"—a name that, after more than a hundred years of use, has lost all of its original significance. Earl Grey was a British nobleman who, during a stint as a diplomat in the Orient, became an investor in the sailing ships that brought teas to Europe. Later, Lord Grey was British Prime Minister. He had a special blend of tea made up for his private use and, later, authorized its sale under his name to the public. After his death, the copyright on his name expired and, today, any tea company can throw together any blend and call the result "Earl Grey," whether the tea be good, bad, or indifferent. This is not to say that some "Earl Greys" put out by reliable firms are not still first-class. But the name, in itself, is no longer any guarantee of quality.

My own uses of my various teas are quite personal. I make different demands of them at different times of the day.

Morning Teas

After being woken up at crack of dawn with the blackest and strongest coffee, I prefer tea with my sit-down breakfast. But it must be a robust and fairly sharp variety. There are some Darjeelings of this type—or, occasionally, I might substitute a Chinese aged Keemun, the black fermented type with the flavor often described as "winey," giving a slight shock to the tongue that, to me, is excellent for the early hours of the day up to mid-morning, or even lunch. Keemun was named for the district of China where it was first grown. Another tea with a suitable morning "shock of aftertaste" is Formosa "Black Dragon" Oolong, a half-fermented half-green type, more delicate than Keemun. Another morning alternative worth an experimental tasting is the so-called High Mountain Ceylon from Sri Lanka, where the leaf matures slowly in the cool ocean breezes and the aromatic oils develop strongly to a rich and almost startling perfume.

Afternoon Teas

Toward the end of the working day, when the stresses and tensions need to be eased, I look for tea that is softer, more delicately flowery, more discreetly perfumed, and there are several Darjeeling types that fill this gently soothing need. Among the Chinese alternatives, the element of floweriness is carried to a peak in Jasmine, in which green or Pouchong teas are blended with dried petals of the jasmine flower. Sometimes in the afternoon, I turn to the extraordinary, delicate smokiness of Chinese Lapsang Souchong, one of the rarest and most unusual of all teas. It was grown originally in a valley of China where the July sun was so hot that the leaves were slightly burnt while still on the bush. Like in other places where it is cultivated, the plucked leaves are deliberately smoked over wood fires to develop the special, strange, complicated flavor balance.

Evening Teas

After dinner, or for the last sip at night before going to bed, there is nothing to equal a great Darjeeling type—from a tea garden at, say, seven thousand feet. At these cool elevations the leaf matures very slowly, bringing a soft roundness of flavor and a marvelous, almost mystical, lingering aroma. There is simply no alternative to Darjeeling.

Brewing a Superb Cup of Tea

It hardly needs to be repeated that buying and brewing tea in teabags has every possible disadvantage and virtually no advantage. The tea deteriorates more quickly when separated by air pockets in small doses. The cost per ounce is usually about double that of the same grade of loose tea. The bag inhibits the proper first quick contact between the boiling water and the tea leaf. The vital fact is that the first dash of absolutely boiling water during the first fraction of a second uncurls the leaf, opens its pores, and brings out the flavor oils. This is the scientific justification for all the ritual. This is why the usually English-made brown earthenware teapot is the best, because it is an insulator to hold in the heat. I avoid teapots of fancy china, heatproof glass, or silver, etc. I have one brown earthenware that holds one pint and another with a capacity of one quart. The Japanese have their "tea ceremony"—I have my own . . .

1. I thoroughly warm the teapot with hot water, empty that out and dry it completely before putting in the tea. Nothing is worse than for the tea to become wet before the moment of scalding. I put in about 2 teaspoons of tea for the pint pot, 4 teaspoons for the quart.

2. The water must come up absolutely to a rolling boil in the kettle. I bring the teapot to within an inch or two of the spout of the boiling kettle and pour quickly at the moment of fierce boiling.

3. Stir at once and then brew for somewhere between 3 and 7 minutes, depending on your taste and the type of tea. Then stir again and pour into a pre-warmed cup. To swamp great tea with lashings of milk and sugar, or to dominate it completely with lemon juice, is a crime. I drink my best teas with nothing in them, but I am not entirely opposed to a single drop or two of heavy cream, to add a slight body with minimum effect on flavor, plus no more than a drop or two of a thin sugar syrup.

Georges Blanc: France's Youngest Three-Star Chef

His intimates among the winemakers have always affectionately called him Le Petit Blanc—Burgundian slang for "a small glass of white"—the reference being to his stature and his youth. Now they are saying that Le Petit Blanc has become *un grand cru!* Certainly, in 1981 the lightning of supreme success struck Georges Blanc and his beautiful *auberge*-restaurant, La Mère Blanc, in southern Burgundy from every direction at once. In January, the prestigious *Gault-Millau Guide France* awarded him its top rating of four red toques and an almost unbelievable nineteen points out of a possible twenty, placing him on an equal level with such decorated French chefs as Paul Bocuse, the Troisgros brothers, Roger Vergé, Michel Guérard, and even the fabled Fredy Girardet of Switzerland. Then, in March, the noted *Michelin Guide* made his the twenty-first restaurant and him the youngest *cuisinier* (at thirty-seven) in France with three stars, their top rating.

I first met Georges fifteen years ago. Jean Troisgros had taken me along on one of his wine-tasting and buying expeditions to Burgundy, and we were driving from Mâcon toward the Beaujolais. Suddenly Jean turned sharp left onto the narrowest of twisting country roads, saying, "I'm taking you to lunch at the restaurant of a young chef friend of mine who has a great future." Within five minutes, we were in Vonnas, the tiniest, most rural of villages, its square dominated by the church and the almost

---

EDITOR'S NOTE: This article originally appeared in the April 1983 issue of *Food & Wine*. The restaurant is now called Georges Blanc and still merited three stars in the 1986 edition of the *Michelin Guide*.

miniature, white-fronted, flower-bedecked *auberge*, Chez La Mère Blanc.

Inside we were welcomed, instantly charmed, and cosseted by a stunningly beautiful, naturally poised young woman: Georges's wife, Jacqueline. As soon as we were seated in the tiny lounge, sipping KirBeaujolais, Georges appeared with a tray of hors d'oeuvre that I can still remember in detail. Included were artichoke bottoms filled with diced foie gras delicately touched by Madeira and port, and an extraordinary concoction of snow-white strips of chicken breast marinated with Cognac, herbs and lemon and truffle juice (see recipe, page 228). From the hot and cold hors d'oeuvre, I knew at once that Georges had the two most basic gifts of every great cook: a sure hand with the balance of aromatic herbs and an absolute mastery of the cooking fires.

There followed a brilliantly imaginative lunch: local baby frog's legs, crisp and juicy under a delicate coating of herbed batter; the classic *poularde de Bresse à la crème* (Bresse chicken in cream), which first made the *auberge* famous (see recipe, page 224); followed by a climactic main course, Georges's invention of roasted squabs filled with a ragoût of the forest—wild chanterelles and morels, forest herbs, and woodland berries—all the different flavors coexisting in harmony, yet each delicately retaining its separate identity.

During such a feast, I could hardly avoid learning a good deal about Georges Blanc—his tranquillity and his strength, an inner steel-like security. The roots of that security are in the history of the house. In 1872 his great-grandparents Jean-Louis and Virginie Blanc opened the *auberge* here at the edge of the Vonnas fairground. They knew it was the site of a market every Thursday and that the poultry farmers and their wives who came in their horse-drawn carts to shop would then come in for a *casse-croûte*, country lunch. Great-grandmother Virginie gave them so precisely what they wanted that word traveled and within a few months Chez La Mère Blanc had become famous in the region.

But it was the next Mère Blanc, Grandmother Elisa, who brought them national fame. She stayed firmly with the rich local cuisine of butter and cream, but she dared to adapt and add her measure of sophistication. In 1930 *Michelin* awarded her a star and Curnonsky (perhaps the greatest gastronomic writer in French history), said of her: "La Mère Blanc is the greatest natural cook in the world." In 1934 the third Mère Blanc, George's mother, Paulette, took command and by 1950 had earned two *Michelin* stars, which she handed over in 1968 to Georges.

If an inner security is Georges's first great strength, then his second, the source of his leadership qualities, is his classical training. His mother was sure that he would be influenced by the revolutionary ferment of our gastronomic times, but she felt he should at least stand on a solid classical foundation. So Georges took the full course at l'École Hôtelière de Thonon-les-Bains, the conservative hotel and restaurant school outside Geneva in Switzerland. Then he apprenticed in restaurants in Paris and the provinces, including La Réserve in Beaulieu-sur-Mer near Nice. Finally, he was sous-chef to his mother for two years. (He whispered to me, "It was very hard having my mother as my boss.")

I became so interested in this young man with the extraordinary balance of instinct and reflection that I have been back to Vonnas virtually every year to observe his progress and, of course, to enjoy some of the best food I have eaten anywhere. As I sampled menu after menu, I became aware of Georges's third great strength: his loyalty to the traditions of his region, of which Vonnas is the central crossroads. Despite all his adapting, changing, creating, and inventing, Georges is as loyal to these regional traditions as was his grandmother.

What a region it is—perhaps the richest gastronomic storehouse of France. To the east is Bresse, which produces the Rolls-Royce of chickens and, among its many cheeses, the great bleu de Bresse; the wide valley of the Ain with its exquisite small yellow cows, its tiny lambs and veal, its almost miniature goats; and the mountains of the Jura with wild mushrooms, snails, and forest fruits. To the south is the Beaujolais and the Pays de Dombes, the wonderful wild country of lakes and marshes, game birds, crayfish, and tiny frogs. To the north are the marvels of Burgundy, including more cheeses, fruits, and vegetables. And to the west, the Charolais, the best beef of France.

Georges Blanc has taken the old dishes of the region and given them a new breadth and subtlety. He has opened up new facets, shown us new concepts, new ideas and possibilities. He has taken traditional regional cuisine and brought it into the twentieth century.

"I leave it to others to say that I have exposed new facets or brought new insights to ancient, traditional cuisines of the Ain; the Bresse, and the Jura," explains Blanc. "I certainly do not believe in reinventing everything and in rejecting the old farmhouse cooking. On the contrary, I admire and respect the *ancienne cuisine* of all our provincial *grandmères*, with cream and butter separated in the morning, with magnificently fresh natural products."

But, Blanc says, he is trying to produce a healthier cuisine. "I deliberately avoid using flour to absorb the fat as was always done in the old days, thus holding all the grease of a dish and making it quite indigestible. In my *poularde de Bresse à la crème*, for example, I use only a quarter as much flour as would normally go into a single breakfast brioche. There is only enough flour to bind the sauce without binding the grease, which, as a result, rises to the surface and can be skimmed off and discarded.

"My preparation of all these ancient dishes," concludes Blanc, "is therefore a much healthier cooking technique than any of the traditional recipes of, say, fifty years ago. Also, I believe that the flavors of my modern versions are more concentrated, better balanced, more pleasurable to the taste buds than in the days when they were overlaid with large quantities of fat-impregnated starch."

Now, it seems that many other young French chefs have also decided that this is the way to go. This trend, which may profoundly affect many of the restaurant kitchens of France, was discussed in a recent issue of the French monthly gastronomic magazine, *Le Nouveau Guide*, under the title "The Return to Regional Cuisine—the Profound Wealth of France." The writer considers the work of twenty-five young chef-restaurateurs in various parts of France who, instead of endlessly imitating and repeating the clichéd dishes of *nouvelle cuisine*, are turning for inspiration back to their regional cuisines, which, the author asserts, "are just as important, just as valuable, and just as essential to keep in up-to-date repair as any of the national monuments of France." To me, Georges Blanc is unquestionably the leading champion of this point of view.

Georges's subtle modifications of the cuisine of his predecessors has recently been accompanied by other changes as well. He has transformed the *auberge* from a charming, minuscule country inn and bistro into one of the most elegant and luxurious small country hotels in France. (At the same time, he changed the restaurant's name to La Mère Blanc, dropping the "Chez" with its homey *auberge* implications.) There is a new dining room alongside the river, with an immense new kitchen, all gleaming and shining with copper and stainless steel and a glass wall that makes the work in progress visible to all diners. The twenty-five hotel rooms have been enlarged and imaginatively redecorated by Jacqueline with authentic antique Bresse furniture, lovely handcrafted pieces of cherrywood or walnut. There are now four sumptuous suites, one with its own private solarium. There is also a heated swimming pool, flower-filled outdoor dining patios, tennis courts and, shades of Hollywood, a landing pad for helicopters. Across the street is La Boutique Blanc, a luxurious shop where the specialties and wines of the *auberge* may be brought to take home.

As to my prognosis for the cooking that goes with all this new elegance and luxury, I have unbounded faith in Georges's future. I can do no better than quote my French colleague, Guy Gentilhomme: "Georges Blanc, I don't quite know how far you're going, but I do know already that it is absolutely necessary for me to go wherever you will be!"

Whenever Georges has served a dish that has particularly delighted me, he has always been willing immediately to give me the recipe. So now I have a "Georges Blanc Collection" to bring me special pleasure in my own kitchen and to delight my friends. The dishes are always among my proudest productions. In the following recipes, the comments and notes are predominantly Georges's.

BRESSE CHICKEN IN CREAM À LA GRANDMÈRE BLANC

4 servings

> 3½-pound chicken
> 4 tablespoons clarified butter
> Salt and freshly ground pepper
> 3 tablespoons all-purpose flour
> About 4 cups chicken stock or canned broth
> 1 medium onion stuck with 1 clove
> 1 medium clove of garlic
> 1 sprig of fresh thyme or ½ teaspoon dried
> 1 bay leaf
> 4 cups heavy cream, reduced by half (see note)
> 3 egg yolks
> ½ teaspoon fresh lemon juice

1. Cut the chicken into 8 pieces as follows: Cut off the legs and separate the drumsticks from the thighs. Using a very sharp boning knife, lift the complete breasts off the carcass. Cut each breast in half crosswise. You now have 8 pieces that you will serve; all the rest of the chicken is to provide flavor for the sauce. Cut off the wings and divide them into their sections. Chop the carcass into fairly large but manageable pieces and set aside.

2. Heat 2 tablespoons of the butter in a large skillet. Add the 8 chicken serving pieces. Salt and pepper them and sauté over high heat, turning, until golden in color, about 5 minutes. Remove with a slotted spoon and set aside.

3. Add the remaining 2 tablespoons butter to the skillet and warm over moderately high heat. Add the reserved chicken wings and bones and cook, tossing, for about 2 minutes, to coat on all sides with butter. Sprinkle the pieces evenly with the flour. Continue to cook, tossing, until the flour is well browned, about 2 minutes longer.

4. Pour in enough stock (about 3½ cups) to cover the wings and

bones. Increase the heat to high and cook, stirring constantly, until the stock boils and thickens slightly, about 6 minutes. Reduce the heat to a gentle simmer, move the wings and bones to the sides of the skillet and place the browned serving pieces in the center of the pan. Make sure the pieces are covered by the stock, add more if necessary.

5. Tuck the onion, garlic, thyme and bay leaf around the serving pieces and simmer gently, uncovered, until the serving pieces are perfectly cooked: the breast meat about 6 minutes, the thighs and legs about 15 minutes. If the stock reduces too quickly, or if any of the pieces are not covered, add more stock to cover. As each piece is done, remove to a warm platter and keep warm.

6. When all the serving pieces are cooked, strain the cooking liquid through a fine sieve into a bowl. Spoon off any excess grease and place 1½ cups of the liquid in a medium saucepan (reserve the remainder for another use).

7. Warm the 1½ cups cooking liquid over low heat just to a simmer. In a medium bowl, whisk the reduced cream with the egg yolks until blended. Remove the pan from the heat and beat the cream and egg yolk mixture into the warmed liquid. Stirring constantly, warm the sauce over low heat until it thickens enough to lightly coat the back of a spoon; do not allow to boil. If the sauce becomes too thick, add more stock, 1 tablespoon at a time. Taste and adjust the seasonings, then add the lemon juice.

8. Return the serving pieces to the sauce just to heat through. Divide the chicken among 4 plates and coat lightly with some of the sauce. Pass the remaining sauce separately.

NOTE: Simmer the cream until reduced by half, about 1 hour.

POTATO CRÊPES VONNASSIENNES

This is the second of the famous specialties of the *auberge*. The recipe was invented by accident by Grandmère Elisa. She was mixing a batch of dough for potato dumplings when she inadvertently threw in more than double the proper quantity of eggs and cream. Not wanting to waste the batter, she decided to fry it in the form of small crêpes. They fluffed up like puffballs and were such an enormous success with the customers that they have not been off the menu for seventy-five years.

Georges says they can be served either as a separate savory course after the meat, sprinkled with salt and pepper, or as a dessert, covered with fine sugar.

6 servings

> 1 *pound baking potatoes*
> 3 *tablespoons milk*
> 3 *tablespoons all-purpose flour*
> 3 *whole eggs*
> 4 *egg whites*
> ¼ *cup heavy cream*
> 1 *cup (2 sticks) butter, clarified*

1. In a medium saucepan of boiling salted water, cook the potatoes until tender when pierced with a knife, about 25 minutes; drain and rinse briefly under cold running water. Peel the potatoes and put them through a ricer or mash until smooth. Beat in the milk. Refrigerate the potatoes until just cool, about 10 minutes.

2. Lightly blend in the flour with a wooden spatula, folding rather than stirring. In the same way, add the whole eggs, one at a time and then the egg whites. Gently blend in the cream, mixing lightly until the potato batter is the consistency of a thick pastry cream.

3. Heat 2 tablespoons of the clarified butter in a large sauté pan. Add the batter by tablespoons to make small crêpes about 2½ inches in diameter. Fry over moderately high heat, turning frequently, until lightly browned on both sides, about 1 minute in all. Transfer to a warm platter and keep hot in a low oven while frying the remaining crêpes. Serve at once on hot plates.

SEA SCALLOPS IN SAUTERNES SAUCE

4 servings

> 12 *large sea scallops*
> 4 *tablespoons unsalted butter*
> 2 *shallots, minced*
> 1 *cup Sauternes*
> 2 *cups heavy cream, reduced by half (see note)*
> ½ *teaspoon salt*
> ¼ *teaspoon freshly ground pepper*
> ½ *teaspoon curry powder*
> 1 *tablespoon fresh lemon juice*
> ¼ *cup green pistachio nuts—shelled, skinned, and coarsely chopped*
> 1 *tablespoon minced fresh chives*

1. Preheat the oven to 500° F. Cut each scallop horizontally in half. Arrange them on a lightly buttered cookie sheet.

2. In a heavy, medium, noncorrodible saucepan, melt 1 tablespoon of the butter. Add the shallots and cook over low heat until wilted, about 2 minutes. Add the Sauternes, increase the heat to moderate, and boil until reduced by half, about 3 minutes. Add the reduced cream. Boil for 2 minutes longer. Whisk in the remaining 3 tablespoons butter, the salt, pepper, curry powder and lemon juice. Strain through a fine sieve and keep the sauce warm over low heat.

3. Bake the scallops for 1 minute. Turn them over and cook for 1 to 2 minutes longer, until just opaque throughout.

4. Divide the scallops among 4 warmed plates and coat each serving with about ¼ cup of the sauce. Sprinkle the top with the pistachios and chives.

NOTE: Simmer the cream until reduced by half, about 45 minutes.

MARINATED CHICKEN BREASTS ALEXANDRE

This is the hors d'oeuvre that so instantly impressed me the first time I visited Georges almost fifteen years ago. Since then, he has substantially developed and improved the recipe. This is the latest version, which he has now named in honor of his younger son. Georges says, "This original concept is very refreshing and is excellent for arousing the appetite. Serve it with a fresh, light, red wine—ideally a Beaujolais nouveau."

4 to 6 servings

>   2 pounds veal bones
>   3 cups chicken stock or canned broth
>   4 skinless, boneless chicken breast halves (about 1 pound)
>   2 tablespoons sherry wine vinegar
>   2 tablespoons white wine vinegar
>   1/4 cup olive oil
>   2 tablespoons corn or peanut oil
>   2 teaspoons Dijon-style mustard
>   1 tablespoon fresh lemon juice
>   1 teaspoon Cognac or brandy
>   2 whole cloves
>   1 medium shallot, finely minced
>   2 tablespoons minced fresh chives
>   2 tablespoons minced fresh tarragon or 2 teaspoons dried
>   Salt and freshly ground pepper
>   1 cup green beans, cut into 2-inch lengths, for garnish
>   1 large ripe tomato, quartered and seeded, for garnish
>   12 very thin slices black truffle (optional)

1. In a large saucepan, simmer the veal bones, 1 cup of the chicken stock, and water to cover for 1 hour, skimming the foam from the top occasionally. Strain and skim off the fat. Measure out 1 cup of the stock to use in the marinade in Step 3; reserve the remainder for another use.

2. In a large deep skillet or heatproof casserole, arrange the chicken breasts in a single layer. Add the remaining 2 cups chicken stock and enough water, if necessary, just to cover. Heat to a bare simmer, cover and poach gently until the breasts are barely pink in the center, 8 to 10 minutes. Remove, drain, and pat dry.

3. Meanwhile, make the marinade: In a small bowl, whisk the reserved 1 cup of stock, the sherry wine vinegar, white wine vinegar, olive oil, corn oil, mustard, lemon juice, and Cognac until blended. Stir in

the cloves, shallot, chives, and tarragon. Season with salt and pepper to taste.

4. With a very sharp knife, cut each chicken breast horizontally into 3 thin slices. Arrange the slices in a single layer in a large noncorrodible pan or baking dish. Pour the marinade over the chicken; turn to coat both sides. Marinate, turning the slices every 30 minutes, for at least 1 and up to 3 hours.

5. Serve the chicken at room temperature, sauced with a little of the marinade. Garnish each plate with some green beans and a tomato quarter, dressed with the marinade. Decorate each piece of chicken with a truffle slice, if desired.

ONE-MINUTE SALMON WITH SAUCE AIGRELETTE

Aigrelette is Georges's jocular name for a sauce of his creation. He argues that if a vinaigrette is made primarily from vinegar, then an aigrelette is mixed mainly from *aigre* (bitter-sour-tart) components. He also calls the sauce "my bastard mayonnaise." It's an extremely good and useful all-around sauce, which can enhance and magnify many different ingredients.

The slices of the fish are so delicate and thin that once they are baked, they simply cannot be lifted from a serving platter to the plates. So they have to be actually cooked on the dinner plates. You should not, therefore, use your best and thinnest china in a 550° F. oven, even though it's only in for a few seconds.

Georges says: "In small servings, this can be an hors d'oeuvre; in larger amounts, it's a light main dish or the dramatic fish course of a grand dinner party."

4 main-course or 6 appetizer servings

  1 *egg yolk*
  1 *teaspoon Dijon-style mustard*
  3 *teaspoons fresh lemon juice*
  ½ *cup peanut oil*
  ¼ *cup olive oil*
  ¼ *cup soybean oil*
  3 *tablespoons dry white wine*
  2 *tablespoons canned chicken broth*
  1 *tablespoon white wine vinegar*
  1 *tablespoon minced fresh chives*
  1 *tablespoon minced fresh tarragon or 1 teaspoon dried*
  ½ *teaspoon coarse (kosher) salt*
  ⅛ *teaspoon freshly ground pepper*
  2 *pounds fresh salmon—boned and cut on the diagonal into about 20 very thin slices (see note)*

1. In a medium bowl, whisk the egg yolk, mustard, and 1 teaspoon of the lemon juice. Gradually begin to whisk in the peanut, olive, and soybean oils, drop by drop, until the mayonnaise begins to thicken. Then continue to whisk in the oils in a thin stream until they are all incorporated. (If the sauce becomes too thick, beat in 1 or 2 teaspoons of the wine, then add the rest of the oil.) Beat in the wine, broth, vinegar,

and remaining 2 teaspoons lemon juice. Stir in the chives, tarragon, salt, and pepper. (The recipe may be prepared ahead to this point. Cover and refrigerate the sauce.)

2. If the sauce has been refrigerated, take it out and let return to room temperature. Preheat the oven to 550° F. Lightly butter 4 or 6 heatproof plates or a platter. Sprinkle lightly with salt and pepper. Arrange the salmon slices on the plates and let come to room temperature.

3. Slide the plates into the oven and bake for about 1½ minutes, until the fish is pale but still rose-colored at its center. Immediately remove from the oven; the heat of the plate will continue to cook the fish.

4. Spoon about 1 tablespoon of the sauce over each slice of salmon and serve immediately, warning guests of the hot plates.

NOTE: Ask your fishmonger to do this. Or if you prefer to slice the salmon at home, put it in the freezer for 10 minutes to firm the fish and make it easier to slice.

BRESSE FARMHOUSE CHOCOLATE CAKE

6 servings

> 7 ounces bittersweet or semisweet chocolate, broken into small pieces
> ½ cup plus 1 teaspoon unsalted butter
> ¼ cup cake flour
> ½ cup plus 1 tablespoon superfine sugar
> 3 eggs
> ¾ cup heavy cream, reduced by half (see note)
> 1 tablespoon unsweetened cocoa powder

1. Preheat the oven to 400° F. Lightly butter an 8-inch springform pan.

2. In a double boiler, melt 4 ounces of the chocolate and ½ cup of the butter, cut into small pieces.

3. In a medium bowl, blend the flour and ½ cup of the sugar. Add the eggs and mix well.

4. Add the melted chocolate and butter to the bowl and, with an electric mixer, beat at high speed for about 5 minutes, until the batter is smooth and forms a ribbon when the beaters are lifted.

5. Pour the batter into the prepared pan (it will be about 1 inch deep) and bake for 15 to 20 minutes, until the cake is set and a toothpick inserted in the center comes out dry.

6. Unmold the cake onto a rack and let cool; it will fall to about half its original height.

7. Meanwhile, in a double boiler, melt the remaining 3 ounces chocolate and 1 teaspoon butter.

8. In a small heavy saucepan, bring the reduced cream to a boil, then whisk it vigorously into the chocolate. Continue whisking until smooth and glossy.

9. Place sheets of waxed paper under the cake and cooling rack. Pour the frosting over the top of the cake, using a metal spatula to spread it evenly over the top and sides.

10. After the frosting has hardened slightly, about 5 minutes, use a long straight knife to mark the top in a cross-cross pattern. Mix the cocoa with the remaining 1 tablespoon sugar and sprinkle it decoratively over the cake before serving.

NOTE: Simmer the cream until reduced by half, about 20 minutes.

Steak with Ten Peppers from The Four Seasons

Reaching one's twenty-first birthday is just as important a milestone for a restaurant as it is for a young man or woman. It means coming of age, the development of character, a degree of maturity, the unfolding of personality, and the beginning of sophistication. All these are equally important to a restaurant—especially if it is as controversial, as famous, as influential in restaurant design, as revolutionary in concept as The Four Seasons, which enters its twenty-first year in 1980* and remains one of the half-dozen top restaurants in Manhattan.

On its opening day in 1959, I sat at a table among the growing trees at the edge of the bubbling pool in the middle of the main dining room. I so much enjoyed the spot that a note was made on my card in the reservations office for me to be given that table whenever I called. So I have been sitting in the same seat for twenty-one years and, like a father watching his child grow up, I am in a good position to remember why the beginning was so noisy and what happened to the food along the way.

In 1958, the glass and steel Seagram Building, thirty-eight floors of ultramodern shape and surface texture, was rising in Manhattan from the designs of the two most experimental architects of the twentieth century, Mies van der Rohe and Philip Johnson. They were quick to conceptualize the restaurant that might be planned within the superb setting of this building. Three floors were set aside for it so the dining rooms could be dramatically tall.

---

*EDITOR'S NOTE: This syndicated newspaper article originally appeared in January 1980.

Johnson designed the interior to be almost futuristic—the walls paneled with polished walnut, a pool bubbling as if it were Champagne, tall trees growing in huge tubs and massive suspended flower boxes creating the atmosphere of a lovely garden, a king's ransom in modern art work (from the suspended ceiling sculpture of Lippold to the huge stage curtain by Picasso), with tall curtains of tiny chains of aluminum, so light they simmer and undulate with the indoor breezes.

But, of course, the traditionalists screamed bloody murder. They called it a deluxe hospital. They said it had a cold and naked look—that it had the atmosphere of a corporation boardroom—that it was a chauvinistic place for men in dark suits and that women in lovely dresses looked out of place.

There also has been a good deal of debate about the food. As the Seagram's people, owners of the building, sold their whiskies and wines to virtually every country in the world, they thought it would be tactful and wise to have a restaurant that offered a melting-pot American menu, with the finest natural products from all over the world absorbed into daily specials of brilliant freshness and quality.

The first menus were worked out by the late Albert Stockli, the Swiss chef who veered away from the classic dishes and who invented off-beat food combinations. Some of these, such as calves' liver with slices of avocado, have been so successful that, after twenty-one years, they are still on the menus.

Over the years The Four Seasons has had its ups and downs. It has been run by some very showy and showoff chefs and managers. Today, when rising costs force simplification in every direction, it is better than ever before. Its two current manager-owners, Paul Kovi and Tom Margittai, stress quiet, professional skill rather than noisy showmanship. They have stripped away some of the decorative fol-de-rols so that you can again see the original architectural design in all its magnificence. But the most significant symbol of change is the current director of the kitchen, Swiss-born executive chef Seppi Renggli, classically trained, charming, gentle, modest yet self-assured.

In the restaurant, he and his staff prepare the best fish and shellfish in New York City. Their steak tartare, lightly laced with Cognac, is superb. Vegetables—including the new sugar snap peas—are crisp, sweet, and wonderful. More or less in honor of the restaurant's twenty-first birthday, Renggli has worked out and perfected an irresistibly attractive variation to the classic "steak au poivre," the steak pounded with cracked black pepper that is a standard offering in most French restaurants.

Renggli uses not one but a spectrum of six or even ten kinds of pepper, so as you cut each mouthful of meat on your plate, you get a distinctive flavor from each variety of the spice. He gave me his restaurant recipe and I have adapted it for home use.

First, you have to get a supply of the various peppers. Most of them are available at local fancy food or spice shops, but, if you have difficulty with, say, the "Grains of Paradise," you can order it (and the others) by mail from the specialist spice suppliers, Aphrodisia Inc., 282 Bleecker Street, New York, NY 10014. Telephone: 212/989-6440.

In spite of the several peppers used in this dramatic preparation, it does not end up very hot on your tongue. This is because a good part of the peppery oils are burnt away during the searing of the steaks, so you can add pepper to suit your own taste. Also, the garnishing with the green and red julienne strips of sweet peppers gentles and softens the taste while adding color, crispness, and juiciness. This *steak aux dix poivres à la Seppi* (steak with ten peppers) is handsome to look at and dramatic to taste—a good reminder, after twenty-one years, of the continuing innovative momentum of The Four Seasons.

STEAK WITH TEN PEPPERS FROM THE FOUR SEASONS

4 servings

- 2 teaspoons whole Lampong black peppercorns, coarsely cracked in a mortar or electric spice mill
- 2 teaspoons whole Tellicherry black peppercorns, coarsely cracked, as above
- 2 teaspoons whole Chinese Szechuan brown peppery berries, 1 teaspoon coarsely cracked, remainder finely cracked (not ground)
- ½ teaspoon whole Mexican Tepino brown chili pepper berries, coarsely cracked
- ¼ teaspoon very hot red pepper flakes, finely crushed, or, if unavailable, use cayenne
  Coarse crystal or kosher salt
- 4 sirloin steaks, of whatever cut, shape, size, and trim you prefer, but each should be about 1½ inches thick
- 2 tablespoons fine fruity olive oil
- 6 tablespoons unsalted butter
- 1 teaspoon whole Cubeb peppery berries, finely cracked
- 1 teaspoon whole Liberian "Grains of Paradise" peppercorns, finely cracked
- 1 teaspoon whole Madagascar dried green peppercorns, finely cracked
- 1 teaspoon whole Montuk white peppercorns, finely cracked
- 1 teaspoon whole Madagascar drained soft green peppercorns, canned in brine, mashed to a paste
- 2 tablespoons corn, peanut, or other vegetable oil
- 2 medium sweet green bell peppers, seeded, deribbed, cut into thin julienne matchsticks
- 2 medium sweet red bell peppers, cut in the same way

Blending the Peppers and Pounding the Steaks

Thoroughly toss together in a small bowl the coarsely cracked peppers: the blacks, 1 teaspoon of the Szechuan, the Mexican, the red flakes, plus 1 teaspoon of the salt. Pound the steaks lightly with a serrated meat hammer or scallopine mallet, or with the back of a clean, heavy frypan to loosen, stretch, and tenderize the meat. Now, using the heel of your hand, press and pound the mixed peppers and salt evenly across and into both sides of each steak. You don't have to use all the pepper mixture, but remember that a good part of the hot oils will be burnt away by the searing heat. Next, gently pat both sides of each with the olive oil so there is an even coating all around. Let the steaks rest at room temperature for 2 hours to absorb the aromatic spice flavors.

During the last 15 minutes or so of this time, heat up whatever method of searing you are going to use. Best, of course, is a charcoal grill—good alternatives are a very hot broiler or a large, heavy, very hot frypan.

Searing the Steaks and Adding the Exotic Peppers

For the fullest appreciation of the aromatic flavors, the steaks should be served properly rare. This means, with correct high heat, grilling, broiling, or frying for about 3 minutes on the first side and about 2 minutes on the second—or a few seconds longer, to your taste. If you fry in a pan, you will need to use the butter—if not, melt the butter separately and dribble it, hot, over the steaks at the moment of serving. While the steaks are being seared, warm up a platter to hold them.

The moment the steaks are done, place them on the platter, leaving them to rest and mature for exactly 10 minutes. During this wait, apply the remaining peppers to the top surface only of each steak. If you have been lucky with your shopping, you now have six aromatic peppers left. Divide the top surface of each steak, in your mind, into six sections and lightly cover each section with one of the remaining peppers. The idea is that, as the steak is cut by the diner, virtually each mouthful will have a different surprise aromatic flavor—a flavor associated with a different Far Eastern nation. Do not allow the peppers to mix or overlap. Sprinkle and pat on, lightly, in turn, the remaining Szechuan, the Cubeb, the "Grains of Paradise," the dried green, the white, then spread the last section with the soft green paste, mashed with the back of a spoon. Let all the peppers rest on the steaks.

Garnishing and Serving

Place a large sauté pan on high frying heat and lubricate its bottom with the corn oil. When it is quite hot, put in, all at once, the green and red pepper julienne matchsticks. Stir and toss them almost continuously, until they are quite crisp and very hot—usually no more than 3 or 4 minutes. Set the pan aside, off the heat.

Finally, at the last moment before serving, set the steaks back under a hot broiler for 10 seconds to soften and toast the peppers, then garnish with the sweet pepper matchsticks, dribble on the melted butter and any pan juices, then serve at once on very hot plates. The ideal accompaniment is butter-sautéed mushrooms.

The Finest Regional Dish in America

Not too many years ago, it began to look as if regional dishes soon would be on the endangered species list. As air transportation took its great leap forward and the world became smaller, no one had to travel to Hong Kong anymore to taste authentic bird's nest soup or imperial shark's-fin stew. It seemed everyone in the world would be eating the same dishes.

It has not quite worked out that way. The strongest force toward preserving regional cuisine has been tourism. Several decades ago, two far-sighted French gourmets, Maurice-Edmond Sailland (who wrote cookbooks under the grandiose pseudonym Curnonsky, Prince of Gourmets) and Austin de Croze, saw the handwriting on the wall. France was going the way of the United States. All the food of the provinces was being shipped to Les Halles, the central market of Paris, from where it was being spread back over the country in a bland, thin, uniform layer— a little bit of everything going everywhere. Regional cooking differences were disappearing. The two realized that, if this happened, the provinces would lose their tourist business. Both French families and visitors from abroad traveled around France mainly for the experience in tasting different foods.

Sailland and De Croze spent ten years traveling around France to virtually every city, town, and village in every region, talking to local restaurateurs, newspaper editors, housewives, and hotelmen, warning them

---

EDITOR'S NOTE: This syndicated newspaper article originally appeared in February 1979.

of what would happen to their tourist income if they failed to maintain and build up their regional cuisines. They formed committees of house-wives to do research in local libraries, to dig out old cookbooks and recipes, to bring them up to date, to see that the dishes were served in local restaurants and publicized in local newspapers. These two men singlehandedly saved the regional gastronomy of France.

Ten years ago, the late editor of *Esquire* magazine, Arnold Gingrich, asked me if I would write a column, "The Movable Feast," that would document whether there were still regional dishes and foods in the U.S. He suggested that I begin in Denver because it was "the largest city farthest from any coast and from most of the agricultural centers." Den-ver would be the supreme test. On my first evening, I found fresh grilled Rocky Mountain rainbow trout on the menu. With my first bite, I knew there was a gastronomic world to explore.

From Denver, I spread out and around North America. In Nova Scotia I found smoked Gaspé salmon. In Boston, codfish cakes and baked beans. In Philadelphia, snapper soup, pepper pot, fish-house punch, and scrapple. In Baltimore, imperial crab cakes, Chincoteague oysters, dia-mond-back terrapin stew, grilled blue crabs with a strip of bacon, and roast canvasback duck. In Florida, stone crabs. In Creole New Orleans, gumbos, jambalayas, pompano en papillote, calas tout chaud, and *café brûlot*.

People who say that there is no great regional food in America are ax grinders, fools, or knaves—or all three. But if I review all the U.S. specialties, I have ever enjoyed, there is one dish, in one place, that ranks above the others. You find it, in its most dramatic and irresistible form, prepared by the Italian-Americans of San Francisco.

· It is a dish that follows a great international tradition. If you charter a fishing boat in the old port of Marseilles for a day of sport on the Medi-terranean, your day will end with a wonderful beach picnic. Your fisher-man will land you in a nearby cove, light a fire, hang a huge old black iron pot over it, put in olive oil, onions, tomatoes, saffron, herbs, and wine, with a carefully balanced mixed bag of fish and shellfish and, within a few minutes, you will be dining on a beautiful *bouillabaisse*. After a day of fishing from Barcelona, your Spanish fisherman will send you home well fed on a zarzuela, his variation of a fish stew. On the Italian Adriatic coast, after a day's fishing out of Ravenna or Rimini, you will end up eating a *brodetto*.

But if you charter a fishing boat at Fisherman's Wharf in San Francisco chances are ten to one, that, as part of the final entertainment on the way back, the master of the boat will pull off the tarpaulin from the marine safety stove on the afterdeck and start preparing the greatest American regional dish—San Francisco cioppino.

Into the big pot built into the stove will go olive oil, onions, garlic, tomatoes, herbs, California wine, crab, shrimp, clams, mussels, and boneless chunks of fish.

If you so much as suggest to chauvinistically proud San Franciscans that the dish and its name may have come from Italy, they will practically scream at you. Of course, such a brilliant dish must be a pure San Francisco invention! Naturally the name is onomatopoeic. All the vegetables and much of the fish have to be vigorously chopped. Those early Italian immigrants who first made it were fairly weak on English. So they pronounced it "chop-ee-no" and spelled it *cioppino*.

There is less romance, but a louder ring of truth in a slightly different story. During the Gold Rush of 1849, it was certainly true that there were already many Italian immigrants running solidly tomato-flavored restaurants in San Francisco and the small mining towns around the Bay. One of the owner-chefs was a Genoese fisherman-sailor named Guiseppe Buzzaro. He brought with him a recipe for a fish stew called, in his native Ligurian dialect, *Ciupin*. I have eaten this dish in small, waterfront restaurants—mainly those popular with sailors—around the port of Genoa. Beyond this logical story, there is no hard proof of the dish's origin.

If cioppino is so supremely good, why hasn't it become an American national dish? The answer, I believe, is that—at least in its commercial-restaurant form—cioppino is like certain wines—it doesn't travel well. I have had a Los Angeles version that included, as alternatives to the usual San Francisco ingredients, rock lobster and white lingcod. The mixture simply did not work. Nor did a glamorous combination called Puget Sound cioppino served in Seattle in a bowl colorful and rich with butter clams and chunks of red king salmon. No. The balance is very delicate. Even in San Francisco, you have to know where to go to get it in its perfect form.

Quite a few tourist traps treat it as a heavily advertised, showoff item, made in large quantities in advance and kept hot on a steam table. Eliminate them instantly. Some of the best noncommercial cooks of the city are its professional firemen, who, on a city allowance of a couple of dollars or so per head per day, cook their own meals while on duty at the firehouses. Among the finer cioppinos I have tasted is the preparation of fireman Art Treganza, now retired from Rescue Company No. 3. Another memorable cioppino was prepared by one of San Francisco's best known characters, an Italian fisherman and fish handler whose real name is Antonio Tedesco but who is universally known, for reasons he keeps strictly to himself, as Mr. Hogan. After almost seventy-five years of catching and selling fish, he and his daughters run a fish market and café, where he will prepare a crab cioppino for any serious student of the delicacy. With the help of my friend Shirley Sarvis, a San Francisco food writer, I have become the proud owner of both Treganza's and Hogan's recipes.

The greatest of all San Francisco crab cioppinos, however, is served to special order on a couple of days notice at Ernie's Restaurant. That is fitting because Ernie's is owned and run by two Italian-American brothers, Victor and Roland Gotti. It is unquestionably the most elegant, famous, finest, and luxurious restaurant in San Francisco and is probably among the three or four greatest truly American restaurants in the country.

Today, Ernie's is a San Francisco legend, a monument, and an enormous tourist attraction. Virtually every visitor insists on dining there, and for the out-of-towners the kitchen endlessly repeats a small group of now-famous specialties led by the chicken in Champagne. Yet, for its local regular, sophisticated, and special clients—who include kings, movie stars, and princes, more or less in that order of importance—the restaurant can provide dinners of supreme elegance and luxury.

Yet, its fame and fortune belie its humble (and questionable) beginnings. Its history is a social climber's dream come true. It began soon after the turn of the century as a simple, unpretentious Italian *trattoria*, serving an excellent cioppino. The name of this little place was Ernie's Il Trovatore, after its chef-owner Ernie Carlesso. It was on the edge of the notorious Barbary Coast red-light district in the building formerly occupied by the notorious 'Frisco Dance Hall. Newspapers of the time said the area was filled with scenes of "wickedness and pollution unparalleled. . . . Beneath the gaudy saloon lights, the streets were filled with . . . fancy ladies." Brothels were reported to be abundant, as were call houses, cheap lodging places frequented by streetwalkers and, of course, the infamous dance halls where the performers "entertained" between their acts in private rooms upstairs.

That there ever were rooms of "entertainment" at the back of the restaurant and on the upper floors of the building never has been proved and is vehemently denied by Victor and Roland, but there is no question that in its early days the restaurant was a kind of early singles bar. The little restaurant was such an enormous successs, that by 1935 Ernie felt he had to have a partner, and he joined forces with one of his waiters, Ambrose Gotti. Soon they were able to buy the building and they rented rooms upstairs to "boarders." So Ernie's continued to be jam-packed every night.

When he finished school, Ambrose's son, Victor, came to work, scrubbing the red wine stains off the floors and washing the dishes. Soon he was joined by his kid brother, Roland. Ernie died and the Gotti family became the sole owners. In 1947 Ambrose died, and Victor and Roland took over.

Then the brothers made a brilliant and fateful decision. They would close Ernie's for a while, rebuild its interior, redecorate and refurbish it. They would make it the most beautiful restaurant in the world. There would be no limit as to what they would spend. But they would not make it modern. They would turn back to the Gay Nineties, to the colorful, elegant, expensive, luxurious bordello era. The first thing they did was to clean up and move the famous long mahogany bar, with its intricate, stained-glass back, to the front of the restuarant. It was the last remaining relic of the 'Frisco Dance Hall. The main dining rooms were decorated with magnificent Victorian crystal chandeliers, the walls covered with maroon Scalamandre silk brocade, the banquettes and chairs in red, the carpets in burgundy, the furniture, antique pieces from some of the great mansions of San Francisco. The ambiance was that loud, supreme elegance in which the wealthiest nabobs of a hundred years ago might have met the grandest of the ladies of the night.

It is now more than thirty years since the great transformation, and it has all been a fantastic success. The great names of the world have dined there. The food can be superb. The greatest and oldest bottles of the wine cellar are beyond replacement. Yet, if you will give Ernie's a couple of days notice, they will still prepare for you, and serve in a magnificent solid-silver tureen, the best San Francisco crab cioppino this side of paradise. And in that beautiful and formal setting, you will still eat your cioppino as if it were a picnic. The waiter will tie an enormous lobster bib around your neck. He will supply you with large bowls for the empty shells. And you will eat with your fingers.

If you can, eat crab cioppino at Ernie's. If you cannot, here is the best possible (and an extremely good) alternative. Victor and Roland have given me their recipe. I have prepared it in my own kitchen, with ingredients bought three thousand miles from San Francisco, and the result, although not quite perfect, was reasonably excellent. I have also tested and tasted the recipes from Treganza and Mr. Hogan, and have dared to commit lèse-majesté by adding two or three clever tricks from their recipes to the great basic preparation of Ernie's. I am, unashamedly, making a slight adaptation to a recipe for use in a home kitchen. Here, then, is my ideal recipe for the greatest American regional dish.

ERNIE'S SAN FRANCISCO CRAB CIOPPINO

6 to 8 servings

FOR THE FISH BOUILLON

- 2 pounds fish trimmings—heads with eyes and gills removed; backbones slightly broken up; fins, skins, tails, etc., of any white-fleshed fish, washed
- 1 large yellow onion, peeled and coarsely chopped
- 2 stalks green celery, with leaves, stalks fairly thinly sliced, leaves coarsely chopped
- 2 medium carrots, scraped and thinly sliced
- 1 whole bay leaf
- 6 whole black peppercorns
- 1 teaspoon coarse crystal salt

FOR THE SOUP SAUCE

- ½ cup top-quality virgin olive oil
- 3 medium yellow onions, peeled and finely chopped
- 3 cloves garlic, peeled and finely minced
- 4 cups finely chopped good ripe tomatoes, first peeled and seeded—or use canned Italian plum tomatoes, drained
- 1 cup dry white wine
- ¾ cup chopped parsley
  Coarse crystal salt and freshly ground black pepper, to taste
- ½ tablespoon chopped fresh basil, or ½ teaspoon dried
- ½ tablespoon chopped fresh rosemary, or ½ teaspoon dried
- 1 teaspoon chopped fresh sage, or ¼ teaspoon dried
- ½ tablespoon chopped fresh thyme, or ½ teaspoon dried

FOR THE FISH AND SHELLFISH

- About 4 pounds large Pacific Dungeness crab—or, if unavailable, the equivalent in hard-shell blue crabs—precooked by being plunged into boiling water for 3 minutes, then immediately into cold water and drained
- 3 dozen large mussels in their shells, scrubbed, washed, and debearded
- 2 dozen small hard-shell clams, in their shells, scrubbed and washed
- 2 pounds steaks of firm white-fleshed fish (cod, haddock, hake, halibut, sea bass, etc.), all bones and skin removed, then cut into large chunks
- 1 pound medium-large shrimp, left in shells, but cut open down back and black intestinal vein scraped out

KITCHEN EQUIPMENT: A very large, perhaps 6- to 8-quart lidded, enameled or stainless-steel soup kettle.

The Bouillon

Spread the fish trimmings evenly across the bottom of your big soup kettle. Pour in (gently, to avoid disturbing your orderly layer) 6 cups of cold water. This should be enough to cover the fish. If not, add a bit more. Heat it up fairly quickly to the boiling point. While it is coming up, continuously skim off the foam and scum that rises to the surface. These, if left, will cause bitter flavors. No more skimming is possible as soon as bubbling actually begins. Then at once reduce heat to gentle bubbling and add the onion, celery, carrots, bay leaf, peppercorns, and salt. Let everything bubble gently, partially covered, for 20 minutes.

Strain the bouillon through a fine sieve into a bowl. In the sieve, press the fish and vegetables with the back of a spoon to extract all possible juices. Throw away all the solids. Hold the flavorful bouillon, covered.

Assembling the Soup Sauce

Thoroughly wash and dry the big soup kettle. Pour in the olive oil in the bowl and set it over medium-high frying heat until a light haze forms over it. Add all the onions at once and sauté them very quickly, stirring almost all the time, until they are soft and translucent, but not brown—usually in about 3 to 4 minutes. Then, at once, stop the frying by turning down the heat and hissing in 4 cups of the reserved bouillon. As it comes to the boil, adjust the heat so that it simmers gently and add the garlic, the tomatoes, wine, ½ cup of the parsley, plus basil, rosemary, sage, and thyme. Let all this bubble gently, partially covered, for 15 minutes. While this is in progress, turn your attention to the crab.

Preparing and Poaching

Each crab will, by now, have been precooked for 3 minutes in boiling water, then, at once, cooled and drained. If you are forced to use frozen crabs, they will, of course, have been completely defrosted. Using a wooden mallet (but not too fiercely), just crack the top shell and, then, holding the crab tightly with one hand, lift or pry off the shell completely. Put out the grey gills and spongy lungs from each side and scrape on its back and, with the point of a small, sharp knife, pry off the pointed flap, called the "apron." Using a heavier knife or a sharp Chinese cleaver, cut away the head in a curving line behind the eyes. Now hold the crab, for a second or two, under gently running cold water. If it is a large crab (1½ to 2 pounds) use the cleaver to chop it into quarters. If it is smaller, chop it into halves. If you are using still smaller blue crabs, leave them whole. When all the crabs have been fixed, hold them aside on a platter. Lightly sprinkle the chunks of cod with not more than ½ teaspoon of salt.

The moment the timer rings for the end of the 15-minute simmer of the soup sauce, put in all crabs, pushing them down with a wooden spoon, so that they form a solid layer on the bottom of the soup kettle. Next, put in and push down the mussels and clams as the next layers on top. Turn up the heat full to bring it all back to bubbling as quickly as possible, but do not let it go beyond gentlest simmering. Cover it tightly. Listen to it carefully without opening the lid, to make sure it does not bubble too hard. Let it simmer for exactly 10 minutes—not a second more.

The instant the timer rings, put in and push down the fish chunks and the shrimp. Taste and adjust the seasonings as needed. Again bring back everything as quickly as possible to gentlest simmering. Cover tightly and continue simmering for 5 minutes more. Never stir but shake the pot occasionally. Then check that clams and mussels have opened, that fish is flaky and that shrimp are pink. If any of these requirements have not been fully achieved, continue simmering for 2 or 3 minutes longer. But do not let one or two recalcitrant clams fool you into overcooking everything. Serve instantly, either in a preheated tureen, or directly onto very hot, deep, and wide soup plates. Sprinkle each serving with the remaining parsley.

PART
·IV·

*Life's Singular
Pleasures*

"Le Snack" Is Also an Art

The first sudden thunderclap seemed to shake the Auberge to its foundations. We were in the dining room, in the middle of lunch. It had grown so dark that Mademoiselle Vivette had come in to turn on the lights and announce that we were about to experience *"la grande tempête des Alpes."* Each rolling boom, multiplied by the echoing reverberations of the valley, seemed to envelop us from every direction. One sensed the vibrations beating down on houses, pastures, trees. . . . As boom followed boom in rapid fire, the bright copper pots and utensils which decorate the rooms of the Auberge began vibrating in a buzzing harmony: the long *poissonière*, the "fish boiler" on the old oaken bread-chest, the tall *bidon*, the ancient five-gallon "milk can" standing in the corner.

The rain came down in almost solid sheets. The windows shook with a steady rhythm. I went up to my room and opened my casement window. Through all the noise and roar there was a sense of solitude, of isolation, of the relaxation of pent-up force and tension. I could hear the water rumbling in the Valley. I imagined the flooded and steaming landscape, the river swelling and overflowing, the roots of plants laid bare, the most private cracks and gullies of the earth penetrated and violated. Then the storm rolled on and away.

I went out into the garden. Shouts were coming up from the village. There was a frothy wind in my face. Overhead, rosy clouds were galloping. There was a damp, rich smell, perhaps from bared roots, sap oozing

EDITOR'S NOTE: This piece is excerpted from *The Auberge of the Flowering Hearth* (Bobbs-Merrill, 1973). The Auberge is in the French valley of La Grande Chartreuse.

from broken branches, the nectar of crushed flowers. . . . I breathed deeply. Soon, I was sure, the crushed flowers would slowly lift up their heads again, the thick blood of the earth would revive everything. Mademoiselle Vivette was loudly announcing that tomorrow morning the woods would be thick with wild mushrooms.

During the storm, the Auberge had filled up with passing motorists, unable to see ahead through the sheets of falling water and afraid of the hairpin bends. The smaller mountain roads, in fact, immediately became impassable—turning into rushing streams a foot deep, with large, rounded, weather-polished pebbles rolling down under water. Alpine storms make no allowances for automobiles.

So the low rattan chairs in Le Hall were filled with gossiping guests, drying and warming themselves before the crackling logs in the open hearth. Listening to their voices one could place the people by their reactions to the storm. The middle-aged husband and wife in the corner had obviously discovered the Valley years ago and had come back again and again. They were joyously uplifted by the dominant roar of Nature in command. The couple with the three young children had, it appeared, stumbled into the Valley by accident this morning. They were awed and overwhelmed. They spoke in whispers. With some guests there was a sense of fear. One man asked about possible rockfalls on the high Sappey road. A young mother discussed the danger of poisonous snakes if the children went for a walk. The leather-jacketed couple who had come in the noisy sports car were asking whether it was safe to leave the Valley after dark by the narrow twisting Porte de la Fourvoirie. . . .

Mademoiselle Vivette bustled among them, handing out her *carte du jour*, taking orders for *le snack*, or pouring drinks behind her small copper-covered bar with its back wall of dark green canvas and its striped canopy of apricot yellow and tulip green behind the wrought iron screen. One could tell more about the guests by what they ordered. The simplest commitment was to that most ubiquitous of all French soft drinks, Pshitt. (The first time I tasted it, I decided its name was precisely right.) Thirstier throats called for tall glasses of beer: the selection ranging from the simple, unsophisticated, locally brewed Kronenberger *blonde ou brune*, up to the luxuriously smooth, world-traveling Carlsberg. Those who had been chilled by the ice-cold rain demanded doubtful French vodka, or safe-and-sound *le Scotch*. But the couple who took delight in the storm were celebrating with one of Mademoiselle Vivette's house-label bottles of *le Champagne, Blanc de Blancs*. An English family, of course, ordered a pot of tea, and Mademoiselle Ray converted it into something quite French with a piled-up dish of her home-made *petits-fours*.

For guests who claimed they were starving at this midway point between lunch and dinner, Mademoiselle Vivette would serve, at a table in the dining room, her basic snack meal—available, in an emergency, at almost any hour of the day or night—*Le gouteron pour le Motoriste*. It consisted of home-baked rustic-style walnut bread, locally churned butter, a platter of paper-thin slices of mountain-cured sun-dried ham, locally made fresh white goats' milk cheese, some of Mademoiselle Ray's superbly light miniature fresh fruit tartlets, a carafe of the house white wine, and coffee. (Incidentally, I have been able to reproduce the imaginatively balanced simplicity of *le gouteron* in New York, with Smithfield ham, my own walnut bread baked from Mademoiselle Ray's recipe, imported French goat cheese, etc.)

Other guests were more demanding. They were willing to wait while Mademoiselle Ray prepared a hot version of *le snack*. Listening to their discussions as they studied the *carte du jour*, I realized how seldom the French think in terms of *le sondvitch*, *le homburger*, or *le hottdog*. (The two latter, of course, are considered merely as variations of *le sondvitch* and thus have to accept their share of the contempt which all Frenchmen feel for all gastronomic things British and all inventions of the Earl of Sandwich.) Instead, these demanding guests wanted something altogether more imaginative. To them *le snack* was a special branch of the culinary art, involving very little compromise from a fancy dinner dish, except that it had to be prepared quickly. I discovered that in this department of the kitchen Mademoiselle Ray was as much the gastronomic master as she was in every other. She has taught me that the French *les snacks* are dramatic, practical, and relatively simple.

COLD ARTICHOKE HEARTS À LA GRECQUE
(Les Artichauts Violets de Provence à la Grecque)

4 servings

In the language of French menus, a vegetable served as a cold appetizer *à la grecque* means that it has been cooked in a sharply aromatic oil and vinegar marinade. Perhaps it was so called because, throughout the Middle Ages, the Greeks were famous for their olive oil. Use fresh artichokes during their season from September to June. At other times, use ready-preserved artichoke hearts. The *à la Grecque* preparation can be done days in advance—they keep for weeks in tightly capped jars in the refrigerator.

> About 12 artichoke hearts, according to size
> 1 cup cold water
> ¾ to 1 cup olive oil
> ¼ to ½ cup tarragon white wine vinegar
> 2 whole bay leaves
> 1 teaspoon whole fennel leaves
> ½ teaspoon dried thyme
> 1 teaspoon coarse crystal salt
> 12 whole black peppercorns
> 3 or 4 sprigs fresh parsley
> 1 bunch fresh watercress
> 1 lemon

Active Preparation About 15 Minutes—Unsupervised Simmering About 20 Minutes

If using fresh artichokes, wash them thoroughly, pull off all outer leaves, cut away chokes and cut off stems. In a 2-quart saucepan, preferably enameled iron or tinned copper to avoid interaction with the acid, mix 1 cup cold water, ½ cup olive oil, and ¼ cup vinegar. Bring up to simmering while adding aromatics: 2 whole bay leaves, 1 teaspoon whole fennel seed, ½ teaspoon thyme, 1 teaspoon salt, 12 whole peppercorns, and 3 or 4 whole sprigs of parsley with stems. Simmer, covered, for about 10 minutes to develop flavors. Then drop in artichoke hearts, making sure there is enough liquid to cover them. If not, add more oil, vinegar, and water in same proportions as above. Continue gently simmering, covered, until artichokes are cooked through—usually in 15 to 20 minutes. Then, let everything cool and pour artichokes and marinade into wide-mouthed screwtop storage jars and refrigerate until needed. If they are to be kept for many days, it is best to strain out and discard the aromatic spices, since they tend to keep on strengthening the flavor.

Serving at Table

Serve artichoke hearts at room temperature with lemon wedges on a bed of chopped watercress leaves. (Incidentally, after using up all the artichoke hearts, save the marinade. It can be reheated with a new batch of artichokes, mushrooms, or other vegetables.)

LE BIFTECK DE GRUYÈRE DES ALPES
(Grilled Cheese Steak of Alpine Gruyère)

4 servings

This is another classic French cheese snack dish. It takes its name from the fact that it is, in reality, a *bifteck* of French Alpine Gruyère cheese cut in the shape of a ½-inch-thick slab about the size of a filet mignon, covered with a fritter batter and baked, fried, or grilled until the cheese is almost melting, so that it is rich and unctuous in the mouth. Finally, the *bifteck* is topped with eggs and aromatic herbs.

10 large eggs
½ cup milk
1 ounce Armagnac brandy
2 tablespoons melted butter
1 cup, or a bit more, all-purpose flour
3 tablespoons superfine sugar
1 teaspoon baking powder
4 tablespoons melted butter
4 slabs French Alpine Gruyère cheese, each cut ½ inch thick, about 5 by 3 inches and weighing 5 to 6 ounces
½ cup light cream
  Coarse crystal salt and freshly ground black pepper, to taste
  A few tablespoons chopped fresh parsley

About 45 Minutes Before Serving—Active Preparation in About 25 Minutes—Unsupervised Frying and Baking for About 20 Minutes

BASIC RULES FOR FRITTER BATTER: Prepare the fritter batter in a large mixing bowl. Break into it 2 eggs and beat them lightly with a fork.

Then mix in the ½ cup of milk, the 1 ounce of Armagnac, and the 2 tablespoons melted butter. Put into a flour sifter the 1 cup of flour, the 3 tablespoons of sugar, the 1 teaspoon of baking powder and sift into the egg mixture, pausing in the sifting to stir in the flour every couple of minutes. The finished batter should be quite thick, so that it will solidly coat each cheese slab. If at first it is not thick enough, sift in more flour until exactly the right consistency is achieved.

In a large sauté or crêpe pan, over medium drying heat, melt 4 tablespoons of butter. Dip each slab of cheese thoroughly into the fritter batter, so that it is very well coated, then quickly fry until golden in the hot pan, turning once with a large spatula. Preheat the oven to 375° F. Choose a low, open baking pan, just large enough to hold the four cheese steaks but not leaving too much space around them, to avoid unnecessary spreading of the following egg mixture.

Break 8 eggs into a mixing bowl and beat them and the ½ cup cream very lightly with a fork. Season them with salt and pepper, to taste. Then when all four now-batter-covered cheese steaks are safely in the baking pan, pour the eggs over them. Place them in the center of the oven and bake them until the eggs are set, with the top surface brown and puffy—usually in 20 to 25 minutes. At this point, the cheese, while still holding its *bifteck* shape, should be just about at the point of melting. With a little practice you can achieve this precisely every time. Needless to say, you must now serve the *bifteck* instantly, on very hot plates, the tops sprinkled with the chopped parsley.

FLAMING CANAPÉS OF MOUNTAIN HAM
(*Jambon de Montagne Flambé*)

4 servings

These are classic French-style canapés, each small slice of ham resting on a crisply fried round of toast, covered with a sauce of sour cream and eggs, touched with the tartness of tarragon wine vinegar and flamed with the robust brandy of Armagnac.

> *About 4 tablespoons butter*
> 2 *large egg yolks*
> 2 *tablespoons tarragon white wine vinegar*
> 12 *neat crustless rounds of bread to be fried in butter*
> *Coarse crystal salt and freshly ground black pepper, to taste*
> 24 *slices of dry-cured, dark-smoked ham, cut to fit the bread rounds*
> 1 *cup sour cream*
> ⅓ *cup Armagnac brandy*

Total Working Time from Start to Serving About 20 Minutes—May Be Prepared About an Hour or So Before Serving

In a sauté pan over medium frying heat melt 2 tablespoons of the butter and lightly brown on both sides the 12 bread rounds. Lay them out at once on a warm serving platter and hold them in a keep-warm oven. Add more butter, as needed, to the sauté pan and quickly brown the 24 slices of ham. Place 2 slices on each bread round. Hiss the 2 tablespoons of vinegar into the sauté pan and bubble it hard for 2 to 3 minutes to reduce it and concentrate its flavor. Then, work in the cup of sour cream, stirring thoroughly and scraping the bottom of the pan. Lightly beat the 2 egg yolks with a few strokes of a fork and blend them into the pan. Now turn down the heat to quite low and, using a wire whisk, vigorously beat the sauce to incorporate air and lightness, until you have almost a fluff—usually in 3 or 4 minutes. While continuing to beat, add salt and pepper to taste. Spoon this sauce, in equal parts, over the 12 canapés. Heat the ⅓ cup of Armagnac to just above blood heat and, in front of your guests, spoon it over the canapés and flame them.

LEEKS IN TOMATO SAUCE IN THE STYLE OF MEYARGUES
(Poireaux de Meyargues)

4 servings

French cooks, more often than Americans, have the courage to start a dinner with an utterly simple, cold cooked vegetable in a subtly spiced sauce that seems to titillate the appetite and clean the palate while providing only a minimum of filling bulk. This way of cooking leeks whenever they are in season (usually the year round, with peak supplies in the spring and fall) is, to my mind, one of the very best examples of this kind of light hors d'oeuvre.

> 4 tablespoons olive oil
> 1 medium yellow onion
> ½ lemon
> 5 tablespoons tomato paste
> 2 cloves garlic, finely minced
> 2 bay leaves, crumbled
>   Coarse crystal salt and freshly ground black pepper, to taste
> 2 pounds white leeks

Active Preparation About 10 Minutes—Unsupervised Cooking About 20 Minutes

The leeks should, of course, be prepared several hours or the day before the meal. It is very important for this dish to use the finest green virgin olive oil. Gently heat 4 tablespoons in a fair-sized sauté pan. Finely chop the onion and gild it in the hot oil. With a small, sharp knife, dig out the pulp from the ½ lemon, chop fine, and add to the sauté pan. Also add, working everything together smoothly, 5 tablespoons of tomato paste, the 2 finely minced cloves garlic, 2 crumbled bay leaves, with salt and pepper to taste. Cover and simmer very gently, to blend and develop flavors, for as long as it takes to prepare the leeks.

Carefully wash and chunk them into ⅜-inch cross sections and drop them, for not more than 15 seconds, into rapidly boiling water. Drain them at once, dry them in a towel and add them to the sauté pan. Make sure that each chunk is well incorporated into the sauce, then let everything gently simmer until leeks are perfectly soft—usually in about 20 minutes. Taste and adjust seasonings. If you think the tomato paste should be stronger, add a few more teaspoons of tomato paste. Then, the entire contents of the sauté pan can be refrigerated, tightly covered, for several days. Always serve at room temperature.

PANCAKES WITH CHEESE AND MOUNTAIN HAM
(*Pannequets au Fromage et au Jambon Montagnard*)
4 servings

These light, small filled crêpes are equally excellent served as the hors d'oeuvre of a party dinner, or as the main course of a lunch or supper. The ideal cheese is the firm, nutty Beaufort of Savoy, but a fine imported Switzerland Gruyère or Appenzeller will do as well.

FOR THE PANCAKES

> 2 *cups all-purpose flour*
> 3 *teaspoons baking powder*
> 1 *teaspoon salt*
> 3 *large eggs*
> *About 6 tablespoons butter*
> 1½ *cups milk*

FOR THE BÉCHAMEL SAUCE

> 3 *tablespoons butter*
> 3 *tablespoons all-purpose flour*
> 1½ *cups milk*
> 6 *ounces cheese, either Beaufort of Savoy, or Switzerland Gruyère*
> *Freshly greated nutmeg, to taste*
> *Coarse crystal salt and freshly ground black pepper, to taste*

FOR THE FILLING AND GARNISH

> *About 4 tablespoons butter*
> 12 *small slices boiled ham*
> 1 *cup sour cream*

About 1 Hour Before Serving—Preparing Pancake Batter in About 5 Minutes

After first sifting flour to measure it correctly, sift it a second time with the 3 teaspoons baking powder and the 1 teaspoon salt into a mixing bowl. In a separate bowl, break the 3 eggs and beat them with a fork just enough to mix yolks and whites. Just melt the 6 tablespoons of butter and measure exactly ⅓ cup. Do not let it get too hot. Using a wire whisk in the main bowl, lightly beat in the 3 eggs and the melted butter. Now, beating all the time, gradually dribble in the milk, until batter has the consistency of thin custard, so that finished pancakes will be very thin. Do not necessarily use all the milk—or, if batter remains too thick, add an extra dash or two of milk. Continue beating until bubbles appear, then let batter rest to develop lightness and texture.

About 55 Minutes Before Serving—Preparing Béchamel Sauce in About 15 Minutes

In a 1-quart saucepan, over medium heat, melt the 3 tablespoons of butter and blend in the 3 tablespoons of flour. Stir until fully blended and very smooth. Then leave on low heat to cook the flour while you heat up the 1½ cups of milk in another saucepan. Now again, stirring continuously, begin gradually blending the milk into the butter-flour roux, continuing to stir until it all thickens and is very smooth. Leave it to bubble very gently while you grate the 6 ounces of cheese. Work half of this cheese into the white sauce, adding a few grinds of nutmeg and salt and pepper to taste. Sauce should finally be fairly thick. If it is not thick enough, continue bubbling and stirring it until it reaches the right consistency. Then turn off heat and cover the saucepan.

About 40 Minutes Before Serving—Griddling and Filling the Pancakes

Heat up and lightly butter the pancake griddle. Give the batter a final beat or two and spoon it onto the griddle in amounts to give you about a dozen thin pancakes, each about 2½ inches across. Cook until brown on both sides. Spread each with the béchamel sauce, lay on a slice of ham cut to fit, then roll up each pancake and place in a single layer in a buttered pan. When all pancakes are lined up side by side, dribble the sour cream over them, sprinkle over the remaining grated cheese and liberally dot them with butter. They may now be held until . . .

About 10 Minutes Before Serving—Gratinée the Pancakes Under the Grill

Turn on the grill. When it is hot, place the pan of pancakes under it and leave them until the cheese is browned and the sour cream is bubbling hot. Serve at once.

CRÊPES FILLED WITH GOAT CHEESE AND RED CAVIAR
(Crêpes de Chèvre aux Oeufs Rouges)

4 servings

At the Auberge in the Valley, the cheese with which to stuff these crêpes is the Père Ernest, a soft, unctuous cream cheese of goats' milk. On this side of the Atlantic there are now some good, soft goat cheeses in the fancy cheese shops—or, as a somewhat blander compromise, one could use the standard cream cheese. A good part of the attractive flavor comes from the grated Alpine Gruyère and the red caviar. These filled crêpes make an excellent hot hors d'oeuvre, served as the first course at table, or, in larger quantities per person, as a luncheon or supper main course.

> One batch of about 2 cups of Crêpe Batter as described in Pancakes with Cheese and Mountain Ham on page 257
> About ¼ pound butter
> 8 ounces, about 1 cup, red caviar, salmon eggs or roe
> 6 ounces goat cheese, creamy soft, shaped into 12 small (1 × ¼-inch medallions)
> ½ cup grated French Alpine Gruyère cheese
> ½ cup heavy cream
> Coarse crystal salt and freshly ground black pepper, to taste

Preparation in Less Than 15 Minutes—Make a Fine Show in a Crêpe Pan Over a Spirit Stove at Table

Prepare a crêpe batter, making it quite a bit thicker than usual, as described in Pancakes with Cheese and Mountain Ham on page 258. Set your crêpe pan (or alternative) over fairly high frying heat and quickly melt 4 tablespoons of the butter. At the same moment, set the oven to a keep-warm temperature (about 175° F) and put in it, to warm up, a serving platter large enough to hold the 12 crêpes. When the butter is thoroughly hot and sizzling, ladle in as many crêpes as the pan will hold, each fairly thick and about 2 inches across. Place at the center of each 1 tablespoon of red caviar. Cover it with a small, not too thick medallion of the creamed goat cheese. Then, sprinkle on 1 teaspoon of the grated Gruyère, 2 teaspoons of the cream, and a grind or two of salt and pepper, according to the saltiness of the goat cheese. Now, at once, cover this construction with another ladle or two of crêpe batter, so that you have a kind of sandwich. Flip each crêpe over and quickly brown the second side. The moment each crêpe is lightly golden on both sides, set it on the serving platter in the keep-warm oven and repeat the frying operation with more butter, as needed. If you are doing this at table, you don't really need a keep-warm oven or a serving platter—far better to serve each guest directly from the pan onto very hot plates.

THE BLACK PÂTÉ OF PROVENCE
(*Tapenado*)

4 servings

This famous hors d'oeuvre from the Mediterranean coast is in season throughout the year. Mademoiselle Ray serves it as a three-colored canapé platter, garnishing the black mound of pâté with concoctions of red—salmon-roe caviar—and green—mashed eggplants. The two principal ingredients of the *tapenado* are anchovies and black Morocco olives, and if you can get both of them fresh from Greek or Italian groceries you will have the finest possible flavor and texture. If not, use the 2-ounce cans of flat anchovy fillets and the best available quality of preserved black olives. For the red and green garnishes, see separate recipes below. Instead of serving only slices of bread on which to spread the pâté, Mademoiselle Ray produced a handsome platter of what the French call *crudités du jardin*, best translated as "raw tidbits from the garden" (see list below).

¼ *pound anchovies, whole fresh in brine, or ½-ounce can flat fillets*
½ *cup olive oil*
¼ *cup Cognac*
 1 *teaspoon English dry mustard, or to taste*
  Freshly ground black pepper, to taste
½ *pound black olives, pitted*
 2 *ounce can tuna fish*
 3 *ounces capers*

Preparation in 20 Minutes or Less

If you are using fresh whole anchovies, first behead, clean, and bone them. Then put them into the jug of an electric blender, with ¼ cup of the olive oil, 1 tablespoon of the Cognac, 1 teaspoon of the mustard, a few grinds of pepper, and all other ingredients. Set the blender on a medium-high speed and at once start dribbling in more olive oil and Cognac. (But do not necessarily use entire amount.) Stop blender frequently and push down ingredients. As soon as everything is completely mixed and has the texture of a coarse, spreadable paste, stop the blending. Check seasoning and texture. If paste is too thick, work in more olive oil. If flavor is not sharp enough, add a tablespoon more or so of Cognac, mustard, and/or pepper. The anchovies, of course, supply the salt. Mold pâté into a neat pyramid on serving platter.

RED CAVIAR GARNISH FOR TAPENADO

This can be made with the normal salmon roe available in jars at most supermarkets. If, however, you are near a Greek grocery and can get the *tarama,* reddish yellow carp roe, it makes a superb variation of flavor and texture.

> 1 *lemon*
> About ½ *cup olive oil*
> 4 *ounces red salmon-roe caviar or Greek* tarama *(carp roe)*
> 1½ *tablespoons tomato paste*
> About ½ *cup breadcrumbs*

Preparation in 5 Minutes, or Less

Squeeze juice from lemon and put it in the jug of an electric blender with ¼ cup of the olive oil, plus the 4 ounces of roe, and the 1½ tablespoons of tomato paste. Blend at medium-high speed. The entire mixture should have the consistency of a stiff mayonnaise. If it does not thicken enough, add breadcrumbs, 1 tablespoon at a time. If it thickens too much, add more olive oil. Serve in piles alongside the *tapenado.*

GREEN EGGPLANT GARNISH FOR TAPENADO

2 medium eggplants
¾ cup olive oil
1 lemon
  About 1 teaspoon dried marjoram
  Coarse crystal salt and freshly ground black pepper, to taste

**Preferably Made the Day Before—Active Preparation About 10
Minutes—Unsupervised Baking of Eggplant About 1 Hour**

Preheat oven to 400° F. Prick each eggplant with fork in about a dozen
places, rub with olive oil, and place in open baking dish in center of
oven. Eggplant will be done when skins begin to crisp and split, while
inside pulp feels soft—usually in about 1 hour. Open up eggplant, dig
out inside pulp with a spoon and put into a saucepan over medium heat.
Mash down pulp and stir continually to evaporate water and thicken. At
the same time, work in ½ cup of the olive oil, the juice of the lemon,
about 1 teaspoon of dried marjoram, plus salt and pepper, to taste. When
mixture has achieved stiffness and texture of mayonnaise, turn out into
storage bowl and chill thoroughly in refrigerator. Check seasonings once
more when it is cold and adjust if necessary. Arrange and serve alongside
black *tapenado* and red caviar.

RAW "TIDBITS FROM THE GARDEN" TO GO WITH TAPENADO
The most dramatic way of serving the *tapenado* is to mound it as a black
pile in the center of a serving platter, and then surround it with two
shallower circles of the red caviar and green eggplant. Finally, the remaining space on the platter can be filled with neatly arranged tidbits,
including all or some of the following: slices of crisp apples, inch-long
slices cut lengthwise from young carrots, cherry tomatoes, shelled walnut
halves, sprigs of watercress, small celery sticks, cucumber slices, etc.
There should also, of course, be French bread for mopping up.

When Lucullus Dines Alone

When modern gourmets describe a magnificent meal as being "a Lucullan feast," they are paying tribute, after more than two thousand years, to the man who has often been called the greatest of all gastronomes of ancient Rome, Lucius Lucullus. He gave some of the largest, most lavish and expensive dinners in history. He also enjoyed dining alone. On one such day he felt that the menu and the preparation of the dishes by his cook were not quite up to scratch. The little roasted birds with which the meal began were not quite crisp enough. The sauce on the fish did not quite have the perfection for which the cook was famous. Lucullus clapped his hands and ordered the cook to the dining room. He bowed deeply and expressed abject apologies when he heard his master's complaint. "But, my lord," he excused himself with a trembling voice, "I did not think it necessary to prepare a supreme banquet when you were dining alone." The voice of Lucullus was as cold as ice: "That is precisely when you must be most careful, for then I have my most critical of all guests—Lucullus is entertaining Lucullus."

Two thousand years later, for precisely the same reason, I find interest and pleasure in dining with myself. I would feel that I was being rude to myself if I turned on the phonograph or the television. On the contrary, now is the moment for special concentration on the fine details of the food, however simple it may be. Now is the moment to experiment with that new and revolutionary recipe that I would not dare to try on my

EDITOR'S NOTE: This piece is excerpted from *Esquire's Handbook for Hosts* (Grosset & Dunlap, 1973).

friends until I had tried it on myself. Now is the time to taste new and highly unorthodox marriages of foods and wines in the hope of discovering some marvelous new combination that no one has ever thought of before.

Yet, of course, there are inevitably many occasions when one must eat, not only interestingly and nourishingly, but also quickly. Then I usually turn to the simple art of boiling water, which can cover a multitude of my Lucullan needs. It boils and poaches eggs. It cooks the most complicated shapes of pasta. It preserves, by its steam, the subtlest flavors of fish and meats. Bubbling water makes the bouillon for rice pilaf, the aromatic risotto, or the *cassoulet* of goose-flavored baked beans. Above all, bubbling water is the essential start of a great soup.

I like to believe that soup is the second oldest of all cooked foods, preceded only by the meat that the hunter brought back to his cave and grilled over the open fire. It is still one of the most essential of gastronomic commodities—especially when Lucullus dines with Lucullus. Soup, made in advance, can be hidden in the refrigerator as insurance against a sudden attack of the hungers. Hundreds of famous soups are highly satisfying one-dish meals. Every important farming region of the world has its own special richly hearty soup, brought to table in a huge earthenware pot, or casserole, or *marmite*, or *olla*, or *toupin*, according to the language of its homeland. All these soups are simple to prepare; they improve with keeping and reheating. I find them much more timesaving, economical, and delicious than the so-called short-cut foods.

Here, then, are a few of my favorite Lucullan soups. I prepare them in a large, old, and handsomely browned earthenware *marmite*; they simmer slowly in a very low oven for hours without the slightest attention, then are stored in the refrigerator as a basic supply from which an instant good meal can be reheated at any hour of the day or night. All of them, of course, are good enough for an informal party.

But dining alone does not have to be tied to even the most succulent of soups. Some of my other favorite recipes follow. The "secret trick" of my Garlic Snail Butter was given me by the brilliant young American chef Jerry East. His recipe, of course, begins, "Take ten pounds of the best butter . . ." but I have cut it down to my size and usually keep a pound or two on hand, not only for snails, but also to spread on hot country-ham biscuits, to use with anchovies as an appetizer dip, or to be added in small quantities for the enrichment of many other dishes or sauces. Once you have mixed your basic butter, you can store it in the refrigerator for days, or in the freezer for weeks, removing only as much as you need at any one time.

THREE GREAT ONE-DISH-MEAL SOUPS

FRENCH POTAGE CHASSEUR
(Hunter's Soup)

Several solo meals

I learned this recipe in the kitchen of a Spanish Catalan family living in one of the more remote Alpine valleys of the High Savoy in southeastern France. The dish takes its name, obviously, from the fact that it can be made with almost any cut of almost any animal brought home by one of the mountain hunters. If you live, as I do, rather far from any mountains, you can use a piece of ham, or smoked pork, or virtually any other meat to add its variety of flavor to this highly flexible stew. It should traditionally be prepared in a lidded earthenware pot, but you can also use an enameled cast-iron *cocotte*, or any kind of soup kettle that will fit into the oven.

3 cloves garlic
2 large Bermuda or Spanish onions
2 medium leeks
1 small green cabbage
1 fairly large green pepper
4 tablespoons plus 2 teaspoons olive oil
1 can (1 pound) plum tomatoes, peeled and seeded
2 cups beef bouillon
2 cups dry white wine
Large ham bone, with plenty of meat on it (about 3 pounds), or a smoked pork butt of the same size
2 bay leaves
3 whole cloves
2 teaspoons dried thyme
Salt and freshly ground pepper to taste

Active Preparation About 45 Minutes—Unsupervised Oven Simmering About 2 Hours

Preheat oven to 300° F and put in, to heat up, the large, empty soup pot. Make ready all the ingredients and hold each separately: peel and finely mince the 3 cloves garlic; peel and slice the 2 onions; thoroughly clean and chunk the white parts of the 2 leeks; peel off the tough outer leaves of the cabbage and cut its heart into 8 segments; wash, seed, and coarsely chop the green pepper. Put 4 tablespoons of olive oil into a fairly large sauté pan, heat it up to low frying heat, and put in the garlic, the sliced onions, and the leeks. Let them gently simmer for about 10 minutes, stirring them often, so that they melt but do not brown. Then add the can of tomatoes, with all their juice, and the chopped pepper. Keep them simmering, stirring occasionally, for about 15 minutes.

Meanwhile, in 2-quart saucepan, heat up the 2 cups each of beef bouillon and wine, with 2 cups of freshly drawn cold water, almost to boiling, then keep hot. Take the main pot out of the oven and put into it the piece of ham or pork, surrounded by the segments of cabbage. Put back into the oven, covered, to let them sweat.

When vegetables in sauté pan have simmered about 15 minutes, again take the pot out of the oven and pour in the entire contents of the sauté pan. Add 2 crumbled bay leaves, 3 whole cloves, 2 teaspoons dried thyme, plus salt and pepper to taste. Pour in the 3 pints of liquid, cover, then put pot back in oven, tightly lidded, to simmer for at least 2 hours. Add more water, if necessary, to keep everything well covered.

Serving at Table

Lift meat out of pot and carve off as many slices as your hunger demands, placing them in your hot soup bowl and sprinkling them with 2 teaspoons of fresh olive oil. Ladle soup and vegatables over meat and finally adjust seasonings to your taste.

ATHENIAN FISH SOUP AVGOLEMONO

Several solo meals

This is a modified, fishy version of the classic Greek egg-lemon soup. It is best when you can get a whole, firm-fleshed fish, with its head on, such as, for example, a red snapper, a sea or striped bass, or a small cod or haddock.

> ½ cup olive oil
> 2 medium yellow onions
> 2 medium green peppers
> 1 bunch green celery
> 1 can (1 pound 1 ounce) Italian plum tomatoes, peeled and seeded
> 1 whole fish, (about 3 pounds), cleaned and scaled, but with backbone and head intact (red snapper is ideal)
> 1 teaspoon dried oregano
> 1 teaspoon dried thyme
>   Coarse crystal salt and freshly ground black pepper, to taste
> ⅓ cup dry white vermouth
> 1 large egg (for each serving)
> 1 lemon (for each serving)
>   Elbow macaroni (1¼ cups, before cooking)

Active Preparation About 30 Minutes—Simmering About 20 Minutes

Prepare this soup in a 3-to 4-quart soup kettle, or stewpot, on top of the stove. Put into it the ½ cup olive oil and heat up to gentle frying temperature. Add the 2 onions, peeled and sliced, the 2 green peppers, seeded and chunked, the heart only of the celery, chunked (including some of the leaves, finely chopped), and the can of tomatoes. Let them all simmer gently, stirring from time to time, until quite soft—usually in 15 to 20 minutes. Meanwhile, see that the fish is cleaned and properly scaled, then cut it across into larger chunks, keeping the head as one of these chunks. In a large saucepan, bring up to boiling 2 quarts of freshly drawn cold water. As soon as vegetables are soft, add fish (including head) to main pot, plus 1 teaspoon oregano, 1 teaspoon thyme, with salt and pepper to taste and the ⅓ cup vermouth. Then pour in only enough boiling water to cover everything and simmer until fish is just firm and flaky—usually in about 10 minutes. Meanwhile, separate 1 egg, putting yolk into small bowl and reserving white for some other use. Beat yolk lightly and hold. Squeeze juice of 1 lemon into another bowl and hold. Set your oven to keep-warm temperature, about 150° to 175° F.

The moment the fish is done, remove chunks from soup, discard head, and keep chunks warm in covered dish in oven. Sprinkle the 1¼ cups macaroni into soup in main pot and stir around to mix. Keep soup bubbling merrily, covered, until macaroni is just done, but *al dente*, still nicely chewy—usually in 10 to 15 minutes. Meanwhile, take out as many chunks of fish as your hunger demands, remove and discard skin and bones, then flake flesh into bite-sized pieces and continue to keep warm. Remaining chunks of fish can now be refrigerated, covered, for future use.

Serving at Table

Warm your soup bowl, but do not make it too hot, or egg yolk will set. Pour egg yolk into soup bowl and at once strongly beat into it with a wire whisk the lemon juice. Now, continuing to beat strongly all the time, dribble in hot liquid (avoiding solids as much as possible) from main soup pot. Egg will begin to thicken. At once beat in more hot liquid, until you have as much liquid as you want for 1 serving. It should be creamy, smooth, handsomely pinkish yellow in color, and nicely lemony in flavor. Now fill up your bowl with as much macaroni and vegetables as you need, plus the flaked fish. Remaining soup will, of course, be refrigerated and, the next time you want to serve it, you can reheat just as much as you need, with more of the fish, plus the egg and lemon thickening beaten into each bowl. If you want to serve it to several people, you should have 1 egg yolk and the juice of 1 lemon for each person, and then it is best to do the beating all together in a warm tureen.

MY MODIFIED VERSION OF SPANISH FABADA ASTURIANA

Several solo meals

This is the famous specialty of the mountainous region of Asturias in northwestern Spain. The name *fabada* comes from the white *fabe* bean, which grows there and is the main ingredient of a magnificent stew with the aromatic local smoked meats and sausages, all surrounded and washed down by Asturian tart hard cider. In place of these purely local ingredients, I use large white haricot beans, with Spanish-style *chorizo* sausage (when I can find it in Spanish, Puerto Rican, or Latin American stores), or the Italian *pepperoni*, long, narrow sausage.

> 1 *pound white haricot or Greek Northern beans*
> *Ham hock, with bone and plenty of meat (about 2 pounds)*
> 1 *bottle hard cider*
> 1 *medium yellow onion*
> 4 *whole cloves*
> 1 *teaspoon dill, dried if fresh not available*
> 1 *teaspoon dried oregano*
> 1 *teaspoon dried savory*
> 4 *large Spanish onions*
> 3 *cloves garlic*
> 1 *medium green pepper*
> ⅓ *cup dry white vermouth*
> 1 *teaspoon saffron in strands*
> 2 *bay leaves, crumbled*
> *Spanish* chorizo *sausage, or Italian* pepperoni *(about 1 pound)*
> 2 *pigs' feet, fresh, cut in half lengthwise by butcher*
> 4 *medium potatoes*
> 1 *small head green cabbage*
> *Coarse crystal salt and freshly ground black pepper, to taste*

The Day Before—Soaking the Beans—Working Time 5 Minutes

In a 3-quart saucepan, heat 2 quarts of water to a rolling boil, then dribble in the pound of white beans slowly enough so that water never stops boiling. Continue bubbling hard for 2 minutes, then turn off heat, cover, and leave to soak overnight.

The Next Day—Active Preparation About 30 Minutes— Unsupervised Simmering About 2 Hours

Drain the soaked beans, saving the soaking water and straining it through a fine-mesh sieve. Wash beans under running cold water and pick them over, discarding any that are broken. Put ham hock on bottom of your large soup pot, surround it with soaked beans, pour in bottle of hard cider, and add just enough of the soaking water to cover everything about 1 inch deep. Peel the yellow onion, leaving it whole, stick 4 whole cloves into it on 4 sides, and add it to the pot. Also add 1 teaspoon each of dill, oregano, and savory. Place pot over high heat and bring rapidly to the boil, then turn down heat and simmer very gently, covered. This dish will be mushed and ruined by any hard boiling. Meanwhile, prepare more vegetables and assemble them together in a mixing bowl: peel and chunk the 4 Spanish onions, peel and finely mince the 3 cloves garlic, core and chunk the green pepper. Into a very small, butter-melting saucepan, put the ⅓ cup dry white vermouth and heat up gently to just above blood heat—so that it stings the tip of the finger. Into this hot liquid put the 1 teaspoon of saffron, stir it around with a small wooden spoon, and leave it to soak and exude its bright-yellow oils until it will be added to soup.

20 Minutes After Simmering Begins

Add the onions, garlic, and green pepper to soup, with 2 crumbled bay leaves, and stir in. Then add vermouth and saffron to soup pot, carefully rinsing out all yellow oils from small pan with a spoonful or two of the hot soup. Cut up *chorizo* or *pepperoni* sausages into 1½-inch lengths and add to main pot. Into a separate pan put the 4 halves of the pigs' feet, cover with cold water, and bring rapidly to boiling, skimming off any rising dirt or scum; simmer them until they are just soft—usually in about 30 minutes. Drain them and add feet to the main soup pot. Peel and coarsely chunk the 4 potatoes and add to pot. While gentle simmering continues, remove tough outer leaves from cabbage, coarsely shred its heart, and set aside. Occasionally check level of liquid in main pot. All ingredients should remain well covered. If not, add more of the soaking water from the beans.

After 1½ Hours of Simmering

Taste 2 or 3 beans for doneness. They should be quite soft. If not, continue simmering another 15 minutes and taste again. As soon as beans are soft, add shredded cabbage to pot. Continue simmering 5 to 8 more minutes, according to whether you like your cabbage crisp or soft. Finally, check soup for seasoning and add salt and pepper to taste. This is always done at the last moment with this dish, since one can never tell in advance how much salt and pepper will be exuded by the meats.

Serving at Table

Make sure, of course, that you get a balanced mixture in your soup bowl of chunks of ham and pig meat, of pieces of sausage, of beans, and everything else in this rich conglomeration. When the main pot has cooled—and before putting it away in the refrigerator—remove and discard all bones, cutting the meat into large chunks. After a few hours of refrigeration, you can also lift off the thin layer of fat that will have solidified on the surface. For the next meal, just heat up as much as you need.

JERRY EAST'S ALL-PURPOSE GARLIC SNAIL BUTTER

About ¼ pound to keep on hand

Although the preparation of this aromatic butter is as simple as the square root of four, the superb balance of its flavors requires accurate measurement. Chef East, being a professional, insists on weighing all his ingredients—even his pepper. Since most of us do not have such accurate scales, I include the closest possible approximation of measurements by cups and spoons. Remember, though, that you will get the best results by weighing.

> 1 pound sweet butter
> 1 ounce (about 8 medium cloves) garlic, already peeled
> 1 ounce (about 10 medium cloves) shallots, already peeled
> 1¼ ounces (about 1¼ cups, fairly tightly packed) parsley, leaves only
> ½ ounce (about 1 tablespoon) coarse crystal salt
> 0.15 ounce (about 1 teaspoon) freshly ground white pepper
> 1¼ ounces not-too-sweet California dessert wine

Preparation and Mixing in About 20 Minutes

The "secret" of this magnificently aromatic butter is the use of the slightly sweet (but not too sweet) wine. You simply mix everything in a large bowl. Put in the butter and let it soften. Finely mince the garlic. Do the same with the shallots. Finely chop the parsley leaves. Add all these and the salt, white pepper, and the wine. Working firmly and indefatigably with a wooden spoon, completely blend everything. Make sure that there are no unmixed pockets anywhere. With spatula and spoon, mold the butter into a tightly lidded crock and refrigerate for later use.

Just Before Serving—Cooking in About 5 Minutes

Measure the precise amount you need and put it into a small sauté pan. Heat up quite gently until butter starts to bubble. Watch bits of garlic and shallot very carefully. They must just be clarified and not, under any circumstances, browned. As soon as the garlic or shallot starts to color, the butter will take on a bitter taste. This must be avoided at all costs. Better to undercook than to brown, but best of all to learn to recognize the precise moment when garlic and shallots have become clear and butter should be removed immediately from heat and served. At this point it is marvelously aromatic and nutty—I am such an addict that I soak it up with soft bits of sourdough bread.

HOT OR COLD COUNTRY-HAM BISCUITS

About 20 biscuits

Whenever I expect to be dining alone, one of my most regular and reliable standby meats is a fine-quality ham, which, if properly wrapped, seems to keep almost indefinitely. By "fine-quality" I do not, of course, mean the mass-produced ham of the average market, which is bland to the point of boredom and over-weighted with fat, gristle, and deliberately injected water. Instead, I insist on getting (ordering by mail direct from the producers, if I can find no local source) one of the fine, American farm-made hams, still being produced in limited quantities in all parts of the country. The king of American hams is the true Smithfield, which must legally be made in or around the town of that name in Virginia. Its meat is dark, nutty-dry, slightly crumbly, almost winy in flavor—the result of the all-peanut diet of the cosseted and pampered porkers of that district. Less dominant in personality and lighter, but still superb in fineness of flavor, are the "country hams"—from porkers fed on a mixed diet of peanuts and grain. Often, when I have some of this type of ham left over, I grind it up and blend it into these irresistible country-ham biscuits . . .

2 cups all-purpose flour, after sifting
2 teaspoons baking powder
¾ cup coarsely ground country ham
    Salt
2 tablespoons bacon or ham drippings
¾ cup milk

Total Preparation About 30 Minutes

Having sifted the flour once before measuring it, put it back in the sifter, sprinkling on the 2 teaspoons of baking powder and resifting together into a fair-sized mixing bowl. Blend into the flour, with light strokes, the ¾ cup of ham and, according to its saltiness, a very little extra salt, to taste. Next, using a pastry cutter, work in the 2 tablespoons of softened drippings, until the emerging dough has the look and texture of coarse cornmeal. Add the milk, dash by dash, using as little as possible to achieve a soft dough.

Preheat your oven to 450° F. Using a gentle touch with your fingers, gather the dough into a ball and set it on a lightly floured pastry board. Knead gently for about 30 seconds. With a lightly floured rolling pin, roll out the dough to about ⅜-inch thick and, with a 1½-inch diameter round biscuit cutter, press out the biscuits.

If Serving the Biscuits Hot—Final Baking in About 15 Minutes

Set the biscuits on a baking sheet and slide into the center of the oven. Bake until golden brown—usually in 12 to 15 minutes. They are also fine served cold.

English French Toast

No one can fool around with the word "royal" in Britain. Whether you are making a product or running a restaurant, you cannot call it royal without the permission of the Administrative Office of Buckingham Palace. Such permission is normally never given unless your product or your services have actually been used by the Royal Family. When I stayed in London at the charming, quiet, small Royal Court Hotel on Sloane Square at the end of the King's Road in Chelsea, the concierge was always prepared to whisper in a conspiritorial tone that "Several of our rooms have been reserved by Buckingham Palace for V.I.V.s"—meaning Very Important Visitors with some connection with Her Majesty the Queen. It was not surprising. The hotel was too small to be grand, but most of its comfortable rooms had bay windows that overlooked the classic square, and its restaurant on the lower ground floor had some of the best food in London, served beautifully and with quiet modesty.

Sunday brunch, beginning at eleven o'clock and continuing through the early afternoon, was always one of the special pleasures of any week at the Royal Court. The menu was large. The side headed "English selections" was very solidly British: grilled Black Angus beefsteaks or Southdown lamb chops, sautéed Cumberland ham or kidneys, a choice of Irish or Scottish bacon, large bowls of whole-grain Irish or Scottish oatmeal porridge with lashings of heavy cream and natural brown sugar, a whole buffet table of slice-for-yourself cold cuts and cheeses, plus dozens of vari-

EDITOR'S NOTE: This syndicated newspaper column originally appeared in August 1978.

eties of breads, fruit preserves, bitter orange marmalades, and coffees and teas from Arabia, China, India, Indonesia, Java. On the other page of the menu were the "French selections," dishes that could be feathery light and lusciously lovely. My favorite among these was Gaston's French toast.

It was like no French toast you had ever seen, tasted, or dreamed of! It was partly prepared alongside your table by the maître d'hôtel, Gaston, who was said to have invented the recipe. He began normally enough by dipping slices of bread in an egg batter and sautéing them in butter—but there the resemblance to standard French toast ended with an alcoholic hiss. Gaston added the spirited excitement of French Calvados apple brandy, the smooth velvety richness of a vanilla egg custard, and the tangy refreshment of a puree of fresh fruits. Finally, he rushed the dish back to the kitchen for a finishing session in a very hot oven so that, when it was placed before you, it was crusty and bubbly—an unbelievably effective waker-upper.

I enjoyed Gaston's specialty for many years. When it came time for him to retire, I begged him for the recipe as a lasting remembrance of the pleasures of our relationship. Now, I often prepare this royal English version of French toast for Sunday brunch. Each person who tastes it for the first time is wowed by it. Old friends, when they are invited, ask: "Will you promise to make your English French toast?"

GASTON'S ROYAL ENGLISH FRENCH TOAST

4 servings

> 1 cup mashed or coarsely pureed fruit in season: apricots, peaches, plums, raspberries, strawberries, etc., or frozen or canned
> 1½ cups whole milk
> About ¼ cup white sugar
> 1 whole vanilla bean, or about 1 teaspoon pure vanilla extract, plus a few extra drops of the extract
> 3 large whole eggs
> ½ teaspoon salt
> 1 long narrow baguette loaf French bread
> 1½ cups half-and-half
> 2 to 3 tablespoons confectioners' sugar
> ⅓ cup French Calvados apple brandy
> 8 tablespoons butter

AVERAGE TIME REQUIRED: about 45 minutes to mash the fruit, boil the egg custard, cut, dip, and sauté the bread, and assemble the dish—a final 15 minutes of baking.

The Fruit and Custard

Wash the fruit and, as needed, remove stalks, skins, pits, stones, etc. Either mash them by hand (possibly passing the puree through a sieve), or run them for no more than a second or two through an electric blender or food processor. Hold the mash, covered. Put the milk into a 1-quart saucepan and stir in the sugar, and heat it very slowly while you prepare the vanilla bean. Using a small sharp knife, cut off and discard the stem of the bean. Slit it in half along its entire length. With the point of the knife, scrape out all seeds on both sides and drop them into the milk. Cut remaining bean halves into ½-inch lengths and add to the milk. (The bean is far superior even to the pure vanilla extract, but if you are going to use the latter, do not add it at this point or it will evaporate during the heating; hold it until later.) Stir the milk and heat almost to boiling, but do not let it actually bubble. Take the saucepan off the heat and let it cool slightly.

Meanwhile, heat water in the bottom of a double boiler to a very gentle, steady simmering. Break 2 eggs into a 1-quart bowl and beat them very hard with a balloon wire whisk, at the same time incorporating ¼ teaspoon salt. While continuing to beat hard, work in 2 tablespoons of the still-quite-hot vanilla milk. Still beating, slowly but steadily pour in all the remaining hot milk. Strain the mixture through a fine sieve into the top of the double boiler. Cook the custard, stirring continuously, until it thickens and coats a metal spoon—usually about 5 minutes. Remove the top from the double boiler and dip it into a bowl of cold water to stop the cooking and thickening. Now stir in pure vanilla extract, if you are using it. Even if you have used a bean, you may now, if you like, add a few more drops of extract to strengthen the vanilla flavor. Now is the time to also add a bit more sugar, if you like. Lightly, but thoroughly combine the custard and the mashed fruits. Taste again and readjust sugar and vanilla. Do not make it too sweet. Finally, cut a circle of wax paper to fit the top surface of the custard and press the paper down very lightly to prevent a skin from forming during the holding time at room temperature.

The Spirited Batter and Bread

Cut the French bread diagonally so you get oblong slices, each, say, about ½ inch thick. How many slices will depend on their size, the estimated hunger of your guests, and the measurements of your flat baking and serving dish. My guess is usually between 4 and 8 slices. In a bowl, whip together the frying batter: the remaining egg, the 1½ cups half-and-half, 1 tablespoon confectioners' sugar, Calvados, and ¼ teaspoon salt. Set a sauté pan over medium heat and lubricate its bottom with 2 tablespoons butter. While it is melting, preheat oven to 400° F.

Dip each bread slice in batter and swish it around to thoroughly soak it. Lightly shake off excess batter and at once sauté on both sides until nicely browned. Do several slices at once, if you can. Keep adding butter to the pan.

Assembling and Baking

You will need at least 1 tablespoon butter to liberally grease the baking pan. Lay each browned bread slice in the pan. Slices can be horizontal, or, if necessary, slightly overlap. When slices cover the pan bottom pour the custard over and spread evenly to completely cover. Sprinkle confectioners' sugar on the top. Bake in oven center until the top is slightly browned and bubbly, about 15 minutes. Serve on very hot plates.

WORKING NOTES: You may be tempted to cut corners on this recipe. Resist—if you want to achieve the maximum "wow effect" on your guests. It is well worth the trouble of finding a vanilla bean in a fancy food or specialty spice shop. The flavor is so much cleaner, fresher, and stronger than even the purest extract. But the worst sin is to make the custard from a packaged, powdered, artificial egg, dessert pudding mix. That could murder the dish! If you cannot easily get French Calvados brandy, you can almost equally well use French Cognac or Armagnac, or a first-class California brandy, such as Setrakian, or Christian Brothers X.O., or the new vintage brandy of Cresta Blanca.

Lou Pastis en Pott

Which is the greatest dish in the world? The question is often asked by culinary beginners. Without getting bogged down in defining gastronomical greatness, surely one would hardly nominate any of the so-called "*haute cuisine* creations" of the famous chefs in their grand kitchens. The dishes that I have found most magnificent, in the anticipation and in the eating, are the regional combinations of everyday foods, not "invented," but gradually developed, often over centuries, by country and farm cooks making the most economical use of the foods at hand.

No one "created" the bouillabaisse of Provence. The Mediterranean fishermen sold the best of their catch in the market for the family income. What they could not sell, and brought home to their wives, were the spiny, bony, ugly fish, not one of them quite good enough to rest on its own in the sauté pan or under the grill. So the thrifty wives began combining them in a stew, balancing one texture against another, lifting dull flavors with the freshness of local vegetables, adding rich body with the local olive oil, and gilding the plain white flesh with saffron. How many thousands of tries, how many inedible failures, before the basic principles of the recipe were established? How many experiments were needed to combine perfectly the tropical fish of the Gulf of Mexico with the superb vegetables of the black-bottom Mississippi Delta and the Choctaw Indian spices into the gumbo of Louisiana? Or the shellfish and meats with the vegetables and rice into the *paella* of Valencia? Or the

---

EDITOR'S NOTE: This article originally appeared in the October 1967 issue of *Gourmet*.

mutton, hot peppers, and wheat grains into the *couscous* of North Africa? No one "invented" the curry of India; the combination of spices was an essential ingredient to preserve and sweeten the meat under the spoiling sun.

Among the dozens of such great dishes, there is one that has been prepared for centuries in a small area of France, but which (perhaps partly because of the strange complication of its name) I have never found listed on any menu, or included in any cookbook. It is called *lou pastis en pott.*

The queer spelling is from the old dialect once universally spoken in the mountain villages of southwestern France. The dialect was called *la langue d'Oc*—the language of Occitania, the western region. Eventually, the area became a single province called the Languedoc, one of the most famous gastronomic areas of France, where *pastis* is the powerfully alcoholic native drink. Thus, translated from the Oc, "the *pastis* in a pot" implies "a drink in a pot," or "potted wine," or "solid wine." It is in the classic tradition of a great regional dish. Even my discovery of it was in the historic pattern of Balzac, Rabelais, and Anatole France.

I was being driven from San Sebastian on the north coast of Spain to stay for a few days with friends in the Médoc village of Margaux in the great wine country, along the western shore of the Gironde estuary. We crossed the French border into Hendaye at the crack of dawn and breakfasted in Biarritz on a perfect *pipérade* of scrambled eggs with peppers, tomatoes, and Bayonne ham. Then we drove for mile after repetitive mile along the wide, wild salt marshes, planning to lunch on the famous local *gravettes* oysters at Arcachon. We lost our way, however, and in the heat of high noon we found ourselves in the deserted central square of a small country town a few miles southwest of Bordeaux. The houses were brilliant under the fiery sun. The only sound was the rustling of the dusty lime trees. We were two hundred miles hungry and did not feel like retracing our tracks. We noticed a tiny café and saw at once, through its window, two uniformed officials, obviously the postal clerk and the railway ticket collector, sipping their apéritifs. Such men, in any town, always know the best place for lunch.

Our judgment was confirmed at the door by a superb aroma of meat cooking in wine. Except for the two officials, the place was empty. *Madame* bustled out of the kitchen and crossed the sanded floor to greet us. *Monsieur,* short, fat, and bald, stood behind the zinc-topped bar, half hidden by a pyramid of glasses. *Madame* was delighted. Certainly, we could have our choice for *déjeuner.* Perhaps, to begin, *les saucissons truffés bordelaise;* followed, perhaps, by an *omelette aux fines herbes;* then some chops of *agneau pré-salé*, the young lamb grazed on the local salt marshes; then we might end with some Pessac strawberries.

Monsieur came out from behind the bar and pointed to the back door, through which came the noonday murmuring of chickens. In five minutes one of those birds could be in the sauté pan.

I asked about the delicious aroma from the kitchen. A moment of silence. *Madame's* voice was a shade uncertain. She wondered whether the dish was good enough. A very plain and simple stew "of the family." I insisted that there was nothing plain about that marvelous smell, and tactfully inquired if there would be enough for all of us. She assured us of abundance, but insisted that we must at least have an hors-d'oeuvre first. We compromised to make her happy.

A few minutes later *Madame* approached us and, with charming warmth, asked if, since we were sharing the family dish, we would permit them to serve the lunch *en famille*. I replied that we would be honored. Several tables were put together and we were formally introduced to "Monsieur le Chef de Poste" and "Monsieur le Chef de Gare."

It was one of the best of all lunches. When the unknown dish was placed in the center of the table, it appeared as an enormous earthenware *toupin*, radiating warmth. The steaming fragrance, when the lid was lifted, made waiting almost unbearable. The gently bubbling stew appeared to be a close cousin of *boeuf bourguignonne*, but was cooked in the red wine of Bordeaux, with many vegetables and several kinds of meat. The first taste was indescribably good. The flavor of the wine was as if it were concentrated and yet softened. This effect was achieved, I was to learn later, by the use of sweet figs. The chunks of beef, pork, carrots, mushrooms, and onions were all covered and unified by a wine sauce thickened, not with flour, but with a distillation of mashed vegetables. Intrigued, I asked our host how long the dish had been cooking. "It has been on our fire for ten years, *monsieur*!" Unbelievingly, I prodded: "In that time, how often has the pot been refilled?" "In ten years, *monsieur*, the pot has never been empty—each time we eat from it, we fill the pot up again with new ingredients, but the base remains the same—this is the concentration of flavor that forms the sauce." I asked about the wine in the pot. "It must be a good red Bordeaux, of course, and the vintage must be exactly as old as the dish."

When we all asked for second helpings, the delight of our host and hostess was unbounded. I thought, as I finished, that the total effect was of eating a dish of wine in solid form. Before we left, I persuaded Madame to write out her recipe for the great stew which was, of course, *lou pastis en pott.*

I have eaten it many times since in that region (but always in private homes) and have learned something of its background. Again and again I have noticed that the serving of it is always surrounded by the same sense of family unity and warmth that I found the first time in the small café. As soon as one's hosts realize that one knows and appreciates *lou pastis en pott* one is no longer a guest, but a member of the family. It has been a family dish for centuries on farms where, in the old days, the cattle and pigs were slaughtered and butchered at home. The best cuts of the meat were sent to market for profit. What remained were dozens of odd, irregularly shaped, relatively unsalable scraps. To make the most economical use of this surplus, the thrifty Médoc farmwife developed her *pott*. She added fresh vegetables and herbs from her kitchen garden. The children brought in mushrooms from the woods. Above all, there was always a superabundance of the local red wine. True enough, the great and famous vintages went to Paris and abroad for high profits, but there was plenty of the medium wine from the lesser vineyards, and that gave the *pott* its character. Since it was so economical, so practical, and so much enjoyed, it was kept going on the back of the wood-burning stove, day after day, month after month, and year after year, refilled with fresh ingredients each time a meal was served from it. As the *pott* grew older, it grew richer and richer in nuances of taste.

It may be true that Anatole France was not thinking precisely about *lou pastis en pott* when he wrote the following, but he might well have been:

> *Je veux vous amener chez [la mère] Clémence . . . où l'on ne fait qu'un plat, mais un plat prodigieux. On sait que pour avoir toutes ses qualités [cela] doit cuire doucements sur un feu bas. . . .*
>
> *[Chez] la mère Clémence [cela a] cuit depuis vingt ans. Elle ajoute de temps en temps . . . mais la marmite . . . contient toujours le même plat. La base demeure, et c'est cette antique et précieuse base qui donne au plat une qualité comparable à ces tons ambrés si particuliers qui caractérisent les chairs dans les oeuvres des vieux maîtres vénitiens.*

"I would like to take you to the establishment of Mère Clémence, who makes only one dish, but a spectacular one. In order for this dish to have its proper quality it must cook gently over low heat. At Mère Clémence's it has cooked for twenty years. She adds things from time to time, but the pot always contains the same dish. The foundation remains, and it is this antique and precious base that gives the dish a quality comparable to the unique amber skin tones characterized in the works of the old Venetian masters."

Naturally, there are dozens of versions of *lou pastis en pott,* and I have combined their best features in my own modern recipe, which is prepared with modern ingredients in a modern pot and cooked in a modern oven. It does not involve slaughtering one's own steer and pig at home. The amounts listed below could, of course, be finished up at one sitting by a party of eight to ten hungry people, but one will never know the true magnificence of this dish unless one keeps it going for a week or two, adding more ingredients (including more wine) as needed to keep the *pott* always full, while the flavor gradually builds up to its true winy richness. Once the dish is thus "rolling along," it has all the much-advertised features of a "one-dish convenience meal." It involves no more trouble in preparation than chunking the ingredients and putting them into the pot in layers. The slow simmering in the oven requires no supervision whatsoever. The dish can be served at once, or it can be kept in the refrigerator for several days, ready to be reheated. It is the nearest thing to the ancient Arabian tale of Mohammed's magical "bottomless cauldron."

LOU PASTIS EN POTT
(Potted Wine Stew)

The First Day

The ideal pot for this modern version is a 5-quart French enameled cast-iron *cocotte* that can be used in the oven or on top of the stove and is good-looking enough to be brought to table. However, one could also use an earthenware or heatproof china casserole, or a bean pot with a reasonably well-fitting lid. Cover the bottom of the pot with ½ pound salt pork or bacon, thickly sliced. Rub one slice around the sides to grease them slightly. Top, tail, and scrape 3 carrots and slice them fairly thinly into the pot, spreading them in an even layer. Put in 3 whole bay leaves.

Cut away the tough stalks of a small bunch of parsley, wash the leaves, and, with kitchen scissors, coarsely snip them into the pot. Sprinkle on ¼ cup fresh thyme leaves, coarsely snipped, or 2 teaspoons dried thyme. Cut in half 6 figs, fresh if available, otherwise dried, and add them to the pot. Divide 2 pounds onions into three parts, peel and slice the first part, and add it to the pot as the next layer. Divide in half 2 pounds lean stewing beef, such as chuck or bottom round, cut into 1½-inch cubes, put half the chunks in the pot, and sprinkle them with salt and black pepper to taste. Peel and slice the second part of onions and place them in a layer on top of the beef. Divide in half 2 pounds lean stewing pork, such as shoulder, cut into 1½-inch cubes, put half the cubes in the pot, and sprinkle them with salt, pepper, and monosodium glutamate. Divide 1 pound mushrooms into 2 parts and pull out the stems from one part, leaving the caps whole. Wipe the caps clean with a damp cloth (never wash mushrooms in water), then gently push the caps and stems into odd corners of the pot. Peel and finely chop 3 garlic cloves and ¼ pound shallots and sprinkle them into the pot. The dish should now be about half full.

Put ½ cup Cognac into a small saucepan, warm it over low heat to just above blood heat, ignite, and pour it, flaming, over the ingredients. Pour in enough red wine barely to cover the ingredients. Put on the lid and set the dish in the center of a moderately slow oven (325° F). Everything must now be gently bubbled until the wine has been reduced by half. In other words, if the wine is 4 inches deep to begin with, the cooking is complete when the wine is 2 inches deep. The time depends on the efficiency of the oven and the type of dish; usually from 2 to 3 hours is required. Check after 1 hour and make sure the liquid is gently bubbling. If not, turn up the oven heat 25 degrees. On the other hand, if bubbling is too fierce, turn the oven down 25 degrees. Never, under any circumstances, stir the ingredients. When the level of wine has correctly fallen, turn off the oven, let the dish cool on top of the stove, then refrigerate it, covered, overnight.

The Second Day

Turn on the oven to the same final setting as the day before. Fill up the pot to within ½ inch of the top by adding, in order: 3 carrots, topped, tailed, scraped, and sliced, the remaining 1 pound beef, salted and peppered, the remaining onions, peeled and sliced, the remaining pork, salted and peppered, and the remaining ½ pound mushrooms, prepared as above. Add more red wine, again barely to cover the ingredients. Put on the lid, set the pot in the oven, and let it bubble until the wine is again reduced by half. The *pott* may now be served at once, but it will be much better, with flavors matured and concentrated, if it is cooled and then refrigerated for about 3 more days. Never serve more than half the dish. Half must be held back as the rich flavor base for the next cycle of cooking.

Method of Serving

Remember that the vegetables and wine at the bottom of the pot are being boiled and concentrated down to a mash, to provide the sauce for the newly cooked ingredients at the top. Therefore, first serve each diner with meats and vegetables from the top, then dig down to the bottom for the wine sauce.

Continuing the Cooking Cycle

After the first meal, fill up the pot again with more of the same ingredients, in roughly the same proportions and in the same order, always adding more red wine barely to cover and cooking the mixture until the wine is reduced by half. Each successive cooking improves the flavor and, in between, the pot may be left in the refrigerator for up to three days. Then, to avoid deterioration of flavor, it should be heated up to gentle bubbling for about 15 to 20 minutes. New wine should not be added for this reheating, but only for new ingredients. Scrupulously attended to, the *pott*, if one correctly interprets Anatole France, will last for twenty years.

Varying the Ingredients

After a few weeks, I sometimes become slightly tired of the repeated flavor of beef and pork. Then, for the next cycle, I may add any or all of the following: a stewing chicken, cut into pieces, including the bones, or a small turkey, treated the same way; chunks of smoked ham in place of the fresh pork; cubes of lean lamb; garlic sausage; various types of German or Polish sausage; and different combinations of fresh vegetables, according to the season. In summer, the dish is excellent cold. There seems to be no limit to the flexibility of *lou pastis en pott*.

Chef Roger Vergé's Secrets of Making Great Fish Soups

Room Five on the second floor of the Old Mill at Mougins is one of the most beautiful bedrooms in Provence. In the early morning, you step out from your bed through tall French windows onto a stone balcony where everything is at once perfumed and vivid and warm from the magical brightness of the Midi sky and sun. Behind you, the red-tiled roof slopes upwards. At your left, the old mill wheel still stands, now dry and silent. Below, on terraces at various levels, under gray-and pink-striped umbrellas, are the tables of Chef [Roger] Vergé's three-star restaurant, Le Moulin de Mougins. Surrounding the garden is a circle of giant oak trees and from the vastness of their greenery comes, morning and evening, the multitudinous orchestra of the singing birds.

A young waiter sets the breakfast tray down on the bamboo table on the balcony. There are half a dozen home-made fruit preserves to try with the brioche, the croissant, the *petits pains*, the black coffee. Chef Vergé comes up to join me for breakfast and to discuss last night's memorable dinner. "If you had carried me down here from Paris with my head in a sack," I said, "I would still have known instantly that I was in Provence by the scent of the garlic in your marvelous fish soup."

"Our Provençal garlic is something quite special," Vergé said. "When it is freshly harvested it has an almost flowery scent and a sweetness as against the bitterness that develops in the old, dried heads. With our newly harvested garlic, we can use as many as eight cloves to each cup of

EDITOR'S NOTE: This piece is excerpted from *Revolutionizing French Cuisine* (McGraw-Hill, 1975).

our fresh green Provençal olive oil. It is this combination of flavors that marries so perfectly to our fresh Mediterranean fish in the great soups of our region. The old idea in Provence was that you loaded everything with olive oil, but I have discovered that, if you control exactly the balance of flavors, you need use only about a quarter of the oil normally called for in the classic Provençal recipes. And since pure olive oil has a much stronger character than butter, less of the oil goes a longer way toward developing a memorable personality in any fish preparation."

Roger explained to me the differences between the three great fish soups of Provence. The best known, of course, is *la bouillabaisse*, which is almost a stew of chunks of a carefully balanced selection of fish and shellfish. It starts with the vegetables more or less melted into a large quantity of olive oil. The great chef, Fernand Point, once said that a true *bouillabaisse* could only be made within sight of the Mediterranean. Vergé goes even further. He never makes *bouillabaisse* in his restaurant because he believes that it is not at its absolute best unless it is boiled in the open air, on the beach where the fish have just been landed, in a huge, black, iron, open "witches' cauldron," over a bonfire of pine branches with the needles, so that the inside of the pot is licked by the flames and everything is slightly smoked by the burning of the resinous wood. "That," said Vergé, "is the marvelous, ultimate effect."

The second great Provençal soup, *la bourride*, must, according to Vergé, "be prepared with what we call *les poissons de landes*," including the *chapon*, the white *rascasse*, the *congre*, and a few *murènes*. These are boiled together with onions and the soup is then thickened with the famous *aioli*, the Provençal garlic mayonnaise. Again, with *la bourride*, oil is a primary ingredient.

"As you know, I am not from Provence," Roger continued, "but once one starts cooking here, with the magnificent products of the Provençal earth, sea, and sunshine, one has to adapt one's techniques to the region. It has always seemed to me that the third great Provençal soup, *la soupe de poisson*, in which all the fish are mashed to a kind of cream, offers the best chance for cutting down on the oil and producing a dish that is digestible, healthy and light, in the tradition of the new cuisine."

Roger gave me the basic rules for his marvelous fish-garlic soup (see recipe, below). It has all the colors, the dominant character, and the warmth of Provence. The fish flavors are magnified by saffron, and fennel, by bay-laurel and thyme—in their strong Provençal versions. The soup is neither very delicate nor very modest in personality. It is, historically, a peasant dish originated by the wives of the Provençal fishermen. Roger took me shopping in the fish market at Cannes and showed me the kind of fish you must buy, wherever in the world you happen to be and whatever the different names of the available specimens. He prefers fish caught with lines along rocky coasts to those dredged with nets along muddy bottoms, because the feeding habits of rock fish give their flesh a special flavor. They should be small and soft-fleshed, because they are going to be puréed in the soup.

On this particular morning, Roger bought: *rascasse*, also called "sea devil of the Mediterranean" or "hog-fish" (also caught off North Carolina, around Bermuda, and on the coral reefs of the West Indies); *rouquier*, the highly colored parrot-fish or sheepshead (or, off the West Indies, the "Slippery Dick"); *girelle*, the rainbow wrasse or goldfinny; *galinette* or *grondin*, also called gurnard, redfish, or sea robin; *cigale*, spider crab or water cricket; *murène*, the spotted moray (also caught off the North Sea coast of Scotland or off the West Indies, where it is called the "hamlet"); *favouille*, tiny rock crabs (also found in the Gulf of Mexico), plus some strictly Provençal fish that simply have no English names, *capoun*, *pageot*, *sars*, and *vielle*.

Roger has been so insistent on what he wants (and his local prestige is so high) that the fishmongers now have barrels of small mixed fish at their stands in the market, labeled POISSONS POUR LA SOUPE. I think that every fishmonger in the United States ought to do the same.

Once Roger gets the live fish back to his kitchen, he gives them only light cleaning and washing to guard their juices and then cooks them in a minimum of oil. To reduce the richness of the soup even further, Roger serves it accompanied by dry-toasted slices of French bread instead of butter- or oil-fried croutons. He rubs the bread with garlic instead of spreading it with the rich traditional *rouille* of Provence, the whipped garlic-egg-and-oil spread. (But, of course, he will make the *rouille* for you if you insist on it.) Finally, he brings the soup to table in wide, deep soup plates with the oval slices of bread floating on the surface like little boats.

THE NEAREST AMERICAN VERSION OF CHEF ROGER VERGÉ'S TRUE FISH-GARLIC SOUP OF PROVENCE

4 to 6 servings

This marvelous soup contains not an ounce of butter, not a spoonful of cream, not a wisp of thickening flour. Its creamy body comes only from the pureeing of the flesh of the fish.

Can it be reproduced in the United States? Well, naturally, not exactly. For one thing, there is a difference of mood between, say, Madison, Marietta, Minneapolis, and Mougins. But I think I have proved to at least a score of my New York friends that my translation and adaptation of the Vergé recipe is an eminently satisfactory variation of the master *cuisinier's* interpretation of the traditional Provençal dish.

The balance of the fish is all-important. In New York, I buy about half a pound each from the following list: butterfish, flounder, gurnard, red mullet, fresh sardines, sea bass, sea robin, sea trout, sheepshead, whiting, plus two or three small whole blue crabs.

For maximum lightness, use only dry-toasted garlic bread as the garnish for this soup. But if you are prepared to risk the added richness of a celestial Provençal *rouille*, the recipe is below. The *rouille* is then spread on the garlic bread. A final note: You can, if you wish, sprinkle grated Parmesan over the soup and I have included some cheese in the recipe. But, personally, I am against the Parmesan. It seems to me to add a slightly clashing Italian note to a soup that belongs, completely, to the Midi of France. The cheese is offered so you can, if you wish, agree to disagree.

Mixed fish, see above, at least 6 to 8 types, all boned and skinned, but bring home bones and skin (about 3 to 4 pounds total flesh and bones)
1¼ pounds yellow onions, peeled and chopped
2 or 3, according to size, small blue crabs, whole in shells
1 cup olive oil, not too fruity
4 medium ripe tomatoes, sliced
9 cloves garlic
Thyme, fresh in season (2 or 3 stalks with leaves)
2 bay leaves, crumbled
2 teaspoons fennel seed
2 tablespoons dry white wine, to soak the saffron
½ teaspoon saffron filaments
Coarse crystal salt, and freshly ground black pepper, to taste
1 loaf French bread, long baguette
¼ pound Parmesan cheese, optional, grated, for sprinkling on top of the soup at table, see above

About 1 Hour Before Serving—Active Preparation About 30 Minutes, Plus Another 30 Minutes of Unsupervised Poaching and Boiling

Wash the bones and skins, then put them into a 4-quart covered saucepan with 3 quarts of cold water and ½ cup of the chopped onions. Do not add salt or pepper. Bring water to a boil and keep simmering, covered, until you need this court bouillon in the main kettle.

Wash and carefully dry all the fish and crabs, then put them, together, in a large bowl. Set a big soup kettle on top of the stove over quite low heat and pour in the 1 cup of olive oil. Add all the remaining chopped onions, stir them around in the oil and let them simmer for 10 minutes. They must under no circumstances fry or brown but simply become transparent and melt into the oil. Watch this carefully as you occasionally stir the onions around.

Meanwhile, add to the fish in the bowl the 4 sliced tomatoes, 8 of the cloves of garlic, whole and unpeeled, the thyme leaves and stalks, the 2 crumbled bay leaves and the 2 teaspoons of fennel seed. Hold until the onions in the big kettle are ready. Into a very small saucepan put the 2 tablespoons of white wine, heat it to just above blood heat, then soak the ½ teaspoon of saffron in the wine, stirring it around to encourage it to exude its coloring and flavoring oils. Hold it off the heat, covered, until it is needed in the big kettle.

At the end of the 10 minutes, when the onions are perfectly done, turn up the heat to quite high and add, all at once, the contents of the large bowl with the fish, etc. Stir it all around quite vigorously, to impregnate everything thoroughly with the onion-flavored base. You should expect the fish now to begin breaking up into smallish chunks. Continue this process, with regular stirring, for exactly 10 minutes. Between stirrings, strain the bouillon from the fish bones and skins and measure it. You will need exactly 3 quarts to add to the big kettle. If it has slightly boiled down, add cold water to make up the 3 quarts.

About 30 Minutes Before Serving—Boiling the Fish

The moment the 10 minutes are up, pour in the 3 quarts of fish bouillon. Stir everything around and begin tasting for seasoning. I usually find that I need, at this point, about a ½ teaspoon of salt. Do not yet add any pepper. Chef Vergé warned me that if the pepper is added too early it can cause a slightly bitter flavor. Keep the heat high under the kettle. The soup must boil hard, exactly as if it were a *bouillabaisse*, with large bubbles ensuring that all the flavors are continuously being blended together. This is the essential trick in making a perfect *soupe*. Do not cover your kettle at this point. Stir frequently. Keep everything bubbling for exactly 20 minutes.

While waiting, prepare the crusts of garlic bread and, if you have opted for the extra richness, beat up the *rouille* (see next recipe, below). Preheat your oven to 275° F. Cut ½-inch slices from the loaf of French bread—about 2 slices per person—and toast them, dry, on a cookie sheet or aluminum foil in the oven. They will usually be nicely browned in about 10 minutes. Then, either rub them with the cut side of the remaining clove of garlic, or hold them to be spread with the *rouille* when it is ready.

During this stage it is helpful to have two people working on the job. When the 20 minutes of hard boiling is up, turn off the heat under the big kettle. Strain out all the solids, set them in a bowl to be pureed and return the liquid to the kettle. Turn on the heat to low just to keep the liquid warm. Split open the crabs, take out what little flesh is left inside them, and add this to the fish, discarding the shells. Quickly puree the solids in two stages. First, pass them through an electric vegetable grinder, or a Cuisinart chopper-churner. Second, rub the ground mash through a sieve, returning the resulting puree of fish and vegetables to the big kettle. The fish fibers that do not pass through the sieve have little flavor left and should be discarded. When this job is completed, thoroughly stir the soup and bring it up to the gentlest simmering. Now add the saffron and its soaking wine. Make sure that all the coloring and flavoring oils of the saffron are gathered up from the walls of the little saucepan by rinsing it with a few tablespoons of the hot soup. Stir the soup again and watch its color change to the warm orange of Provence. Taste again and add more salt, if needed. This is the moment to grind in plenty of black pepper—in my case, usually 16 to 20 grinds. Keep it all gently simmering, covered, until ready to serve.

Serving at Table

Present *la soupe de poisson* in wide soup plates, or in gumbo bowls of not less than 8 inches diameter. Bring the garlic-covered bread slices to table on a serving platter. The diner then has the choice (according to his or her love of garlic) of biting into the bread separately or soaking and working it and its garlic into the soup. If you are going to use Parmesan cheese, sprinkle it on. With this memorable dish, Chef Roger Vergé served me a dry, fruity, light white wine of the Côtes de Provence. You can serve instead a dry, light California Pinot Blanc.

AN AUTHENTIC PROVENÇAL GARLIC ROUILLE FOR LA SOUPE DE POISSON

2 egg yolks
3 cloves garlic, peeled and mashed
    About 8 tablespoons light oil, preferably Provençal grape
    Coarse crystal salt and freshly ground black pepper, to taste
    A few teaspoons hot fish soup, from previous recipe, for slight thinning
    Toasted bread, from previous recipe
    About 1 teaspoon Hungarian sweet paprika

Preparation Time—About 5 Minutes

Arm yourself with a smallish round-bottomed beating bowl and a balloon wire whisk. Put in the 2 egg yolks and give them a few beats to break them up. Next, beat in the mashed garlic. Then start beating in the oil, teaspoon by teaspoon at first, making sure that each teaspoon is thoroughly absorbed before the next is added. As the yolks expand, the oil can go in tablespoon by tablespoon. If you beat hard and fast, with lifting strokes, getting in plenty of air, the *rouille* will soon become very fluffy and stiff. Beat in salt and pepper to taste. Then dilute the *rouille* to the thickness of a not-too-stiff mayonnaise by beating in a few teaspoons, one at a time, of the hot soup.

Serving

Spread the *rouille* on each slice of toasted bread and decorate each piece with a sprinkle of paprika (Chef Vergé thinks not more than two rounds per person, or the *rouille* will begin to dominate the soup). Serve these rounds on a separate plate.

Once you become a *rouille* aficionado, you will want to use it also in other ways: with potatoes, all kinds of green and yellow vegetables, cold meats, fish, poultry, even in picnic sandwiches. Dr. Johnson might easily have said, "Mayonnaise is for boys, *aïoli* is for men, but *rouille* is for heroes!"

Pissaladière Niçoise

If it is really true—though no historian has ever proved it—this is one of the most fantastic stories from the ancient world of royal feasting. In 1295, Marco Polo returned home to Venice after traveling for years in Asia and visiting the court of the emperor of the Tartars, Kublai Khan, at his palace in Cambuloc (now Peking).

Polo gave a big dinner for his friends to entertain them with his stories of the wonders he had seen. He served some of the dishes he had eaten in the halls of Kublai Khan. One specialty of the Tartars was a large, round, flat loaf of bread, topped with slices of meat and cheese. You can still find it in certain parts of China. It is called—believe it or not—*peen-zah*.

The Venetians did not adopt Marco Polo's bread. They prefer a low-starch diet. But the idea traveled southward through Italy until it reached the starch-loving, pasta-eating city of Naples.* The Neapolitans started making their version of *peen-zah*, using the ingredients they had at hand: anchovies, mozzarella cheese, mushrooms, olives and olive oil, sliced pepperoni sausage, tomatoes. They called the result—do I have to tell you?

Having come all the way across Asia from Peking, pizza did not stop in Naples. It went up the west coast of Italy to Rome, then to Genoa and, finally, to France. Of course, the French version of pizza had to be radi-

---

EDITOR'S NOTE: This syndicated newspaper column originally appeared in June 1978.

* EDITOR'S NOTE: There is evidence that the ancient Greeks baked a flat bread with a topping, and that the ancient Romans adopted this practice some one thousand years before Marco Polo's return.

293

cally different. (No French gourmet would admit that any foreign dish was even edible.) They threw out the bread dough—too heavy. They kicked out the peppery sausage—too rough for sensitive French tongues. And so on. Instead of the bread, they turned to their own Alsace-Lorraine idea of a light, buttery, quiche tart shell filled with their own bounty in the South of France—anchovies, olives, onions.

The name pizza, of course, had to be dropped. No French tongue has ever been able to manage the impossible Italian double-Z. Fortunately, the French had a word of their own. Along the Mediterranean beaches around Nice, when fishermen find a glut of anchovies in their nets, their wives conserve the extra fish with oil and spices in large stone crocks. This anchovy conserve is known locally as *pissala*. So the pizza of Naples was transformed and reborn as the *pissaladière* of Nice. It was spread over France with dozens of variations. (Incidentally, an exact copy of the French version has traveled back to Italy, where it is served in the restaurants of Genoa as *pizzaladina*. Perhaps it will, one day, get back to Peking.)

My recipe, below, is the original French version from the professional kitchens of Nice. Serve *pissaladière* exactly as if it were a quiche, as an irresistible appetizer with the drinks before the meal, as a dramatic hors d'oeuvre course at table, or as a snack anytime.

PISSALADIERE NIÇOISE

4 servings as main supper dish; 8 as appetizers

   15 *tablespoons butter*
 1½ *cups sifted all-purpose flour*
   1 *teaspoon salt, and more, to taste*
   2 *pounds yellow onions, peeled and thinly sliced*
     About 3 to 4 tablespoons top-quality olive oil
     Freshly ground black pepper, to taste
  24 *flat boneless anchovy fillets, usually from three 2-ounce cans, or bulk anchovies from barrels at Greek, Italian, or Spanish neighborhood grocers (see working notes)*
     About 24 (½ pound) black olives, pitted, preferably from same ethnic stores as anchovies

KITCHEN EQUIPMENT: Bowl, pastry cutter and blender, wooden spatulas and spoons (or food processor), cutting board and sharp knives, sauté pan with cover, pastry board, 10-inch pie plate.

AVERAGE TIME REQUIRED: Make it the day before; about 15 minutes for mixing the pastry dough; about 45 minutes, with little supervision, for simmering the onions; about 20 minutes to assemble the tart; and 30 minutes of unsupervised baking.

Mixing the Pastry Dough

Bring 14 tablespoons butter to room temperature. Have ready in your freezer about 2 tablespoons of ice water, but do not let it freeze. Put flour into a large bowl; sprinkle salt over; then cut in butter with knives or a pastry cutter, sprinkling on a minimum of ice water, a few drops at a time, until there is no dry flour left and it all looks like niblet corn. (Or you can do the whole job in a food processor.) Gather the dough lightly into a ball; wrap loosely in wax paper and refrigerate at least 1 hour, or longer, until needed.

Simmering the Onion Filling

You need a sauté pan large enough to easily hold all onion slices at once with enough room to spare so that they can be stirred around. Lubricate its bottom with 3 tablespoons of olive oil; heat it up to gentle frying temperature; then add the onions and stir them thoroughly with a wooden spoon to coat every slice with oil. Now comes the secret trick of making a great *pissaladière*. The onions must be cooked gently to a golden color while remaining chewy. If you cook them too fast, they'll fry and brown; too slow, and they'll mush into a puree. Stir gently and regularly. Do not let the bottom of the pan dry out. Dribble in more oil as needed. The onions should be golden in 10 to 15 minutes. Then cover and lower the heat so they just gently simmer about 15 minutes. They are perfectly done when still slightly chewy, but gentle and smooth in flavor. Season to taste with salt and pepper.

Assembling and Baking the Pissaladière

Use the last tablespoon butter to lightly grease a pie plate. Preheat oven to 400 degrees. Quickly roll out the dough about ¼ inch thick on a floured board, and line the pie plate. Some dough will be left over. Neatly place 18 anchovies on the bottom of the tart shell. Fill with onions. Gather together the remaining dough; roll it out ¼ inch thick and cut it into strips about ⅜ inch wide. Make a neat, lattice-work grill across the top surface of the onions. With the 6 remaining anchovies make a star in the center. Now press a pitted black olive into each open space between the lattice grill. Also make a ring of black olives all the way around the outer edge of the tart. If the olives are large, you may halve or slice them. Or you may work out your own design. Bake the pissaladiere until the lattice crust is nicely brown, usually 25 to 30 minutes. You cannot serve this hot from the oven because the crust will be too crumbly to cut. Let it cool to room temperature, then refrigerate, lightly covered with wax paper, until needed. Let it come back to room temperature before serving, cut into narrow pie wedges.

WORKING NOTES: Let me again extol the virtues of anchovies and olives bought in bulk from Greek, Italian, or Spanish neighborhood groceries. The anchovies are almost always displayed as small, whole fish (each 2 to 3 inches long) tightly encrusted with salt in an open barrel. About ½ pound would be plenty for this recipe. It is a matter of a few seconds to scrape off the salt, behead and tail them, split them down the center, and remove the backbone. You will then have two large fillets of a quality and taste that will surprise you.

You will feel the same about olives. Those that come in cans or jars have to be pasteurized and this seems to destroy most of the bite of their flavor. A first-class Greek grocery will probably display about 15 different kinds of olives in open barrels: black or green, enormous or miniscule, dry and crinkly or fat and oily, biting sharp or soothing, soft, soaking in brine, or oil, or light vinegar—the variety is dazzling. You taste from one barrel after another before you decide which you prefer. The names of the varieties speak of Mediterranean islands. You will wonder how you ever got along with just plain cans. Try making this *pissaladière* with sun-dried Moroccan olives.

NOTES ON A FRENCH MENU FOR BASTILLE DAY: July 14 is France's greatest national holiday, Bastille Day, celebrating the uprising in which Parisian workers burned down the old prison, the symbol of royal dictatorship. We like to join the celebration, wherever we happen to be, by inviting some friends to a French summer supper. It is usually a cold buffet, but starting with a warm cup of soup for each guest to stress the welcome—a cup of creamed consommé Bretonne, half-and-half clear chicken bouillon and clam juice, garnished with a tiny dollop of whipped cream made rosy with a sprinkling of paprika.

The *pissaladière* is followed by a molded spiced fish mousse with a tomato sauce. The main entrée might be an impressive chunk of boneless beef rump, stuffed with aromatic vegetables, then decorated and molded into a wine aspic.

The ideal festive dessert (as French as it is American) is the largest watermelon you can find, cut in half lengthwise, hollowed out, then filled and piled high with fresh fruits glazed to a brilliant shine with sugar syrup, garnished with bright lemon sherbet and dotted with snowflakes of white meringue—as if it had just passed through a winter storm.

In honor of our abiding admiration of French wines, we would offer each guest a glass of the sherry of France, the *vin jaune*, the yellow wine of the Jura mountains, the Chateau Chalon, which is not a trade label but the name of the village where several producers make this extraordinary wine in the stangely shaped bottles. We would also drink it with the *pissaladière*. With the fish, we would pour a white Burgundy, or a Mâcon Pinot Chardonnay. The great beef certainly deserves a great red, château-bottled Bordeaux. With the watermelon basket of fruits, nothing less than a noble, dry Champagne. And with the coffee, a fine old Cognac, or Armagnac.

Red Cabbage with Apples and Chestnuts from a Farmhouse in the Jura Mountains

It was a few years ago, but I remember it as if it were yesterday. I had spent Christmas in Paris, and during the few days until the New Year, I was driving with a couple of friends in the Jura Mountains, along the border of France and Switzerland.

We were following a narrow, precipitous valley. It was snowing so hard that it seemed as if there were a solid white wall in front of us. The cold was so fierce that in spite of the warmth from the engine, my legs were numb and I was beginning to chew over bitter thoughts—not a good diet for a gourmet.

Suddenly—disaster! Our engine failed. We were out of gas. It was hopeless to think that anyone could walk in this blizzard. We appeared to be miles from the nearest village. For a couple of hours, we ran a small electric heater off the battery, but that, too, failed.

Evening was coming on. I was just beginning to think about freezing to death when we heard the roar of our saviours approaching. We all jumped out and waved wildly in the glare of their oncoming headlights. It was a big snow-buggy, with huge wheels, balloon snow tires, the growl of a powerful engine, and a snow-tight body as warm inside as an orchid hothouse. We needed just one invitation to jump in.

The man driving was accompanied by two ladies; all were dressed for a country party. They said they could hardly help us with gas because that would take time and they were already late for a New Year's Eve supper

EDITOR'S NOTE: This syndicated newspaper article originally appeared in December 1979.

at the big farm at the low end of the valley. Then the man said, "Why don't you come on with us and have a bite to eat? Then we'll see what we can do for you later. Our hosts will be delighted to have you as their guests—if you can accept and enjoy a simple peasant meal!" Clearly, he had already noted my thin city shoes, so unsuitable for mountain snows. I disregarded the gentle sarcasm and accepted the invitation with gratitude and relife. My shoes were waterlogged. My feet were blocks of ice.

The farm was huge. The buildings were long and low. To make sure that the snow slid off the roofs, they were steeply raked and came down so low that the houses seemed to grow out of the earth. They formed three sides of a square courtyard with a fountain in the center now, of course, frozen solid. I sank into the snow almost to my knees as I took the few steps to the kitchen door. We were graciously received by Madame, the proud queen of her huge kitchen domain, with its several woodburning stoves, its battery of huge, shining, copper pots, and a brigade of helpers, for it was an important occasion. I was taken to a bedroom by one of the children and, in place of my soaked shoes, I was installed in a pair of toasty-warm carpet slippers. Then we were all seated at the enormous table in the dining room.

In the convivial, hospitable, and warm atmosphere of that great old farm, amid the lonely silence of the mountains, with the snow falling heavy and thick outside, how could that unforseen grand supper be anything but memorable?

There was rich farm cream in virtually every one of the many courses—in the thick soup that sent a glow of warmth through my whole body, in the sauces of the various fish and meats, poultry and game, the dressings of the salads, the cream cheeses, and in the wonderful desserts. Our host boasted that every single ingredient came from this farm, except the coffee, pepper, and salt. Even the wines were from his vineyards.

"But, *monsieur*," I said, putting on the nonchalance of Sherlock Holmes, "what about the sugar in that most excellent tart filled with your walnuts?" He slapped me down instantly: "That was sweetened with honey from my bees."

New lines of conversation and new courses of food continued for hours. Some of the details have become dim in my mind. But one dish was so right for the occasion and the setting that it has remained with me, loud and clear! It was—and still is, to my mind—the winter vegetable dish *par excellence*. After the fish that had been caught in the farmer's lake, after the chicken from his farmyard and the ham from his smokehouse, there was a roast of wild boar shot in his forest and, to accompany it, came this magnificent casserole of red cabbage with apples and chestnuts. With the first aromatic scent as the lid was lifted, with the first taste on my tongue, I was sure it must be an old family recipe, prepared and served hundreds of times at this table—each time improved in some slight detail and brought a little but nearer to perfection. After supper I asked Madame about it. She had, in fact, learned it from her mother. No recipe had ever been written down, but she was very willing to tell how it was done.

That was many years ago. It is still one of the most prized recipes in my personal notebook. It is still a great winter vegetable casserole. It is still the best possible accompaniment to game and other strong meats. But it is so good, so rich, so solid, that I often serve it as the main dish in its own right for lunch or supper. Another advantage is that any left-over can be held refrigerated for a few days, then gently reheated with a noticeable improvement and ripening of its flavors.

Ideally, you should use fresh chestnuts and learn the trick for zipping off the tough outer peel and the multicreased inner skin without too much time and trouble. But you can, with some compromise in taste and texture, use the imported Italian dried chestnuts. They have to be soaked as if they were dried beans. The best winter apples for this dish should be tangy and tart—Midwestern Greenings, Western Newtown Pippins, New England Northern Spy, Eastern Rome Beauty or Winesap, or Southern York Imperial.

This New Year, let us go back to the snowbound French Jura and to that great old farm at the bottom of the valley where they are probably serving this gorgeous version of le chou rouge aux pommes et aux chataignes.

RED CABBAGE WITH APPLES AND CHESTNUTS

4 servings

> 2 pounds whole chestnuts, fresh or dried
> Up to 3 tablespoons vegetable oil
> ⅓ cup heavy cream
> Up to 4 cups whole milk
> Coarse crystal salt, to taste
> About 2½ pounds young red cabbage, either 1 larger or 2 smaller with
> plenty of tender leaves and minimum of hard stalks
> ½ pound dark-smoked, thick-sliced lean bacon
> 3 tablespoons butter
> 3 tablespoons soft white pork lard, or low-cholesterol margarine
> Up to 2½ cups clear beef bouillon
> 3 or 4 large winter apples, according to size (see story)
> Freshly ground black pepper, to taste

KITCHEN EQUIPMENT: Heavy frypan with metal handle to heat chestnuts for peeling; 3-quart lidded saucepan for cooking chestnuts; cutting board and sharp knives; wooden spatulas and spoons; large lidded casserole, French-style *cocotte* Dutch oven, or stewpot, preferably of enameled cast iron for use in oven and on top burner and handsome enough to come to table as the serving dish.

Early on the Day—Peeling and Preparing the Chestnuts

Shelling and skinning fresh chestnuts is fairly quick and simple once you know the how. Preheat your oven to 350° F. With a short-bladed oyster knife, gash a deep X on the flat side of each chestnut. Put them into the heavy frypan over medium-high frying heat and sprinkle them with 2 or 3 tablespoons of the oil. Move them around to coat the shells on all sides with the oil. When they start seriously sizzling, set the pan in the oven and bake until the shells puff out and the inner skin is crisp—usually in 10 to 15 minutes.

Then turn off the oven, bring out the chestnuts, and let them cool. As soon as you can handle them, crack off the shells and, with a small knife, pull and scrape off the furry inner skin, making sure to get it out of all the crevices. If you do this while the chestnuts are still hot, the skin will come off easily and quickly.

(If you use the Italian preshelled and preskinned dried chestnuts, they will need 6 hours of presoaking. In your 3-quart saucepan, bring about 2 quarts of water up to a rolling boil. Meanwhile, wash the chestnuts under cold running water. When the water in the saucepan is boiling hard, dribble the chestnuts into it slowly enough that the bubbling does not stop. When all the chestnuts are in, continue boiling them hard for 4 minutes, then turn off the heat and leave them soaking in the hot water for about 6 hours. Finally, they can be drained, rinsed, and will be ready for the next step.)

Whether you use fresh or dried chestnuts, they are to be gently simmered in the cream and milk. Rinse out the saucepan, put in the chestnuts, wet them with the cream, pour in just enough of the milk to cover them, salt them, and simmer gently, covered, until the chestnuts are just soft, but still whole and chewy—bearing in mind that they will get more cooking with the cabbage in the big pot—usually about 15 to 20 minutes. Let them cool in the milk.

About 4 Hours Later—Preparing and Sautéing the Cabbage

Wash the cabbage under running cold water, pull off and discard the tough outer leaves, and cut it, across its axis, into slices about ½-inch thick. Where necessary, neatly trim out the hard central stalk. Hold the slices for the moment. Cut the bacon into ½-inch squares and hold them. Set your large stewpot on medium frying heat and melt in it the butter and pork lard. Add the bacon squares and sizzle them gently until they are lightly crisp. Now add the cabbage slices, coating each with the fat, then pack them loosely so the steam will be able to circulate between them.

Assembling and Simmering the Main Dish

Wet the cabbage down with the first 2 cups of the beef bouillon. Heat it to gentlest simmering, cover it, then keep it going on very low heat, listening to make sure of the lightest bubbling.

Next, immediately, peel the apples, then slice them. Spread the apples in a layer on top of the cabbage. Salt and pepper, to your taste. Again adjust the heat for gentlest simmering, cover, then keep it going (listening, occasionally to make sure that the bubbling is not creeping up) for an hour.

At this point, check the bottom of the stewpan to make sure that it is not boiling dry. If necessary, add another ¼-cup of bouillon. By now the apples will probably have melted down to a mush. Using two large spoons, turn the entire contents of the stewpan over, so that the apple mush is now on the bottom. Return it all to gentlest simmering, again cover and keep it going for another hour.

Then, again, check for dryness, add more bouillon, if needed, and turn the whole mass over once more. Continue gentle simmering, covered, for another half hour.

Now drain the chestnuts from their milk; cut in half. When the timer rings, spread the chestnuts as a layer on top of the cabbage. Let the chestnuts steam gently, covered, for a final half hour.

Last of all, check and adjust the seasonings. Then, if possible, bring the entire pot to the table and serve from it onto very hot plates. Even if this luxurious version of red cabbage is being used as an accompaniment to a main meat course, it is best to serve the vegetables on a separate hot plate.

Guérard's Puree
of Spinach and Pears

Once upon a time, spinach was the vegetable most disliked by most people and—especially—most children. When I was growing up in London, I agreed completely with the famous cartoon in *Punch*, the satiric weekly, showing a mother furiously upbraiding her young son at table: "I say it's good for you and you're going to eat it!" The small boy, chin out, replied, "I say it's spinach and I hate it."

Then there was an American agricultural expert who said, "If God had intended us to eat spinach, He would have flavored it with something."

Spinach took its first big step toward popularity—at least with me, as a boy—with the cartoons of Popeye, the sailor, who "fights to a finach, 'cause I eats me spinach . . ." Popeye would produce a can of spinach, drink it down as if it were root beer, the muscle in his right arm would swell to Herculean proportions, and with one blow of his fist he would stop an express train at full speed or flatten an army of villains.

But spinach, many years earlier, had been accepted by the rarefied arbiters of French high cuisine. That country's most famous gastronomic philosopher, Brillat-Savarin, was mayor of Belley at the edge of the Jura Mountains. Every Sunday after attending mass, he would lunch with the priest, Canon Chevrier. This holy man, a brilliant cook, had discovered a way of simmering chopped spinach in butter for five days so that, as water was expelled from each pound of spinach, it would absorb at least three-quarter pound of butter. The final result was a luxurious, velvety-smooth dish of spinach.

EDITOR'S NOTE: This syndicated newspaper article originally appeared in August 1980.

More recently, spinach was given its crowning glory in French high cuisine terms by the late chef Fernand Point of the three-star Restaurant de la Pyramide. He lightened buttered spinach by working whipped cream into it, and eliminating the slight bitterness of the spinach by adding some sugar.

But today, in terms of the strictly low-calorie *cuisine minceur,* such things as butter, cream, and sugar are out. So it's proper that the ultimate modernization of an elegant spinach dish should come from chef Michel Guérard, the inventor of *cuisine minceur.* In his recipe, he replaced butter, cream, and sugar with—of all things—a puree of Bartlett pears. To understand the brilliance of this idea, you have to know a little about this pear.

It was discovered in 1770, growing as a wild tree in England, by a schoolteacher on a stroll. He told a friend named Williams, a nurseryman, who took cuttings from the wild tree, propagated them, and soon was selling small trees for a fruit he called the Williams pear. That name still is used throughout Europe. The tens of thousands of bottles of pear brandy and pear liqueur made in France, Germany, Italy, Switzerland, and Spain all are called Williams pear *[poire William].*

About 1800, some pear trees were planted near Boston. The next owner, Enoch Bartlett, did not know the name of the pears growing in his new garden. So he sold some young trees under his own name and that was how it became the Bartlett pear in the United States. It is at its best, and at its lowest cost, during August, September, and October.

Guérard estimates that each portion of his spinach dish has only 150 calories. I decided to publish it not for that reason but because it is an imaginative way of serving spinach, with an unusual and memorable balance of tastes.

MICHEL GUÉRARD'S PUREE OF SPINACH AND PEARS

4 servings

>   2 tablespoons fresh lemon juice
>   2 pounds ripe Bartlett pears or, less good, other soft eating pears
>   2 pounds young spinach leaves, tough stalks discarded, or, less good,
>   equivalent frozen or canned
>   Coarse crystal salt and freshly ground black pepper, to taste

Poaching the Pears

Put about 2 quarts cold water into saucepan, and stir in lemon juice. Peel and core pears and quarter lengthwise. Drop into lemon-water and heat to a gentle simmer. Simmer until pears are just cooked, usually about 2 minutes. Drain and reserve.

Cooking the Spinach

The perfect cooking of spinach goes so fast that it works best with two persons—one washing it and the other stirring it with a long wooden spoon in a big, deep pot on the stove. Place pot over high heat. Wash handfuls of spinach under fast-running cold water to remove all sand. After washing, do not shake out the leaves, just throw them into the pot. The only coating liquid is the water on the leaves. Keep adding handfuls of spinach to pot as fast as possible. As each handful falls into the pot, press it down hard with the wooden spoon, at the same time sprinkling in plenty of salt. Within several minutes, all the spinach will have wilted. Remove pot from heat at once. Let spinach cool in the pot until it can be handled.

Using hands, remove spinach from pot and squeeze out as much juice as possible. Place spinach on chopping block and coarsely cross-chop it.

The Final Pureeing

Put pears and spinach into food processor. Process until mixture is smoothly pureed, but not liquefied, usually in about 6 to 9 seconds. Taste puree, working in a good grinding of black pepper. Gently reheat it. At this point, if there is a bit of liquid, simmer the puree gently a few minutes to cook off excess water, or drain it.

Salads at Speed and Vegetables with Vitamins

No one is suggesting for a moment that you should change your normal way of preparing a green salad—tearing the crisp leaves by hand and tossing the dressing into them with a wooden fork and spoon. No machine can help you with that ancient, delightful, and formal exercise. But there are salads and salads. Some are made up of an almost infinite variety of chopped, shredded, or sliced cooked or raw vegetables, and for these the shredding and slicing disks of the Cuisinart, as well as its chopping blade, can be of considerable help in terms of efficiency and speed. You can produce by machine an immense variety of marvelously refreshing and tasty mousses and purees of raw or slightly cooked vegetables with none of their minerals or vitamins boiled away. Also, the ingredients of salad dressings are amalgamated more completely and finely in the machine than by any amount of hand beating. The following recipes will teach you the basic principles. Once you have mastered them, you will be able to invent dozens of your own variations.

EDITOR'S NOTE: As this selection has been extracted from Cooking with the Cuisinart (McGraw-Hill, 1977), the brand name is mentioned throughout. Needless to say, any food processor may be used.

ALMOST-INSTANT RICH SALAD DRESSING

3 cups

This is a luxurious, general-purpose dressing, which can be stored in the refrigerator for many days. It is particularly good over cold or hot cooked asparagus. We have adapted the recipe that came to us, originally, from Chef Jean Vergnes at the Restaurant Le Cirque in New York.

> ¼ cup imported French mustard
> 1½ teaspoons coarse crystal salt
>   Freshly ground black pepper (about 10 grinds of the pepper mill)
> ½ teaspoon Worcestershire sauce, preferably Lea & Perrins
> 2 drops Tabasco
> ½ cup tarragon white wine vinegar
> 1½ cups salad oil, blended vegetable and peanut
> ¼ cup water
> ½ cup best-quality virgin olive oil

Prepared in About 10 Seconds

Simply put everything into the Cuisinart bowl and churn it until it is perfectly amalgamated—usually in 10 seconds. Transfer to a covered jar and store in the refrigerator.

SHREDDED SALAD OF YOUNG GREEN BEANS AND ESCAROLE

4 servings

This is one of the simplest and most refreshing of green salads. We have adapted the recipe given to us originally by the brilliant young Chef Georges Blanc at his country *auberge* in the French village of Vonnas in southern Burgundy. He served this salad to us as the first course of a memorable lunch. It would also shine as one of the accompaniments at any meal, simply family or luxurious party.

> 1 *pound green beans, small and young, boiled in salt water until just crispy-soft*
> 2 *heads escarole, whole heads, washed and thoroughly dried, not torn apart*
> 4 *tablespoons vinaigrette salad dressing (see previous recipe)*

Active Work of Preparation About 15 Minutes, Plus About an Hour of Refrigerator Chilling

It is best to boil the beans a few hours ahead—they are usually dead right in about 10 minutes—so that they an be drained, dried, and thoroughly chilled in the refrigerator. The whole escarole heads, too, should be washed, thoroughly dried, and completely chilled. Also, put your salad serving bowl in the freezer to chill. When you are ready to start preparing the salad, fit the slicing disk into the Cuisinart bowl. Remove the pusher from the cover chimney and fill the chimney with the beans, cut in lengths so that they will fit exactly, sideways, in the chimney. Start the motor and push down gently with the pusher. Almost faster than you can see it, the beans will be "French cut" into long thin slices. Refill the chimneys as many times as may be necessary to slice all the beans. If the bowl becomes too full, empty it into the salad serving bowl.

Next, deal with the escarole in more or less the same way. Push each head, upside down, into the chimney. If one head is too fat, cut it in half vertically. The chimney should be full, but not jammed tight. Start the motor and push down gently with the pusher. The escarole will be thinly shredded into the bowl. If the bowl again becomes too full, empty it into the salad serving bowl.

Finally, lightly toss the salad with the dressing and serve, nicely chilled, on chilled plates.

INDIAN SALAD OF CUCUMBER, MINT, ONION, AND YOGURT

4 servings

An Indian family would call this *dahi raita*, meaning a "yogurt refresher." Certainly, served ice cold, it is one of the most refreshing side-dish salads in the world and goes wonderfully with almost any main dish. When a colorful bowl of it is in front of you on the table, you will find it positively habit forming. The chopping of the ingredients used to be quite troublesome—now the machine does the work.

Naturally, we prefer our cucumber unpeeled, but if it is the waxed kind that usually comes from supermarkets this artificial covering will have to be removed.

> 1 *medium cucumber, washed, preferably unskinned (see above)*
> 1 *medium purple onion, peeled and sliced*
> 2 *cups yogurt*
> ¾ *teaspoon caraway seeds*
> *Mint leaves, fresh or frozen (enough to fill 1½ tablespoons)*
> ¾ *teaspoon salt, fine-grind*
> *About ½ teaspoon paprika, preferably Hungarian medium sweet, for decoration*

Active Work of Preparation About 10 Minutes, Plus About 2 Hours of Refrigerator Chilling

Choose a pretty, preferably ceramic open serving bowl with a capacity of about 1 quart. Put it in the freezer to chill. Or you could use 4 individual bowls. Slice the cucumber by first cutting it with the medium slicing disk. Then remove the slices from the work bowl and put the steel blades in position. Put back the cucumber slices into the bowl and whirl the blades in 1-second bursts until the cucumber is not too finely diced—usually in about 2 bursts. Drain and transfer it to a covered storage dish and hold it in the refrigerator. Now repeat this operation with the onion. Transfer the onion to a covered storage dish and hold in the refrigerator. Without rinsing the Cuisinart bowl, put in the 2 cups of yogurt, the ¾ teaspoon of caraway, the 1½ tablespoons of mint, and the ¾ teaspoon of salt. Run the machine until these are all perfectly mixed and the mint leaves have been not too finely chopped—usually in about 4 to 6 seconds. Transfer to a mixing bowl and quickly work in with a wooden spoon the diced onion and the shredded cucumber. Taste as you work and add more salt, if necessary. The whole thing should be crisp and tangy. Now cover the bowl with aluminum foil and set it in the refrigerator to chill for at least 2 hours. Do not stir any more. Just before serving, lightly sprinkle the top surface with some of the paprika—just enough to give it a bright red glow. Serve ice cold in small chilled bowls.

JAPANESE SALAD OF CHICKEN WITH EXOTIC VEGETABLES

4 servings

This is a most delightful and unusual salad with, we are assured by our Japanese friends, the authentic delicacy and subtlety of the gastronomy of Japan. If you are lucky enough to have a Japanese grocery within range of your shopping excursions, you will have no difficulty in finding all the proper Japanese ingredients. In case that is not possible for you, we propose Western alternatives, which will still give you a very fair idea of the dish. It will certainly be a focus of attention on any party menu—both because of its lovely coloring and its unusual and memorable balance of flavors.

1 package (2 ounces) Japanese dried wild mushrooms, or Chinese, or
  Italian (or can be replaced by ¼ lb of standard fresh mushrooms, sliced)
  About 6 ounces chicken breasts, skin discarded
2 tablespoons sake ("Japanese rice wine") or Spanish dry sherry
3 small carrots, scraped and julienned
  About ¼ cup bamboo shoots, cooked fresh or canned, julienned
  About ½ cup burdock root (gobo) from a Japanese grocery, peeled (if
  unavailable, can be replaced by raw parsnip, peeled and julienned)
  About 6 ounces Japanese cellophane noodles, or Chinese
  Small handful of watercress leaves
3 tablespoons salad oil
¾ cup clam juice
3 tablespoons white granulated sugar
  Coarse crystal salt, to taste
2 tablespoons Japanese light soy sauce

Active Work of Preparation About 25 Minutes, Plus About 2 Hours of Unsupervised Chilling in the Refrigerator

If you are using dried mushrooms, soak them in a small mixing bowl with warm water until they begin to soften—usually in about 20 minutes. A Japanese traditional cook would laboriously scrape the chicken breasts with a knife to produce fine little shavings of the meat. It might take him half an hour. We can do it in the Cuisinart machine in about 4 seconds. Chunk the raw chicken meat into the work bowl, then whirl the steel blades until the flesh is quite finely minced—usually in about 3 to 6 seconds. Transfer the choppings to a covered storage dish and pour over them the 2 tablespoons of sake or sherry, stirring thoroughly to make sure that all the meat is well soaked. Leave it until you need it later. When the dried mushrooms are soft, drain them and squeeze them out, then cut them into julienned strips about 1 inch long with the fine or medium serrated slicing disk, to match the carrots and bamboo shoots. (If you are using fresh mushrooms, they should be wiped clean, trimmed and very thinly sliced.) Slice the burdock root as thinly as you can by shaving the pointed end diagonally with a knife, turning the root as you go, as if you were sharpening a large pencil. The cellophane noodles are so light and thin that they are perfectly cooked simply by having boiling water poured over them and then being drained immediately. After draining, put them into the Cuisinart bowl and chop them coarsely by whirling the steel blades for usually no more than 1 second. Transfer the noodles to a covered storage dish and hold them. Rinse and dry the Cuisinart bowl and put into it the small handful of watercress leaves, then whirl the blades until the leaves are quite coarsely chopped—usually in no more than 1 second. Transfer the leaves to a covered storage dish and hold them.

Now heat the 3 tablespoons of oil to quite high frying temperature in a wok or a sauté pan, then plunge-fry, for hardly more than a second or two, the burdock, carrots, and mushrooms. Turn down the heat and at once hiss in the ¾ cup of clam juice, 3 tablespoons of sugar, 2 tablespoons of soy sauce, and salt, to taste—for us, usually, ½ teaspoon of salt is about right. Stir in thoroughly and let it gently bubble for about 5 minutes. Put the minced chicken and its sake marinade into a 1-quart saucepan and simmer it until the tiny bits of chicken are just firm— usually in no more than a couple of minutes—then, with a slotted spoon, remove all the vegetables from their boiling bouillon and add them to the chicken. Hold the bouillon to use as a dressing. Turn off the heat at once, then transfer the chicken mixture and the bouillon to two covered refrigerator containers and chill them for about 2 hours. Last of all, a few moments before serving, toss the salad with a couple of table-spoons of the chilled bouillon and incorporate the crisp and fresh water-cress.

A VARIETY OF MOUSSES
AND PUREES—
VEGETABLES WITH VITAMINS

Certainly the pureeing of vegetables is nothing new. Which of us does not remember the pounding in a mortar and the slow, slow rubbing of fibrous mixtures repeatedly through fine sieves. Sometimes it seemed as if the hard, arm-aching work went on for hours. Now it is all a matter of a few seconds.

The work rules are quite simple. Different vegetables, prepared in different ways, serve two distinct and carefully balanced purposes in the finished mousse or puree. Some of the vegetables are soft to begin with, or are baked or boiled until they are soft, so that they will provide the smooth base of the mixture. Other vegetables are hard and are very finely grated, so that they add a lightly crispy texture to the soft mix. The result, when there is exactly the right balance between crispness and softness, can be a memorable side dish—an irresistible balance between crackle and velvet on the tongue. The pieces of whatever vegetable goes into the Cuisinart bowl should be no more than an inch square. Normally, do not put in more than a total of 2 cups at a time. But, of course, you can do as many batches as you need. Soft vegetables should be run for about 4 seconds. Then check and continue pureeing, if necessary, for a few seconds more. With experience, you will soon learn the precise timing of every combination you use regularly. If some of the vegetables stick to the side of the bowl, stop the machine and scrape them down with a spatula. Then continue running the machine until the mixture is as smooth as velvet.

As a starter, try this one: Preheat the oven to 374° F. Lightly rub the skins of 2 medium onions with butter or oil and set them, uncovered, in an open baking pan in the center of the oven. Wash 2 medium zucchini, rub their skins with butter or oil, wrap them in foil, including inside the wrapping a few sprigs of fresh dill or other fresh herbs, then set the package in the baking pan in the oven alongside the onions. With no further supervision whatsoever, both vegetables will be about perfectly done in 45 to 50 minutes. Meanwhile, to supply the texture, open a 3-ounce can of Chinese water chestnuts, drain and dry them, chunk 3 or 4 of them and put them into the Cuisinart bowl. Run the machine in one-second bursts until they are very finely minced—almost a crispy-crunchy grain—usually in about 2 to 4 bursts. Transfer them to a storage dish and hold them. As soon as the onions and zucchini are done, peel the onions and chunk them into the Cuisinart bowl. Chunk the zucchini and add to the onions, with a ¼ teaspoon of English mustard, a teaspoon of mayonnaise, with salt and pepper, to taste. Run the machine until you have a velvet puree—usually in about 3 to 4 seconds. Transfer to a mixing bowl and stir in with a wooden spoon tablespoon by tablespoon of the grated water chestnuts until you have the near-perfect balance of crispness and velvet. Put this mousse into a covered serving dish and keep it warm in the oven at about 200° F until serving time. Please note, with satisfaction, that no butter or cream is added to this mousse, so that it is quite low calorie!

Now that you know the basic principles, you can start experimenting with other vegetables, both hard and soft, cooked and raw. Among the soft vegetables: lightly boiled green beans or broccoli tops, brussels sprouts, an eggplant baked with garlic slivers, a baked sweet potato or yam, young spinach leaves, baked acorn squash . . . Among the aromatic and garnishing ingredients to be added to the purees, try almost any of the fresh leaf herbs, fresh ginger root, Chinese Szechuan pepper, a tablespoon or two of yogurt . . . Among the hard vegetables to be ground in advance in the Cuisinart for texture, an excellent mixture includes finely chopped salted peanuts, scraped raw carrots, or chunked raw white turnips, or, during their short season, raw Jerusalem artichokes. The possible combinations are almost endless. Here are two more examples from famous young chefs in France . . .

BUTTERED AND CREAMED MOUSSE OF ROMAINE LETTUCE

4 servings

We have adapted this recipe from the original, which came to us from the young, imaginative Chef Gérard Vié at his restaurant in Versailles, outside Paris.

> 2 small or 1 large head romaine lettuce
> Up to 6 ounces Gruyère cheese
> ¼-pound stick butter
> Up to 6 tablespoons heavy cream
> Coarse crystal salt and freshly ground black pepper, to taste

Active Preparation 20 Minutes, Unsupervised Draining 2 Hours, and Chilling Overnight

You start the day before. Tear apart 2 small (or one large) heads of romaine, cutting away the tough base and lower stalks. Plunge the leaves into salted water at a rolling boil for 5 minutes. Then they must be completely dried by letting the water drain out of every crevice for several hours. Tear the leaves and put them into the Cuisinart bowl, batch by batch, running the machine until the lettuce is smoothly pureed, usually in about 3 to 6 seconds. Stop during the process and push the mixture down with a spatula. Again, drain the puree by transferring it to a fine-mesh sieve and leaving it to drip for several more hours. The mousse can now be refrigerated, covered, overnight. Meanwhile, grate ¼ pound of Gruyère cheese in the Cuisinart with the medium grating disk. Then, shortly before serving, put the mousse back in the bowl of the machine with a ¼-pound stick of butter, sliced, 4 tablespoons of heavy cream, and the grated Gruyère cheese. Run the machine until it is all completely mixed—usually in about 2 to 4 seconds. Transfer the mousse to a saucepan and gently heat it up, stirring continuously, until the butter and cheese melts and the mousse solidifies and thickens. Taste and adjust the seasonings. Adjust the texture by adding more cream to thin it, or more grated cheese to thicken it. Serve it quite hot.

PARISIAN PUREE OF JERUSALEM ARTICHOKES

4 servings

We have adapted this recipe from the original by one of the most famous of the younger Paris chefs, Alain Senderens.

  1 pound Jerusalem artichokes
  ¼-pound stick butter, sliced
  6 tablespoons heavy cream
    Coarse crystal salt and freshly ground black pepper, to taste

Preparation from Start to Serving About 35 Minutes

Thinly peel and gently boil the artichokes in salted water until they are quite tender. Try them with a fork after the first 15 minutes. Drain and dry them completely, then chunk them into the Cuisinart bowl, with a ¼-pound stick of butter, sliced, 4 tablespoons of heavy cream, with salt and pepper, to taste. Whirl the steel blades until the mixture is smoothly pureed—usually in about 3 to 6 seconds. Transfer the puree to a saucepan and gently heat it up, stirring continuously, adjusting the seasonings and thinning it, if necessary, with a few more teaspoons of cream. Serve it very hot.

CONCENTRATED AROMATIC PUREE OF TOMATOES

4 servings

We learned this superb trick with tomatoes originally from the "great master" himself, Paul Bocuse, at his superb, three-star restaurant outside Lyon. Our adaptation for the Cuisinart needs, for complete success, tomatoes that are beautifully ripe and sweet. When your local tomatoes are hard and tasteless, as they so often are these days, you can improve matters by preparing this recipe with half fresh tomatoes and half imported Italian canned plum tomatoes, which will add color, flavor, sweetness, and texture. Drain off, of course, as much as possible of the liquid from the can.

5 shallots, whole, unpeeled
2 cloves garlic, whole, unpeeled
   Tomatoes (see above) (total 1½ pounds)
3 tablespoons butter
   Coarse crystal salt and freshly ground black pepper, to taste
   About 1½ teaspoons sugar
1 teaspoon dried basil or 1 tablespoon fresh leaves
1 teaspoon marjoram, or 1 tablespoon fresh leaves
   About 5 good sprigs parsley, leaves only

Prepared in About 30 Minutes from Start to Serving

Put the 5 shallots and the 2 cloves of garlic into the Cuisinart bowl and run the machine until they are not too finely minced, starting and stopping in usually about two or three 1-second bursts. Transfer them to a covered storage dish and hold them. Cut each fresh tomato in half and, squeezing each half gently (as if it were a lemon), get rid of the juice and the seeds. With the Cuisinart, there is no need to skin the tomatoes as the skins are disintegrated by the whirling blades. Chunk the tomatoes into the bowl and run the machine until the tomatoes are finely diced, but not quite pureed—usually in about 2 to 4 seconds. Leave the tomato mixture where it is for the moment. Heat up a 10-inch frypan over medium drying heat and melt in it the 3 tablespoons of butter. As soon as it is reasonably hot, put in the minced shallots and garlic, stirring them around for hardly more than a few seconds. At once add the tomato mixture and adjust the heat so that it bubbles merrily, getting rid of its excess water and concentrating its flavors. Encourage this process by stirring it almost constantly. At the same time, blend in salt, pepper, and sugar, to your taste. Continue the bubbling until all the water is out and the tomatoes have thickened to a nicely solid puree. This should be achieved in about 20 minutes of steady but not too strong bubbling. Meantime, if you are using fresh basil, marjoram, and parsley, rinse and dry the Cuisinart bowl and put the herbs into it, mincing them not too finely in about two or three 1-second bursts. As soon as the tomatoes have thickened and have a beautifully concentrated flavor, stir into them the minced herbs. (Dried herbs, of course, will not need to be chopped.) Finally adjust the seasonings and serve the puree very hot.

MOST LUXURIOUS WAY OF SERVING POTATOES—A FRENCH GRATIN

4 servings

We learned this superb method with potatoes from the great three-star French chef-brothers, Jean and Pierre Troisgros, at their marvelous restaurant in central France. A *gratin* involves slicing the potatoes and baking them in ½ pint of heavy cream. If that sounds an awful lot, let us say without hesitation that we would gladly do without cream in our coffee and over our fruits all through the year, just so that we could consume it all at once in this irresistibly lovely dish. It represents the humble potato glorified into a heavenly body!

1 *pound potatoes, starchy rather than waxy*
2 *cloves garlic, whole, unpeeled*
5 *tablespoons butter*
2 *medium yellow onions, peeled and chunked*
1 *cup heavy cream*
  Coarse crystal salt and freshly ground black pepper, to taste

Active Work of Preparation About 15 Minutes Plus About 1 Hour of Unsupervised Baking

Thinly peel the pound of potatoes and, if necessary, cut them to fit easily down the chimney of the Cuisinart cover. Fit the medium slicing disk into the workbowl and slice all the potatoes, pushing them down quite gently so that the slices will be nice and thin. As the bowl fills up, empty it, batch by batch, into a large mixing bowl filled with cold water. It is essential to immerse the potato slices at once in the water to wash away their starch and to keep them from discoloring in the air. Choose an open baking dish, about 2 inches deep and 9 inches across, preferably of enameled iron or tinned copper, so that it can be used on top of the stove as well as in the oven. Preheat the oven to 275° F. Cut the 2 garlic cloves in half and thoroughly rub each half all over the inside of the baking pan. Then butter it liberally, using at least 2 tablespoons. Rinse and dry the Cuisinart bowl and put into it the chunked onions and the remains of the garlic cloves. Then run the machine until they are mashed to a puree—usually in about 3 to 6 seconds. Add the cup of cream and run the machine for another 2 seconds to amalgamate completely the cream and onions. Hold the mixture where it is. Drain the potato slices and dry them thoroughly with a cloth, then layer them neatly in the baking pan, carefully overlapping each layer so as to leave room for the cream to run between the slices. Lightly season the layers as you build them with salt and pepper. Pour all around and over the top the creamed onion mixture and set the baking pan over gentle heat on top of the stove. Adjust the heat so that the cream comes to a very gentle simmer and keep it going, uncovered, for exactly 10 minutes after the first bubbling begins. Then dot the top with the remaining 3 table-spoons of the butter and set the pan, uncovered, in the center of the oven. The secret for persuading the potatoes to absorb the cream is to cook everything extremely gently for about 2 hours. If, at any time, the cream begins to bubble too hard, turn the oven temperature down 10 degrees. Taste a bit of a potato and, if it is now quite soft, turn up the oven to 425° F to brown the top of the gratin to a gold crust—usually in 5 to 10 minutes. Bring the baking pan to the table and serve the gratin on very hot plates. It can be the accompaniment to the main dish, or, better still, we think, it can be a course on its own after the main entrée.

From One Who Loved Food as Much as Sex: An Easy Lemon Pie

Food often has been an important part of fiction. It might be one of the gastronomic orgies of James Bond, or Nero Wolfe, or their French counterpart, Inspector Maigret. But few writers have used food with such supreme skill to delineate the personalities of their fictional characters as the great modern French "novelist of love," Colette, who wrote, among so many books, *Gigi* and *Cheri*. In the twenty-six years since her death in 1954, as fine American translations of her novels, articles, autobiographical essays, and reminiscences have become available, we can see the roots of her skill with food. She was, in herself, as passionate about eating as she was about love and sex.

She remembered every detail of how she came to Paris still almost a schoolgirl, an earthy child of the French provincial land, in love with strong-smelling cheeses, the velvet of hot chocolate, the perfume of perfectly ripe fruit, the tang of freshly baked lemon tarts, and spicy bourgeois casseroles. . . . With her hair in braids, she married the dishonorable Willy, who discovered her writing talent and locked her in her room for four or five hours each day, until she had filled about 20 pages. Her only demand was that she must have, at least in summer, a bowl of ripe strawberries in her room and a dish of honey in which to dip each one. Thus imprisoned, she completed her first series of immediately successful novels at the rate of one a year.

But she got no credit for them. Willy put his name, as the author, on

---

EDITOR'S NOTE: This syndicated newspaper article originally appeared in February 1980.

each manuscript. Hardly surprising, Colette left Willy—and, in turn, two later husbands—and she went through almost innumerable love affairs—all of them framed and recorded for posterity with lyrical, sensuous, vivid descriptions of magnificent meals.

The heroine of the first series of novels, a sexy young lady of sixteen named Claudine, obviously is modeled on Colette herself. When a young man in love with Claudine tells her she is like a Greek goddess and goes into raptures about the complexity of her soul, tough little Claudine gives him a look of icy, piercing detachment and says: "You are entirely wrong, M'sieur. My soul is simply full of white haricot beans and little strips of crackly bacon." Almost every one of the paragraphs about food is a taste experience for the reader.

In her novel *Cheri*, Colette writes of the lovers, a twenty-three-year-old young man and a forty-nine-year-old woman, who do their loving, their quarreling, their admiring of each other's bodies, their eating and drinking in a huge brass bed in a rose-pink, sunlit bedroom. I feel sure that it must have been in such a setting that Colette enjoyed what is always said to be her favorite dessert—a freshly baked, still-warm-from-the-oven, soft, tangy, and velvety *tarte au citron*, a lemon tart of buttery-creamy-rich taste and texture. I can imagine the cook silently bringing it in, cutting it into wedges on a side table, serving it on delicately thin china plates, and handing it to Colette and her partner in the enormous bed. The great American writer and gourmet Marjorie Kinnan Rawlings once said of this kind of pie: "I hope to be offered a piece of it on my deathbed, and then I shall refuse to die!"

When I was in Paris recently, I became involved in an extraordinary accident—a meeting with "a friend of a friend of a friend of a friend of a friend"—the result was that I suddenly and amazingly had in my hand what is alleged to be the original recipe for that favorite *tarte au citron* of Colette!

She always believed that the simplest recipes were the best—in fact she often railed against the show-off complications of the high cuisine of the luxury circles of Paris—and this lemon tart recipe certainly meets her specifications in terms of a perfectionist simplicity. She also always demanded that every ingredient of every dish should be of the finest and freshest quality—and that, too, is an essential if this dessert is to be not just average and mediocre, but is to have about it a memorable magic. As for practical details, the ingredient amounts are for a pie pan of 9 to 10 inches in diameter and 2 inches deep. (Or, since this is a French recipe, you can use a French tart pan of about 26 centimeters diameter and 5 centimeters depth.)

NOTE: The secret is to magnify and uplift the lemon flavor and perfume by adding to it and underpinning it with a small amount of orange-flower water, an exotic North African flavoring available in the fancy-food sections of most department stores, or in specialty food shops, or in Middle Eastern and North African grocery stores.

I have slightly adapted this recipe to the modern American kitchen. If you want this *tarte au citron* to be a serious reminder of Colette—of her victories as a woman, her self-conquest, her supreme skills as a gourmet, a lover, and a writer—you should shop for these ingredients with determination, prepare this recipe with dedication, serve the lemon tart still warm from the oven, and eat it with sensuous delight—even if you don't own a huge brass bed and a pink bedroom. . . .

FRENCH TARTE AU CITRON IN HONOR OF COLETTE

4 to 6 servings

FOR THE PIE-SHELL PASTRY IN A FOOD PROCESSOR

1¾ level cups unsifted all-purpose unbleached flour
    Extra flour for sprinkling
    A couple of pinches coarse crystal salt
9 tablespoons unsalted butter, chilled, cut in small pieces
    Small piece of softened butter for greasing pan
1 large egg yolk, chilled
    Up to 3 tablespoons orange-flower water, ice cold (see note above)

FOR THE LEMON CREAM FILLING

4 large eggs, yolks and whites separated
14 tablespoons superfine-grind white sugar
2 large fresh lemons, with good skins, outer yellow rind peeled off and finely minced, juice squeezed
1½ teaspoons cornstarch

KITCHEN EQUIPMENT: Food processor for pastry, pie plate, as noted above; beating bowl; mixing bowl; wooden spatulas and spoons; electric beater (or balloon wire whisk); zester or swivel-peeler for lemon rind; sharp mincing knife; juice squeezer; double boiler; aluminum foil; weights for prebaking pie shell; silver knife or needle for testing lemon cream.

AVERAGE TIME REQUIRED: About 40 minutes for food processor blending of pastry and resting it, plus about 30 minutes for preparing filling while prebaking pie shell, plus about 25 minutes more for final baking, and about 10 minutes for cooling—total about 1¾ hours, but pastry can be made ahead.

Blend the French Pastry in a Food Processor

With the steel blades in position, spread the flour evenly across the bottom of the workbowl of the food processor and sprinkle in the salt. Switch the motor on and off for a split second to fluff up the flour and, in effect, sift flour and salt together. Now dot evenly around on top of the flour the small pieces of cold butter. Run the motor for 1 second, then check, then continue with 1-second bursts, checking in between each, until butter and flour are combined into the texture of niblet corn—usually, in my Cuisinart, in a total of about 3 to 6 seconds. Separately, in a smallish bowl, lightly beat together the chilled egg yolk and the first 2 tablespoons of the ice-cold orange-flower water. Restart the motor and at once open the feed chimney in the lid and pour in the yolk-orange-water mixture. If this is not quite enough liquid, dribble in the third tablespoon of orange-flower water. Within a few seconds the dough will be formed and will knead itself into a single ball, which will ride up on top of the whirling blades—usually in 4 to 8 seconds. Take out the ball of dough, place it on a lightly floured pastry board, knead it by hand for no more than 1 minute. Then gather it into a thick disk, dust it lightly with flour, wrap it in waxed paper or plastic, and refrigerate it for at least 30 minutes, or longer, until you are ready to roll out the pie shell. Meanwhile, start mixing the filling.

Prepare the Lemon Cream While Baking the Pie Shell

Preheat your oven to 350° F. Put the 4 egg yolks into the mixing bowl and the 4 whites into the round-bottomed beating bowl. Beat into the yolks, either electrically or by hand, 7 tablespoons of the sugar, until the mixture is pale yellow and creamy smooth. Next, lightly beat in the juice and minced rind of the 2 lemons, plus the 1½ teaspoons of cornstarch. Let it all rest while you complete the pie shell.

Roll out the dough, butter and lightly flour the pie pan, line it with the pastry, thoroughly prick the bottom with a fork, line it with aluminum foil, and weight it down with aluminum "beans," real beans, rice, or any way that you prefer. Bake the shell until it is just set, but not yet beginning to color—usually in about 15 to 20 minutes. Then remove the foil and let the shell cool slightly.

As soon as you have put the shell into the oven to bake, give the egg mixture a final beat and transfer it to the top of a double boiler in which the water in the lower half is at the point of gentlest simmering. As the egg mixture heats up, stir it continuously with a wooden spoon, meticulously scraping every corner of the bottom and sides. Don't stop stirring, even for a moment. When the mixture shows clear signs of thickening—so that it solidly coats the spoon—lift the pan out of the double boiler and plunge it into a bowl of cold water to stop the cooking and thickening process. Keep stirring another couple of minutes. Then cover the pan (to prevent formation of skin) and hold it while you beat the whites.

As you beat—preferably by hand, since the longer strokes enclose more air—sprinkle in, one spoonful at a time, the remaining 7 tablespoons of sugar. When you have the requisite stiff peaks, fold the whites and the yolk mixture together, as if you were making a soufflé. First stir a few spoonfuls of the whites into the yolks to lighten them. Then, large spoonful by large spoonful, lightly and quickly fold and incorporate the yolks into the whites.

Bake the Tart and Serve It

Raise the temperature of your oven to 375° F. With spatula and spoon, lightly and evenly fill the tart shell. Smooth the filling, but do not press down on it or stir it, to avoid squeezing out the imprisoned air. Slide the tart into the exact center of the oven and let it bake until the top surface is handsomely browned and a bright silver knife plunged into the center of the lemon cream comes out dry—usually in about 20 to 30 minutes. The filling normally will puff up like a soufflé and then fall back down. The moment the tart is done, turn off the oven, leave the door slightly ajar, and let the tart cool slowly in the oven. When it is no longer hot, but still quite warm, with a lovely, just-baked, lemon-orange perfume, serve it.

PART
·V·

In High Spirits

The Scotch Would Like to Take You to Bed

Dinner at one of London's great French-style restaurants is still as formal and traditional, as stiff and starchy, as if Queen Victoria were expected to drop in for coffee and Cognac. British fancy eaters remain devoted to a conventional wisdom about high French dining that is at least a hundred years out of date and has virtually disappeared from France. London these days is a good deal more French than Paris. After all, Escoffier spent the major part of his working life in London, and one of his most inflexible rules was that at the end of a great meal, with the coffee, you sipped a spirituous *digestif* to settle the stomach and soothe the soul. And there was only one perfectly acceptable *digestif*, the prince of brandies, French Cognac.

So I was quite startled when, after a good meal at the Mirabelle in Mayfair, with the coffee just poured, the wine waiter approached my table and said: "May we offer you a Cognac, sir? Or, perhaps, a Scotch malt?" Since Scotch whiskey is not a brandy and has never claimed royal connections, it seemed at that moment as if Goliath were being arrogantly challenged by David.

Admittedly, Scotch malt is not the same thing as Scotch. Malt whiskey (or single malt, to give it its full legal appellation) is something quite special. It is, so to speak, the vintage estate-bottled original whiskey of Scotland made in about ninety small distilleries dotted among the glens, lochs, and offshore islands in some of the most beautiful and wildest parts

EDITOR'S NOTE: This article originally appeared in 1977 in *Esquire*.

of the Highlands. These distilleries are controlled by just about the tightest appellation laws in the world. Each single malt is strictly the product of a single distillery in a single place, unblended with a single drop of any other spirit from anywhere else. Each must be labeled with the name of the place where it was made and is different from every other single malt because each depends for its character and personality on its local earth, local water, and local weather. Single-malt whiskey bears about the same relationship to average Scotch that Château Lafite-Rothschild does to Hearty Burgundy.

The devotion of the Scots to their single malts is extreme to the point of being unnerving. When a Scots baby has croup and appears to be coughing himself to extinction, its mother will give it a lump of sugar soaked with a full teaspoon of malt. Loaded in a hot toddy, it is the universal Scots medicine for bronchitis. It is dabbed onto the skin of children with chicken pox. Scots teen-agers regard it as a sure cure for acne. A Glasgow banker told me that if there were another Arab oil embargo, the solution would be to run automobiles on pure single malt. "You would certainly get combustion," he said.

For almost five hundred years, single malt was the only whiskey in Scotland, but since each tiny distillery could produce very little—and since the thirst of all Scots was interminable—there was never enough of the great stuff to go around. The solution to this terrible problem came in the 1850s, when a whiskey distributor named Andrew Usher, in Edinburgh, conceived the idea of making a little single malt go a long way by heavily diluting it with tasteless corn-grain spirit. Usher's hunch may have been the most profitable and successful single commercial idea in the history of world trade. It was the birth of so-called blended Scotch, or what we all now simply call Scotch. Before long it was being exported to the world by the millions of gallons—in bottle shapes and under label names (from Cutty Sark to White Horse) that have become household words everywhere. But Scotsmen remain fiercely loyal to their single malts. "I always approach a blended whiskey," said a Scot I met recently in a bar in Perth, "rather as I approach a sausage—with caution and a certain degree of suspicion—in case it is trying to hide something."

It was not the ordinary Scotch but those vastly superior single malts that I found in the top London restaurants, being offered as alternatives to Cognac. Malt was suggested by the wine waiters at Keats, Parke's, Carrier's, and even at those other citadels of the French cuisine in London, Le Gavroche, Le Coq d'Or, and Chez Solange. Each time, the persuasive words of the wine waiters were so suspiciously alike, I thought there had to be some master planning in the background. Britain and

France have been regularly warring with each other for at least a thousand years. Was this a new outbreak?

The matter was clinched for me by a full-page ad in a London magazine. Under a handsome color picture of a dinner table with coffee, a snifter glass, and a bottle of whiskey, the message rang out loud and clear: "After dinner, try a very smooth, very subtle change. As any pure malt-whiskey drinker will tell you, there's more to life than brandy and port. There's Balvenie, an uncommonly fine malt. You'll find the smooth and subtle taste an extremely satisfying change. In fact, we believe there's really no finer way to end a meal."

I am addicted to Scotch single malt, so I invited the wine waiters in those London restaurants to pour it for me. The two labels most widely available (and, incidentally, most heavily pushed by the waiters) were indeed the Balvenie of the ad (a label not imported into the U.S.) and the ubiquitous Glenfiddich. Since both are produced by the redoubtable, still entirely family-owned distilling firm of William Grant & Sons, I decided to find out if there were any Grants around to answer a few pertinent questions. There were. I talked to David Grant, an impeccable young Scot who is chief of the London office and president of the single-malt division of the firm. (Grant also has a blended-whiskey division whose products are in competition with such famous blends as Dewars', Haig, Johnnie Walker, etc.)

I got right to the point with David Grant. Is there a war being declared between Scotch malt and French Cognac? "Well, let's not go too far too fast," said Grant in a voice that was a model of polite British reticence. "We wouldn't want anyone to get the idea that Scotch malt isn't the perfectly right drink for absolutely any hour of the morning, noon or night. But if you're talking about that precise moment at the end of dinner when one needs a reviving and settling digestive—well, yes, we do happen to be putting on a bit of a push. We're trying out a few things experimentally in Britain and then, if they work here, we'll introduce them—on a much larger scale, of course—in the United States."

The backbone of the drive for malt instead of Cognac will be an ad campaign in snazzy magazines stressing every possible angle on the advantages of sniffing and sipping malt whiskey after dinner. Readers will be encouraged to send in their ideas and reactions. (One enthusiastic British drinker wrote: "Sipping malt feels as if Elizabeth Taylor were sliding down my throat in velvet pants.") There will be an "incentive campaign" to encourage maîtres d'hôtel, captains, and wine waiters at top restaurants to suggest single malts at the end of dinner. A special malt-tasting glass has been designed—not quite like a Cognac *ballon*, but modeled after the professional tasting glasses used in the whiskey industry. Each will be engraved with a drawing of an ancient battlemented and turreted Scottish castle and the initials of the recipient. There will be various consumer competitions and the prizes will include free vacations in Braemar Castle in Scotland, free dinners at expensive restaurants (with, of course, malt at the end of every meal), and sets of the tasting glasses packed in red-velvet-lined caskets and accompanied by a bottle of single malt. A U.S. opinion survey has already been completed on the feasibility of starting up a kind of supergourmet society (with plenty of Scottish ceremony, maybe even with skirls of a bagpipe or two during dinner), to be called, perhaps, The Academy of Single Malt of Saint Andrew in the New World.

I suggested to David Grant that it was all very well to persuade people to try malt whiskey after dinner as a new experience, but would the habit take hold? Wasn't there such an immense difference in character and personality between Cognac (based on a distillation of grapes) and single-malt whiskey (based on a distillation of barley) that they were in different leagues and could not possibly compete? Grant replied that even apart from all considerations of marketing and price, even in terms of pure taste, the quality of malt whiskey had been so much improved by new production techniques that it was now richer, silkier, smoother, subtler, more mellow and fragrant to the nose and around the tongue. He said: "For centuries, Cognac in England has always clothed itself with a prestigious aura of something very special, something rare, an important and memorable part of the high art of dining. Well, now Scotch single-malt whiskey is presuming to think of itself in those terms as well. And we're encouraging that thought at every stage of our new production technology." When I asked him to explain precisely what they were doing that was different, he invited me to go up to the northern Highlands with him to explore what is absolutely new in the malt distilleries.

A few evenings later, David and I boarded The Royal Highlander, the crack night train from London to the northern Highlands, settled down in the club car with a bottle of single malt between us, and talked about Scotch in general and malt in particular. The key factor behind all the marketing maneuvers of 1976, Grant told me, is the fact that by April there had occurred a turning point in the thousand-year history of distilled spirits. By April, the sales in the United States of the so-called white goods, particularly vodka, surpassed the sales of other spirits, even including American homegrown bourbon. Grant's theory is that the tastes of Americans are gradually polarizing into two camps. One group seems to require its drinks (possibly also its foods) to be simple. These people want their drinks lighter and lighter, with less and less taste. They turned to the light whiskeys and then rejected them in favor of vodka, which is required by U.S. law to be a "neutral spirit . . . without distinctive character, aroma, taste or color." The opposite group (still in the minority, but steadily growing) seems to be made up of people who look for some character and personality in food and drink. These are turning in droves to Scotch single malts. They are deserting the middle-of-the-road drinks, including the Scotch blended whiskeys, sales of which were down during the past year by as much as 8 percent.

Grant gave me some of the historical background of the present trend. Up to the early 1960s, almost all drinkers at bars and in restaurants in the U.S. simply asked for Scotch, or Scotch on the rocks, or Scotch and soda. Then, gradually, they became aware of the differences between blended and malt whiskeys. Next, they began developing judgments on specific label names—especially in terms of malts. "Almost immediately," said David Grant, "our Glenfiddich began outstripping all the others in sales. Bear in mind that it was originally the only whiskey that my great-grandfather made. He did no blending whatsoever. Glenfiddich was our family whiskey—made the way we liked it. We have never been able to find out what the factors or qualities are that have made it the most popular single malt all over the world—with forty percent of world sales. We simply don't know whether it's the lilt of the name—which means 'valley of the young deer'—or the triangular bottle, or the taste of the whiskey itself. We've spent hundreds of thousands of dollars on opinion surveys, but they have never really given us a definitive answer. Meanwhile, Glenfiddich just keeps on growing."

If the progress of single malt is so satisfactory, I wonderd out loud, why was there the need for a declaration of war on Cognac? Grant, of course, instantly denied that there was any question of war. He preferred to call it healthy market competition. The entire Scotch-whiskey industry was currently depressed. So it was perfectly natural that it should probe for any soft spot in the world market where it might expand. The current opportunity was largely a matter of price.

There is no secret about the present financial problems of the French brandy people. When I was recently in Cognac I heard the groans and moans from every side. The prices the growers have been getting for their grapes have been rising steadily and steeply. So the distillers have had to bounce the price of their spirits. At the same time, the value of the U.S. dollar was falling in relation to the French franc. All the factors conspired to skyrocket the price of a fine bottle of Cognac in U.S. stores. You can't get a very good bottle now for anything less than twenty dollars, while great bottles may cost anything from fifty to seventy-five dollars, and a few superb labels have been selling for up to four hundred dollars a bottle. Cognac may now be pricing itself out of all but the richest part of its market.

Against this, the entire Scotch industry is benefiting from the cata-strophic devaluation of the British pound. Most of the best single malts—at about twelve dollars a bottle (see chart on page 336)—are now selling in the U.S. at below replacement cost. "But price would be of small importance," David Grant said firmly, "if it weren't for the fact that a great single malt can compete directly in terms of its bouquet and taste. More and more people are drinking it after dinner in exactly the way they drink Cognac, without freezing its flavor with ice cubes or chill-ing its character with carbonated water. They are sniffing it—or nosing it, as we say in Scotland—and appreciating its superb bouquet. They are sipping it, rolling it around on the tongue, spreading it across the taste buds of the mouth and the throat with judgment and understanding. It is because a single malt can be a great, dry, liqueur spirit that it is compet-ing openly with the greatest of the great brandies." With that philosoph-ical thought—and finding that the bottle of whiskey between us was empty—we decided to turn in and sleep through the rest of the journey.

In the morning, in bright sunshine, we stepped out into the clear, pure mountain air of the Highlands with the salty sea breeze blowing in from the Moray Firth at the small-town capital of Highland whiskey, Dufftown, and walked across to the Balvenie and Glenfiddich distilleries, which are side-by-side on the banks of the Fiddich River. I spent the next couple of days with another member of the owning family, the informal technical director, Charles Grant Gordon, and the chief chem-ist, Dr. George Wilkin, discussing the qualitative foundations of the bat-tle with Cognac. The basic fact is that a single malt is the most complex spirit of all Scotch whiskeys. In every dram, or glass, or shot of malt, there are at least two hundred fifty different organic chemical compo-nents and virtually every one of them—even those that are only trace elements—has a measurable effect on the body, the bouquet, the charac-ter, the personality, and the taste of the whiskey. For more than five hundred years, no one knew what these elements were. Making good whiskey was a matter of trial and error, of day-to-day luck and avoiding the mysterious pitfalls that seem to surround the entire operation. "Even ten years ago," Charles Gordon said, "we didn't really know how to control the chemistry of malt-whiskey production. Today, if we knew everything, I can assure you we wouldn't bloody well be way up here in the Highlands; we'd be making the stuff in a modern plant somewhere near Glasgow or Edinburgh, where we wouldn't have to truck the whiskey over mountain roads. But part of the mystery is still up here—in the air, in 'the bugs in the walls,' as we jokingly refer to the free-floating wild yeasts."

But, while there may still be a few unanswered questions, there has been extraordinary progress during the last ten years in identifying the organic components of malt whiskey and in controlling the balance among them. The detective work has been done by the experimental biologists, organic chemists, enzymologists, and just plain maltsters. They have isolated the bad guys and good guys among the organic elements of malt whiskey—the aldehydes, congeners, furfural, fusel oil, esters, ethers, ethyls, etc.—and the role of each in the production process is being precisely charted. They are using a new, highly sophisticated electronic analysis system called gas-liquid chromatography, which vaporizes the various volatile liquids, measures their minutest elements, and produces a kind of fingerprint chart showing, in peak-and-valley patterns on a sheet of photographic paper, the chemical makeup of each sample of whiskey. The problem now is to associate each of those elements with particular wanted or unwanted smells and tastes. I was shown a veritable F.B.I. most-wanted-criminal-type list of test tubes of the destructive elements that have to be (and are being) eliminated, from amyl acetate, the notorious banana oil (which was the scourge of whiskey makers up to twenty years ago and can still, if it suddenly appears accidentally, ruin a whole batch of new whiskey), to butyric acid, which can give a batch of whiskey the smell and taste of rancid butter. There is also a Good Samaritan list of the organic elements that are being encouraged to develop during distillation because they are the sources of the strong recent improvements which now enable malt whiskey to challenge Cognac.

The drive for positive progress has gone right back to the farmers who grow the barley. The eventual conversion of the starch depends largely on the latent supply of enzymes within that grain. New varieties of barley are now being grown with better strains of enzymes, more powerful in the basic elements of the alpha-amylase and beta-amylase, to produce a purer grade of barley sugar. This natural conversion was traditionally encouraged by spreading out the barley on the malting floor and turning it over by hand for six days. Instead, today, the barley is sprouted in huge revolving drums under precisely controlled conditions of agitation, humidity, and temperature. Then, when the barley is smoked over burning peat, the phenol elements in the smoke are analyzed by the chemists so that the rougher coal-tar constituents can be eliminated. After the barley has been ground, mashed with hot water and cooled, it is seeded with the yeast for fermentation; here, again, there has been important progress. New strains of yeasts are being selected out and bred toward a better conversion to smoother, richer whiskeys.

The chemists now know that the softness of the nose of a great malt whiskey is largely controlled by the proper balance of the esters—particularly between the methyl acetate and the ethyl acetate—and this can now be controlled during distillation. When you lift a glass of malt whiskey to your nose, it is the esters that vaporize and give you the sensuous pleasure of the bouquet. For the first time in whiskey-making history, the producer is in a position to control the balance of "the brew." This balance makes the body, the bouquet, the silkiness, the smoothness, the overall taste of the malt whiskey, which is finally finished and rounded by aging in oak casks. It all seems to point to the possibility that the Scotch malt-whiskey boys may be able to achieve in twelve years the degree of perfection that has taken the Cognac boys about seventy-five years. It is, in short, technology thumbing its nose at prestige and tradition.

The next morning, as David Grant drove me to the airport in Aberdeen for my return flight, he was not talking about chemistry, or perfectionism, or the supremacy of quality. He was taking the pragmatic Scots point of view. "The Scottish rule is, every day, one before lunch and two before dinner. If we could now add to that, one after dinner, why, we would then have increased our sales by thirty-three percent."

QUALITY RATING CHART FOR SINGLE MALTS OF THE SCOTTISH WHISKEY INDUSTRY

There are over ninety different single-malt whiskeys made in the Highlands of Scotland and their merits are discussed and debated by Scottish drinkers in much the same way the French discuss their great château and estate wines. There is even an established vocabulary for judging Scotch malt. It may be said to be clean, or dry, or fruity, heavy, light, oily, peaty, smoky, solid. Geography plays an important part in the character and personality of the whiskey. Almost all the famous and luxurious types come from a small area around Dufftown in the main valley and up the tributaries of the River Spey; these are known as Speyside malts. A more smoky group comes from the western island of Islay (pronounced Eye-lah) and these are known as Islay malts. Others come from the Outer Hebrides and from the northern islands of the Orkneys. Another group, now somewhat out of fashion—there were nineteen distilleries here, now there are only two—comes from the southwestern corner of the Highlands, on the Mull of Kintyre, around the village of Campbeltown, and are known as Campbeltown malts. Where a single malt comes from is a good advance indication of its character.

The greatest experts on the single malts are, of course, the big blenders with their huge lowland factories around Glasgow and Edinburgh. They buy the single malts in large quantities and use them to add the authentic Scotch flavor to the famous-name, blended, grain Scotches.

In fact, the big blenders are in direct competition with consumer drinkers of single malt and some of the most famous labels have virtually disappeared from the market. Take, for example, what is considered to be perhaps the finest of all single malts, Talisker, made on the Island of Skye. Not too many years ago, Talisker was bottled under its own label and sold all over the world. Then the distillery was bought, lock, stock and barrel, by one of the giant conglomerates and, today, very little Talisker is bottled. Most of it goes, in the barrel, to the immense Glasgow distilleries, where a bit of Talisker is put into each bottle of Black & White, Dewars', John Haig, Johnnie Walker, White Horse, etc. But not quite all of it goes to Glasgow. Some bottles of Talisker are still filled and sold locally on Skye to the workers in the distillery and the local shops of the island. (Fewer still find their way to shops in other ports of Britain or the U.S.) The corporate owners in Glasgow are well aware that if Talisker disappeared completely from Skye, there might be a danger of revolution.

What follows is part of a confidential chart that is circulated among the blenders of Scotland to help them decide which of the single malts to buy for their blends. The malts are rated by the industry as Supreme de Luxe and, in descending order, first, second, third, and fourth classifications. There is a separate listing for Campbeltown, Islay, and other smoky malts. We list the Supreme de Luxe group, because these are the ones most widely available in the United States. Their prices average from ten to thirteen dollars a bottle.* To the listing we have added, in the column at the right, our own blind-tasting quality-points score. Whiskeys rated from 37 to 42 are Noble; 43 and above, Great.

---

*EDITOR'S NOTE: According to the Scotch Whiskey Information Center, 1986 prices for single malts range from eighteen to thirty dollars a bottle.

Supreme de Luxe:	Author's blind-tasting ratings:
Aultmore (from Speyside)...............................	*
Balvenie (from Speyside)	*
Dalmore (from Moray) 41	
Glendronach (from Speyside)........................43	
Glenfiddich (from Speyside)........................46	
Glen Grant (from Speyside)........................43	
The Glenlivet (from Speyside)........................47	
Highland Park	
(from Orkney Islands)........................	*
Lagavulin (from Isle of Islay)........................	*
Macallan (from Speyside)........................40	
Mortlach (from Speyside)........................46	
Strathisla (from Keith)	*
Talisker	
(from the Island of Skye)........................48	

Available in Britain

From the first classification, Cardhu and Glenmorangie (both from Speyside) are often available here. Cardhu rates a Fine 34, Glenmorangie, a 35.

The Islay malts have such a special flavor that they hardly challenge Cognac. But they can be an attractive and interesting acquired taste if you enjoy smoky foods—smoked ham, smoked turkey, smokey tea, etc. Laphroig is the most widely available and rates a 43.

Apart from the relatively well-known names listed above, there are more than seventy other single-malt distilleries dotted around in all parts of the Highland mountains. Some of them produce magnificent whiskey. When you are traveling in Europe (especially, of course, in Scotland), if you search diligently you may be able to pick up a few bottles. Or they may be ordered from such famous stores as Gordon & MacPhail in Elgin, Moray, Scotland (this famous shop, in the heart of the whiskey country, has no less then fifty-five single-malt labels on its shelves), or you can find about forty labels at Lambert Bros. in Edinburgh, or about the same number at Fortnum & Mason or Harrods in London. You can also find a fair selection at the London airport shops.

Rum:
The Summer Spirit

Ernest Hemingway once said that rum, which is the alcoholic essence of sugar—the name comes from *saccharum*, Latin for "sugar"—has a greater variety of colors and characters, flavors and bouquets, strengths and textures, than any other distilled spirit. Whiskeys and gins are made from almost every sort of grain. Brandies come not only from grapes, but from a whole range of fruits. Yet all these vary much less than do the rums. One rum may be as colorless and very nearly as tasteless as water, while others have the color of distilled gold, with a rich and smooth taste to match. Still others are dark mahogany and among the most powerful of all spirits, with more than 75 percent alcohol.

Yet, despite the variety, only three or four carefully chosen bottles of different rums in the home bar can be turned into a dramatic array of mixed drinks. Rum may come an hour before lunch as a "fizz" of fluffy white velvet. Or in midafternoon as a tall, fruit-decked punch. Or as a shockingly frosty Daiquiri before dinner. Or in a brandy snifter after dinner. Or in a party punch bowl at any degree of convivial strength. And, since good rum has a special affinity for the refreshing citrus juices and enough character not to become tasteless when served close to freezing, it is my choice as the ideal spirit for hot summer days. Yet no rum drink can be dramatically successful without the "secret factor," which is the right degree of "rumminess."

This is the problem. Few people seem to know how to choose the right rum for the right purpose. Going to the corner liquor store and asking for

EDITOR'S NOTE: This article originally appeared in the June 1968 issue of *House Beautiful*.

"a bottle of rum" is about as useless as going to the butcher and asking for "a piece of meat." The late Harold J. Grossman, an authority on the subject, once said that the rums with the greatest character do not speak Spanish but have the lilting accents of the British Caribbean colonies, coupled with the foggy cockney of London. What he meant was that some of the finest rums have, for more than two hundred years, been shipped from the West Indies to England to be aged in casks (sometimes for fifteen years or more) in the cold, damp atmosphere of the bonded warehouses of the London docks, before being blended, bottled, and shipped all over the world. This luxuriously costly operation has been seriously undermined—in fact, the whole rum industry has been turned topsy-turvy—by three cataclysmic upheavals of the last thirty years.

First, the German submarine warfare in the Atlantic during World War II virtually cut off for almost six years the shipments of Caribbean rums to London and started the irreversible trend toward aging and bottling on this side of the ocean. Also, the same German submarines prevented Scotch whiskey from reaching the U.S., creating an enormous demand for rum—a demand partially met by the virtual "explosion" of mass-production rum industries in Puerto Rico and the Virgin Islands. (These American rums, not subject to the U.S. alcohol import tax, have a considerable price advantage over their imported competitors.) Also, large quantities of light rums were imported from Cuba.

Then, the coming of Castro eliminated Cuban rum from the U.S. market and gave another enormous boost to the Puerto Rican and Virgin Islands industries.

Last, the granting of independence to the British Caribbean colonies (especially Jamaica, Guyana, and Barbados, in terms of rum) led to the breaking of centuries-old commercial ties, to the disappearance of famous rum names, and to the seizure of old estates by new owners with new ideas about making and selling rum.

Experts say that there are three main factors in the production of a great rum. First is the mineral content of the soil, which affects the sap of the growing cane. Second is the live yeast, which must trigger the fermentation of the mash. In certain areas (notably Barbados, Haiti, Jamaica, and Martinique), spores of live yeast are actually floating in the air and settle naturally on the surface of the rum-to-be in the open vats. In other areas, the yeast has to be cultivated in a laboratory and injected into the mash. Third is the natural quality of the water used for refining. When there is an affinity and unity between local soil, a local strain of yeast, and pure local water, a great rum is generally the result.

But many steps precede this greatness. The traditional method of production was to press all the juice out of the cane, using the entire crop for rum. This luxurious and wasteful process is still used by less than half a dozen producers in the entire world. Among the best known of these luxury rums are Plantation Saint James from Martinique, Barbancourt from Haiti, and Eldorado from Puerto Rico. These are much too subtle for mixed drinks. They are best sipped from a brandy snifter after dinner.

The more efficient method, used for probably 99 percent of all rums, is to make them as a by-product of the manufacture of sugar. The cane juice is boiled down until the sugar crystallizes. The remaining molasses is fermented, refined, and distilled. This may be done slowly, over as long as twelve days in a pot still, or very quickly, in as little as twelve hours in a mass-production column still. The first way keeps the natural character of the rum. The second purifies the rum until it has neither color nor taste. The final smoothness comes from years of aging in oak casks and highly skilled blending. Each producer tries to keep the same character in his brand year after year. But among the hundreds of different labels, no two rums in the world are exactly alike.

CHOOSING THE RIGHT RUM

One man's rum is another man's poison—the decision is a matter of personal preference, but there are a few basic rules:

1. There is a certain family resemblance among the rums from a particular area. Get to know which of these families you prefer. Taste the aged golden rums for which Jamaica is famous. Try the dark Demeraras, grown and distilled in Guyana but aged and blended in London. (Demerara, incidentally, is the name of a river, a town, and a valley.) Test the light rums from Barbados. And these are only a beginning.

2. Within each area, there are usually two or three famous family names that are a reliable guarantee of quality. Start with their products as a standard of comparison. My personal list of the best-known names in alphabetical order: from Barbados, Mount Gay; from Guyana, Lemon Hart; from Jamaica, Appleton, Lemon Hart, Myers, and Wray & Nephew; from Puerto Rico, Clemente, Fernandes, and Serrales.

3. Remember that the large firms bottle a range of rums for different purposes:

White rums: the lightest, least "rummy," and often the least satisfactory. Some are deliberately colorless and tasteless, made to be inexpensive competitors of the dry gins and vodkas. The better white rums, in my experience, come from Barbados and Jamaica. They are fine for light daiquiris and other short cocktails, but less suitable for tall drinks and punches.

Golden rums: the all-purpose mixers, varying in a wide sweep from the lightest and palest to the rich, aromatic, and full-bodied, which are a specialty of the great rum estates of Jamaica.

Dark Demerara rums: the most aromatic and powerful, with a velvet smoothness that comes from years of barrel aging. They are too dominant for cocktails, but fine for superpunches with a super punch.

Luxury rums: for sipping straight or on the rocks. The label should specify how many years of aging. Eight years is a good average. Fifteen years makes them soft and silky. Apart from those already mentioned, my favorites include Lemon Hart's "15-year Golden Jamaica" and Puerto Rican "Ron del Barrilito."

MIXING RUM DRINKS

The Calypso entertainers of Barbados often sing this basic recipe for a rum drink:

> *One of the sour*
> *Two of sweet*
> *Three of strong*
> *And four of weak.*

The sour is almost always freshly squeezed lime juice, which has an extraordinary affinity for rum. A few recipes require lemon, grapefruit, or other citrus juices.

The sweet can always be superfine white sugar, but the secret of wowing one's guests is learning to improvise with the various syrups and liqueurs. There are three multipurpose syrups available almost everywhere. Falernum (a generic name, used by several producers) is a highly aromatic sugar syrup imported from the West Indies, flavored with almond oil and ginger. Grenadine is the sweetened juice of the pomegranate and gives its rich red color to any drink that contains even a few drops. Orgeat (another generic name, from the French *orge*, meaning "barley") is a thickened sugar syrup delicately flavored with almonds, orange blossoms, and rose petals. Also, many of the sweet liqueurs can make interesting variations, including maraschino, banana, or orange Curaçao.

The strong may be straight rum or a mixture of spirits.

The weak is usually the crushed ice, but may also be club soda or dry Champagne.

Mixing tools ideally include a cocktail shaker, an electric blender, an ice crusher, and the usual bar measures. Everything must be ice-cold. Put tools and glasses into the freezer and all ingredients into the refrigerator well before mixing time.

THE FAVORITE RECIPES OF A RUM AFICIONADO

Apéritifs and Other Short Drinks
(Amounts given for 1 drink)

MY PERFECT DAIQUIRI

Put into ice-cold shaker: ½ ounce freshly squeezed lime juice, ½ ounce falernum, 1½ ounces 86-proof Jamaica white rum, plus coarsely cracked ice. Shake vigorously for not more than 15 seconds, then strain into ice-cold, 4½-ounce tall-stemmed glass.

QUICK FROZEN DAIQUIRI IN AN ELECTRIC BLENDER

Put into ice-cold blender jug: ½ ounce fresh lime juice, ½ ounce falernum, 2 ounces 86-proof Jamaica white rum, plus measured ⅓ cup chipped ice. Blend at high speed until ice has consistency of stiff sherbet, usually in about 2 minutes. Do not overblend, or ice will melt to syrup. Mound into ice-cold glass and serve instantly with a short straw.

BARBADOS PINK FIZZLE

My own combination of the New Orleans Fizz and the West Indian Swizzle.

Put into ice-cold blender jug: 1 ounce fresh lime juice, 1½ teaspoons orgeat, 1½ teaspoons grenadine, 3 ounces 90-proof Barbados white rum, 2 dashes Angostura bitters, white of 1 egg, 1 ounce heavy cream, plus measured ¾ cup coarsely chipped ice. Blend at highest speed for 10 to 15 seconds, no more. Pour into frosted silver mug, or glass. Add a splash or two of club soda.

SHERRY-RUM FLIP

What to do with the egg yolk left over from the Fizzle.

Put into ice-cold shaker: 1½ ounces dry Spanish Sherry, ½ ounce orgeat, 2½ ounces 86-proof Jamaica white rum, ½ egg yolk, plus measured ⅓ cup chipped ice. Shake vigorously 15 seconds, then pour, including ice, into ice-cold, tall, 12-ounce glass. Float pinch of ground nutmeg on top.

MODERNIZED OLD ENGLISH DAISY

Perhaps less a cocktail, more a late-evening refresher.

Put into ice-cold shaker: ½ ounce fresh lemon juice, ½ ounce lime juice, 2 ounces orange juice, 1 ounce sweet banana liqueur, 2 ounces 86-proof Jamaica golden rum, plus measured ⅓ cup chipped ice. Shake vigorously 15 seconds, then pour, including ice, into frosted mug, or Old Fashioned glass. Add dash of club soda and swirl with muddler or silver spoon.

Long Refreshers and Fruit Punches

(Amounts given for 1 drink)

MY BASIC PLANTER'S PUNCH

Pour into ice-cold, tall 12-ounce glass, half-filled with ice cubes: 1½ ounces fresh lime juice, juice of ½ orange (having first cut off and reserved 1 slice for decoration), 1 ounce sweet pineapple juice, ½ ounce falernum, 2 ounces 86-proof dark Demerara rum, 2 dashes Angostura bitters; then stir vigorously. Decorate with minimum frills—say, a fresh sprig of mint and orange slice on edge of glass. Fill up with soda and float pinch of nutmeg on top. Serve with long spoon and straw.

SUNDAY MORNING MILK PUNCH

Put into ice-cold shaker: ½ ounce sweet banana liqueur, 2 ounces 86-proof dark Demerara rum, 1 cup milk, plus measured ⅓ cup chipped ice. Shake vigorously 15 seconds, then pour, including ice, into ice-cold, tall 12-ounce glass. Serve with straw and float pinch of nutmeg on top.

Party Punches
(Amounts given for 10 people)

MODIFIED U.S. ARTILLERY PUNCH

There was a note attached to the original recipe that said: "When serving this to other than artillery men, dilute with an equal quantity of water." We prefer to reverse the instructions. If this is to be served only to artillery men, double the alcohol!

Put into 2-quart kitchen mixing bowl: grated outer rind of 1 lemon, ¾ cup superfine white sugar, then vigorously mash and pound together with pestle or wooden spoon. Blend in the juice of 2 lemons, juice of 2 oranges, plus 1¼ cups hot, not-too-strong tea. Stir thoroughly, and set in refrigerator to cool. Then add: 1 bottle 86-proof dark Demerara rum, same amount of dry Spanish Sherry, ½ cup medium-priced French Cognac, stir thoroughly, cover, and mature in refrigerator for at least 6 hours. Serve in iced punch bowl, adding, at last moment, ½ to 1 bottle ice-cold dry Champagne, to taste.

MODIFIED CHARLESTON JOCKEY CLUB PUNCH

A modern, lighter version of the drink Southern cotton growers used to serve to English and French buyers just before negotiating a contract.

Put into 2-quart kitchen mixing bowl: grated outer rind of 1 lemon, ¾ cup superfine white sugar, then mash and pound together with pestle or wooden spoon. Add: juice of 5 lemons, 1 bottle medium-priced French Cognac, 10 ounces 151-proof dark Demerara rum, 4 ounces dry peach brandy, 2 measuring cups hot, not-too-strong tea, then stir thoroughly, cover, and mature in refrigerator for at least 12 hours. Serve in iced punch bowl, adding, at last moment, ½ bottle ice-cold dry Champagne.

AND FOR A PARTY FOR 2,000 PEOPLE?

This recipe was actually used by a millionaire host in the Victorian days in Trinidad.

Build a marble pool specially for the occasion in the garden. Pour in: 1,000 bottles dark Demerara rum, juice of 2,000 lemons, 100 pounds cane sugar, 500 bottles sweet Spanish Malaga wine, 200 ground nutmegs, 300 quarts boiling water. Now launch onto the surface of the pond a miniature Venetian gondola carrying a small boy in appropriate (?) costume (and preferably wearing a gas mask). Let him stir the mixture for a while with his paddle, then glide to the side, take up a silver ladle, and serve the punch to the guests. When the gondola is grounded on the bottom of the pond, the party is about over.

The Cognac Nose

Why You Can Never Have One and How to Imbibe the Best Anyway

It was a *scandale*—a shocking moment around the dining table in the Bordeaux château. The boy's mother blushed scarlet. His father, through tears of shame, glanced from face to face around the table, watching for the reactions. Everyone knew, of course, that five-year-old Yann was absolutely right. The red wine had gone bad. Its bouquet and taste were slightly musty from the accident of a gently rotting cork. So why was Uncle Maurice Fillioux smiling so proudly?

The Fillioux family, for more than two hundred years, has been cultivating its vineyards in the Charente region (a few kilometers north of Bordeaux) where the principal business is the distillation of the local wines into Cognac. The Fillioux, in the Charentais tradition, sip their Cognacs at the end of dinner, but, with the food, they proudly drink the wines they think are the best in the world, those of their Bordelais neighbors. So the Fillioux were extremely impressed by that important and wealthy father-in-law who had migrated to Bordeaux and had become the owner of a magnificent château. Once a year—usually around Christmastime—when he invited the entire family to a festive lunch at the château, they accepted in a body, with deferential excitement. On this particular occasion, the party included Michou and Pierre Fillioux, their five-year-old son, Yann, and Pierre's brother, Uncle Maurice. In the Bordelais tradition, when the red wine was poured, there was a miniature glass for Yann. At once, as they lifted their glasses to their noses,

---

EDITOR'S NOTE: This article originally appeared in the April 1975 issue of *Esquire*.

the guests knew that the wine was slightly corked. The host did not notice the fault. He was almost eighty years old and was concentrating on acting out the part of *le grand seigneur*. No one dared to say a word about the wine. No one except little Yann, who piped up: "But, Papa, I cannot drink this wine. It smells of rotten cork." In the hush that followed, Uncle Maurice was heard to whisper to Papa Pierre: "That decides Yann's future. He has the nose for a chief taster at Hennessy!"

To realize the earth-shattering significance of that whispered remark made twenty-three years ago, you have to understand the extraordinary role of the human nose in general in the making of Cognac, and of the Fillioux family noses in particular, in the making of the one kind of Cognac that is among the most widely distributed around the world. Almost every bottle of Cognac easily available at the local store is a blend of dozens (sometimes hundreds) of different spirits, all distilled from wines made from grapes grown in the legally delimited areas of the Charente. Each of the great Cognac houses—the companies that put together their own blends and label millions of bottles with their names—buys almost all the original spirits in small quantities from thousands of individual growers. Each grower submits a small sample bottle. The instantaneous decision whether or not to buy that particular lot is made by the chief taster of the company, generally in a matter of a few seconds. When the barrels of spirit are delivered, the taster decides whether or not the contents are up to the original sample and may, if his nose tells him to do so, instantly reject the delivery.

Every one of hundreds of thousands of barrels of spirit in storage in, perhaps, a dozen different cellars has to be opened and tasted for progress at least once a year. Finally, "the mix" that goes into the bottles has to be put together from hundreds of different barrels with every crucial decision made by the chief taster. Perhaps in no other business on earth is the computer more useless and the human nose and throat more paramount. One of the directors of Hennessy, referring to its present chief taster, Uncle Maurice Fillioux, told me: "He is one of the chief pillars of our house."

But what happens when Maurice Fillioux comes to the end of his working career? Surely the search for a successor with the same extraordinary gift of nose and taste, with the intellectual capacity to absorb the training in an infinity of complications—the search for a new taster must be almost impossibly difficult. In the case of Hennessy, not at all. The Fillioux family, from father to son and uncle to nephew, has been able to provide a Hennessy chief taster continuously for seven generations and well over two hundred years. This fantastic performance is about as if Babe Ruth had had a son with the capacity to be trained to hit home runs as easily and frequently for the Yankees as his father, and that this son, in turn, had produced a grandson of the Babe who could do the same, and that this sequence had continued for the Yankees for more than two hundred years. And who will dare to say that hitting home runs is more difficult than putting together a Cognac blend of several hundred parts, or of deciding, on the basis of a sniff and a sip, how a young spirit will taste fifty years later?

At the time of the now famous lunch at the Bordeaux château, there was a crisis in the Fillioux family. Uncle Maurice, who was then about to succeed his father as chief taster, had flagrantly flouted the holiest of family traditions and had remained a bachelor. Perhaps the great line of Fillioux tasters would have to end with him. Then little Yann had piped up, and the crisis was ended. A new Fillioux taster had been found. No one, of course, bothered to explain the deep significance of his words to Yann. No one asked him whether he would like to be a Cognac taster. But his life, from that moment on, was firmly bent to serve the essential honor of the Fillioux family.

Yann is now the assistant taster of Hennessy under his chief taster uncle. Yann is the eighth generation of Fillioux to offer their noses and throats in the service of *la maison*. In Cognac recently, I asked Maurice about this extraordinary family performance. He said: "I do believe it is a gift. If you think of music . . . there always has to be a gift. However hard the young musician may study, success does not come without the gift. Remember the family of Johann Sebastian Bach. They were leaders in the musical life of Europe for two hundred sixty-five years!

"Our Fillioux family gift, I am sure, comes from our closeness to the earth of the Charente. My father, my grandfather, each generation of Fillioux, has always married a Charentais girl of a family involved in the growing of grapes and the distilling of Cognac. The secret of our success, you might say, is sex and blood. That has been true since the very beginning."

The beginning was in 1740, when a young Irish mercenary, Captain Richard Hennessy, having been kicked out of Ireland by the British as a dangerous revolutionary, and having completed his term of service in the French armies of Louis XV, decided to settle down in the sleepy little town of Cognac. At just about the same time, a young French farmer, Christophe Fillioux, also came to Cognac from the Vendée region to the north toward the mouth of the river Loire. His mission was sex. He was chasing a lady who had everything, even money, since she owned a vineyard in the village of Javrezac, a mile or two outside Cognac. Captain Hennessy got into the Cognac business, buying the brandy in barrels and shipping it for a fair profit to his friends and neighbors in Ireland, where it was appreciated so much more than the rough local whiskey that, within quite a short time, Hennessy was looking for a partner. Mainly, he wanted someone to ride out into the vineyards to taste and judge the various Cognacs that the grower-distillers had for sale. The job went to Christophe Fillioux, who had married his lady and moved into her vineyard.

It was very soon clear that Christophe had an extraordinary gift for nosing and tasting each young spirit and judging whether it would develop, with age, into something beautiful and special. Since then, while seven generations of Hennessys have built and directed one of the largest Cognac-shipping firms in the world, they have had, without a break, seven generations of Fillioux doing the nosing, the tasting, the buying, and the blending.

"We became a family with a mission in Cognac," Maurice Fillioux said. "Each of our children, generation after generation, has been immersed in the atmosphere of the Charente, in the daily discussions of the merits of the Cognac at the dinner table, in the philosophy and the work of making and tasting our *eaux-de-vie*. And always, when our boys reached the age of sexual attraction, they were led to marry Charentais girls."

Did the parents, I wondered, provide their boys with official lists of eligible local girls to walk out to the hayloft on a summer evening? What happened to a Fillioux boy if he rode into Bordeaux and picked up a red-wine girl? There must have been some pretty stormy family meetings before an approved marriage contract was settled. The Fillioux sexpolitik must have been pretty rough!

I asked Maurice Fillioux about the education of Yann since the famous lunch in Bordeaux. "Yann will not become a chief taster at Hennessy because he is a Fillioux, or because he is alleged to have a gift. He must prove himself after years of study. He must develop memories of smells and tastes, in the way an artist memorizes sights or a mathematician holds memories of arrangements of equations. He has already spent ten years in practice and study. It may take him ten years more of tasting, tasting, tasting. . . ." Needless to say, Yann Fillioux does not smoke.

On my latest visit to Cognac a few weeks ago, Maurice anad Yann allowed me to be one of their assistant tasters for a few days. It made me realize how much there is to learn about Cognac. I reported at ten in the morning to *la salle de degustation*, the tasting room, at the heart of the Hennessy headquarters building, a high-ceilinged room with oil portraits of previous Fillioux tasters. Its walls are covered with glass shelves on which are hundreds of laboratory-style small glass bottles labeled and numbered for the identification of each sample spirit; there is a huge oak table surrounded by chairs and beside each chair a gravel-filled bucket spittoon. Chimney tasting glasses are dark blue so that no taster will be influenced by the color of each sample and each glass is washed by hand in sterile water, then rinsed inside and out with Cognac (never wiped dry with any kind of cloth), and hung upside down on racks. When work is in progress, the door is locked and the telephone cut off. No man may enter the room with any kind of perfumed hair pomade or after-shave lotion; no woman may wear any perfume or cosmetics, least of all lipstick. The day's tasting does not begin before ten so as to allow for the full digestion of an "always light breakfast."

The art of tasting Cognac, with its large element of highly volatile alcohol, is entirely different from the universal method with wine, and my first lesson was in the proper technique for judging both the blended and unblended spirits. The right way is so efficient and practical and involves so little actual drinking, that I now use it to judge every bottle of Cognac I buy. You pour not more than half an ounce into a four-ounce chimney tasting glass (which does not, for average amateur use, have to be blue), stick your nose into the glass, and breathe in slowly, remembering your most important first impressions. You then take the tiniest sip—no more than a fairly large drop—which you slap with your tongue onto the roof of your mouth, then immediately spit out the excess liquid. Swallow, then open your mouth and breathe in through it, slowly, steadily, deeply. Assemble your impressions—think about each one separately—then put them together and judge the whole.

Over and over, in Cognac, I asked the tasters of the great houses what I should look for in a fine, noble, or great bottle. First, as soon as you pour it there should rise up from the glass a dominant and enveloping bouquet; a complicated and subtle blend of refreshing fruitiness, of perfumed power and of a subtle sweetness; a complicated balance of impressions in the nose, interpreted by each taster in a different and personal way. Next, the first, smallest sip should have the feel on the tongue of silk and velvet. The first contact of even the tiniest amount of the liquid with your throat should instantly expand and sharpen the first impressions of your nose, with, at the back of your throat and down your chest, not the slightest bite or harshness. Then, as you breathe in through your mouth, there should be the lasting impression of cleanness, refreshment and, as Maurice Fillioux put it, "a sense of amusement, charm, excitement, all combined into the purest of pleasure."

With Cognac, unlike wine, you should judge the color last, since it is not a true measure of age and quality. The color, primarily, should be a brilliant gold—the natural effect of long aging in the oak barrels. It does not have to be a deep color. Many of the best Cognacs are quite pale. Always beware of an exceptionally dark color. This is usually induced artificially—often to make a young Cognac seem older—by the addition of caramel or burnt sugar. I consider it one of the more unfortunate French laws that permits the addition of up to 2 percent of "cane sugar or caramel," which can both color and soften a harsh young spirit and give it, artificially, a slight sense of age. Even worse, in my opinion, is the addition of le boisé, an essence from an infusion of oak chips. By soaking these chips in a strong spirit, one can very quickly extract their color and tannin, and small quantities of this liquid essence, after filtering, may sometimes be added to the Cognac for a kind of "instant aging," but without the softness that comes only from decades of breathing oxygen through the pores of a barrel. In spite of all the denials, these additives (rarely used by the reputable houses) do affect the pristine purity of the flavor.

Words are almost useless in trying to describe the infinite shadings of smells and tastes. Yet Maurice and Yann (and the other professional tasters of Cognac) must instantly communicate their impressions to each other. So they have invented a vocabulary of special words with special meanings—a kind of secret code of the Charente region. When they say that a spirit has verdeur, greenness, they mean that it has the acidity, the bite, the lemony sharpness of unripe fruit, of grapes picked too early. If they were picked two or three days too late and there is even the slightest beginning of rotting, it comes out in the distilled spirit as goût de pommes, a taste of apples, the sense of slightly fermented apples in a glass of cider.

If a spirit is boisé, woody, it has drawn too much tannin from the oak barrel. I heard them say that one sample of spirit had a nose of pain chaud, new bread hot from the oven. Another, quite noticeably different in nose, was pain brulé, slightly burnt bread. They even use local Charentais dialect words not found in any dictionary. They say that a spirit is fraichin—a word used by river fishermen to describe a just-landed pike as it lies wriggling in the grass—a country smell, but ever so slightly fishy, which, in an eau-de-vie, is usually caused by storage in a badly cleaned barrel where a small amount of stale water accidentally remained before the barrel was filled with new spirit.

We had a session of tasting for inventory control in one of the vast, silent, dark, fortress-like aging cellars. A portable tasting table had been set up for us in the entrance space. We faced about thirty thousand barrels in row after row, sometimes stacked seven tiers high, each with its date and defining code.

The master of the cellar and his assistants drew out the samples from each barrel with a metal tube that looked as if it were a twelve-inch, sawed-off section from the barrel of a shotgun suitably called *le fusil*, the gun. It was sealed at its bottom end and lowered into the barrel dangling on a length of wire; each time it brought up a precise measure of spirit. (In slang talk of working cellarmen, lowering the sinker tube into a barrel and having a sly drink is known as giving oneself *un coup de fusil*, a gunshot.) The chief taster had, in front of him on the table, the huge cellar book in which was recorded the life of each barrel from the day it had arrived, perhaps forty years before. We tasted. We discussed. We decided. He wrote into the book his current evaluations and instructions.

There are, as virtually every regular Cognac drinker knows, two other great houses closely and fiercely competing with Hennessy in terms of quality, volume, and worldwide distribution: Courvoisier and Martell. They produce, among the three of them, about one out of every two bottles of Cognac exported from France. In the U.S., one of their labels is on about three out of every four bottles sold. They all operate, in general, by the same system of buying from small growers, of slow aging for decade after decade and of skilled blending by the Cognac Nose. Martell also has a famous family of tasters which has been serving the company for several generations and of which the latest member is the present chief taster, François Chapeau.

So much for sheer size. It is a cardinal principle in the Charente that the largest producer does not automatically make the best Cognac. When you step down to the second rung of the volume ladder—the group of houses led by the redoubtable Rémy Martin—you find strong differences in philosophy, clearly reflected in the wording on the labels. There are laws governing French Cognac labels and, if you are interested in getting the best value for the price you pay, it is pretty important to know how to recognize the significance of the legally definitive words.

The official map of the Charente region (the only region permitted by law to use the name "Cognac") looks roughly like the target of concentric circles at a rifle range. The bull's-eye area, the land around the town of Cognac where the soil is at its chalky best, is called the Grande Champagne district. (The word *champagne*, in the Charente, has nothing to do with the sparkling-Champagne district of northern France. It is the ancient use of the word—spelled *champain* by Milton, Shakespeare, and Tennyson; *campagna* by the Italians—converted to *campagne* in modern French and meaning the open, rolling farm country, as against the forests and woods, the latter called, in the Charente, *les bois.*) If a Cognac label is marked Grande Champagne, or Grande Fine Champagne, it must come, one hundred percent, from the best district. The next target circle surrounding the bull's-eye with soil slightly less ideally chalky, is the Petite Champagne. If a Cognac is made as a blend of the Grande and the Petite, with 50 percent or more of the Grande, it may legally be labeled a Fine Champagne (without the word *Grande*)—still a very good Cognac. (Incidentally, beware, on a label, of the tricky English phrase "Fine Cognac," which has no legal significance whatsoever.) Surrounding the two best districts there are others, in larger circles, where the soil is progressively less chalky, less basically good.

Since the house of Rémy Martin and the smaller houses of Bisquit, Delamain, Marnier-Lapostolle, and others do not have to buy as much new spirit as the giants, they loudly proclaim that they buy only from the two best districts and make only the superior qualities. The giants reply that obviously this is impossible for them at their volume of production, and that the argument is all vague nonsense anyway, since modern technological developments in agriculture have largely evened out the quality differences of grapes of one district and the other. So the big boys are replacing the legal definitions on their labels and, instead, now give proprietary names to most of their Cognacs. This gives them the freedom to blend the spirit of any district with that of any other. Meanwhile, Rémy Martin and its friends stick to their guns and, tasting their superb Cognacs, one has to admit that they have a lot of clout to their argument.

On the last day of my most recent visit to the Charente, I had a rare and memorable tasting of a group of extraordinary Cognacs produced by an almost entirely different system. Above the village of Ambleville, at his hilltop Domaine de la Voute, I met the remarkable Marcel Ragnaud, who is, at seventy, perhaps one of the last of a unique type of grower-distiller. The Ragnaud family, for five generations, here on this hilltop, has grown its own grapes in the surrounding vineyards. They have made their own wines and have distilled them into *eaux-de-vie*, which they have aged in their own cellars over a period of one hundred twenty-five years. They have never blended them with any spirit from any other distiller. In outstanding years they have sometimes made that rarest of Cognacs, a single vintage from a single estate. Finally, they have insisted on bottling and shipping their own products under their own labels in open competition with the worldwide distribution of the big houses.

The Ragnaud system of making and selling Cognac is a difficult and risky tour de force. It involves the capital problems of holding back one's products for as much as a hundred years before selling them, the dangers of evaporation and fire, and the limiting inflexibility of single-estate production without cross-blending, for the sake of quality decades ahead. It can only be worthwhile on the basis of supreme results.

When Marcel Ragnaud began working for his father fifty years ago, they had one serious competitor, a neighbor, also an independent producer, Gaston Briand, who had no son, only a daughter. Marcel married the daughter, so that when old Gaston died about ten years ago,* the two estates, with all their irreplaceable and priceless stocks of *eaux-de-vie*, were united. But the spirits in the barrels were never united. They continued to be aged and developed separately, so that the Ragnaud and the Briand Cognacs could continue to be bottled, each under its own traditional label.

As I tasted, one by one, Marcel Ragnaud's Cognacs—rising from the youngest to the oldest—I felt as if I were climbing, step by step, to the ultimate peak of Cognac quality. There was the twenty-year-old Réserve Spéciale, the thirty-five-year-old Fontveille, the Old Source—the fifty-year-old Gaston Briand. There was the Cognac Ragnaud had inherited from his mother, Héritage Madame Paul Ragnaud, a blend of spirits produced here in 1902, 1903, and 1904. Finally, the best Cognac I have ever tasted, the Gaston Briand Le Paradis, made from grapes harvested in 1880, before the phylloxera epidemic, but now so delicate and gentle that they had to be slightly "refreshed" by the addition of some "younger" spirits from the first post-phylloxera harvest of 1900. I was overwhelmed by an unimaginably complicated blend of sensuous impressions: of gold, of a distantly indefinable perfume, of silk and velvet, of elegance, of force, of poise, of smoothness, of the skill and wisdom of almost a century.

"But you must understand," said Ragnaud, "that we sell in one year no more than what one of the big houses sells in one day. I do not want my *eaux-de-vie* to develop quickly. In my cellar, my nose tells me how they are progressing and I hold them back. The slower they develop the more perfect they will be eventually. In Cognac one can achieve nothing without time."

LATEST NEWS FROM COGNAC: Yann Fillioux apparently is a young man of the twentieth century not prepared to be bound by ancient family rituals or medieval-style control of his personal life for the greater glory of the family name. For two hundred years it has been the Fillioux tradi-

---

*EDITOR'S NOTE: Approximately 1965.

tion that a taster's son must marry a girl of the Charentais earth and vineyards in order to produce children who will be candidates for future tasting honors because they have the spirit of Cognac in their blood. My news is that the tradition has been broken. Yann has married a girl from Paris and brought her to his Cognac home. I called Uncle Maurice and asked him what he thought. He said: "Yann and Betty will have to produce many children—from whom we will hope to choose."

Cordials and Liqueurs: Most Luxurious of Drinks

"Drink this, my friend, and you will never forget it!" Then, drop by drop, with the minute care of a lapidary counting pearls, the priest . . . poured into the glass a green liqueur, gilded, warm, scintillating, exquisite. The first sip bathed my stomach in sunshine. "It is the elixir of Père Gaucher," he said, triumphantly. "They make it at the monastery of the Prémontrés. . . ."

Thus the great French writer, Alphonse Daudet, begins his famous short story, which tells how a poverty-stricken small monastery in the South of France quickly achieved wealth and world fame after one of its young monks had succeeded in re-creating from an old family recipe an alcoholic cordial distilled from the aromatic herbs growing on the local hillsides. Daudet's details are obviously fictional, but the underlying theme is true. Some of the greatest liqueurs were invented by monks and are still made from secret recipes in distilleries controlled by church organizations. These herbs and spice cordials and the fruit liqueurs are among the strongest and sweetest, the most luxurious and velvety, the most extravagantly colorful and irresistibly complex of spiritous drinks.

Is there a difference between a "cordial" and a "liqueur"? Some experts say that the word "cordial" properly belongs to the ancient herbal drinks, originally made not for pleasure drinking, but as medicines and pick-

EDITOR'S NOTE: This article originally appeared in the November 1967 issue of *House Beautiful.*

me-ups for ailing monks. The Oxford dictionary defines "cordial" as a medicine, or beverage which invigorates the heart and stimulates the circulation. Later, when commercial producers began concocting fantastic essences of fruits and flowers, more for the pleasure than the health of the drinker, these were called "liqueurs."

There are right and wrong times, and ways, to serve cordials and liqueurs. A sweet drink should obviously not be served immediately before a main meal. Even after dinner, if served too soon, a very sweet liqueur can bring an uncomfortable feeling of oversaturation. Better, at that point, to serve a dry Cognac. This general rule, of course, is flexible, since some liqueurs are drier and lighter than others.

One ideal use, I think, is for the guest who drops in (or is invited in) for a short visit. "Cordial and cake" is ideal for mid-afternoon. Another charming invitational variation is to say: "Come in tonight at nine for coffee and cordials." After a formal dinner, the strategic moment at which to bring out the liqueurs is often an hour or two after the meal, when the guests are showing the first signs of being "talked out." The liqueurs can re-spark the party with their brilliant range of colors and festive ambience. A cordial is fine to speed the parting guest and keep him warm on his winter way home (but it is not, of course, for the driver). Thus cordials and liqueurs are useful tools for the sensitive hostess—an essential part of the "cellar" in any hospitable home.

There are several problems about finding one's way in the wide world of cordials and liqueurs. First, there are just so many of them. Second, one must learn to distinguish between the proprietary names of the liqueurs, made by only one producer, and the generic names of basic flavor mixtures, which are made by many producers. It also helps to know the names of the great companies, how they developed their products, and how they make them today.

Apart from the efforts of the monks in their monasteries dating back to the twelfth century, the commercial development of liqueurs is inextricably intertwined with the family names of pioneer chemists and merchants. In 1575, an Amsterdam trader with the East Indies, Erven Lucas Bols, decided to use some of the spices he imported to make a flavored gin and thus founded the House of Bols, which is today the largest liqueur producer in the world. Another Amsterdam merchant, Wynand Fockink, started his small distillery in 1679 and founded the second oldest of the great Dutch firms. In 1695, a cooper in Rotterdam, Jan de Kuyper, decided to make some of his own gin to go into his own barrels; today his is the third-oldest of the famous Dutch names.

In France in 1755, Marie Brizard, daughter of a carpenter, made an anisette cordial that was enjoyed by King Louis XV and, with her profits from the court, she founded the company that still uses her name. An-other of the great liqueur families is that of Cusenier, first in Ornans in the Jura Mountains, then in Paris. Some other historic French family names in liqueurs were, and still are, Bardinet, Cointreau, Dolfi, and Garnier. In Italy, the family associated with liqueurs is that of Lionello Stock, who started his distillery in Trieste. In Germany, the important family names were, and still are, Gilka, Mampe, and Riemerschmid.

After repeal of prohibition here and the start of super-high taxation of imported alcohol, there was a major new development in the liqueur business. If the liquid inside the bottle can be made within the U.S., then the bottle can be sold for less than the imported version. This hard fact has led some of the great European names to take out, so to speak, American citizenship. They have set up their own manufacturing here, and today the names of Bols or de Kuyper do not necessarily mean a Dutch import. The names of Cointreau and Garnier no longer always mean a French product. These names compete with purely American labels like Hiram Walker. How to choose? A difficult question, because so much depends on personal preference. Let us begin by classifying cor-dials and liqueurs into six fairly broad groups.

1. THE ANCIENT, SECRET-FORMULA, MIXED-AROMATIC CORDIALS

The name familiar to connoisseurs everywhere and always the powerful contender for first place among all cordials is green Chartreuse, owned by the Carthusian monks and made by them in only two places: in their monastery of La Grande Chartreuse at Voiron, near Grenoble in south central France, and at their monastery in Tarragona in Spain. The secret formula, said to contain about one hundred thirty aromatic herbs, was developed in the sixteenth century and has been made for sale by monks since 1735. About a hundred years later, they developed yellow Char-treuse, a lighter and sweeter version said to be "for the ladies," but there is a saying in France that all yellow Chartreuse would rather be green if it could.

The other great name is, of course, Benedictine, developed by the monks at the Abbey of Fécamp on the coast of Normandy. There is a record of the drink having been served to Francis I when he visited the abbey in 1534. After the French Revolution when the abbey was pil-laged, the secret formula was lost for almost a hundred years. Then it was rediscovered, and for the last hundred years, Benedictine has been made by a commercial firm but still in the cellars of the old abbey at Fécamp.

About thirty years ago, noting that many people like to mix their Benedictine with brandy, the company developed B & B, a delicious half-and-half mixture of the two drinks.

The famous Basque cordial of Spain, green Izarra, is actually distilled across the border in France, but its aromatic herbs are picked on the Spanish slopes of the Pyrenees. There is also a lighter and sweeter yellow Izarra.

Other proprietary, herb-flavored cordials worth investigating include, from Italy, the bright yellow Galliano and the slightly citric, highly aromatic Strega; from Spain, the brown-gold Cuarenta y Tres (Forty-three); and from the Bordeaux district of France, Vieille Cure (green or yellow).

2. THE CORDIALS WITH A SINGLE, DOMINANT AROMATIC SPICE

The most well-known aromatic cordial is, of course, crème de menthe, a generic name used by dozens of producers. When it comes from the distillation, it is crystal clear, and I firmly believe (although many will disagree) that the taste is slightly better in this natural state called "white" on some labels. Most brands, however (including the famous Cusenier Freezomint), are colored green, some rose-pink, or even gold. There is also a lighter, always clear version produced by several makers, called "peppermint schnapps."

The second most famous spice cordial is anise or anisette, generic words used by all major producers. An unusual version comes from Badalona, Spain, under the name Anis del Mono. Another spice cordial, famous in Eastern Europe for hundreds of years, takes its name from its principal flavoring, cumin seed, and is alled "kümmel," but it also has the added flavor of caraway and coriander.

3. THE FRUIT LIQUEURS

These are the true liqueurs in the classic meaning of the word. Different fruits react differently to infusion with alcohol, but above all, the orange, produces the outstanding and most universally accepted liqueur. The word most often linked with orange liqueurs is Curaçao, the name of the Dutch West Indian island. Soon after the Dutch took control of it in 1634, they discovered that a small, sour, wild orange there had such an abundance of flavor oils in its greenish skin that it could be distilled into a marvelous liqueur. There was soon such an international demand for orange Curaçao that seeds of the orange were planted in other tropical countries, and their cultivation has become an international industry. There is a double-strength version called Curaçao Double, and a triple-strength, much drier orange brandy called Triple Sec. All these names are generic. Though there is still one distillery on the original island (its product is imported under the name Senior's Curaçao of Curaçao), magnificent orange Curaçaos are sent to us from France to add to our excellent domestic types.

Not every maker, however, uses Curaçao oranges. Some use Valencias, and the label then reads simply "orange liqueur." Two world-famous proprietary orange liqueurs use neither the word "orange" nor "Curaçao" but are known simply by the names of their makers—Cointreau and Grand Marnier. Another variation of the orange liqueur uses the tangerine, and the liqueur is always labeled in French as "crème de mandarine."

The sweet cherry takes second place to the orange in popularity as the informing flavor of a liqueur. The cracked pits are generally included in the infusion to add a slight but dramatic bitterness in the aftertaste. Again, the liquid as it comes from the distillation is clear, and the Swiss versions are sold without added coloring as kirsch (the German word for "cherry"). Without question, the most popular cherry liqueur is a proprietary brand from Denmark, Cherry Herring, the second word being the name of the family who founded and has run the Copenhagen company for more than one hundred fifty years. Other competing producers have launched proprietary names, such as Cherry Marnier or Cherristock.

As to other fruit flavors, all the names are, of course, generic and almost all the producers make them. Apricot is sometimes called "abricotine" or "apry," and the Hungarian version, Hungaria Baracklikör is always superb. The blackberry's flavor comes through brilliantly in a liqueur, as does that of the black currant. The peach makes a gentle and subtle drink. The less familiar sloe berry, generally imported from England, is usually labeled "prunelle" or "Crème de Prunellia" in France. Raspberry is generally labeled either "crème de framboises" (in French) or "Himbeer liqueur" (in German). Strawberry is almost always "crème de fraises."

4. LIQUEURS FROM THE ESSENCES OF FLOWERS

It can be an extremely interesting experience to taste a bouquet which one has known all one's life only as a scent. There is a crème de rose, a crème de violette, and a combination of flower essences with a name at which cynics scoff: Parfait Amour. It is imported from both France and Germany, and there is also a domestic variety.

5. A MISCELLANY OF OTHER FLAVORS

This category begins with a group that includes Drambuie, based on the Scotch whiskey, flavored with heather honey, one of the most popular liqueurs in the world. When the base is Irish whiskey, the liqueur is Irish Mist. When the base is American bourbon, and the secret flavorings seem, to at least one regular drinker, to be a combination of Southern peach and honeysuckle, the name is Southern Comfort.

In the second most popular group are the liqueurs flavored with coffee, made in romantic places and known by poetic names. The long list of favorites includes Tia Maria from Jamaica, Kahlúa from Mexico, Espresso Coffee (with even a caffeine-free version) from Anacona, Pasha Turkish Coffee from Istanbul, and others with the added flavors of chocolate and mint. Pure chocolate liqueurs are traditionally called "crème de cacao," and almost every producer has his own version.

6. CONVERSATION-PIECE ODDITIES

There are some famous off-beat liqueurs, which achieve such a dramatic appearance that they have a value greater than their taste—a surprise factor for the entertainment of the guests at a party. The first is one of the oldest of all liqueurs. In 1549, King Zygmunt of Poland is said to have visited an ancient monastery in Danzig where the monks offered him a magnificent, clear liqueur, which he liked so much that he christened it *"zwota woda"* (gold water). That gave the monks the idea of garnishing the water with floating flakes of gold leaf. About fifty years later, one of the old harbor houses used for curing salmon was converted into a distillery for making and selling the first commercial goldwasser, called Der Lachs (salmon brand). There is no longer any copyright on the word "goldwasser," but only one type, now made in Germany, may still call itself Danzig (Der Lachs) Goldwaser and still has a salmon on the label. Danzig is now Polish, and its government exports a cordial known as Polmos Zwota Woda.

There is a liqueur from Italy called Fior d'Alpe (because it is said to be flavored with aromatic Alpine flowers), which carries inside every bottle a small green branch from a living tree. Then, by a secret manufacturing process, sugar crystallizes out from the liquid in the bottle and forms tiny, rock-candy crystals growing like buds all over the branch.

There is a chocolate liqueur from Switzerland called Marmot Chocolat Suisse, which has, floating in it, literally hundreds of neatly rounded chips of Swiss chocolate. I once poured a two-ounce jigger onto a dinner plate, and counted. There were sixty-five "niblets" of chocolate. It's hard to decide whether one is having a drink or eating a snack.

Finally, there is a Swiss liqueur made from the Williams pear, which is bottled with pure magic. Suspended in the liquid inside the bottle is a full-size pear, obviously ten times too large to get through the narrow neck of the bottle. The pears are actually grown inside the bottles. Late in May, when the petals fall off the flowers and the tiny pears appear at the tips of the stems, the men slide the empty bottles over the pears and up the stems and securely tie the bottles to the branches. Sometimes as many as thirty bottles are suspended from each tree. Each pear grows rapidly inside its private little hothouse. Usually about mid-August, when each pear is fully grown, it is carefully snipped from its stalk and allowed to slide gently down to the bottom of the bottle. The same day, the bottles are delivered to the distillery to be filled with the pear liqueur, which preserves the color and freshness of the living fruit almost indefinitely.

THE PERFECT POUSSE-CAFÉ

The unique drink of the liqueur world is the Pousse-Café, in which several flavors are put together in a glass, yet do not mix. My recipe came many years ago from one of the oldest bars on Bourbon Street in New Orleans, where the drink originated. There are now dozens of variations but this is the original, from The Old Absinthe House, New Orleans.

POUSSE-CAFÉ

Each drink is made individually. You need a tall Pousse-Café glass, about 5 inches high, ¾ inch at the bottom and expanding to about 1½ inches at the top. Into this glass you must pour seven liqueurs in an exact order, so that the heaviest remains on the bottom, the next lighter rests on top of it, and each in turn is lighter still. The final result is a gently swaying vertical rainbow of colors.

You have to pour each so gently on top of the previous one that there will be no blurring of the demarcations between the layers of color. There are various ways of pouring:

1. Slide the measured amount of liqueur down the side of the slightly tilted glass.
2. Pour them onto the back of a spoon inserted inside the glass.
3. Pour them down the blade of a knife.
4. Use a large-size eyedropper, a bulb-controlled measuring pipette (from a chemical supply store).

I would practice at least once before trying it out at a party.

The other important point is to know the weight of the various liqueurs. This is generally controlled by the alcohol and sugar: the less alcohol and the more sugar, the greater the weight of the liquid. However, various makes of the same flavor may vary in sugar content, so you must experiment before you launch out into your own variations. Here is a specific formula that works (use these exact brands, ice-cold, in this order):

2 *teaspoons Marie Brizard Crème de Cacao—brown, the heaviest*
2 *teaspoons Bols Crème de Banana—yellow*
2 *teaspoons Cusenier Freezomint—green*
2 *teaspoons Bosch Anis del Mono—clear*
2 *teaspoons Cherry Herring—red*
2 *teaspoons Galliano—bright yellow*
2 *teaspoons Cointreau—clear, the lightest*
1 *teaspoon heavy cream*

Gently pour the liqueurs into the Pousee-Café glass in exactly the order listed above. Top with the cream. Drink the Pousse-Café without shaking it, so that you taste the various flavors separately.

On the Martini

I suppose I can say that I drank my first Martini when I was eleven years old. I had overeaten. I was feeling sick. My mother's standard cure for this condition was a glass of London gin with a drop or two of Angostura bitters to make the whole thing slightly more palatable and, as Robert Benchley would say years later, "to take away that ghastly watery look." Since that day I calculate that I must have drunk (sometimes even against my better judgment) at least 10,467 Martinis and have developed a strong philosophy on the subject.

I know exactly, for myself, the right number to drink, the right place, the right time, and above all the right reason. I am convinced that a dry Martini of proper strength is not an apéritif to be consumed before a fine dinner. It does not whet the appetite. It dulls it. It refuses to play second fiddle to food. It is a meal all to its liquid self. I am willing to consume it at breakfast time, at midmorning, in place of afternoon tea, immediately (and especially) at the end of the day's work, at midnight or at four in the morning, but never within an hour of a good lunch or dinner.

At these proper times (and assuming the essentially correct techniques of preparation), I divide my dry Martinis into four types: first, the safe and sound; second, the special occasion; third, the intensely intimate; and fourth, the downright dangerous. The first is the kind one offers to new friends at the first meeting, before one has any idea of their capacity or sophistication. I make it of three parts of London gin and one part of Italian dry vermouth, cooled by gentle stirring over ice, poured into frosted, long-stemmed glasses holding not more than two ounces, with the requisite droplet of oil of lemon sitting on the surface, the remaining

EDITOR'S NOTE: This piece is excerpted from *Esquire's Handbook for Hosts* (Grosset & Dunlap, 1973).

lemon rind wiped around the lip of the glass, and the dropped-in green olive stuffed with red pimiento. It is all quite conservative and mild, but, in interesting company, it can be excellent.

My second version is made in the same way, but with some differences in the ingredients. I use four parts of Dublin gin to one part of French dry vermouth, with the same arrangement of the lemon zest on the surface and around the lip, but with the green olive stuffed with a chewy bit of salted almond. And then, a few seconds before serving it, my secret trick is to add to the glass, from an eyedropper, a single drop of raw onion juice. This is what I would serve, on a festive weekend, to my guests at five o'clock, when dinner is planned for eight. This is what I would try to get from my favorite barman at the best bar in any city of the world, when I was meeting the loveliest lady of the region and would be taking her two hours later to the best local restaurant to dine with a group of fascinating friends.

My third, intimate dry Martini is never served in public and never at any party larger than myself and one other person. Let us suppose that my friendship with the lovely lady has flowered and that the next time we are to dine she invites me to call for her at her apartment. The bottles, glasses, and ice are ready on the silver tray. She commands me to mix the drinks. I would mix five parts of an aromatic British gin to one part of Chambéry vermouth, with the inevitably essential routine of the lemon zest and the green olive, this time stuffed with a pearl onion. I would pour three ounces per person and my "secret trick" would be to add, from the eyedropper, two drops of juniper-flavored Holland Genever gin from its ice-cold stone crock. After this I would hope for at least two hours of intimate conversation before departing for a superb dinner.

Finally, there might come the day when the lovely lady agrees to dine *à deux* in my apartment and an entire evening of peacefully relaxed communication of two sympathetic spirits stretches before us. This would be one of the rare occasions for my fourth, my dangerous Martini, for which I would have on hand a bottle of the finest and rarest Holland gin available. The bottle would be kept in my freezer, so that at mixing time it would have an almost glycerin thickness.

THE SECRET OF AN EXTRAORDINARY EFFECT

There are no parts to my recipe. I simply measure, pour over the ice, and gently stir until intensely cold, four ounces of imported Russian vodka and serve it in freezer-chilled Champagne glasses, with no more than four or five eyedropper drops of the driest Chambéry vermouth, with the lemon zest on the surface and around the lip as usual and, instead of the olive, a tiny, orange-reddish Tuscan pepper, about the shape and size of a large pearl.

Finally, a second or two before the first sip, I gently suffuse into each glass two eyedropper drops of the Genever, which is so heavily solid that it rolls down to the bottom of the glass and adds an entirely indefinable perfection. The liquid is so cold that one feels the approaching chill on the tip of one's nose. Alongside this drink of extraordinary uplifting force, I would serve a tiny dish of pearl onions, each speared on a miniature toothpick and all resting on a bed of finely crushed snowy ice. Perhaps it is the contrast between the solid ice in the dish and the liquid fire in the glass that is the ultimate drama of this extraordinary drink.

It is something very private. It cannot be taken lightly, or drawn out for too long, or, worst of all, repeated too often. I seldom find the occasion more often than, say, three or four times a year. In the right company, it can bring a brief sense of peace. It can provide a calming of the human spirit by the distilled essence of the spirit of the fruits of the earth. Soother or stimulant—it is the nearest thing I know to the perfect dry Martini.

PART
·VI·

The Oenophile
at Large

What Goes with What?

The "Perfect Marriage" of

Food and Wine

Should Allow Room for Infidelity

Even the finest dinner is made more memorable by the proper serving of the right wine. In fact, most expert hostesses nowadays agree that a truly successful dinner party is impossible without the inclusion of at least one wine. The proof of the point is the extraordinary U.S. "wine explosion"—in 1971, we will have drunk about 275 million gallons. I sometimes wonder how many of those gallons will have been properly enjoyed, in the proper setting, at the proper time, with the proper food.

I am always being asked about the "perfect marriage" of food and wine. But is "marriage" the right word? It does imply complete fidelity—the same two partners always together—their relationship controlled by fixed and immutable rules. The partnerships of food and wine are not at all like that. They can change almost every night. They involve wildly undisciplined romance—a trial love affair joyously started one evening, abandoned as a total failure the next. There is almost unlimited fickleness, infidelity, variation of mood. It may be the spice of variety. It is not the continuity of marriage.

Some people try to enforce a shotgun marriage with a straitjacket of fixed rules. White wine, they say, with white chicken and white fish. Red wine with red meat. Pink wine with pink lamb. This is the lunatic fringe of menu planning. It can lead to dinner table disaster—perhaps

EDITOR'S NOTE: This article originally appeared in the November 1971 issue of *House Beautiful*. The appended chart is taken from *Esquire's Handbook for Hosts* (Grosset & Dunlap, 1973). According to *The Wine Spectator*, a trade publication, Americans were drinking 2.2 gallons of wine per capita in 1985.

even to divorce! Try serving a great white 1964 Steinberger from the Rhine with a delicately poached fillet of sole. The fish will taste like blotting paper. Or try matching a rare steak of venison in rich *marchand de vin* sauce to a beautiful, young, bright raspberry-colored Beaujolais of last year's harvest. The charming wine, perfectly delightful with the right dish, will taste like watery red ink.

To find the perfect wine partner for your menu, you must think of more than color. There can always be, of course, an element of romance. How often does the lilting name of a lovely wine add to the glamorous moment when a beautifully decorated dish is presented? A bottle of Valpolicella de Verona, for example, seems to exude the ambience of the city where Romeo and Juliet fell in love. Too, the wine can help you establish the mood of your party: informal and simple or luxuriously spendthrift. But the most decisive factor will be the character and personality of the wine.

The never-ending marvel of the world of wine is that almost every vineyard is in some way different from every other and produces a slightly different wine every year. Yet there are strong and continuing family resemblances between wines of the same district in the same region. Whether they be red or white, dry or sweet, still or sparkling, some wines are gentle, light, modest, uncomplicated in bouquet and taste, while others are irresistibly dominant, masterful and powerful, subtle and complicated on the tongue. Foods also can be delicate and gentle or powerful and spicy. The menu-planning trick is never to allow a too-dominant wine to overpower a gentle dish (as the Steinberger above did to the simple sole) or a too-dominant dish to overpower a gentle wine (as the venison did to the Beaujolais).

I have incorporated these and other vital principles into a basic food-with-wine chart on the following pages. It is a very flexible reference chart—not a set of rules, but an invitation to experiment. Once you know *why* you are putting wine X with food Y, you can make up your own rules as you go along and then break them whenever you are struck with an idea for an interesting experiment. In fact, in the right-hand column of the chart, I suggest a few of these unusual, off-beat combinations for each of the wine types. They are marvelous stimulants of conversation at the dinner table. One friend said to me the other day: "I don't believe anyone can call himself a true gourmet until he has tried red wine with fish." Perhaps he is right.

A few notes of explanation. The chart begins (left-hand column) with the three major types of white wine because these are the most universally available, have the widest range of uses and are, in general, the best with which to start experimenting. Then follow the two major types of red wine, the not-so-universal rosés, and the two sharply different types of sweet wine. Naturally, within each of these broad definitions there is an infinity of variations between districts, regions, and countries. I try to indicate this enormous variety in listing (in the second column) some of the specific wines to look for in your local wine shop. The countries are in alphabetical order, from France through Germany, Italy, and Spain to the U.S. Within each country, I list the wines approximately in the order of their importance. I have, of course, tasted charming and good wines in many other places besides those listed (for example, in Algeria, Australia, Austria, Chile, Greece, Hungary, South Africa, Switzerland, and Yugoslavia), but these wines are not yet sufficiently well distributed across the U.S. to be included here.

In the third column, I try to define in words the character of the wine type to help you in planning your experiments with the various foods suggested in column four.

EXPERIMENTS AND REWARDS

Certainly, for me, experimentation has been the essential key to my education in wine. I remember a beach picnic on the Mediterranean coast of southern France, a few miles from Marseille, when I had my first truly authentic *bouillabaisse,* the world's most wonderful fish stew.

That day, I learned one of the primary lessons: how good it is before a fine meal to drink, as an apéritif, a bottle of bone-dry, ice-cold white wine. We began with an Alsatian Sylvaner (the name of the grape) that both cooly slaked the thirst of our throats and, with its faint touch of acidity, stimulated our appetites. It was accompanied by small canapé slices of goat cheese, ripe black olives, and unsalted nuts—an ideal combination before even the most formal dinner.

Now the *bouillabaisse* was ready—a superb gastronomic experience that taught me how to recognize the subtle combinations of different types of fish with various wines. We opened several bottles at a time and then, taking a single mouthful of each fish in turn, noticed how an added sip of one wine would bring out a certain taste quality, while a sip of another wine would produce a different effect. The Chablis of Burgundy and the Muscadet of the Loire are, of course, the classic wines with fish, but there are at least a dozen other dry whites worth trying, from every wine-producing country in the world.

These dry types (which are, shall we say, the workhorses of the wine world) are followed up the power scale by the mellower wines with stronger personalities (which can stand up to the richer and spicier foods) and, at the top, by the most dominant and powerful whites. The greatest of these can provide surprises—sometimes even shocks.

My first discovery of the impact of the aggressively strong whites came at a superb dinner at the three-star country restaurant of Paul Bocuse a few miles outside Lyon, the city that rules the gastronomic heartland of France. Chef Paul served me some of the fishy riches of the Saône and Rhône Rivers (including the marvelous local crayfish) prepared with incredibly rich sauces and served with a range of the noble white wines from his enormous cellar. He showed me the elegance and power of the Alsatian wines made from the Riesling and Gewürztraminer grapes; the forceful beauty of the Bordeaux whites, led by such great château names as Carbonnieux, Domaine de Chevalier, Laville-Haut-Brion and Olivier; the dominant grace of the fine whites from the village of Meursault in Burgundy, from Vouvray on the Loire, and from the famous Hermitage hill on the Rhône. Finally, we opened a bottle of the white wine I consider to be one of the most powerful in the world, the 1964 Le Montrachet from the Côte d'Or slopes of southern Burgundy. I found it so irresistibly dominant in personality that I asked Chef Bocuse whether it would not go well with red meat. His eyes twinkled and, as a shocking experiment, he served it with the main course of our dinner, a rare and red *tournedos aux champignons*, a beefsteak with a creamy-rich brown sauce, garnished with wild cèpe mushrooms. I took my first bite of the meat, then lifted my glass of the great white wine while Chef Bocuse watched with a wicked grin. Red meat and white wine—a near-perfect partnership!

When it comes to red wines, the idea of a beautifully colored château-bottled Bordeaux with red beef is so basic and universal that it needs not a word of discussion. The problem in menu-planning is how to differentiate between the gay and charming light reds and the big, powerful red wines.

A VINTAGE VISIT

Last year I stayed several days at one of the greatest vineyards of the world, Château Latour, in the Médoc district of Bordeaux. I spent most of my time with wine master Jean-Paul Gardère, whose discussions and demonstrations were a memorable revelation. He planned the food every day with the brilliant cook of the château, Madame Jeanne Verger, to prove the perfect partnership of the Bordeaux wines with a wide range of simple to complicated dishes. The first major point he proved was the vital importance, in wine quality, of soil and weather. Because of its soil, each château vineyard has a certain basic similarity of character in all its wines. Therefore, if you taste the wines of various châteaux, you will very soon begin to know which labels strike the best balance between your taste and your pocketbook. But then, you should also remember that, depending on the amount of sunshine and rain each summer, the wines of each château will be lighter or heavier, gentler or stronger. So, with practice, you will learn to buy both by the château name and vintage year.

In cold, dry, and sunless years, even such normally great wines as Châteaux Lafite, Latour, or Margaux can be relatively gentle, light, and comparatively inexpensive. In those years, they can be bought and used as if they belonged to the "light reds" on my chart. For example, at Château Latour, we drank the light and modest 1951 vintage with the white meat of chicken in *poulet bordelaise* and the almost equally light and unpretentious 1963 vintage with a delicately creamy preparation of veal sweetbreads.

My education in the reds of Burgundy has come mainly from my friends the brothers Jean and Pierre Troisgros, the two great Burgundian-born chefs, at their three-star Troisgros Restaurant in the small town of Roanne, also near Lyon. Although they now live and work on the banks of the Loire, they have kept their contacts and their family friendships among the Burgundy growers, and they seem to get the best wines before anyone else has heard about them.

They showed me, in a series of tastings, that many of the lightest and softest Burgundy reds come from the city of Beaune (labeled "Beaune" or "Côte de Beaune" or "Côte de Beaune-Villages") or take their names from the village of Volnay, a few miles to the south. They also proved how fine a young Beaujolais can be when it is carefully produced and bottled by a single small vineyard, such as, for example, Château de la Chaize in the village of Brouilly.

When I arrived for a visit with the Troisgros last October,* at the start of the hunting season, Chef Pierre had spent the weekend in the forests of the Garenne and had brought back a *marcassin* (a young wild boar), wild duck, large hares, rabbits, and partridges. For the next few days, we tasted these prizes, superbly prepared and perfectly matched to some of the big, dominant Burgundy reds, which—with only a few exceptions—come from the villages to the north of Beaune. The names to remember are Chambertin, Clos Vougeot, Grands Echézeaux, Musigny, Richebourg, Romanée-Conti, La Tâche. Our biggest dinner involved the

---

*EDITOR'S NOTE: De Groot refers to October of 1970. Jean Troisgros died on August 8, 1983.

three-day preparation of one of the greatest of all Burgundian game dishes, a *civet de lièvre à la royale*, the hares marinated in brandy and red wine, then filled with a supremely aromatic stuffing and slowly simmered for twenty-four hours. When the enormous and magnificently decorated platter came to table, the meat, with its garnishes and sauce, proved to be too dominant in flavor for the 1964 Grands Echézeaux, a moderately light year. The wine seemed slightly sharp and thin. Chef Pierre instantly replaced it with a much bigger Burgundy, the 1966 Pommard, Hospices de Beaune. This, a more dominant wine, stood up to the power of the food.

For dinner on my last evening, the Troisgros brothers served me a surprise—an off-beat combination to prove that even fairly strong red wine *can*, in a properly planned way, be matched with fish. They prepared a Burgundian *meurette*, a richly luxurious stew of local lake and river fish, all marinated with Burgundian Marc brandy and gently simmered in red wine. It was served with a red 1967 Bonnes Mares from the Burgundian village of Chambolle-Musigny.

I found another surprising, but successful, partnership of red wine with fish at a small mountain inn among the High Alps near the Swiss border, The Auberge of the Flowering Hearth. The excellent cook, Mademoiselle Ray Girard, had a large, pink-fleshed salmon-trout, caught that morning in Lake Paladru, near Grenoble. Mademoiselle Ray decided to prepare it *a la genevoise*, which means, on any menu in any country, "as they do it in Geneva," that is, in red wine. The whole fish was gently poached in the locally produced light red, Gamay de Savoie, which was sharp enough to cut the oily richness of the fish. Then it was served with a red sauce and a lightly soft red wine from the Rhône, made from the grapes that grow on the hillsides so hotly bathed by the sun that they and the wine are called Côtes Rôties, or "roasted slopes."

At this point, some readers may be thinking: "Why bother with a chart? Just serve rosé wine. It goes with anything!" This is nonsensical. Most inexpensive *vin rosé* has so little character that it does not add anything to anything at any time. You might as well drink a glass of colored water. The making of a good rosé is a delicate process. It is, more or less, like making a fine red wine from red grapes with a well-developed character but stopping the production process before the red color has deepened. This delicate operation is ignored in the making of the poor rosés. They are simply a characterless mixture of red and white wines.

How can one find the best rosés? They are made in a specific place, from specific grapes and the producers are legally required to put the names on the labels. See the chart for a list of them. Is there a place for a good rosé in menu-planning? Indeed there is. It can help to unite several different kinds of dishes on a cold buffet table. It can stress the informality of a picnic. It will not be killed by the peppery sauces of a Texas-style barbecue, a Mexican dinner, or an Indian curry.

PÂTÉ AND SAUTERNES

During the 1970 harvest in Bordeaux, I was invited to a memorable lunch by Monsieur and Madame Henri Woltner at their great Château La Mission-Haut-Brion in the Graves district, just outside the city. After the main meat course, a superb roast of veal, there was served, of all things, a rich pâté de foie gras and with it, believe it or not, a lightly sweet Sauterne wine. I winced, but as I tasted the two together, I realized the wine cut the richness of the goose livers while magnifying their flavor. The pâté almost eliminated the sweetness of the wine. It was pure magic!

When I asked Madame Woltner why the foie gras, normally an opening course, was served *after* the meat, she laughed gaily and said: "Because people will eat less of the expensive stuff at this point!" She was, of course, putting me on. She went on to explain that when planning a menu, her husband and other Bordeaux producers always decide first on the wines they want to show off, then choose the foods that will best go with them.

THE LIGHTLY SWEETS

You will find that apart from the famous, honey-sweet Bordeaux wines, there are many lightly sweet wines—yellow rather than golden in color, the products of smaller vineyards and less-sunny years—that have all kinds of special uses in menu planning. They can be served as a buffer between the meat and the dessert or equally well at the start of a meal. I have used this trick many times at my own dinner table—a lightly sweet wine as a cutting edge against some richly unctuous dish.

These lightly sweet wines are very different, of course, from the great vintages of Château d'Yquem and the other world-famous Sauternes châteaux. Their wines can be almost as sweet and thick as honey but with a marvelously spicy character. Their classic use is with desserts that are not too sweet, so that the aromatic sugar of the wine is not overpowered. You should never serve them with ice cream, which slightly freezes your taste buds so that you cannot fully appreciate the wine. Nor should they ever accompany any dish containing chocolate, which, as you chew it, also clogs your taste buds. I think the finest of the sweet wines, including the great sweet wines of Germany, are best drunk in place of liqueur after dinner, either by themselves or with candies, unsalted nuts or those fine, jumbo-size muscat raisins that come in bunches from Australia.

A final note on cheese with wine. It is invariably a fine partnership. Professional wine shippers always say: "Let me sell wine with cheese, but buy it with apples." They know that cheese brings out the best from any wine, but that the sourness of an apple shows up the worst qualities and provides a wholesale buyer with the ammunition with which to cut down the price that he will have to pay. Even with cheeses, the rules about domination and strength still apply.

APPLY THE RULES

Always remember that the bland and simple cheeses should be matched with the less-powerful whites, the medium-strong cheeses with the lighter reds. Only the extremely powerful blues and "stinky" goat cheeses (as well as such "loud" items as Liederkranz or Limburger) are strong enough to do battle with the most powerful reds. My chart gives a few of the names and will help you to choose your cheeses to match your wines.

I hope I have said enough to persuade you that menu-planning with wine is one of the most irresistibly fascinating of hobbies, just because there is such an infinity of possible variations. I have never found any hobby to be really worthwhile unless it presents a certain challenge to one's ingenuity and skill.

THE BASIC WINE AND FOOD AFFINITIES

TYPE OF WINE	SPECIFIC WINES	GENERAL CHARACTER	TRADITIONALLY SERVED WITH	UNUSUAL (BUT VERY GOOD) SERVED WITH
Dry whites Dry Champagnes and other sparkling wines (serve chilled)	Chablis or Pouilly-Fuissé from Burgundy Muscadet or Pouilly-Fumé from the Loire Sylvaner from Alsace Crépy or Seyssel from the French Alps Light Moselle from Germany Soave from Italy White Rioja from Spain Johannisberg Riesling or Pinot Blanc from California	Dry and refreshing, almost lemony Thirst-quenching	Canapés before a meal Clams and oysters Nonoily fish, grilled or poached Cold chicken or turkey Or with all dishes in a simple meal	Canapés made with soft goat cheese Olives and unsalted nuts as appetizers

Wine		Character	Foods	
Medium dry whites Softer Champagnes (serve chilled)	White Graves from Bordeaux Corton-Charlemagne or Meursault from Burgundy Light Vouvray from the Loire Light Hermitage from the Rhône Niersteiner, Forster, Bernkasteler, or Wehlener from Germany White Chianti or Orvieto Secco from Italy Alella from Spain Sauvignon Blanc from California	Gentler and softer; fruity, less sharp Grapy, rather than lemony	Smoked salmon Bisques or cream soups Fish with cream sauces and fried fish Hot chicken or turkey with gravy Cold lamb or veal Roast pork Sweetbreads or kidneys	Main dishes with cheese, such as veal Cordon Bleu, veal Parmigiana, macaroni and cheese, spaghetti with meat balls and cheese sauce, cheese omelet with herbs or mushrooms Nutty cheeses such as French Tomme de Savoi or Swiss Gruyère
Rich, powerful whites Sweet Champagnes (serve ice-cold)	Montrachet from Burgundy Gewürztraminer from Alsace Rich Vouvray from the Loire Johannisberger, Steinberger, or Vollrads from Germany's Rheingau	Very dominant Aromatic and spicy, sometimes faintly sweet Rich and velvety on the tongue	Rich preparations of crab and lobster Roast pheasant Baked or boiled ham Simple grills, roasts, or stews of lamb, pork, or veal	Turtle soup Red meats such as beefsteak with natural gravy Simple cheeses such as Dutch Edam or English Cheddar

Rich, powerful whites Sweet Champagnes (*cont.*)	Orvieto Abboccato from Italy Pinot Chardonnay from California		Rich, oily fish such as salmon or Salmon-trout *à la genevoise*
Light, young, relatively uncomplicated reds (serve at room temperature)	Médoc, Red Graves, or Saint-Emilion from Bordeaux (simple recent vintages) Beaune, Volnay, or Beaujolais from Burgundy (soft recent vintages) Côte Rôtie from the Rhône Gamay de Savoie from the French Alps Bardolino or Valpolicella from Italy Rioja Clarete from Spain Cabernet Sauvignon or Barbera from California	Fruity and gay, a bit feminine Lovely in color, straightforward in personality	Simple preparation of red meat, such as steaks with natural gravy or red-wine sauce Oven or pot roasts Simple stews or casseroles Lamb or veal with rich, creamy garnishes or wine sauces Roast duck Richly prepared capon, goose, guinea hen, pheasant, squab, or turkey Medium-strong cheeses, such as Alsatian, Muenster, Normandy Camembert, Parisian Brie, or Savoy Reblochon

Powerful, dominant reds (serve at room temperature)	Médoc, Graves, Pomerol, or Saint-Emilion from Bordeaux Chambertin, Clos Vougeot, Musigny, Pommard, or Vosne-Romanée from Burgundy Châteauneuf-du-Pape or Hermitage from the Rhône Barolo or Chianti Classico from Italy Rioja Clarete from Spain Pinot Noir from California (all fine old vintages)	Dominant and strong, with a very powerful personality Smooth and velvety, almost heavy on the tongue	Red meat with rich sauces, such as Beef in Burgundy and other winy casseroles All kinds of game birds, such as wild duck, wild pheasant, or wild turkey Richly stuffed goose Strong goat cheeses such as Alpine St. Marcellin goat, Loire Chabichou or Ste. Maure, or Valençay goat, or very strong blue cheeses such as English Stilton, French Roquefort, or Italian Gorgonzola *Meurette*, the Burgundy fish stew
Authentic rosés (serve ice-cold)	Tavel from the Rhône Pinot Rosé from Alsace Light young Beaujolais from Burgundy Rosé de Cabernet from Anjou or Touraine in the Loire Grenache, Gamay, or, in lesser quantity,	Light, refreshing, and uncomplicated (but they do *not* go with everything)	Cold buffet Barbecued foods Picnic foods Rich, oily fish (as above) Buttery cheeses such as Dutch Gouda or Italian Fontina

Authentic rosés (cont.)	Cabernet and Pink Zinfandel from California			
Lightly sweet, yellow wines (serve chilled)	Young regional Sauternes from Bordeaux Gewürztraminer or Riesling from Alsace Light sweet Anjou or Vouvray from the Loire Light sweet Moselle or Rhine from Germany Light sweet Muscatel or Sémillon from California	Rich but not cloying Refreshingly light on the tongue	Light desserts	Pâté de foie gras Rich pâtés and terrines of game meats Very rich soups Rich and creamy preparations of lobster
Honeyed, golden wines (serve almost freezing)	Sauternes from Bordeaux Gewürztraminer from Alsace Sweet Anjou or Vouvray from the Loire Sweet Moselle or Rhine from Germany Muscatel or sweet Sémillon from California (Only the great old vintages achieve this status)	Magnificently aromatic, heavily honeyed	Rich desserts Fruit- or nut-filled soufflés (But *never* ice cream or any dish with chocolate)	Candies, nuts, and raisins as a liqueur after dinner

Why Shouldn't I Buy One Bottle at a Time?

And "Shake It Up Good"

on the Way Home to Dinner

My friends Celia and Henry are charming and sophisticated hosts. Both are excellent cooks. They would not dream of inviting me to dinner without serving at least one bottle of wine. But they refuse to make the effort, or take the time, to learn something about wine. In the early afternoon of the day when they are going to serve, say, a fillet of sole baked in a cream sauce with mushrooms, followed by a grilled rack of lamb with fresh vegetables, Celia goes to her local wine merchant, tells him her menu for the evening, and asks him to suggest a bottle. The condition of that wine by the time it is poured at table was best described one day by Celia's fourteen-year-old son, who, holding a bubbly glass of cola in one hand and a glass of wine in the other, said, "I like wine best when you shake it up good."

I am always telling Celia and Henry that buying wine one bottle at a time is the worst possible way. It is overexpensive and inefficient in terms of matching the wine to the food, and above all boring, dull, 'and uninteresting in terms of the fascinating game of exploring the extraordinary range and variety of the pleasures of wine.

To save money, to be able to open better bottles more often, to serve exactly the right wine with the right food—in short, to gain the reputation among your friends as a memorable host in terms of wine also—I believe it is essential to set up some kind of storage arrangement at

EDITOR'S NOTE: This piece is excerpted from *Esquire's Handbook for Hosts* (Grosset & Dunlap, 1973).

home, even if you live in a one-room studio apartment and open only a couple of bottles a week. Let us not become involved in nonsensical cliché talk about "building a wine cellar." The ridiculous word "cellar" ought to be eliminated from the modern vocabulary of wine. Obviously it is an anachronistic impossibility in a city apartment, in a single-level ranch house, or a beach cottage on stilts. If there is a below-ground-level space in the modern home, it probably houses the furnace, the brightly lit, often smoke-filled playroom, or the buzzing vibrations of the power-driven home workshop—hardly right for the slow aging of wine, which requires coolness, darkness, the absence of any smell or smoke, and a silent, vibration-free stillness.

Recently, when I visited the great Château Latour in Bordeaux, I found that its enormous, classic "cellars" were not really below ground at all, but were a series of block-long granite sheds. After walking, it seemed, for miles along the lines of barrels and among the racks of bottles, my guide, the cellar master, opened a side door and there we were, at grass level on the sloping hillside looking out across the waters of the Gironde. If Château Latour doesn't need an underground cellar, I certainly don't.

What every good home drinker of wine needs is what I like to call a "wine library." The parallel is precise. You buy your favorite books according to your taste. There are so many possibilities in the shops that you must learn to pick and choose. You develop loyalties to certain kinds of books, to certain authors, certain subjects. Sometimes you buy an extremely expensive book because it is so magnificent that you feel you must have the experience of owning it. At other times, by diligent searching, you find a little book at a giveaway price that brings you a pleasure far beyond its value. As you gain experience in collecting books, you learn the two most fundamental rules. First, never let yourself become a victim of high-pressure promotion—never buy a show-off book simply because it is the fashionable thing to do, simply because you think its ownership will give you prestige among your friends. Second, never choose a book by its price tag—if it is a bad book, it is a bad book at any price. The principles are exactly the same for the wine library.

Every sound rule of wine-buying points to the advantages of the home wine library. At the simplest level, there is that automatic 10 percent discount on a case of twelve bottles—even, at most stores, on a mixed case of your own choice. You can take immediate advantage of the "special offers" many stores advertise as an enticement to bring in new customers. If you study the sales catalogs and search diligently from store to store in your neighborhood, you can often find unusual and remarkable buys, sometimes for as little as half the normal price, which, if you have reasonable storage space, can give you enough inexpensive bottles to last for several months.

Then there is the problem of "shaking it up good" on the way home for dinner. No good wine—and especially not a fine old red wine—should be moved around or violently jogged shortly before it is opened. There is often a slight, sometimes almost invisible, powdery sediment in the wine, which should be left at the bottom of the bottle and not consumed as floating dust in the wineglass. So I keep every important bottle lying on its side, with the label facing upward, in my wine library for at least a month. By always remembering to keep the label up when removing the bottle, carrying it to the table, and gently removing the cork, one avoids rolling around any sediment that might have quietly settled. I would never dream of consuming today the bottle I bring home today. I choose from the small backlog in my wine library.

There remains the question of "the perfect marriage" between the wine and the food. Your local merchant—even assuming the excellence of his goodwill and knowledge, and discounting his natural desire to increase his profit by selling you a more complicated and more expensive bottle—can never, without an intimate knowledge of your cooking style, give you more than the standard clichés about white wine with white meat and red with red. But how rich is the sauce that accompanies your white fish? Will your red steak be served with its natural juices, or with a béarnaise or other luxurious sauce? It makes a big difference to the wine. The creamier and richer the dish, the richer and softer should be the wine. It isn't the color that counts—it is the aromatic dominance of the food against the power of the personality of the wine. You will never learn about "the marriage that makes the meal" if you buy only one bottle at a time, here and there, haphazardly, and probably a different bottle every time. Your wine library should provide you with an immediate range of choices of wines you already know, from the most delicate, light, and subtle, up to the most dominant and powerful—so that you can choose, with the assurance of previous experience with these particular wines, the precise companion to the particular dish of tonight. This kind of service should be built into your wine library.

Finally, there is the much-debated question of aging wines at home. I am not suggesting for a moment that any of us can or should hold noble wines for twenty, thirty, or forty years, as rich connoisseurs did years ago. Comparatively few wines are now made with such lengthy "home cellaring" in mind and yet it is still possible to buy a fine young wine, at a relatively reasonable price, with the near certainty that it will improve enormously in both quality and value with up to four or five years of careful keeping. Thus, at a time when wine prices have nowhere to go but up, if you can keep such an aging program going, on a rotating basis, setting aside some wines every year, you will always be able to offer your friends currently expensive wines with the knowledge that you did not pay expensively for them. Let us take a specific example.

In January, 1960, the 1959 Château Latour, only three months old and still, of course, in the barrel, was offered for sale at $3.50 a bottle for U.S. delivery in 1962. By 1961 the price had risen to $5 a bottle. In 1962, upon U.S. delivery, the price was $7 a bottle. By 1964 the price was $10 a bottle. In 1973, approaching its peak, it sold, if you could find it, for between $60 and $85 a bottle. Such treasures are simply unavailable anywhere in the commercial market. (And what more perfect gift to honor, say, the birthday of a friend, than one of your irreplaceable bottles.)

My own wine library is divided into three parts. Close to my dining area, in a spot I can reach with hardly more effort than stretching out my hand, I keep a metal rack that holds up to two dozen bottles of what my French friends call *vins de consommation courante du jour*, wines of current, day-by-day consumption. But don't be fooled by the French definition. Usually at least half of my everyday, inexpensive wines—wines instantly ready to slake a sudden thirst, bottles to be opened to pour a glass to accompany my luncheon tray at my desk—at least half of these simple wines in my rack nowadays are American: from California, Maryland, New York, Ohio, or Wisconsin. Many of them still work out at less than two dollars a bottle. Very few are above the three-dollar mark. I say "work out," because, of course, I sometimes buy them in gallon or half-gallon jugs, although as soon as the jug is opened I pour the remaining wine into standard bottles, tightly recorked for better keeping. Such wines—in fact, any bottle, once opened, whether it contains red, white, or any other color—will, in my opinion, hold their character for a day or two if refrigerated. A red bottle from the refrigerator, of course, should be given two hours to come back to room temperature before being reopened and repoured.

The second division of my wine library is a honeycombed "wine wall," facing away from the light in an air-conditioned room, where the temperature is never allowed to rise much above 70° F. I deliberately store these "here-and-now party wines" at from ten to fifteen degrees above the normally accepted temperature in order to age them slightly more quickly for use within the current year. This wine wall of mine can hold up to twenty cases of wines of the middle range of price and quality, with enough varietal sweep of character, personality, and power that, for any dinner-party menu, I can pick exactly the right wine for that "perfect marriage" for which one is always trying.

How many wines do you need for this pursuit of perfection? You certainly do *not* need as many as my two hundred forty bottles. I am sure that, with careful and regular choosing, you could provide yourself with a sufficient variety within the scope of a minimum of four cases, forty-eight bottles. Here again my favorite California wines are given status equal to those of France, Germany, Italy, Spain, and Switzerland, while the best wines of Australia, Chile, Greece, Hungary, and Portugal are never far behind. Let me say that my devotion to our American wines has nothing to do with national pride. I choose and buy my wines entirely on the basis of "blind comparison" in terms of quality and value. In this vast middle range of the wines of the world, our California varieties are now generally the equals of their imported counterparts, while some Californians have special qualities of freshness and fruit that are unduplicated in foreign wines.

Perhaps for this reason, I usually find (without especially thinking about it) that my "party wine wall" is usually one-third to one-half full of California bottles. In this middle-range category, one has to say California, because when the noble wine grapes of Europe (the varieties from which all the finest wines of the world are made) were brought to the United States, they thrived only in the temperate, mist-soaked, richly earthed, rolling valleys of the West Coast. In other parts of the country—among the Finger Lakes of New York, along the Ohio shores of Lake Erie, in Maryland and other grape-growing areas—the winters are just too fierce for the delicate European vines, so the wines of those regions (often attractive, country-style wines for simple meals) are made from our native grapes, which were growing wild here long before the coming of the Colonists.

The third division of my wine library is a locked "secret closet," with a miniature air conditioner keeping it always at 55° F, where my great wines can rest comfortably and age gracefully, year after year, as the magical and mysterious development of supreme wines demands. There are never very many of these bottles at any one time. The great wines have now become as sought-after and valuable as rare jewels. Unless one rides on mountains of money, one has to wait for the exceptional opportunity, the chance to buy a young wine of great promise, or a suddenly supreme vintage of a relatively unknown producer. My secret closet is never opened, no bottle is ever gently lifted from the racks, without serious consideration. The occasion must be important. The menu must be special. The guest of honor must be a worthy connoisseur. The qualities of the greatest wines are so complex, so subtle, so much a matter of fine shades of personal opinion and taste, that I can see no point in offering them to unskilled amateurs. I am absolutely opposed to the host who offers a Château Lafite, a Château Latour, a Schloss Johannisberger, or a Château d'Yquem of a truly great vintage simply for the prestigious show of these famous labels. The old proverb may have put it harshly, but "pearls before swine" is still a philosophical truth. Great wines should always be wedded to great occasions.

This is the wine library that best suits my needs. Many connoisseurs keep much larger stocks—sometimes up to three thousand bottles, or even more. I am often asked my opinion as to the minimum practical wine library, when there are sharp limitations of money and space. I would still keep to my three divisions. I would begin by spending, say, fifteen dollars on six inexpensive bottles for immediate daily use—three reds, three whites. For the medium-priced "party selection" wine wall, I would spend, let us say, two hundred fifty dollars on forty-eight bottles— perhaps twenty reds, eight first-class rosés, and twenty whites. As to great (or potentially great) wines, it is almost impossible to give detailed advice. The opportunities are so varied and the range of prices so wide. I do know, for example, that at this time of writing, I could buy a bottle of noble to great wine in New York, already reasonably aged for current drinking, for a price somewhere between twenty and thirty dollars a bottle. I could pay as much as one hundred dollars a bottle. A less well known label, but with good prospects for future greatness if properly stored for a few years, might cost as little as eight or ten dollars. This is how it works. These are the pleasures of the exploration, the investigation, the gamble. The tracking down of leads. The sifting of the evidence. The pitting of one's present judgment against future prospects. All the endlessly fascinating rules of the great game of setting up and maintaining one's own wine library.

What Wine with Spicy Food?

I sometimes suffer through an agonizing nightmare. I am dining in a beautiful restaurant. The table is set to perfection and the wine steward pours into the glinting glasses two very great wines: a red 1961 Château Lafite and a white 1972 Le Montrachet of the Marquis de Laguiche. My taste buds tingle in anticipation.

The waiter sets before me the hors d'oeuvre of small slices of darkly glistening beef in a luxuriously thick reddish sauce. The first taste tells me that this is the *yam neua* of Thailand, so utterly incendiary with red chili peppers that my mouth instantly feels on fire. Desperately, I drink the white wine. It "wets down" the furnace, but I fail to taste the elegant flavor of this great wine. I try the Lafite. I find no pleasure in it either!

The next course is a soup—the Korean *cho-kay tang* of sesame seeds and bean-thread noodles, the bouillon so heavily laced with hot chili oil as to be virtually volcanic. Again, I desperately seek refuge in the wines, but taste nothing and receive no relief.

The nightmare continues with a Hunanese fried crispy whole fish with hot and spicy sauce—a tearjerker that might discourage Beelzebub. Then there is a Mexican *enchiladas estilo Guadalajara*, the chili almost vibrating with peppery heat, and an Indian *vindaloo*—perhaps the most dangerously explosive mixture in town. But everything fades into gentleness before a Szechuanese *ma p'o tou fu*, in which the minced beef and chilies look like red ants crawling over the diced cubes of bean curd—surely the hottest dish in the world!

EDITOR'S NOTE: This article originally appeared in the June 1983 issue of *Food & Wine*.

Finally, my thirst and desperation over not being able to appreciate these great wines become uncontrollable. I throw the glasses into the air, overturn the table, rush out of the restaurant—and wake up in a cold sweat with a dry mouth.

My nightmare, of course, stems from the difficult problem of matching wines to exotic spicy foods and my conviction that a serious dinner demands the accompaniment of a planned sequence of wines, not an escapist choice of beers or whiskeys. After considerable experimentation I have come to the conclusion that wine is both possible and preferable to frame and uplift even the most exotic menus.

Since many people tend to try these cuisines in restaurants, the first step is to solve the inevitable problems encountered there. Almost invariably—especially if the food is Asian, Middle Eastern, or African— the wine list is quite limited, often nonexistent. You have to arrange to bring your own wines. The second problem is the family style of serving, traditional in many cuisines: The waiter puts all the dishes on the table at once so that the diners may pick and choose in any combination and order. This makes matching food and wine almost impossible. You must organize banquet-style service, with each important dish presented singly and separately.

At least half the dishes of the exotic cuisines are quite gentle. A majority of the main dishes are simply spicy, not peppery. My theory of the successful marriage of wine with these cuisines is to know (and separate) the gentle dishes, the spicy dishes, and the fiery dishes. The menu is then planned so that each group of dishes is paired with the wine that adds certain essential contrasts and harmonies.

Best of all, of course, is to prepare and serve such a meal yourself. Apart from the foreign cuisines most of us seem to know already, there is nothing particularly difficult about the attractive and decorative party dishes of, say, Burma, India, Indonesia, Korea, Laos, Malaysia, Morocco, Thailand, or Vietnam.

START WITH WINE OF PERSONALITY TO LEAD INTO THE GENTLE OPENING COURSES

When the taste buds are to be aroused, shocked, and titillated by unusual combinations of spices, the introductory apéritif wine should have a stimulating character, an elegant shimmer of fruity refreshment. I like to begin with a tangy Sauvignon Blanc from Sancerre in France's Loire

Valley, for example, Les Tuilières of Redde or a still demi-sec Vouvray of Brédif. Or I'll serve a German wine, a superb Schloss Vollrads (the relatively less expensive blue-gold seal) from the Rheingau, or from the Palatinate region a Wachenheimer Goldbächel Kabinett of the famous Bürklin-Wolf family. Or I'll choose a Napa Valley Riesling of Joseph Phelps or a soft California Chenin Blanc of Charles Krug.

For the opening courses, I might start with such uncomplicated things as Shanghai chicken with walnuts and silver bean sprouts or Vietnamese shrimp broiled on sticks of sugar cane or Indonesian *gado-gado*—vegetable salad with velvety peanut sauce.

ENTRY OF THE DOMINANT SPICES

The middle courses of our dinner should be dishes forceful with the dynamic blending of spices, but not fiery with pepper. What is needed to balance, smooth out, and even uplift these foods is a wine of firm and simple construction, with a sense of fruit and a recognizable overtone of natural grape sugar.

Some of the wines most perfectly balanced between lovely fruit and delicate sweetness come from Alsace and from the German regions of Rheinhessen, the Upper Mosel, the Palatinate, and the Saar valley. Those I have tried with success along with these spicy dishes include the Alsatian Gewürztraminer, produced by Trimbach and the one made by Willm, and a number of German wines—the Niersteiners from the great vineyards of the Franz Karl Schmitt family, the Bishop of Riesling of Rudolf Müller in the Bernkastel district, the Deidesheimer Paradiesgarten of the Bassermann-Jordan family in the Palatinate and the superb Scharzhofberger of Egon Müller from Wiltingen on the Saar. From the United States, a velvety Chenin Blanc from Wente Bros., a smooth Fumé Blanc of Chateau St. Jean, and a soft Semillon of Chateau Ste. Michelle have all been excellent.

Some of the dishes I have matched with these wines include a Szechuanese shrimp in spiced garlic sauce, an Indian lamb braised in yogurt curry, a Malaysian beef in coconut cream curry, and a Moroccan shad stuffed with dates, almonds, ginger, green peppers, and palm sugar.

The advantage of preparing these dishes at home is that, without losing authenticity, you can adjust the spices to "fine tune" the balance of the dish with the wine. For example, the traditional Moroccan *couscous* is normally accompanied with an incendiary *barissa* sauce. It is a good blockbuster uplifter for Muslims who do not drink wine; but when there are the grace notes of the fruit and sweetness of, say, a memorable Rhône Tavel Rosé, such as a Château d'Aqueria, the *barissa* blocks this perfect marriage of *couscous* and wine. I simply eliminate the *barissa*, arguing that *couscous* with the right wine is a far, far better thing than *couscous* with dead wine and a sauce guilty of vinous murder.

Or take Peking duck, one of the greatest Chinese dishes. With its skin as crackly crisp as spun sugar, its breast flesh juicy and subtly aromatic, it is the perfect partner for a fine, rich, fruity, velvety, and delicately sweet white wine. Unfortunately, the Chinese tradition is to serve a dominant sweet-spicy hoisin sauce on it, which instantly kills the wine. Since I have thought for a long time that this sauce is a gastronomic mistake, I discard it and replace its fruity, tangy qualities with the almost sweet overtones of an accompanying wine: from the German Mosel, a Graacher Himmelreich of Prum or a Brauneberger Juffer Sonnenuhr of Thanisch; or a superbly rich Chardonnay from California, either a Stony Hill from the Napa Valley or a Gundlach-Bundschu Special Selection from Sonoma or a Chalone from Monterey. Any of these, to my taste, etches and frames the Chinese duck into a great work of culinary art.

But there is one clear-cut exception to my general rule for wines to pair with these spicy dishes. A few of them are so sharply musky and tangy with fruit—for example, Cantonese lemon chicken, Szechuanese orange beef or a Moroccan *tagine* of lamb with fermented lemons—that the fruity, sweet impression of the wine is overpowered. What is needed in the wine is a sharp refreshing citrus tang. Fortunately, a new wine meets the requirement. The famous French Champagne house of Laurent-Perrier has started making in the United States a still wine called California Chardonnay Blanc de Blancs. It is crisply refreshing and strong in character—exactly right for exotic dishes with dominant fruit flavors.

Most of the time, the best accompaniment to spicy food is cold white wine; red wine can also be matched dramatically with at least one spicy dish: the classic Mexican chicken or turkey *mole poblano*, in which the sauce is slightly thickened with a small amount of bitter chocolate. Montezuma was unable to keep the secret of his chocolate and Cortez carried it back to Spain, from where it crossed the Pyrenees to the French city of Bayonne. Today in this region, they still thicken their meat sauces with bitter chocolate and drink with them Cabernet Sauvignon–based wines from Bordeaux. In the United States, one of the best of our Cabernets is the Heitz Martha's vineyard, which has an extraordinary, distant flavor of wild peppermint. The combination of this with the subtle cinnamon-chocolate *mole poblano* is one of the memorable marriages of exotic gastronomy.

THE MENU GOES UP IN FLAMES

Most exotic menus reach their climax with the incendiary, mouth-burning torrid curries in which the black, green, and red chilies are the masters. When the dish is a Malaccan devil's curry, a Szechuanese sour pepper soup or an Indonesian chicken broiled in peppers, we are whistling in the dark to hope that wine can be anything more than secondary. Yet the right wine, if it has a clear enough character to cut through the heat, will refresh the mouth and help to separate and balance the flavors of the food. The wine should be low in alcohol so that we can drink a lot of it without discomfort, and it helps greatly if it has a slight *pétillance* or sparkle to it. One recently released example is Almadén's Light Chablis. It has about 7 percent alcohol (roughly half the normal). No one claims that this is a wine of stature, but it has the definite flavor of Chenin Blanc and French Colombard grapes, and I find it excellent for putting out chili fires. You could also serve an inexpensive, ice-cold sparkling wine from California or New York State, one of the French "Champagne types" from Saumur on the Loire (try Bouvet Brut or Gratien et Meyer Brut or the delightfully refreshing sparkling wine from Seyssel in the High Alps, Caves Saint Germain).

An exotic menu almost always ends with the soothing comfort of tropical fruits, and these—if you still have the ambition—can be accompanied with sweet dessert wines and liqueurs. Thus, after the daring of the spices and the excitements of the fires, we return, full circle, to the elegant normalcy with which we started, leaving our guests with the best possible impression of our cellar and our good taste.

The Royal Riesling

Greatest of Grapes for
Warm-Weather Wines

It all started with the Emperor Charlemagne at the end of the eighth century—the breeding of fine German white wines. He was "master of Europe." From Spain to what is now Poland, from Saxony in the north to Lombardy in the south, he ruled from his Palace of Ingelheim on a hill overlooking the valley of the Rhine.

One spring day, standing on the watchtower, the emperor looked out at the incomparable view of the great river and the towering slopes of the far side. On one of them, he noticed that the snow was melting in a curious way: softening at the top, while still hard at the base. Charlemagne said to one of his nobles: "The sun strikes that slope from a high angle. It would be a good place to plant vines. See that it's done."

The hill was found to be covered with wild black currants (called *Johannisbeeren* in German), so they named it Johannisberg. In 1100 it was given to the Benedictine monks, who worked patiently for seven hundred years to improve the grapes and make better wines. By selecting and grafting, they gradually developed a special strain of vine with tight little bunches of small yellow-green grapes that ripen to deep golden. At maturity, they have an incomparable aroma, an entrancing taste, which seems to be compounded of the essences of all other fruits: of black currants, peaches, of pineapples, blackberries, and walnuts.

The monks called their vine the Riesling—a name which today can claim to be the greatest among the world's white wine grapes. Greatest,

EDITOR'S NOTE: This article originally appeared in the May 1969 issue of *House Beautiful*.

not only because of its supreme position in Germany, but also because it has successfully traveled to all the other major wine areas of the world. Everywhere it has adapted itself to different climates and soils, producing different wines, yet all with a certain regal richness of character.

But on the Johannisberg it still grows best. In 1801, all church properties were seized by the state, and ownership of Johannisberg passed to the emperor of Austria, who gave it to his favorite minister, Prince von Metternich. He built his *schloss* (château) on the summit. The family still lives there and still makes the world's most famous Riesling wine, now called Schloss Johannisberg. It is closely challenged by two other nearby vineyards, the thousand-year-old monastery of Steinberg ("stone mountain"), now state-owned, and the moated, fairy-story castle of Schloss Vollrads.

Fortunately for all of us, enough of these greatest of Riesling wines are made each year for them to be distributed virtually everywhere. At any well-stocked wineshop, you should find the tall "steeple" bottles with the colorful labels. Schloss Johannisberg has the coat of arms of the Metternich family or a picture of the castle on the mountain. Steinberg has the heraldic black eagle. Schloss Vollrads has the gold-and-red crest of its owners, the family with the unpronounceable name, Matuschka-Greiffenklau. But before buying these and all other German wines, it is important to learn a few basic, reasonably simple rules.

Along the valleys of the Rhine, the Moselle, and their tributaries, the weather varies enormously and unpredictably from year to year. So the wine growers do not harvest the grapes all at once (as is usual in France or California), but, beginning near the end of September, they send skilled pickers with long scissors through the rows of vines to cut only those grapes that are ripe. These are pressed at once into a wine that is kept in separate vats. The following week, more ripened grapes are picked and pressed. This continues, week by week, as long as there is sunny weather; in very good years, the selective picking continues through October and into November.

This means that almost every German vineyard produces not one, but half a dozen wines each year. The earlier ones are dry, slightly lemony, lighter, and less expensive. The later wines, from the more developed gapes, become increasingly softer, stronger in alcohol, and more expensive. Finally, if sunny weather continues long enough, some of the grapes will begin to dry out on the vine, becoming almost like raisins and producing a wine that is wonderfully sweet and rich. It is more suitable for drinking as a liqueur after dinner than as an accompaniment to the food.

THE LABEL PROBLEM

These various wines are signaled on the labels by the use of certain German words, and it is well worth learning a few of them, since they tell you exactly what is inside the bottle. The word *Auslese* means "specially picked," indicating that the wine was made from selected, riper bunches of grapes. Some vineyards subdivide this class of wine into three degrees of quality. First *feine Auslese* means, obviusly, the finer selected grapes. Second *hoch-feine Auslese* means extra fine. Third, *feinste Auslese* means the finest, and this is not just a sales gimmick. Each wine is made, quite separately, from grapes of increasingly better quality.

According to German wine-labeling law, when the grape harvest has been in progress for at least three weeks, if there are still some grapes left on the vines, they may be made into wines which are labeled as *Spätlese*, meaning "late picked" and indicating that the wine is softer, mellower, and, again, stronger in alcohol. Near the very end of the harvest, the final grapes are picked, not bunch by bunch but single grape by single grape, and wine made in this laborious and expensive way (it takes one man a full day to pick enough grapes for one bottle of wine) may be labeled *Beeren Auslese,* meaning "picked berries." But the top of the class belongs to the *Trockenbeerenauslese* (sometimes shortened just to *Trockenbeeren*) meaning "dry grapes," showing that the wine is an after-dinner sweet type.

VILLAGES AND VINEYARD NAMES

Always remember that on a German wine label the word in the largest type is usually the name of the village where the grapes were grown. The second biggest word is usually the name of the particular vineyard. Some of them are quite fantastic, often reflecting incidents in the local history of the region. One famous wine, for example, is called (freely translated from a perfectly straight-faced label) "The Bishop's School for Priestly Convicts." The story goes that the rich owner of the vineyard willed it, upon his death, to the local church. The income from the sale of the wine was used to support the bishop's favorite charity, a seminary where ex-convicts who *really* wanted to turn over a new leaf could be trained as priests!

After the village and the vineyard, if there is no other descriptive word, you can assume that the wine is dry and light. But if you see one of the "wine words" mentioned above, you will know what to expect.

There are basic differences between the Riesling wines of the Rhine and those of the Moselle. (Incidentally, if the wine is from the Rhine, the bottle is of brown-red glass; when it is from the Moselle, blue-green.) Perhaps one can say that the Moselle Valley being narrower and steeper, gets a little less sunshine and has slightly less rich soil, so it produces lighter, more delicate wines with, in the good years, a quite lovely floweriness of bouquet and taste.

Among the thousands of German Riesling wines, your preferences must eventually be a matter of personal taste. But, as a starting guide, the chart on page 400 lists those wines I have recently drunk that seem to me to be above average in quality and value. One can pay less than two dollars for a good bottle, or as much as ninety dollars a bottle for one of the greatest *Trockenbeeren* liqueur wines.*

THE RIESLING IN FRANCE

When the Riesling started its world travels, perhaps it was to be expected that it would first jump across its native Rhine and establish itself as the "King of Alsace," along the French side of the great river. Here, as everywhere else, the Riesling has proved that it makes the best wines when it grows in cool corners on steep, stony slopes, where the grape is small and undernourished, rather than fat and rich.

The finest wines come from the hills above the lovely old villages of Riquewihr, Hunawihr, Ribeauville, and Bergheim—and these are the names to watch for on labels. The rules for buying the Alsatian bottles are different from those of the German. You should look first for the Riesling name on the label. Then, since almost all the wines are blended, the name of the responsible and skilled blending and bottling firm is more important than that of the vineyard. After many years of drinking and loving Alsatian Rieslings, I have come to know and trust certain firms whose wines seem to maintain a high standard year after year (see chart).

A CHANGE IN PERSONALITY

As the little yellow-green grape began to flourish in other and more distant places, it became generally known as the "Johannisberg Riesling," in honor of its illustrious birthplace. This name is, of course, misleading, for the Riesling naturally produces a Johannisberg wine only in Johan-

---

* EDITOR'S NOTE: De Groot is quoting 1969 prices.

nisberg. The grape takes on a new personality wherever it grows in different soils and under different weather. What *can* be said for this marvelous grape is that, whatever the variations in various countries, the wines are always fine—and often great.

Cuttings from Johannisberg were planted in Switzerland, along the upper valley of the River Rhône, east of Lake Geneva in the Canton of the Vallée. Today, although the output is small and not much is exported, I have found these Swiss "Johannisbergs," in local inns, and they are the best of the district. One can play the same tasting game in the northern mountain valleys of Italy, where two separate strains of Riesling often grow side by side: the Riesling Renano (meaning of the Rhine) and the locally grafted Riesling Italico.

The Riesling went eastward into Austria and then on to Hungary, where I have seen many acres of the Balatoni Riesling growing along the shores of Lake Balaton. Drinking it there in village cafés one notes that the wine has taken on a golden ambience from the rich Hungarian soil and sunshine. In Yugoslavia, it is called the "Riesling Renski" (of the Rhine) and makes the best white wines of the famous Lutomer district of Slovenia and also in the Serbian wine areas near Belgrade. In Rumania, there is a fine Riesling at Tirnave and another at Perla. I have also heard of, but not tasted, Riesling wines in Australia—and you could hardly get further from the Rhine than that. Very few of these Rieslings are imported here, but you can try them on their native soils.

IN THE AMERICAS

The Riesling reached the New World first by crossing the South Atlantic and establishing itself in Chile, where it produced that country's finest white wine—the most widely accepted Latin-American wine to be imported (in its fat flagon bottle) into the United States.

Finally, in 1853, the Riesling grape arrived in Northern California and settled down in the cool, foggy valleys around San Francisco Bay. Here it seems to have felt more happily at home than in any other place on earth, except on the banks of the Rhine. The California White Riesling or Johannisberg Riesling (here, these two names mean the same thing), can be as fine and fresh a wine as any Riesling—except the very best of Germany and France.

It ought to be easy to buy California Riesling, since all the better producers name the grape on the label. But unfortunately there are some confusing complications.

Problem one: The true "White" or "Johannisberg" Riesling will grow satisfactorily only in certain cooler areas in the Napa and Sonoma valleys. However, other vineyards in warmer parts of the state also want to be able to make wines with the magic Riesling name. So several other varietal strains (or "clones," as they are technically called) of the Riesling grape have been cultivated in California.

THE RIESLING COUSINS

Some of the strains are newly grafted by the research botanists. Others are grown from imported European roots. A few older types have been renamed to include the word "Riesling." Most of them, when properly harvested and vinified, make very fair wines, but they do represent a compromise and they lack the glorious freshness and gay personality of the true Johannisberg Riesling. There is a "Grey Riesling," an "Emerald Riesling," and a "Sylvaner Riesling" (also sometimes called a "Franken Riesling"). Even an American native wild grape called "Elvira" has been renamed the "Missouri Riesling." Any of these may be labeled "Riesling," but not "Johannisberg."

Problem two: The requirements of California law. If the label names a Johannisberg or White Riesling *and* if it also states that the wine is "estate bottled," then you have a fine wine, for the usual custom is that it must be 100 percent from the named grape. However, if the words "estate bottled" are missing, you are not nearly so safe, for the law then requires that only 51 percent of the wine need be from the named grape: 49 percent can be any other added wine. Again, even if the words "estate bottled" are on the label but the grape name is simply "Riesling," then there is no guarantee that you have a single drop of true Johannisberg, as the wine may be entirely or partly from other less good Riesling types. Once you have acquired a taste for the true wine of the true California Johannisberg, you will consider it well worthwhile to buy labels that are specific on this point (see chart, page 400).

THE TASTING GAME

It is one of the most fascinating of wine-tasting games to trace the multitude of Riesling wines. Start by tasting a German Riesling against a California estate-bottled Johannisberg. The German has an extraordinary and subtle sweet-sour balance. The Californian is less complex, less delicate, but has its own interesting qualities of masculinity and power.

Few people appreciate this fine California wine more than Dr. Harold

Berg, head of the Department of Eenological and Viticultural Research at the University of California. He told me: "It should be drunk young, when it is still fresh and fruity. It should seldom be more than from one to three years old. Some of the dry white Rieslings from our best areas are among the outstanding products of our vineyards."

And I like to think that G. K. Chesterton, the wine-loving English author, was thinking of a Riesling when he wrote:

> *Feast on wine or fast on water,*
> *And your honour shall stand sure*
> *If an angel out of heaven*
> *Brings you something else to*
> *drink,*
> *Thank him for his kind attentions,*
> *Go and pour it down the sink.*

Personally, I am not nearly as pessimistic as Chesterton. I am sure that, if an angel visited me with a gift from heaven for this month of May, he would bring me the finest Riesling of a great year. As I poured it ice-cold into my long-stemmed glass, it would be refreshing, agreeable, and gay. It would come forth from my glass with the bouquet of wild flowers and the freshness of lovely youth. The perfect drink for spring and summer days.

A PERSONAL SELECTION OF RIESLING WINES*

GERMANY

The Three Greats
Schloss Johannisberg
Steinberg
Schloss Vollrads
*Fine vintage years, currently
available: 1962, 1963, 1964*

Others Along the Rhine
Deidesheimer Kalkofen
Eltviller Sandgrub
Erbacher Marcobrunn
Forster Kirchenstück
Geisenheimer Altbaum
Hattenheimer
 Engelmannsberg
Niersteiner Oelberg
Rüdesheimer Bischofsberg
 Schloss Groenstyn
Wachenheimer Gerümpel
Wormser Liebfrauenstift
 Langenbach
*Good vintage years, currently
available: 1964, 1966, 1967*

From the Moselle Region
Bernkasteler Meister-krone
Brauneberger Juffer
Eitelsbacher Marienholz
Graacher Domprobst
Leiwener Laurentiuslay
Maximin Grünhaus
 Herrenberg
Oberemmeler
 Jesuitengarten
Piesporter Güntherslay
Wehlener Sonnenuhr
 Diedenhofen
Wiltinger Scharzhofberg
*Good vintage years currently
available: 1964, 1966, 1967*

FRANCE

The Rieslings of Alsace
Dopff & Irion—Château
 de Riquewihr
Hugel of Riquewihr—
 Réserve Exceptionnelle
Jerome Lorenz of
 Bergheim—Cuvée
 Spéciale
*Be sure to get the label
marked Riesling. Good
vintage years available:
1966, 1967*

U.S.A.

*The True White Reislings
of California*
Almadén Johannisberg
Beaulieu Johannisberg
Christian Brothers
 Johannisberg
Concannon Johannisberg
Louis Martini Johannisberg
Wente Johannisberg
*The good wines are marked
with vintage years. Good
years available: 1966, 1967*

*EDITOR'S NOTE: As this article was published in 1969, de Groot recommends vintages only through 1967.

Index